THE AMERICANS

THE AMERICANS:

A Conflict of Creed and Reality

RONALD SEGAL

NEW YORK / THE VIKING PRESS

TO TONY GODWIN

Published in England under the title
America's Receding Future: The Collision of Creed and Reality

Published in 1969 by The Viking Press, Inc.
625 Madison Avenue, New York, N.Y. 10022

Library of Congress catalog card number: 69-12253

Printed in U.S.A. by Vail-Ballou Press, Inc.

CONTENTS

Introduction   *vii*

1. Violence and the Divided Hope   *3*
2. The Solitary Sex   *51*
3. The Open and Shut Society   *100*
4. The Insurrectionists   *178*
5. The Unhappy Americans   *281*

   Reference Notes   *325*
   Index   *333*

Gatsby believed in the green light, the orgiastic future that year by year recedes before us. It eluded us then, but that's no matter—tomorrow we will run faster, stretch out our arms farther. . . . And one fine morning—

So we beat on, boats against the current, borne back ceaselessly into the past.

—F. Scott Fitzgerald, The Great Gatsby

INTRODUCTION

"If they aim at something and do not get it, they think that they have been deprived of what belonged to them already; whereas, if their enterprise is successful, they regard that success as nothing compared to what they will do next. Suppose they fail in some undertaking; they make good the loss immediately by setting their hopes in some other direction. Of them alone it may be said that they possess a thing almost as soon as they have begun to desire it, so quickly with them does action follow upon decision. And so they go on working away in hardship and danger all the days of their lives, seldom enjoying their possessions because they are always adding to them. Their view of a holiday is to do what needs doing; they prefer hardship and activity to peace and quiet. In a word, they are by nature incapable of either living a quiet life themselves or of allowing anyone else to do so."

Thus, according to Thucydides,* spoke the Corinthian envoys to their Spartan allies about the Athenians, at the moment when Athens stood on the heights of its riches, its power, its vigor, before the fall into despotism, defeat, and despair.

How rich, how powerful, how vigorous America is. In the thrust of her industry and the accumulation of her treasure, along the

* *The Peloponnesian War,* translated by Rex Warner, Penguin Books, p. 51.

highways that command the huge horizons and among the lights inundating the night, she seems to proclaim the infinite promise of American man. Corporations that control the economies of distant nations; regions of wheat or corn, cotton or cattle, copper or coal, that stretch themselves like so many separate countries; art galleries, libraries, and museums that contain a display of human accomplishment such as no other single society has ever possessed; factories and bridges, airports and dams that are the modern wonders of skill and energy: all express the material triumph. The secular exults, exalted to the sacred. Skyscrapers, those peculiar symbols, stand in the day like altars raised to one another; like so many still pillars of fire in the dark.

Is this not the most magnificent empire of them all? In the Catskills, where New Yorkers of appropriate means and tastes retreat from their ordinary exertions, is the Concord, a hotel of red plush, gilt, and crystal, with a profusion of facilities for exercise and entertainment. It confounds the past in a clutter of classical nomenclature: the Imperial Room; the Forum Hall, with Athenian, Spartan, Roman, Grecian Rooms; the Columns, with Doric, Ionic, and Corinthian Rooms. Two years ago, when I visited it, it seemed full of people standing or sitting about and waiting, for someone, for something, anyone, anything, to come and snatch them from themselves. And moving among them was a hostess with a notice, suspended from a rope of large artificial pearls round her neck, reading in black block letters: SMILE!

I was in New York a few days after the killing of Martin Luther King. Several cities, including the country's capital, still flamed with rioting, and knots of police seemed to be everywhere in the Manhattan streets. I was sitting with a publisher in the lobby of the Hotel Algonquin, and as the evening cocktail murmur around us hesitated, we heard a man, at the telephone near the entrance crying, "I can't take the violence any more! I can't take the tension!"

The rate of what is regarded as normal violence in America is startlingly higher than the rate of similar violence in similar advanced industrial societies. The inhabitant of a typical American city has more than ten times the chance of being murdered than has the inhabitant of a typical British one. On an average day some 400 people die violently: 150 on the roads, 170 in other accidents, 50 by suicide, and 30 by murder *—some 150,000 victims a year. And year by year the relative increase—in the case of murder, some 10 per cent—far outstrips the more reputable indices of progress, let alone the rate of population growth. Furthermore, and less and less regarded as abnormal, there is the violence of foreign war and domestic riot, the multiplying casualties of America's character and commitments. How long can the society sustain such accumulating pressures? The American mind has begun to listen for the break. Every new act of known violence does more than add another unit to the total; it promotes in a sort of geometric progression the mood of fear, bewilderment, and dismay.

The future, which for so long seemed so docile, seems now not just refractory but malignant. Continued American political and economic supervision of a world of tumultuous poverty promises to expand the expenditure of American resources immeasurably beyond the limits already held by many Americans to be materially excessive where not morally ruinous. The economy, since the start of the Second World War apparently equal to any effort demanded of it, is showing such disquieting signs of strain that foreigners, abandoning their long devotion to the dollar, are dancing round the golden calf instead. Yet America must either be prepared to sacrifice ever more of her men and money or submit to the very spread of popular upheaval and socialist experiment abroad that she has exerted herself with such a sense of service to prevent.

Alongside the rising violence of deprivation without is the rising violence of deprivation, especially by race, within. And this violence, incredulous or contemptuous of reform and crying for revolution, is assailing the assumptions on which American civilization is based. Department-store arson and the sabotage of power lines prefigure a Negro fury that cannot be confined to the ghettos and managed by troops with the latest instruments of riot control.

* Report in *The Times,* London, April 10, 1968.

It does not need enormous numbers of men, provided that they are
sufficiently determined, trained, equipped, and careless of the consequences to themselves of capture, seriously to damage the functioning of a complex industrial society. The weight of the economy
must make it the more vulnerable, as the weight of a combatant in
judo is exploited by his adversary to throw him. And those driven
so far by the torturing of their ideals as to venture at all on such an
endeavor are in general unlikely to be daunted by the probable
responses of authority or mob. Such insurgency by its nature must
be conducted by a tiny minority, though one that requires the
shelter of a substantial population. To be sure, the black community in America is only one-ninth of the whole. But that, even on
its own, constitutes no insignificant base for such insurgency, not
least since so much of it is concentrated in the centers of the major
cities. And other communities, like the Puerto Rican and the
Mexican, suffering an ethnic discrimination, are becoming mili-
tantly disaffected. Virtual genocide of the colored American is
practical only in theory.

Experience of urban guerrilla warfare in other places at other
times does reveal what resilience a society, with a government of
sufficient will and rigor, can possess. People are incalculably
capable of adapting themselves to protracted periods of social disruption. But they cease in the process to be the people they were.
It is not impossible to imagine an America in which a regime of
ruthless repression would preserve some semblance of order, even
prosperity, in the face of sustained racial rebellion. But it would
not be America any longer.

The New World was never a promise of this. It was a promise of
man's victory over his environment and his own failings, not of
defeat or an exhausted stalemate; a commonwealth of the free and
the equal pursuing happiness here and now, not a citizenship of
acquiescence staring blindly beyond life. America was a profoundly human progress and achievement. Yet what is America
now? Everything that Americans have been taught to believe about
their past and their purposes interacts with their experience to

intensify their disappointment and distress. The mounting violence of reality contradicts their whole collective meaning.

Americans have often enough felt themselves besieged by problems before, but their reaction has traditionally been to regard their resources and resolve as more than adequate to the challenge. Now there are more and more Americans who see the problems of America as so massive and so many, with the resources and resolve of America so inadequate to the challenge, that they are ready to accept defeat and learn only how to live behind its barbed wire. But there are Americans, too, more and more of them, especially among the young, excited anew by the American idea, who see the problems of America as the needless failure of Americans themselves to follow the proper priorities of their creed: who maintain that victory is still possible if Americans will only redirect their energies, in a revolution of their relationships.

Such Americans, though they may hand out leaflets for one Presidential candidate rather than another, and demonstrate their opposition to one or other policy of government, are concerned not so much with particular American wrongs as with what they believe to be systematically wrong with America. For them, the totalitarianism of private profit, with the independent power of property and the moral separation of the individual from corporate acts, is the source of a national sickness, whose manifestations are the growing estrangement of people from each other and from themselves, the growing distance of the individual from the decisions affecting his life, the growing violence of personal assertiveness and despair. For them, the millions humiliated by poverty are a rebuke, as the millions humiliated by riches are a warning. For them, America is increasingly the home of loneliness and terror, futility and a relentless sense of loss. As for the first Americans, so for these, it is individual liberty that constitutes the core of their repudiation and search. And for the first time in American history, it is the young who are in the forefront of revolt. Tomorrow is confronting tomorrow.

It is true that the spread of violence, the isolation of people from each other and from the institutions that order their lives, the sense of helplessness and desolation are, like the angry discontent of the young, only too evident in other industrial societies, not all of them capitalist by profession. The world of material triumph seems to be entering a new, supra-industrial age, of blandly manipulated self-indulgence, a civilization of disintegrated personality and computerized appetite and opinion, where the classic techniques of control have become obsolete, and the technocrat will accomplish a despotism that eliminates even the desire for dissent. But the consequent conflict, between those who promote or, perplexed, succumb to the process, and those who defy it as a violation of their humanity, has been pioneered in America. And this is not solely because the process itself seems to have reached furthest there; it is because such a process denies the avowed purpose of America in history, and because the Americans are fitted, by the creed of their identity, supremely to resist.

It needs not a little boldness to write about a society so immense, so complex, which has been and is being written about so generously by such generous talents. Inevitably, I have drawn on the works of others. Some of them are lost in the reading of years; some are on my bookshelves still; some of my sources were met on buses, in hotels, across executive desks and lunch counters, at meetings and marches—Americans eager to share with a stranger their visions of America. If I have ventured to add my book on America to all the others, it is to record these visions, finally for my own sake. Americans represent much of what is most destructive and ugly in man. But they represent also much of what is most creative and beautiful. If there is no hope in America, where is there hope? For hope was the very conception of America. It is this hope which I, in finding America, have found, and which I have set out—the excuse for my boldness—to encourage as I can.

RONALD SEGAL

1968

THE AMERICANS

CHAPTER 1

Violence and the Divided Hope

When I was a fighter pilot for the FBI I discovered God as a hard-boiled egg in my lunchbox. I ate him.—Among the graffiti in the men's room of a beer-garden in Austin, Texas

The American character has excited interest—not least among Americans, who early displayed an inexhaustible inquisitiveness about themselves and the opinions held of them by others—since American society first seemed to have assumed an individual form, and this interest has inevitably increased alongside the increase in American power and influence. Observers of deep purpose and insight, as different as de Tocqueville and Dickens, agree with tourists and native evangelists in descrying an American identity; but if they all agree on the existence of this identity, they disagree extensively over its essential nature.

Doubtless much of what one sees in America, one sees—so as to sustain or assail it—in the development of industrial civilization and liberal democracy. For America has long been the pace-setter for both. Movements started and still led by American industry, such as automation and the mass manipulation of consumer appetites, affect the character and direction of industrial society everywhere, just as the vast expansion in the power of the American political executive, promoted by the vast expansion in the functions of the American government, is reflected in the character and direction of other established liberal democracies.

It is necessary, therefore, to guard against defining as peculiarly

American qualities common enough in other, similarly organized societies. The Yankee reverence for earthly reward has been ceaselessly remarked; yet the phrase "Time is money" comes from Britain, not America, and neither the Scandinavians nor the Japanese seem to place the labor for riches low down on the list of priorities for leading the good life. It is true that Americans display an exaggerated respect for mechanical inventiveness—they pay their Patent Office the sort of demanding devotion that in other countries surrounds the shrines of saints—but the same may no less truthfully be said of the Russians. Much that has been recorded as peculiarly American is peculiarly Western, or peculiarly urban, or simply peculiarly human. What is peculiarly American is a peculiar combination of qualities, some widely shared abroad, some uniquely native in their force, and all by their interaction producing an individual culture. And the importance of appreciating this culture lies not only in the power and riches of the American state, with their impact on everyone everywhere, but also in the likelihood that, as many of the circumstances which have helped create the American combination spread across the world, so too may spread much of the American character.

To talk of the American character at all is, of course, to generalize. Happily for mankind, men can be intractably dissentient, and nowhere are they showing themselves more so now than in America. There are millions of Americans so unlike whatever one considers the typical American to be, millions indeed who quietly or clamorously reject what they themselves consider to be the American type, that to ignore them is to distort the whole nature of America, its failures and successes alike. Yet their very dissent helps to give form and meaning to a cultural identity, just as a cultural identity helps to give form and meaning to their dissent.

Ask an Indian or a Nigerian, a Frenchman or a Brazilian, who recognizes a peculiar American culture at all, to identify a major manifestation, and he will more likely than not suggest the Western, that saga of courage and cruelty, innocence and corruption, that surges across the cinema screens and crackles from the television sets in so many countries. And the Western, surely, is the first view of an American identity that American children get; space travel, a contender for the toy and television market, is shared with the Russians, while the Revolution and the message of American citizenship must usually wait for school to engage attention of any comparable measure. No culture, indeed, combines history, myth, and entertainment in a way more easily assimilable, especially by children.

The Western itself has two main forms: the conflict between Paleface (settler or soldier) and Indian, and the conflict between Good Cowboy and Bad. The first belongs to early America, in subject and development; it was the form exploited by literature before the coming of either the cowboy or the film, and its theme was starkly a racial—the white tribal—triumph. The second followed the invasion of the plains and the growth of a cattle culture, and its theme was the sanctity of property. That the two themes were scarcely consistent, however, did not prevent a mingling of the two forms to produce the ultimate romance of Cowboys and Indians. For the two forms had one crucial element in common: they depended overwhelmingly for their action and effect on violence. Violence was the medium, and the medium became the message.

Violence remains the essential constituent of the Western, whether it is the first form, or the second, or the blend of both that sets the scene. It is never outside the action; when it is not in the forefront, it broods in the wings, awaited or remembered, always the protagonist. It is the cause, the climax, and the consequence; it is, far more consistently than skin or purity of heart, the definition of the heroic. Recently, indeed, sophistication has produced the Indian hero, and even the anti-Western, the Cowboy as material for farce. But such aberrants remain relatively rare; possess an impact precisely because of the force still possessed by the original forms; and, above all, center still, seriously or flippantly, on violence.

The formal American identity, however, does not enter history with the Western. It enters with the Declaration of Independence in 1776. And the significance of this Declaration to the development of the American character can hardly be exaggerated. The assumptions it made inform the American Constitution, which was adopted twelve years later and which, with its various Amendments—not least those of 1791, comprising the Bill of Rights—is the groundwork of American government. And they reside in the popular mind as the very gospel of democracy. They are contained in two main pronouncements, generally decried when encountered in the world of the late eighteenth century, and by no means universally accepted today.

The first such pronouncement was "that all men are created equal, that they are endowed by their Creator with certain unalienable rights, that among these are Life, Liberty and the Pursuit of Happiness." The assumption of natural equality was extraordinary enough. Authority in nearly all of Europe would not entertain it till the disruptions of the First World War, and for orthodox Hindus today it is as sinful as it is absurd. But far more extraordinary was the assumption that among the unalienable rights of man must be counted the pursuit of happiness. It is extraordinary still. Order, yes; service to state or god or the future, yes; liberty and equality, perhaps; but happiness? At least happiness, as the context makes clear, of a personal, distinctly secular kind, with the implication of feasible attainment? For Marxists the possibility of happiness exists deep in the future, when the proper organization of society has been achieved and the state itself has withered away; for traditional Christians, Moslems, Hindus, Buddhists, Jews, the possibility does not exist at all this side of the grave. It is impossible to know, and fundamentally does not matter, whether Jefferson himself or those who signed the Declaration with him intended more than a flourish of rhetoric; what matters profoundly is that successive generations of Americans have grown up to believe that the pursuit of individual happiness is their right, and that such happiness is attainable here and now.

The second main pronouncement stemmed from the first. "Whenever any form of government becomes destructive to these ends, it is the right of the people to alter or abolish it, and to institute new government, laying its foundation on such principles and organizing its powers in such form, as to them shall seem most likely to effect their safety and happiness." And here it is relevant to recall that the Declaration itself was no mere exercise in propaganda; it was a deliberate and concerted act of treason, the proclamation of revolt. Nor was it a revolt intended to effect change by peaceful means. There were no Gandhis among the signatories to the Declaration, and satyagraha as a form of struggle would take some 180 years to make a substantial American appearance. The American people took sovereign shape in violence, and a violence commemorated regularly ever since in the ritual of patriotism.

The tie between disappointment and violence was thus intrinsic to the very inauguration of the American identity. And the tie has persisted to the present, acknowledged by assiduous specialists on urban society and race relations, as Negroes riot in one American city after the other, burning buildings, looting shops, stoning and sniping at police. Every American government has sought to break the tie—at least where its own aspirations have not been involved; has denounced violence as an improper and profitless means of effecting change. But its own origin, within the origin of the republic, has argued otherwise.

The violence of the Revolution was disappointment, because the very meaning of America was hope. The promise that had drawn by far the most part of those who had come from the Old World was of the freedom and equality, the peace and compassion that they had for so long been denied. To those who fled from the Europe of the time, and to many of those who remained, America was a second chance, an opportunity to rearrange the relations of men to each other and to God without the accumulated restraints of precedent and power. Sir Thomas More placed his *Utopia* in the New World, and successive groups of settlers sought to establish their particular versions there. Surely at few times in history can there have been such an outpouring of idealism, of longing and endeavor for collective liberation, for a hope that was inclusive and infinite.

But the settlers brought along with them, as well, the Old World instruments of property and ordered leadership. And the instru-

ments soon began adapting the purposes of America. One man's
Utopia emerged as another's Chaos, and too many Americans
early displayed a patience only with their own opinions. That the
original idealism survived was due to the generosity of the American environment and the confinements of British dominion. The
settlers had come upon the richest stretch of vast yet sparsely
populated land in the world. There was always another part of the
country to claim for a refuge. Indeed, so many ways of worship
were soon implanted that an established religion, let alone an established church, could not reasonably be contemplated, and it
was no less than the survival of the United States required, that the
first article in the Bill of Rights should have declared: "Congress
shall make no law respecting an establishment of religion, or pro-
hibiting the free exercise thereof." And the experience of secular
repression, in the native lands of many American settlers and within America under British rule, combined with a multiplicity of
political outlooks to promote constitutional safeguards of apparently ample scope for personal liberty and dissent.

Yet in the very inauguration of the formal American creed there
were those busily turning it to their private advantage and making
of hope an individual rather than a collective concern, a desire and
an expectation that excluded rather than encompassed. The propertied leadership of the struggle for independence had no intention
of allowing a political revolution to become a social one. Like
its predecessors in Presbyterian New England and its successors
in the liberalism of the consensus, it used rhetoric to disguise
reality.

For the challenge to long-established authority in the American
revolt and the general turbulence of the ensuing warfare promoted
the conditions for a drastic reapportionment of power, economic
no less than political. The revolution soon to follow in France
would move swiftly from political reform to a fundamental disturbance of social relations. And the uprising in 1786 of impoverished Massachusetts farmers—led by Captain Daniel Shays, a
recent soldier of the rebellious colonies—to prevent the attach-

ment of their lands for debt was clear enough warning of a dangerous social unrest.

The rich and resourceful, backed by the mounting alarm of all conservative Americans, intensified their efforts to achieve a strong national government which would protect the existing eminence of property. Most of the delegates to the Constitutional Convention of 1787 were themselves public creditors, in fact, and understandably afraid that the loose confederation of states framed by rebellion would disintegrate under the strains of conflicting interests and so reduce their bills to scraps of paper. In the event, the Convention did better than the most sanguine of its participants could reasonably have supposed. It associated the objectives of property with the popular sentiment against a single disposal of power. And the result was a political system exceptionally pliable, that would contain enormous changes in the nature of the economy and the functions of government, while securing the dominance of private capital and the acquiescence of labor.

Yet at the very start public acceptance was far from certain. Sixteen of the fifty-five delegates refused to sign the proposals, and though the Convention high-handedly determined that only nine of the thirteen states would have to ratify the Constitution for it to take effect, even this number seemed doubtful. It needed sedulous support from the nation's pre-eminent heroes, Washington and Franklin, the efforts of such astute propagandists as Madison and Hamilton, the conversion of crucial state leaders by the promise of federal jobs, and—above all—the undertaking to add a Bill of Rights to the Constitution, before distrust of a strong central government that would be dominated by the rich could be sufficiently overcome. And there were some who remained unconvinced. Patrick Henry, the patriot from Virginia who had cried out in colonial days for liberty or death, now opposed the Constitution as dangerous to American liberties, claiming that it "squints toward monarchy" and that the Congress, by its power of taxation, would "clutch the purse with one hand and wave the sword with the other."

The successful Federalist leadership did not itself entertain, however much it fostered, the common illusions. Madison rejoiced in the establishment of a Senate whose function would be "to protect the minority of the opulent against the majority." And Alexander Hamilton, who would do so much to form the character of American government in its most impressionable years, had small respect for the democratic rabble. "Your people," he declared, "is a great beast." [1] He saw progress for the republic only in economic expansion under the resolute control of a governing class, and as first Secretary of the Treasury he promoted the power and prestige of this class—the old large-landed families, the merchant shipowners, the manufacturers, the financiers, the public creditors—by a policy that openly favored its interests. If Washington himself was elected first President for quite other reasons, his reputation as the richest American of the time was not without its symbolism for the course of the Revolution.

In the end, accordingly, there was no real disturbance of the social structure. No class was expropriated—the property of loyalists was confiscated, but only so as to enrich another set of proprietors—slavery was not abolished, and the relationship of classes to one another remained unchanged. But if the combination of self-interest, skill, flexibility and, to be sure, idealism that was the new Constitution warded off social turbulence, it was not solely responsible. It succeeded only so far as it suited the prevalent American mood of hope. Patrick Henry himself foresaw that the Constitution was in its very clarity equivocal, and that provisions apparently framed to protect the people from predatory wealth would be employed by a conservative President or Congress, and interpreted by conservative courts, to protect predatory wealth from the people. But the mass of Americans, in the very bounty of their deflected idealism, accepted the definition of hope that their leadership furnished. The class of property was not closed: what was to prevent any American with enough talent and application from entering it? The rhetoric of the Declaration of Independence offered so firm and general a promise, and the Constitution so straight a way for insuring that the promise would be kept. It was the wholeness of their commitment that made so many Americans institutionally conservative. The competitive hope of the rich became a competitive hope among the poor.⌐ *Myth*

Within a decade, indeed, both the Declaration and the Constitution had been raised above suspicion or skepticism to become sacred, objects of a ubiquitous veneration, so that every political party claimed power in their name, as the proper guardian of their principles. And men over much of the world found cause and encouragement in the American example. Most of the great reform agitations in the nineteenth century, and most of the nationalist movements, from Ireland and Germany to Latin America, based their doctrine and appeal on the Declaration, while the Americans themselves saw their revolution as a turning point in the history of mankind. Franklin sent the text of the Constitution to a friend in France with the comment: "If it succeeds, I do not see why you might not in Europe carry the project of good Henry the 4th into Execution by forming a Federal Union and One Grand Republic of all its different States and Kingdoms." Lincoln was to declare that the United States, with its experiment in liberty, was "the last, best hope of earth." And lesser Americans were no less satisfied of their system's superiority and universal relevance.

Inevitably, as the New World prospered, it seemed more than ever an escape from the oppressions of the Old and an entrance to a life of suddenly infinite possibilities. America was no longer merely the promise of some distant Utopia; it was in the process of establishing a material one, which all might enjoy for the price of no more than a transatlantic ticket. If the proclamation of innate equality, with the enjoyment of suffrage and the protection of individual liberty contained in the Constitution, obviously did not apply to slaves, this was of little moment to the discontented of Europe, who ran no risk of being seized for sale on the auction block. As yet, only a few of the more unworldly supposed that Utopia should be color-blind. For the rest, America meant not only religious and political freedom, but the more substantial offering of bread. The Europeans themselves became the most effective propagandists of the American promise.

There is room for every body in America: has he any particular
talent, or industry? he exerts it in order to procure a livelihood, and
it succeeds. Is he a merchant? the avenues of trade are infinite; is he
eminent in any respect? he will be employed and respected. . . . Is
he a labourer, sober and industrious? he need not go many miles,
nor receive many informations before he will be hired, well fed at
the table of his employer, and paid four or five times more than he
can get in Europe. Does he want uncultivated lands? thousands of
acres present themselves, which he may purchase cheap. Whatever
be his talents or inclinations, if they are moderate, he may satisfy
them. I do not mean, that every one who comes will grow rich in a
little time; no, but he may procure an easy, decent maintenance, by
his industry. Instead of starving, he will be fed; instead of being idle,
he will have employment; and these are riches enough for such men
as come over here.[2]

So wrote Hector St. John de Crèvecœur in the 1780s, and his
sentiments would be echoed again and again, not least eloquently
by many who immigrated to America themselves.

Between 1790 and 1850 the population of the United States
increased nearly sixfold, from four million to twenty-three million.
The construction of canals and railways, with the penetration of the
West, produced a demand for cheap labor, and conditions in
Europe produced a flow of immigrants abundantly to meet the
demand. From the few hundred refugees of the abortive Polish
revolution in 1830–1831 to the hundreds of thousands who fled
from the Irish famine of 1846, they came to nourish and be nourished by America, the hopeful hopeless of the Old World. In the
1830s some 600,000 arrived, and in the 1840s more than one and
a half million. Whether, like the Irish, they settled in the cities of
the Northeast or, like the Germans, went West to farm, most of
them did better than they had done in their homelands before and,
doing better, sent for their relatives and friends.

Not that new arrivals stepped ashore to a rapturous reception.
Nearly all the Irish and many of the Germans were Roman Catholic, and hostility to the church of Pope and painted images, so
much a part of the Puritan tradition, allied itself with a common
distrust of the different in a formidable, often fierce, front of
prejudice. Some immigrants, reaching America penniless, became

public charges, while many were prepared to work for lower wages than those prevailing, at the very time when American labor was taking its first uncertain steps in collective pressure for better pay and working conditions. And inevitably now there were already many Americans eager to keep the milk and honey of the Promised Land from any more such greedy foreigners as they or their forefathers had been.

But the immigrants were not without protection. They had the need for their labor in a fast-expanding economy, and in due course the franchise. Political bosses in the big cities, with an efficient hierarchy of lesser bosses below them, dispensed jobs, welfare, and advice to the new Americans, and in turn took their votes to plunder the public treasury for themselves. If they made of democracy a profitable business, however, they were only interpreting the Constitution in a way which many of its original signatories would well have understood. Their peculiar corruption of republican government did not lie in the exploitation of public service for personal enrichment, or even in the exploration of new opportunities for graft; it lay in the employment, whenever patronage proved insufficient, of intimidation to secure their popular bases of power. The violence of the battlefield had established the republic; the violence of the back street now entered the conduct of its institutions and encouraged that coalition of public service and organized crime which has by no means disappeared from local politics in America today. Yet the political bosses in the main sustained immigrant hope. They taught millions of bewildered arrivals how to keep afloat in the American mainstream, and not a few of them how to swim. Overwhelmingly, therefore, the immigrants retained the expectation alongside the desire with which they had come, and were soon rather more convinced exponents of American democracy than those with prosperous American pedigrees who wondered if liberty, equality, and the pursuit of happiness were not being taken too far.

The Atlantic was for the new immigrants, as it had been for the old, a rupture with time. Left behind in Britain and France, Germany and Scandinavia, were the reminders, in history and legend, of a terrible past, of persecution and warfare, plague and famine, rebellion and massacre. Once in America, there was a different history and a different folklore to be assumed, celebrating victory and not defeat—the Pilgrim Fathers, the Boston Tea Party, the life and battles of Washington, the triumph of the Constitution, the continuous yielding of the West. And the future promised to be as beneficent as the past; would prove so, indeed, for the nation at large—with the single major exception of the Civil War—until the shock of the Great Depression. America expanded to the Pacific with an ease that corroborated the belief of her citizens that history was on their side. For $12 million the Jefferson administration bought from France the vast and sparsely settled province of Louisiana, advancing the boundary of the United States from the Mississippi to the Rocky Mountains without loss of a single life. The war with Britain in 1812–1814 procured little glory for either participant, and American pride experienced a serious setback in the burning of Washington by British troops, when some 7000 militia, of the 95,000 summoned to protect the capital, appeared, only to turn and run after a scattering of casualties. But the war proved relatively cheap—fewer than 2000 American soldiers and sailors fell in all the fighting—and if America was forced to realize that she could not capture Canada, she shattered much of the remaining Indian power in the West, revealed the ripe vulnerability of the Spanish empire by an invasion of Florida, and insured that Britain would henceforth be wary of tangling with her. She purchased Florida from Spain for $5 million in 1819; annexed Texas, after a squalid settler war with Mexico, in 1845; and by 1848, after a further, more formal war with Mexico for which her own responsibility was only too plain, had added New Mexico (including present-day Arizona) and California to her possessions. A treaty with Britain in 1846 resolved the long-standing Oregon dispute and gave America her northwest boundaries.

By 1850, therefore, America was sprawling across the continent to lie along two oceans, having grabbed or bought an area several times the size of the original thirteen states at a trivial cost to herself in men and money. And new events and legends had been added to the history of triumph, such as the patriotic martyrdom at the Alamo, when fewer than 200 men, many of doubtful character and most of ravenous ambition, were massacred by Mexican troops while defending the settler snatch of Texas. Such events and legends revealed the figure of violence while disguising its face. The ease with which America extended her dominion could not conceal the existence of a price; but it could attempt to mask the price itself with amenable romance. And just as the plantation regime of the South sought to cover the violence of Negro slavery with the myths of an Athenian civilization, so expansionist nationalism sought to cover the violence against Indian and Mexican with the myths of pioneer innocence and martyrdom. But if the myths transformed the appearance of violence, they emphasized its existence, and indeed its meaning for America, in the process of doing so. The connection between violence and advantage, both individual and national, was made with all the allurement of romance for successive generations, and this would have the most profound effects on the development of American society. The very subsequent transformation of Western romance from Settler against Indian to Cowboy against Cowboy mirrored an inexorable truth.

The Indians themselves certainly proved far less of an obstacle to the spread of white settlement than the Declaration of Independence or the Constitution's Bill of Rights might properly have suggested. No sooner had a treaty been concluded with them than the insatiable appetite of the settlers for land began consuming its provisions. Jefferson himself, when President, encouraged the seizure of Indian lands to nourish westward migration and the spread of agricultural power, and while dutifully protesting benevolence toward nature's noble savages, looked to moving them all across the Mississippi. His purpose was competently accomplished by Jackson, the first American born in a log cabin to be elected President, whose attitude to the Indian and the Negro was even less charitable than that of his high Virginian predecessors had been. During his two administrations, between 1829 and 1837, many thousands of Indians were removed from their land,

by trickery, bribery, or force, across the Mississippi, with a new
treaty always available to provide a legal gloss and to guarantee no
further removal.

Respected by the powers of Europe, bordered either by the
ocean or by countries much weaker than herself, and with no
internal resistance of much account to the consolidation of her
conquests, white America had ample reason to feel supremely
secure. And for millions of immigrants this was not the least important prop to hope. The Europe of perpetually disputed borders,
of shifting alliances and the elusive balance of power, the Europe
that seemed on the edge of war even when at peace, gave place to
an environment where frontier was another word for opportunity.

In the wake of the ships there vanished, too, that sense of confinement produced not only by Europe's closely ordered societies,
but by the pressures of population and, commonly, of climate. For
those who came from northern Europe, America was a release of
high skies and a space that it seemed impossible ever to enclose.
Even those who lived in the swelling cities of the American Northeast, with their squalid tenements and harsh winters, knew that the
West was there, waiting, always an escape. And the West gave soil
and timber and ore, so that the supply seemed only to increase
with the taking. Even the desert gave, first a little gold, then a flood
of silver, leading the imagination on further, to the new profusion of
the Pacific coast. Europe with its clutter of civilizations, its resources explored beyond much possibility of surprise, seemed to
dwindle as America grew. And there grew alongside America, in
the American character, a reverence for size, a view of bigness as a
virtue in itself, offering liberty its scope and ambition its challenge.

History appeared beneficent because, to be sure, it was so. The
opening up of the country coincided with the rapid development of
industrial techniques, and the value of American resources was
commensurately raised. In another age enterprise would have
sought for spices and gold and turned aside from the prairies and
the coalfields. Now America sold wheat to Europe and fed coal to
her own factories. Furthermore, her political system, the promise
no less than the practice of her democracy, promoted the thrust of

industrial capitalism far more than did the hierarchies, of hope as well as of skill and status and power, in Europe. Of course, the rage for profit produced in America, as it did in Europe, the squalor and disease of industrial slums, the subjugation of men, women, and children to machines, the blind mass degradation of the factory culture. But where capitalism in Europe seemed to frustrate mass faith in progress, the sheer scale and speed of industrial advance in America furthered it. America's share of the world's industrial production soared from the insignificant in 1800 to 20 per cent by 1860 and over 40 per cent by 1913. There were sporadic depressions, especially in agriculture; the exploitation of men and resources was relentless; and the misery of the poor was only emphasized by the ostentation of the rich. Yet the growth in national wealth was such as to produce a substantial class of moderate prosperity, which in itself sustained the cause of capitalism and encouraged many Americans below it to continue confident of their capacity to rise.

The very vastness of the private fortunes accumulated and the seeming suddenness of their accumulation dazzled most Americans, who were less embittered than excited by their display. In the absence of a titled ruling class, and with at least the rhetoric of democracy assailing inherited privilege, the self-made man became the symbol of American achievement. And the self-made man was essentially the man who made money.

The Puritan pioneers had themselves bestowed a righteous regard on the heaping up of treasures in this world. In searching for some sign of God's grace in the workings of Calvinist predestination, they turned with impatience from the clumsiness of the camel and the corruptions of the moth to seize upon material success. As manifestly one of the elect as Cotton Mather admonished the Christian of his double calling—to serve Christ and to pursue his own *"Particular Employment,* by which his *Usefulness,* in his Neighbourhood, is distinguished."

A Christian should follow his *Occupation* with INDUSTRY. . . . It seems a man *Slothful in Business,* is not a man *Serving the Lord.* By *Slothfulness* men bring upon themselves, What? but Poverty, but

Misery, but all sorts of Confusion. . . . On the other Side, a man
by *Diligence* in his Business, What may he not come to? *A Diligent*
man is very rarely an *Indigent* man. Would a man *Rise* by his
Business? I say, then let him *Rise* to his Business. . . . I tell you,
With *Diligence* a man may do marvellous things. *Young* man, *Work
hard* while you are *Young:* You'll Reap the Effects of it, when you
are *Old.* Yea, How can you ordinarily Enjoy any Rest at *Night,* if
you have not been well at Work, in the *Day?* Let your *Business*
Engross the *most* of Your Time. . . . Come, come For shame,
Away to your *Business:* Lay out your *Strength* in it, put forth your
Skill for it; Avoid all impertinent *Avocations.*[3]

Yet the Puritans had, too, an immense respect for learning, and
not even the most prosperous New England entrepreneur could
compete in public esteem with a leading minister. Harvard College
was founded by funds from the Massachusetts public treasury in
1636, only sixteen years after the arrival of the *Mayflower,* and
not only did every seventeenth-century New England village have a
primary school, but a dozen of the larger towns supported secondary public schools, on the English model, by taxation. The zeal of
Puritanism, so hot during the first trials of colonization, gradually
cooled, however, and hardened at last into the established faith of
the propertied classes. The clergy were still learned, but their
learning was hollow, without the fervor and imagination of the
early ministers. And then, in the middle of the eighteenth century,
came the "Great Awakening," when revivalism swept America and
devalued the exchange rate of learning. Salvation was no longer to
be sought in classic commentaries on the Scriptures or the textual
explorations of local divines, but in the moving of the spirit at the
eloquence of a new preacher, or simply in the private reading of
the Bible. As the differences between the established clergy and the
revivalists deepened into mutual enmity, learning itself was increasingly attacked as obscuring the simple truths of Christianity
and feeding the pride of the soul.

This depreciation of learning was secularly promoted by the
opening up of the West. The early Puritans had not merely respected education; many of them had been highly educated. For
every forty or fifty families, indeed, there had been one university-

trained scholar, generally from Cambridge or Oxford. But the large majority of those who later took the wagon trails to the West were either new immigrants, whose condition in Europe had provided them with little if any schooling, or those Americans whose circumstances or absence of skills discouraged them from the crowded competition of the Eastern Seaboard. Moreover, within the settlements of the West—whether tiny farming communities on the prairie, brawling mining camps in the mountains and the desert, or cattle ranches on the Great Plains—the struggle was to grow or to find or to raise, with neither means nor material for the culture of the cities. Many, without education themselves or more than the rudiments for their children, made a virtue of necessity and proclaimed the superiority of practical experience to learning.[4]

Allied to this was the whole cult of primitivism, whose heroes were unsophisticated enough, but some of whose most persuasive propagandists came, like James Fenimore Cooper, from the richer, leisured layers of the middle class. Certainly there were those who in departing for America consciously repudiated European civilization as decadent and despotic. But there was at work as well a troublesome inferiority complex. Many who felt themselves slighted by the cultivation of Europe, the plenty of artists, scientists, and centers of learning, sought compensation in advancing the claims of a uniquely American culture, even while they connived at the plunder of Indian land and cursed the backwoodsman for meddling in politics. The mating of Rousseau's noble savage with the predatory white settler produced some very strange cult heroes indeed, whose virtues lay far less in what they stood for than in what they stood against. Not improperly, their ultimate representative—now immortalized in celluloid and comic strip—was Davy Crockett, professional frontiersman and traveling salesman for himself, whose ignorance masqueraded as innocence, and who fell gloriously at the Alamo, the American white primitive translated by Mexican bullets from plunderer to patriot.

It was politics, however, that gave the cult of primitivism its strongest thrust. As settlement spread through the West, and in-

creasing numbers of recent immigrants were enfranchised, the
influence of the old families and patterns of power declined.
Andrew Jackson, born on the Carolina frontier in 1767 to immigrant parents from northern Ireland, became a lawyer in Tennessee, accumulated extensive lands, and led Americans to one of
their few clear victories against Britain in the War of 1812. In the
Presidential election of 1828 he ran against John Quincy Adams,
the White House incumbent and bearer of one of New England's
proudest names, whose father had been Washington's Vice-
President and then second President of the United States. Jackson's triumph, for all the complex factors that produced it, seemed
simply, for many Americans, the triumph of popular government,
an end at last to the long rule of the gentlemen, with their smooth
progress from Cabinet to White House. And Jackson's personality
was crucial to this assessment, as it had been to the electoral
contest. He had no time for book culture; he did not know, or
care, how to spell the name of Washington Irving—whom he
called Erwin—one of America's very few authors eminent abroad.
Indeed, the donkey was first used as a symbol for the Democrats
by their opponents in allusion to Jackson's ignorance—he was, of
course, anything but ignorant of the way to wealth or political
power in America—and the Democrats were electorally glad
enough of the allusion to assume the symbol as their own.

Jackson in office was no champion of the downtrodden, and his
policies did nothing to arrest, let alone reverse, the process of
relentless economic competition. Paradoxically, his election,
despite its debt to the slaveholding South and his rejection by
nearly all of the industrial Northeast, presaged the collapse of
plantation power and the dominion of industrial capitalism.
Popular rule was in reality less a fact than a front. As Jackson's
own career reflected, it was money, not birth or cultivation, that
would increasingly command America. Yet a front of popular rule
would not become any the less advisable, and the association by
the mass of voters of their suitable representative with the industri-
ously unintellectual was a lesson not lost on the class of capital. A
century and a quarter later, an election like that of 1828, with

differences of a consummate irony, was to stir America. It would be the Republican party, supported by the bulk of big business, which would make great electoral play with the intellectualism of the Democratic candidate and the homespun contrast represented by its own nominee. Eisenhower, like Jackson a former general, would attract many votes with his trail of military glamour, and Stevenson would just as surely repel many with his reputation as an "egghead" and his trail of elegant phrases.

If learning ceased to rival money as the object of reputable American ambition, so too did all but the highest reaches of a public career. Politics had not been the profession of America's heroes; they had risen to public notice and demand as scholars or soldiers, farmers or financiers, and generally as men of means. Jackson himself continued the tradition; if he went from log cabin to White House, it was by way of success in land accumulation and war. Only Lincoln, of all the impressive Presidents, achieved renown, without impetus from family or finance, in politics alone, and the circumstances of his rise to supreme office were, like those of his accomplishments there, scarcely normal. Indeed, the Presidency was more likely to impoverish than to enrich. Jefferson entered politics with substantial estates and left the White House with debts of $20,000; threatened with bankruptcy, he was saved in the end only by a national subscription. If the White House was the summit of supposed American desire, the climb usually required more than political equipment, and the slopes seemed to the common eye not seldom strewn with dollars.

To be sure, money—and sometimes a great deal of it—could be made at the lower levels of public service, in Congress and notoriously in local politics; but not by too tender a regard for the law or the obligations of office. And if political corruption seemed in the main safe from disclosure and scandal, it was not always so, while business corruption ran virtually no risks at all. A bribed legislator, discovered, ceased at once to be socially acceptable; a bribing businessman, discovered, was no worse than a shrewd operator taking proper advantage of opportunity. Above all, why should ambition choose the minion instead of the master? Politicians were so openly employed in promoting the interests of the rich that it was scarcely surprising if public opinion despised politics as subservient to money.

And money was not only power, it was progress. The spectacular fortunes were generally made in industry or in the stock speculation and banking associated with its growth. Railways, steel mills, canning factories, the signs of American advance to the material millennium, were connected with individual capitalists. A Cyrus McCormick was regarded as entitled to his millions; his reaping machine, after all, revolutionized farming. And if the methods of some capitalists seemed unduly depraved, the extent of their achievements staggered criticism. Cornelius Vanderbilt corrupted legislatures and courts, but he built boats and ran railroads and by the end of the Civil War was the first man in America to be worth more than $20 million.[5] The American reverence for size found an inexhaustible object in riches, and much was forgiven the possessor of the largest fortune in the country.

Money became the national morality. Indeed, Mark Twain saw it as the established religion.

> What is the chief end of man?—to get rich. In what way?—dishonestly if we can; honestly if we must. Who is God, the only one and true? Money is God. Gold and Greenbacks and Stock—father, son, and the ghost of same—three persons in one; these are the true and only God, mighty and supreme: and William Tweed * is his prophet.

It was not merely that enough money excused all but the most outrageous, and exposed, ruthlessness and even dishonesty in making it. Poverty itself seemed a sign less of misfortune than of vice. As the Puritans had seen in riches a mark of election, so the temporal moralists saw in riches a mark of merit. Journalist, scientist, and statesman, one of the main authors of the American republic, Benjamin Franklin represented his own career as reflect-

---

* The political boss of New York, who with his associates—the Tweed Ring—plundered the public, from 1869 to 1871, of a sum estimated at between $45 million and $200 million. Exposed largely through the efforts of *The New York Times,* he was tried, found guilty, and sentenced to twelve years' imprisonment.

ing the principle of material reward. He wrote his autobiography to record his rise "from the poverty and obscurity in which I was born and bred, to a state of affluence and some degree of reputation in the world," while his *Poor Richard Improved,* published in 1757, was a popular manual to prosperity.

> *If time be of all things the most precious, wasting time must be,* as Poor Richard says, *the greatest prodigality;* since, as he elsewhere tells us, *Lost time is never found again; and what we call time enough, always proves little enough.* Let us then be up and doing, and doing to the purpose; so by diligence shall we do more with less perplexity. *Sloth makes all things difficult, but industry all easy.* . . . If we are industrious, we shall never starve; for, *At the working man's house hunger looks in, but dares not enter.* . . . What though you have found no treasure, nor has any rich relation left you a legacy. *Diligence is the mother of good luck, and God gives all things to industry.* . . . Methinks I hear some of you say, "Must a man afford himself no leisure?" I will tell thee, my friend, what Poor Richard says, *Employ thy time well, if thou meanest to gain leisure; and, since thou art not sure of a minute, throw not away an hour.* Leisure is time for doing something useful. . . . But with our industry we must likewise be steady, settled, and careful, and oversee our own affairs with our own eyes, and not trust too much to others. . . . Trusting too much to others' care is the ruin of many; for *In the affairs of this world men are saved, not by faith, but by the want of it.* . . . So much for industry, my friends, and attention to one's business; but to these we must add frugality, if we would make our industry more certainly successful. A man may, if he knows not how to save as he gets, keep his nose all his life to the grindstone, and die not worth a groat at last.

If such were the peculiar Yankee virtues, which had made not only their practitioners rich, but America herself so vigorous and successful, the corollary was not missed. The poor were poor because of their laziness, credulity, and extravagance. It was an interpretation that excused exorbitant differences in living standards between rich and poor, and naturally the opposition of the rich to any public welfare at their expense. Organized relief would only encourage the poor to believe that they could get something for nothing and so confirm them in their reluctance to work and save. The existence of rich and poor was necessary and beneficial; it provided the proper incentive for the diligent and the proper punishment for the refractory.

The effect of such beliefs, of course, was to promote the social indifference, and human ravages, of money. The hustlers of industry and finance fell upon land, labor, and the gullibility of their fellow Americans with a rigorous devotion to their own enrichment. They leveled forests in bland disregard of the encroaching desert; treated whole communities as no more than a source of labor, to be abandoned when the purpose of their exploitation ceased to be sufficiently profitable; polluted water and air with the refuse of their factories; despoiled private investors and the public treasury by manipulation and fraud. Financial scandals, like those which followed the crash of 1929, revealed not only that men of assured and enormous wealth, the controllers of American business, engaged in dishonesty and deceit, but that they saw nothing wrong in what, after all, long custom allowed.

The gospel of money was a gospel of violence. There was violence of the obvious kind. Men shot each other for mining claims, land deeds, water holes. After killing or driving off the Indians from the Great Plains, cattlemen and sheepherders fought each other across the West, in Arizona, Montana, Wyoming. Rival railroads sabotaged each other's tracks and rolling stock, while intimidating, when they could not bribe, such public officials and private citizens as stood in the way of their expansion. Industry and commerce employed special police to deal with troublesome labor. And since money mattered far more than the means by which it was made, crime grew alongside America. It developed organization and style. It became a business, big business—like any other, in pursuit of the American promise—with its own stockholders, executives, labor; dividends, salaries, wages; concentration of control through mergers, take-overs, and the ruin of undercapitalized competitors. Behind a respectable façade of hotels and restaurants, bakeries and laundries, it would soon operate a form of private enterprise whose success might be measured in hundreds of millions of dollars a year, enviably exempt from income tax.

The violence of acquisitive America went far deeper than such street-level manifestations, however. To the passion for enrichment Americans brought their traditional idealism, an innocence that saw money not merely as useful but as good in itself. Where a more cynical Old World sought it as a means to possessions and leisure and security, the New sought it as an end, the meaning and purpose of the individual and his social relationship. De Tocqueville reached to the essence: "I know of no country, indeed, where the love of money has taken stronger hold on the affections of men, and where a profounder contempt is expressed for the theory of the permanent equality of property." [6] It was true; the Americans had fallen in love with money.

Yet money, by its nature, embezzled the idealism invested in it. It defrauded America out of those very ideals—liberty, equality, and the pursuit of happiness—deposited with her in the establishment of her identity. America meant more and more a hope not merely divisive, personal achievement at the expense of other people, but a hope necessarily divided, between a desire and an expectation that collided. Desiring liberty, equality, and above all happiness, the American expected money to supply them, and found only, inevitably, that it squandered them instead.

Jefferson, that archetypal American in the perplexity of his career, saw and denounced the corruption of riches for the nation, and for the nation pursued them. As philosopher, he sought freedom in an environment of simplicity and rejected economic and territorial aggrandizement as fatal to an agrarian republic governed by mild laws and cherishing equal opportunity. As planter, he possessed slaves himself, and, as leader in Virginia, led no movement to emancipate the state from the sustenance of its economy. As President, he sped the expulsion of the Indians from their land, continued Hamilton's fiscal policies with their encouragement of industry and commerce, extended federal authority by spending federal funds on public works, and killed all prospect of a simple agrarian republic by the expansionism of the Louisiana Purchase. Where he had reluctantly gone, who would not follow? And how much of the original idealism would survive the march of the railroads and the factories across America? Liberty and equality were forsaken as "manifest destiny" went hotfoot after power and prosperity instead.

It was not a choice that could be made without doing violence to much of human, and especially American, character. It was less what Americans found than what they lost in the search for riches that seemed more and more to matter, bewildering them with the elusiveness of satisfaction and gnawing at apparent success with the hunger of guilt. Between the rhetoric of the compassionate Utopia and the reality of the marketplace lay a no man's land of frustration, restlessness, and waste. America promised happiness and sometimes gave, as it was asked to give, money. It was not the same thing. The very infinity of the American hope depreciated anything as finite as money. How much money was enough? Could any amount be enough, if there was someone somewhere who had more? If riches and success were relative, they were for that reason alone finally unattainable.

The American imagination was fascinated and tormented by money, its power and glory, its delusions and devastations. And the two periods of American history over which money held particularly splendid and predatory sway—the Gilded Age that followed the Civil War, and the Jazz Age that followed the First World War—fittingly produced two great writers who realized, in their lives and in their work, this ultimate ambiguity.* Both Mark Twain and Scott Fitzgerald came from backgrounds of the money dream: Twain from a bankrupt father and a childhood of poverty, a home where sudden riches forever hovered; Fitzgerald from a middle-class uncertainty, an eccentric mother and a father failed in

---

* Henry James must be mentioned alongside any other American mythologists of money. So many of his heroines are symbols of the New World—in their innocence, their idealism, their independence, and their fortunes. It is their money that makes them modern princesses, the repositories and source of so much power and romance. It is their money that seems to give them so much freedom, so much promise. And it is their money that provokes their betrayal, the violence done to their trust and their love. Thus it is her surprise inheritance that enables, persuades, even causes Isabel Archer to affront her destiny in *The Portrait of a Lady*. It is her money that subjects Milly Theale in *The Wings of the Dove* to deceitful friendship and marriage.

business, a home where the social dominance of the rich was a
constant spur and a constant rebuke. For both, love seemed always
to demand the surety of material success. Twain's wife, Olivia
Langdon, was the daughter of new money, of a father who had
found in coal and iron the riches that Twain's own father, in coal
and iron too, had so unsuccessfully sought; for the rest of their
lives together, Twain would want to show her that she had not lost
by the exchange of protectors. Fitzgerald, in his first important
love, for Ginevra King from a rich family in Chicago, was told by
someone, "Poor boys shouldn't think of marrying rich girls." [7]
And when he married Zelda Sayre, the daughter of a Southern
judge, it was only after the assured success of his first novel, in the
knowledge that "a life of poverty and struggle" would have put
"too much strain upon her love." [8] As he was to write in 1936,
when exploring his past:

> The man with the jingle of money in his pocket who married the
> girl a year later would always cherish an abiding distrust, an animos-
> ity, toward the leisure class. . . . In the years since then I have
> never been able to stop wondering where my friends' money came
> from, nor to stop thinking that at one time a sort of *droit de
> seigneur* might have been exercised to give one of them my girl.[9]

Both Twain and Fitzgerald earned enormous sums of money,
and inevitably whatever they earned was never enough; both sank
into debt, and Twain, like his father, into bankruptcy. Both, in
their need, turned from their books—Twain to lecturing and business, Fitzgerald to hurriedly written stories for popular magazines
and to film scripts; for both, money seemed to ravage, as it rewarded, their talent. Both died worn out by the ambiguity they
pursued.

In the writings of Mark Twain money is an all but invariable
presence, potent, mysterious, an idol around which men and
women dance in hilarity, in depravity, in sacrifice. As a recent
biographer sees it:

> To know money was to eat of the forbidden tree. . . . The loss
> of sexual innocence, by Mark Twain's standards, was the equivalent
> of a total collapse of morality; by a process of displacement, money

plays the role of sex in his work. He was notoriously reticent about depicting mature sexual and emotional relationships, but he did write a kind of pornography of the dollar.[10]

Indeed, in *The Man That Corrupted Hadleyburg,* the darkest portrait ever done of an America in love with money, Twain drew a people in the ubiquitous corruption of original sin.

Yet money was the very civilization of America, and to abandon it was exile from society, a wandering loneliness. Such was the dilemma that Twain made into myth with *Huckleberry Finn.* Huck, who is significantly the "I" of the story, starts by abandoning his father and renouncing the trust fund that represents, with its 6-per-cent return, the objective and meaning of organized society; he helps "Miss Watson's big nigger" Jim to escape, and so strikes at the whole economic basis of the community to which he belongs; and he returns only to reject the society again. "But I reckon I got to light out for the Territory ahead of the rest, because Aunt Sally she's going to adopt me and sivilize me, and I can't stand it. I been there before." It was a repudiation necessarily condemned by the American conscience. And Huck recognizes it. "All right, then, I'll *go* to hell," he accepts, in deciding at last against betraying Jim. It was a repudiation that Twain himself imaginatively sought, and in reality—guiltily, destructively— renounced.

It was money that Fitzgerald saw as the mildew of the American dream. At the end of *The Beautiful and Damned* Anthony and Gloria have been made by their pursuit of money what they hoped, through its attainment, to escape ever becoming—he lonely, broken, old, "his very craving for romance . . . punished"; she "sort of dyed and *unclean.*" And to the whole novel Fitzgerald gave the citation: "The victor belongs to the spoils." In *Tender Is the Night* Dick Diver is drained of his generous trust in himself, his ideas, and his talent, his very personality, by his rich parasitic wife. And in *The Great Gatsby* American idealism is lured to its death by money. It is money that makes Daisy so dazzling to Gatsby.

"She's got an indiscreet voice," I remarked. "It's full of . . ." I hesitated.

"Her voice is full of money," he said suddenly. That was it. I'd never understood before. It was full of money— that was the inexhaustible charm that rose and fell in it, the jingle of it, the cymbal's song of it. . . . High in a white palace the king's daughter, the golden girl. . . .

They are destructive, the rich. "They were careless people, Tom and Daisy—they smashed up things and creatures and then retreated back into their money or their vast carelessness, or whatever it was that kept them together, and let other people clean up the mess they had made. . . ." Gatsby, with his "heightened sensitivity to the promises of life," his "extraordinary gift for hope," his "romantic readiness," is their natural victim. He is the American dreamer dreaming the wrong dream, and he ends, rightly in violence, consumed by his dream.

Dallas was a city of violence long before it leaped into the headlines as the site of President Kennedy's assassination. And it has continued to be so since. Even by American standards, the murder rate is alarming: 10.3 per 100,000 in 1965, compared to 6.9 for Chicago; 6.1 for Los Angeles and New York; 5.5 for Philadelphia; and 2.8 for Boston.* In Liverpool and Manchester, British provincial cities similar to Dallas in size, the murder rate in 1965 was around 0.5 per 100,000.†

Yet Dallas has one of the lowest levels of unemployment among major American cities. The 1960 Census found a percentage of 3.2 for the metropolitan area, compared to 3.8 for the metropolitan area of Boston, 4.3 for Chicago, 4.7 for New York, 4.9 for Philadelphia, and 5.7 for Los Angeles. There is—as where is there not

---

* FBI figures.

† By British standards, indeed, the murder rate in America as a whole is staggering. In 1965 there were 9850 murders in the United States, and 171 in England and Wales, with a population one-quarter that of the American. The Metropolitan Police District of London, dealing with some 8,500,000 people, had 36 murders, or as many as would have occurred in an average American community of less than 750,000. By 1966 the number of American murders a year had risen to 10,900, or a rate of 5.45 per 100,000. The number of what the FBI termed "serious crimes" had reached 3,250,000, or a rate of 1 per 60 for the entire population of 200,000,000 men, women, and children.

in urban America?—a Negro slum. But West Dallas is not Harlem or Watts. There is—or so far has been—no such ghetto turbulence as marks so many cities, big and small, in the West and North. And if Dallas belongs to the South—Texas was among the seven original Confederate States—it does not belong to the Black Belt, where the civil rights insurrection has struck cities such as Atlanta and Birmingham. Negroes comprise a smaller and less assertive element in Dallas than in most American cities. The unusually high incidence of violence cannot properly be attributed to the peculiar extent of poverty, or of racial rioting, protest, and repression there. Relatively, too, there are very few foreign-born. Where the percentage in New York is 17.4, in Boston 12.4, in Chicago 9.7, in Los Angeles 9.1, and in Philadelphia 6.8, it is in metropolitan Dallas a mere 1.5.[11] Whatever Dallas is, is native American.

And Dallas is, above all, money. Proudly it proclaims itself so in the banks and insurance companies that dominate its skyline, thrusting above one another like churches competitively plucking at the ear of God. There is no natural reason why the city should exist at all. It is a long way from the sea, and its local river is either flood or dust. The black land around is grudging, without the oil and gas and sulphur that have burst through the surface of Texas elsewhere in sudden skyscrapers. No treaty was signed and no battle fought at Dallas; until a President was killed there, it had no claim on the American tourist. It hustled itself into a city, and it hustles still.

Dallas exists by assiduous promotion. In the 1870s, with a population of less than 4000, it bribed and badgered its way into becoming a railway stop. And from that first success it never looked back. It sold itself as a center of commerce and finance, enticing banks and shops, insurance and utility companies, by pioneer techniques of collective advertising. When, in 1936, Texas was to celebrate its centennial, Dallas must have seemed the least likely of all the large cities in the state to be chosen as the site. But leading citizens hurried down to the state legislature at Austin with $3,500,000 in hand, a program of entertainments to intimidate where it did not excite, and the determination of doorstep salesmen. They took the centennial to Dallas, and Dallas to the country as the most important city in the state.

Today photographs of the city skyline, with captions crying "It's Great to Live in Dallas," exhort passers-by from shop windows. Why high banks and insurance companies should provide any guarantee of "great living" may puzzle the stranger; but Dallas itself seems sure enough of the alluring implications. There is culture too, of course. The city takes pleasure in calling itself "The Athens of the Alfalfa Fields." But the sprightly-looking Dallas Theater Center, designed by Frank Lloyd Wright, is largely given over to musicals and domestic comedies of the television type. The Dallas Symphony Orchestra is grandly compared by the local press, industrialists, and merchants, to the New York Philharmonic, and the Dallas Civic Opera makes a seasonal show by importing some of the most expensive singers in the world for gala performances. But there is an obvious air of diligent social leadership about attendance. There are few intruders from the middle, let alone the lower, income levels, and few if any of the young. The museums have some of the most celebrated paintings ever bought to reduce inheritance tax, but they hang forlorn before the flat earnestness of the visiting city. There is, in the whole prosperous metropolitan area of over one million people, not a single bookshop of excellence—though there is one of dutiful dimensions—and less than a handful above the standard of railroad-station newsstands. Culture is, essentially, a branch of the Chamber of Commerce, a civic attraction, like the tax rate, itself promoted as the lowest for any major city in the United States. Dallas comes straight out of Sinclair Lewis, the Zenith with its tone set by Chum Frink's talk to the Boosters about the need for a symphony orchestra.

> . . . Culture has become as necessary an adornment and advertisement for a city today as pavements or bank-clearances. It's Culture, in theaters and art galleries, and so on, that brings thousands of visitors to New York every year and, to be frank, for all our splendid attainments we haven't yet got the Culture of a New York or Chicago or Boston—or at least we don't get the credit for it. The

thing to do then, as a live bunch of go-getters, is to *capitalize Culture;* to go right out and grab it.[12]

Fiction? It was R. L. Thornton, Chairman of the Mercantile National Bank, who more than any other man was responsible for providing Dallas with its symphony orchestra. Once assured that he would never be asked to attend a concert, he headed a drive to raise the required funds.

> He was convinced that a symphony orchestra was absolutely necessary to the economic growth of Dallas and he sold the orchestra on that basis and on that basis alone. In doing so, he gave a pattern to the raising of money for various artistic endeavors in Dallas. Most of the leaders of arts campaigns begin by stating that they themselves couldn't care less about the arts, but that it is good for the city to have them. In my seventeen years in Dallas, I have never heard a man try to raise money for the orchestra on the basis that he loves music.[13]

And the author of that comment should know; he was an executive of Neiman-Marcus.

Certainly far more intrinsic to the quality of Dallas than the arts, and on a level of public awe with the largest insurance company or even the Alamo (which belongs, after all, to a competing city), is Neiman-Marcus, a department store of infinite pretentiousness that teaches Dallas, and much of Texas, the delights of taste. The store has no sense of humor about itself—its owner, Stanley Marcus, calls it "a magic land"—but then the citizens of Dallas have no sense of humor about the store either. From its aggressively condescending advertisements, weekly fashion shows, special exhibitions, and sales staff, they discover how to dress, what to talk about—a handbag is a "conversation starter"; an art show, a "conversation leader"—where most fashionably to dine or retreat for the winter. Those who cannot afford to take the more costly advice settle for salt cellars and art shows and yearn for better days. But for richer or poorer, Neiman-Marcus is the guide.

> Information no opera-goer should be without, concerning what to wear for each performance, the right accessories, and even what your husband should wear. . . . Opening Night. "Il Trovatore" by Giuseppe Verdi. You wear a full-length dress (here, Dior's yellow

lace sheath, $495.00); your escort, white tie and tails. Saturday Afternoon, the beloved "La Bohème," by Giacomo Puccini. Attend it in a sophisticated print, such as this Traina-Norell dotted surah, $210.00. Your husband should wear his newest dark silk suit. Saturday Night, hear Renata Tebaldi in Verdi's "La Traviata." Go gala in short, flowing chiffon by Traina-Norell, $485.00. Your husband? In dinner jacket, of course. Sunday Afternoon, the delightful "La Périchole," by Jacques Offenbach. Plan ahead—wear a silk ensemble like this Blotta design, $265.00. You'll shed the jacket for a final opera celebration Sunday evening.[14]

It thrives not only, like Dallas, by constantly selling itself, but by recognizing the individual insecurity, the terrifying suspicion of personal meaninglessness, in a city that must sell itself constantly to survive. Dallas is a commodity, packaged and promoted for appeal to the customer, and the people of Dallas more and more see themselves as commodities too, individual goods on the counter of the collective identity. Indeed, it is not what they are— for what *are* they?—that matters to the customer, who must be persuaded to buy them; it is what they appear to be. And just as price is what fundamentally distinguishes one commodity from the other, so it is price that distinguishes the people of Dallas from one another. Money is not merely part of the individual personality; it is the dominant part, if not the whole. And since in salesmanship, after all, the illusion is secondary to the reality, the commodity to the packaging, it is the appearance of money that counts—the clothes one wears, the car one drives, the house one owns, the district one inhabits—rather than the money itself. "This is the town of the four-flusher," one wry citizen told me. "Money is what runs it. And if you haven't got it, you'd better make as though you have. The people here pay their country-club dues before they pay the paper boy."

Neiman-Marcus enjoys the prestige it does because it supplies the price tags, the appearance of individual identity. Women recognize a meaning in one another by the Neiman-Marcus labels on their coats or the Neiman-Marcus provenance of their tablecloths, while their husbands do the same with their Neiman-Marcus suits and wallets, tie clips and after-shave lotion. Neiman-Marcus has been called a state of mind. It is, rather, a state of mindlessness. The shops of Dallas become a substitute for thinking, a substitute even for sex. Some of them have the deliberate decor of nightclubs, red plush and hushed lighting and a distant music, lending to the spending of money a sly titillation, a promise of illicit adventure and discovery. To buy is more than to acquire. It is to live. It is to be.

Money is thus not just the business of Dallas. It is the faith. The most sacred days are neither religious nor national occasions, but those on which the bank returns are announced, to reveal whether Dallas is still the city with the most money on deposit in the state. There are reports that Dallas banks lend money to one another when the returns are calculated, so that the same large sum may appear in two ledgers simultaneously, as due for deposit while not yet drawn. These originate, perhaps, in the malice of rival banking centers. But certainly the citizens of Dallas seem, profoundly and personally, to need the knowledge that theirs is the richest city in the state. Allusions to it stud their conversation. It gives them, as empire once gave Britons of all classes, a sense of individual splendor by participation. Even those whose price tags are low can take pride in belonging to the stock of Neiman-Marcus instead of Woolworth's.

Naturally, too, money is the government of Dallas. For who are better qualified to rule a city of money than those who have more money than anyone else? The Athens of the Alfalfa Fields is much closer to the Athens of the Thirty Tyrants than to the Athens of Democracy. The city is in effect governed not by its elected representatives but by a private group of leading businessmen called the Dallas Citizens' Council. This council's membership, of some two hundred, is too unwieldy for local principles of firm efficiency, however, and the essential command is exercised by a much smaller group, the power core of the council, which consists of those at the head of the biggest businesses. Just how many such commanders there are excites much respectful speculation in Dallas; estimates stretch from seven to thirty, but prevalent opinion supposes some figure between seven and ten. Undoubtedly

among them are the heads of the two main banks, the Republic
National and the First National; the president of the Dallas Power
and Light Company; the board chairman of Tom Thumb Stores, a
chain of food shops; the board chairman of the important electronics corporation, Texas Instruments (Mayor of Dallas for the
past few years); the president of Industrial Properties, a real-
estate firm; and the publishers of the two Dallas daily newspapers,
who own the two Dallas television stations as well. Most local
power-watchers would add the heads of the two largest insurance
companies and, despite his reputation for relative liberalism,
Stanley Marcus.

Through the Citizens' Charter Association, the Citizens' Council
controls the City Council; and through the Dallas County Democratic Committee, the state legislators from Dallas County, and the
county commissioners, the whole local one-party dominance of the
Democrats. Through the Greater Dallas Council of Churches, it
keeps the white preachers in line; and through the Dallas Ministe-
rial Alliance, the Negro ones. Through the Dallas Chamber of
Commerce and the Dallas Real Estate Board, it supervises business; and through the Southern Methodist University, whose
president is a member, and the Committee for Good Schools, education. Through the Dallas County United Fund, with its recipient
"social agencies," and the Community Arts Fund, it dispenses and
regulates benefactions for charity and culture.*

"The most efficient mercantile oligarchy since the Medici," one
of my Dallas informants called the system. But it is doubtful
whether the Medici were ever quite so thorough or so bland. For
what astonishes the prying visitor is not so much the extent of
control exercised by the Citizens' Council, but its precision and the
all-but-ubiquitous civic acceptance it enjoys. The right of money to
rule Dallas is seen, if not always as divine, at least as proper and
plainly justified by results. From its genesis in raising the three and
a half million dollars to capture the Texas Centennial for the city,
the council, it is generally agreed, has got things done. When the

---

* The author's sources of information included past and present members
of the Citizens' Council itself.

civil rights struggle threatened to reach Dallas in the early 1960s, the Citizens' Council acted to produce quick token integration. A substantial sum of money was quietly collected, and a program of persuasion launched under the command of two council members, C. A. Tatum of the Dallas Power and Light Company, and Sam Bloom, head of an advertising agency. A film entitled *Dallas at the Crossroads* displayed the likely misfortunes that would attend any defiance of integration, while newspapers, television and radio, churches and businessmen's clubs busily disseminated the same message. Indeed, with Neiman-Marcus in the van of the campaign, token integration became good taste. And no one was left in any doubt of the council's motives. The appeal was not to the Bill of Rights or the requirements of real democracy, but to the prosperity of Dallas, which would be endangered by any such incidents as had already disturbed several Southern cities. Capital and industry were not to be enticed by race riots.

After all, Dallas maintains, the system works. Does it matter that the open meetings of the City Council are mere ceremony, since all serious decisions are taken at closed luncheons beforehand? Or that the exclusion of party politics—in practice, of any challenge to the Democrat establishment—secures the domination by a few very rich conservatives of the city's whole influence and resources? (This has significant national implications, since Dallas has one-ninth the population of Texas, and Texas ranks fifth among the states in number of voters.) Intrinsic to the American identity is competition—of opinions, associations, powers—as the ultimate guarantee of popular government and individual liberty. Yet "the leadership of the community has set a theme of 'loyalty to Dallas' which has repeatedly functioned to unite divergent segments, thereby preventing competition." [15] The system works. But for whose benefit? It is true that big business promotes the prosperity of Dallas in promoting its own; that its ability to take snap decisions on behalf of the city has snatched industry and investment capital from rivals; that its control of propaganda and the institutions of power has forced expedient measures of urban development and racial accommodation through barricades of prejudice; that government is on the surface cheaper and cleaner, as civic life is on the surface more orderly, than in the vast majority of American cities. "Few cities can afford to buy what Dallas has had without cost. We have here a case of business subsidizing government." [16] Yet the cost is not to be calculated solely in the city's financial ledgers.

Dallas has one of the poorest public transport systems in urban America, mainly because a better system would drive up the alluringly low tax rate for commerce and industry. The rich, after all, don't take buses as a rule. Similarly, the city police force is, despite the high crime rate, grossly undermanned, because the rich employ private police to protect their businesses and homes. Near the center of the city are two virtual islands, the independent fashionable townships of Highland Park and University Park, with their own public schools; residents of rich North Dallas, inside the city administrative limits, support costly private schools with generally high teaching standards and a profusion of amenities. And the public-school system of the city as a whole, starved of adequate funds, steadily decays. The rich see no reason to pay taxes for the education of other people's children, and the City Council is not indifferent to their views. The Citizens' Council would scarcely approve of municipal socialism, and in any event, since city councilors are elected by the city at large, the rich northern district, with its superior resources, usually dominates the poll.

Dallas is, beyond the concentration of economic and political control, not a single city at all, but several different cities, separated from one another by the purchasing power of their inhabitants and the commensurate quality of their services. The informed citizen will readily identify, with satisfaction or reverence, the cost of houses in any particular area, pointing out the precise street or pavement that constitutes the boundary between different economic groups. It is doubtful whether class differentiation has ever been taken further in a formal democracy. And it is not wonderful that, under such stable command by business as Dallas is, this should be so. The power of money is so unchallenged that the proudest demarcation by income—or, at least, expenditure—

seems no more than propriety demands. The inhabitants of poorer and more poorly served neighborhoods appear less resentful of the rich and the richly served than eager one day to earn a place in such exclusive regions themselves. Labor is traditionally white-collar in attitude even when blue-collar in job, and gives Dallas capital little cause for offense. Local businessmen complain that the city's reputation for hostility to organized labor is unfair, since Dallas can hardly be blamed for the apathy or contentment of its labor force. Indeed, they say, the city suffers, because manufactures such as cars and air-conditioners, sent from parts of the country where labor is unconscionably militant, sometimes arrive missing essential pieces or otherwise sabotaged. Yet Dallas gladly and profitably sells itself, to capital in search of a congenial home, as a city of tractable labor.

If the tractability owes little to coercion of the body, it owes much to coercion of the mind. For this is among the most destructive aspects of the city's smooth money sway—the virtual paralysis of thought. The two Dallas newspapers are all but unrivaled, within the press of America's major cities, for tedium, not because they are so patly conservative in editorial comment—most American newspapers are—but because their reporting is so overwhelmingly drab. Their coverage of foreign and national affairs is slanted by and for a business leadership of narrow interests and undernourished ideas, and so all the more intolerant of dissent. But if this is not exceptional among American newspapers, the lack of any real local muckraking is. The Dallas press is intrinsic to the machinery of civic promotion, and "loyalty to Dallas" discourages the exposure of scandals. Moreover, as the Dallas press proprietorship is only too aware, muckraking, that traditional feature of American journalism, has frequently, whatever its motivation, succeeded in undermining established power by undermining public complacency or indifference. "Loyalty to Dallas" and "loyalty to the Citizens' Council" are interchangeable concepts. Yet the press is only one major manifestation of a communal condition.

In America, the majority raises very formidable barriers to the liberty of opinion: within these barriers an author may write whatever he pleases, but he will repent it if he ever steps beyond them. Not that he is exposed to the terrors of an *auto-da-fé,* but he is tormented by the slights and persecutions of daily obloquy. . . . He yields at length, oppressed by the daily efforts he has been making, and he subsides into silence, as if he was tormented by remorse for having spoken the truth.[17]

The barriers raised by the majority in Dallas—or, in practice, by the oligarchy to which the majority defers—exclude from decency, when not from tolerance, all opinion to the left of the Citizens' Council. For such opinion appears to represent not just a different emphasis within a secure discussion, but a dissent that threatens the very structure of society, the whole Dallas way of life. Occasionally such dissenters are persecuted: a petroleum-company executive who wrote for a national magazine that the prevailing mood in Dallas had been conducive to the assassination of Kennedy was dismissed from his job and effectively run out of town. But this is rare: the likelihood of social ostracism usually suffices to intimidate liberal criticism. The pressures to conform are everywhere in evidence. The dinner and the cocktail party, the businessmen's luncheons and women's club meetings greet expressions of liberal opinion with unease, then distrust, then open displeasure. The correspondence columns of the local press are clamorously conservative, and a liberal letter is drowned in a torrent of hostility. The sheer intensity of disapproval appalls dissent. And in a society where approval is so important, as the acceptance of one's salesmanship, the purchase of one's identity, there are few who rebel into dissident thought and far fewer who risk censure, let alone the prospect of social and economic banishment, by disclosing that they have.

The superiority of action to thought, of the practical to the contemplative man—with the accompanying distrust of intellectual inquiry, not to speak of criticism—is prominent in the money strain of the American character, but nowhere more so than in areas of strong fundamentalism and frontier culture. The funda-

mentalist churches dominate Dallas, and it is only appropriate that
Billy Graham, the most prosperous of contemporary American
evangelists, should have his parish there. In politics and religion
alike, speculation and doubt are dissipated by a simplicity of
choice and rejection. One stands up for capitalism as for Christ.
There are no intricate explanations necessary for events, no sub-
jections of belief to perpetual test. The right-minded citizen carries
his ideology around like a pocket ruler, to measure events, opinions, people, by its clear and rigid divisions.

And Dallas is a frontier city—not of the traditional, but of a
modern, still developing type that belongs more than anywhere else
to that stretch of America from Texas to southern California. It is
a frontier not of wagon trails and Indian raids, but of mass migration and a new society, with its explorations, dangers, and insecuri-
ties, none the less. Where the older cities of the East and Midwest,
even taking the suburban swell into account, had a population
increase in the 1940s and 1950s generally below the national
average, the cities in the Southwest and southern Far West had one
far above it.

It was to California and Texas, Arizona and New Mexico that
the vast war and postwar movement of industry and people, from
the migration of scientists for work on nuclear weapons to the
establishment of middle-class retirement centers, was directed. It is
here that the vast contemporary movement of mind and machine
—in the new politics, with its collaboration of capital, labor, and
government for the greater glory of private enterprise; in the new
economics, with its development of automation, electronics, space
research, and its dependence on managed consumption and military expenditure—seems above all to be taking place. And Dallas,
with its peculiar self-promoted importance as a center of finance,
commerce, and advanced industry; its low unemployment, generally high incomes, and, of course, still higher credit facilities; its
white- rather than blue-collar labor force, deferential to paternalist
corporations; its whole smoothly ordered society; seems the
symbol, as it was in some ways the precursor. Its Graduate Research Center, so richly endowed, with its total subjugation to the

Standard Metropolitan Statistical Area	Percentage Increase	
	1940–50	1950–60
United States (212 areas)	22.6	26.4
Boston, Massachusetts	9.1	7.4
Chicago, Illinois	13.3	20.1
Cleveland, Ohio	15.6	22.6
New York, New York	9.8	11.9
Philadelphia, Pennsylvania	14.7	18.3
Albuquerque, New Mexico	109.9	80.0
Dallas, Texas	41.0	45.7
Houston, Texas	52.5	54.1
Los Angeles–Long Beach, California	49.8	54.4
Phoenix, Arizona	78.2	100.0

Source: U.S. Census. See Wattenberg and Scammon, *This USA* (New York: Doubleday, 1965), pp. 402–406.

requirements of private enterprise and profit, represents science in the new society. The sway of the fundamentalist churches represents the security of the organized individual quest for faith; a renunciation of that old, dangerously disturbing quest for charity, compassion, and joy. The Dallas Citizens' Council represents the concentration of economic and political power for social manipulation, the techniques of business become the techniques of government. Dallas, with its air-conditioned individualism, its cowboy fashions carrying Neiman-Marcus labels, its suburban ranch-house architecture, seems to many Americans a survival, if a largely artificial one, of the old frontier. It is, far more, a pioneering of the new. For here is the America of basic social conflicts seemingly resolved, the consummation of conservatism in a communal pursuit of ordered material progress.

Since President Kennedy's assassination and the literature that has flourished around it, Dallas—like Los Angeles, or Phoenix, Arizona, or other stretches of the new frontier—has come to be regarded by many Americans defensively, as the habitat of cranks. Yet Dallas has a stronger claim to being the tomorrow of America that the America of today approaches than New York City or Cedar Rapids, Iowa. And nowhere is this claim more strongly to be measured than in the violence which belongs to Dallas as to a Western, always a presence, awaited or remembered when not itself holding the stage.

If Dallas is a center of conservatism, it is no less a center of the Far Right: the home of such prominent extremists as retired Major General Edwin Walker and oilman H. L. Hunt; the scene of two tumultuous demonstrations against leading Democrats—fellow Texan Senator Lyndon Johnson in 1960, and Adlai Stevenson in 1963; the city where in general America seemed least surprised that President Kennedy should have been assassinated. Its Far Right has long lent Dallas a reputation for political violence. Yet Dallas is not, after all, Jackson, Mississippi, or Birmingham, Alabama, where such violence is a predictable snapping of racial tension and emanates in the main from among the frustrated and frightened poor whites. Racial issues are not dominant in Dallas, and those there who belong to the Far Right come from the middle-income levels in the main, with many more of the richer than of the poorer among the remainder. The demonstrator who jostled and spat at Johnson and Stevenson was much more likely to have been dressed in the model rooms of Neiman-Marcus and to have driven down coolly from Highland Park than to have bought clothes off the peg at a chain store and to have sweated on a bus from the shabby end of town.

Along most of the new frontier, from Dallas to Los Angeles, indeed, it is this middle-class surge that has given the Far Right its most significant successes in producing the crests of conservatism. (New Mexico, largely through the voting strength of its Indians and the traditional local romance between white and Indian tribal culture, has so far proved an exception. But continuing white middle-class immigration may soon bring the state into line.) Arizona is Barry Goldwater's political base, and California, through the massive support for him in the middle-class suburbs of the south, gave him his crucial victory in the Republican primary of June 1964. The same middle-class suburbs swept Ronald Reagan to nomination as Republican candidate for Governor of California, and then to election in November 1966. In Texas itself, from Houston to El Paso, middle-class support for the Far Right presses the conservatives into periodic purgings of the Democrat consensus and into the assumption, ceremonially at least, of yet more militant posturings.

Those who belong to the Far Right generally consider themselves conservatives. And to be sure, the boundary between conservatism and the Far Right is often enough blurred. Goldwater and Reagan have both straddled it; conservative in personal outlook and in the management of power, they have exploited the enthusiasm of the Far Right and borrowed from its vocabulary of violence. Yet the difference between the two political terrains is an essential one. The leaders of conservatism, in command of business, the boardrooms of government, and the allegiance or indifference of the consumer democracy, put consolidation before change, order before opposition. Their strategy is manipulation rather than force, as their objective is the acquiescence rather than the defeat of those still outside their commitment. They are the principal beneficiaries of society as it is, and their conflict with the liberals, whose policies they themselves have found so rewarding, lies in their desire to arrest reform where it is rather than run the risk of social disturbance. Their expressed hostility to the expanding power of the state is in part an anxiety that the expansion may outstrip their capacity to exploit it, and in part a maneuver to secure their rear by an alliance of rhetoric with the Far Right.

The adherents of the Far Right, however, see themselves as the victims, present or potential, of society as it is. They put change before consolidation, opposition before order, and their strategy is intimidation or force rather than manipulation, as their objective is the defeat rather than the acquiescence of those who do not share their commitment.

Some of them are old, or old as the America of relentless competition and obsolescent skills has labeled them old, and are now in middle-class retirement in the sun. They feel their hard-won economic security eroded by inflation—which they blame, or are led to blame, on the big spending by the big government of liberals, though it is the conservatives of big business and big investments who profit the most—and their whole way of life endangered by movements and events that they do not understand but recognize as hostile, from the black rebellion at home to spreading turbulence abroad. They want not merely to arrest but to reverse change, to recapture a simplicity and—despite the cruelty to others in their outlook—a compassion that their own material aspirations have helped to destroy. Moreover, America is peculiarly inconsiderate of the old, unless they are rich enough to be rampant consumers. Her whole emphasis on consumption and growth esteems the new and discards the used, the worn, as necessarily expendable. Those old faces in Pasadena, California, and Tucson, Arizona, and Dallas, crumpling in hatred and fear at mention of the United Nations or those liberals in government who constitute for them the fifth column of Communism, yearn for an America that is as far from the society of the present as is the extended family system in village India.

Others are among the very signboards of success along the new frontier—those who have made a great deal of money recently and rapidly. The hick who discovers oil on his land and at once starts to collect air-conditioned Cadillacs is a figure of Texan folklore; but he is, if rare, real—as are his counterparts in more conventional business from Dallas to Los Angeles. These new rich are tormentedly insecure; they see society as unstable. And they doubt the validity no less than the permanence of their achievement. For they have denied, in the speed and ease of their success, the traditional American morality of money, by which riches result from long and arduous effort, from thrift and prudence, from sustained sacrifice. To insecurity, therefore, is added guilt, and both are revealed, in the attempt to conceal them, by self-justification. Why should the rich be required to pay high taxes, as though in punishment for their talents and industry, to subsidize the lazy and incompetent poor? Why should those who have failed to live up to the American promise through their own inadequacies command such power by the mere social burden of their numbers? (Though H. L. Hunt's proposal to distribute votes by income is regarded, even in Dallas, as idiosyncratic, the sentiments behind it are the reserve currency of the Far Right.) If the rich feel insecure, is it not because they are, in fact, threatened by a conspiracy against their riches, and a conspiracy which has as its ultimate aim the betrayal of America herself to international Communism? And who advances this conspiracy if not the liberal intellectual, frustrated by his own inability to make money and so pursuing instead the compensations of power? Is it not this alliance of the intellectual and the numerous gullible poor that has made government so big and taxation so high? And are big government and high taxation not signs that this conspiracy, to subvert America and her ideals of individual enterprise, is succeeding? The whole authority of popular government, which the old rich smoothly manipulate for their own purposes, represents a challenge to the new rich, and they yearn for a society where money will be openly supreme, the recognition and reassurance of their personal achievement and value.

But most of the recruits to the Far Right are neither the merely old, nor the merely new rich; they are the merely, restlessly, average searching for an identity. More of them are women than men. For men can seize some identity from their jobs, some meaning— however superficial and finally suspect—from their place in a corporation hierarchy. But women can borrow this from their husbands with assurance only at the extremes; in the vast middle region they must make an identity for themselves, by their clothes, their homes, their opinions. And as in the shops they find a ready-to-wear identity of body, so in the Far Right, with its distaste for the poor and failed, its distrust of the apparently independent intellectual, they find a ready-to-wear identity of mind. If they, too, display a distaste for the poor and the failed, will it not seem, to themselves no less than to others, that they are rich and successful? If they cry their distrust of—more, their contempt for—the intellectual, will they not depreciate, in their own eyes no less than the eyes of others, the education and independence of judgment that they are without? To be only conservative, satisfied in the respectability of their opinions, does not suffice. By outstripping the very leadership of society, in acclaiming the morality of money and chasing down its transgressors, they assert their rights to an equal dominance, deny the inferiority of their own social meaning and purpose.

Yet their search is implicitly for more than a social identity. They may choose the one recognized form of dissent that runs no risk of social stigma, since its allegiance to the supremacy of business is beyond doubt. But they are dissenters none the less. And for many—perhaps, in some degree, all—dissent is sought in itself, as intrinsic to the search for individual identity. For the new frontier is essentially a closed one, a tight management of society for stratified consumption and power that enslaves the very individualism it pretends to serve. The Far Right seeks to retain the material progress of American capitalism while removing some of its crucial causes and consequences—as though a bridge could be made to change part of its function by blowing up part of its supports and part of its exit. But that such a policy is inconsequent, irrational, and—with its demand, in a world of nuclear terrorism, for greater aggressiveness abroad—infinitely dangerous, does not seem to matter much to its exponents. One suspects that its very inconsequence, irrationality, and danger have a purpose, in insuring popular rejection of the policy and so its indefinite dissidence. For the adherents of the Far Right, it is the mood rather than the idea that counts. The process of disagreement itself, the expression of hostility, especially when violent, satisfies a trinity of needs. It provides an outlet for individual frustration, an affirmation of individual identity, an experience of individual liberation.

Such dissent reflects an inherent attribute of the new frontier— its inexorable encouragement of rebellion. The still surface of Dallas civic life only magnifies the turbulence in the depths. "It's Peyton Place in a clerical collar," a rich industrialist confided sardonically to me over lunch in the august Petroleum Club. "The Baptists command the expression on our faces, but behind, take it from me, we're on our own." The Vice Squad painstakingly patrols the streets, and women walking without escorts after the shops and offices have shut are more likely than not to be stopped and commanded to identify themselves and their motives. But in the call-girl racket, by common account, the city leads even more impressively than in bank deposits, and businessmen readily admit to the ease of supplying appropriate sexual entertainment to visitors from out-of-town corporations or the Department of Defense. "They like to do their buying here," a broker explained, stopping suddenly to secure his reflection in a shop window and turning away puzzled. "We make them feel that Dallas is nothing like home."

The closeness of the old frontier is widely held to explain the exceptionally high rate of violence in Dallas and the rest of Texas. And to be sure, the violence of the old frontier provides the violence of the new with a romantic tradition, of impatience with the law, defiance of authority, and a regard for the propriety of personal requital. A husband who kills his wife, or a wife her husband —preferably by shooting—for adultery, or even in less substantially incited jealousy or rage, scarcely ever suffers the full punishment of the law and not seldom escapes altogether. Indeed, trial for murder is itself significantly rarer than the charges, let alone the known incidence, of murder, would suggest. Dallas grand juries have in recent years dismissed from trial as many as one-third of those brought before them for murder. The traditions of violence in the past sympathetically accommodate traditional violence in the present.

Yet the high and ever-rising murder rate right across America, and the peculiar contemporary nature of so much murder, as of other types of violence, suggest that closeness to the old frontier is of minor and diminishing importance. Murder and serious assault, without apparent reason; rape; the destruction of property in hatred, rage, for excitement, fun: such crime represents an increasing proportion of the total today, with small sanction in the romance of the West. This is the violence of vengeance, against not a person but people, against society itself; and it is the violence of

a fundamental, if wholly negative, personal affirmation. It is collec-
tively evident in much of the racial rioting that has burst through
so many American cities. The attack on whites, not only police or
soldiers, with guns, knives, stones, clubs, bare hands, is in the
main still—for a leadership of political calculation is fast developing behind it—an enjoyment of otherwise aimless hatred and
revenge, an explosion of repressed emotions. Rioters burn or break
what they cannot carry away, and often plunder shops merely to
dump the goods in the gutters outside.

In 1966 two instances of a crime peculiarly American in extent,
coming within a month of each other, stirred the country into a
blaze of dismay. In July a young man stabbed and strangled eight
Chicago hospital nurses; at the beginning of August another, having killed his mother and wife, went to the top of a tower at the
University of Texas in Austin, killed two women and a child there,
and then shot at people on the ground below, killing ten and
wounding thirty before being shot dead himself. The outcry that
followed these seemingly motiveless mass murders, reinforcing the
outcry that had followed the assassination of Kennedy in Dallas,
centered on the need for stricter control over the purchase and
possession of guns.

The past of violence is not a preserve of Dallas. It is all-
American, and its message reaches into every schoolroom and
home. Moreover, the two traditional romances, of national development and the winning of the West, are augmented by two contemporary ones, the romance of crime and its detection, and the
romance of America's foreign frontier. Every device of communication, in print and picture and voice, brings continually before
Americans recitals of violence, from Cowboy against Indian to
Green Beret against Charlie. The significance of such exposure is
scarcely possible to exaggerate; but it is less, surely, as in itself a
provocation to violence, than as an encouragement to the violence
provoked by the personal experience of America. It is the pressures to violence within the present that seem paramount, finding
their nourishment rather than their birth in the past. But perhaps
such a distinction is necessarily finally false. The past and the

present are inseparable. It is the whole long continuous and continuing formation of the American character that makes history, folklore, entertainment, propaganda, and news a record of, a sanction for, and an impulse to individual violence.

Dallas is an extreme of the American development, in the degree of social manipulation for private material profit that it represents; in the degree of violence it provokes by denying the very individualism it excites. It is the legendary scorpion stinging itself to death with its own tail. But this is true of all America that pursues, close behind, the all-consuming morality of money. For the rich, there comes a bewildering sense of entrapment in success, the elusiveness of satisfaction, the need to make more, do more, so as to be more, still. Violence for them is an exploration of power, a reassurance of meaning. For the poor, there is a challenge to be met in their very defeat. Some respond with a sense of outrage, at a national promise broken, an obligation betrayed, and their violence is a vengeance, against people and property as the representatives of that betrayal. Some acquiesce in the American diagnosis of their defeat. They blame themselves and sink into listlessness and dismay, surrendering to the sense of personal inadequacy and inevitable rejection. Theirs is a violence against the self. And some, perhaps most, defy their defeat with a confusion of outrage and despair, hatred and self-disgust. For them, violence is a release and a punishment, a striking at others that is a striking at the self. And in between the rich and the poor are those for whom violence is a search for some identity, for an escape from the meaninglessness that is neither the delusion of success nor the despair and outrage of failure. For all, violence is an affirmation of their independent, their individual existence in a society of divided hope, where the gulf between desire and expectation, between personal fulfillment and the means supposed to promote it, is so great and seems forever only to be growing greater.

"The essential American soul," wrote D. H. Lawrence, "is hard, isolate, stoic, and a killer." [18] As a description of the American confronting the impossibility of finding happiness through the contrivance of money, this could scarcely be bettered.

Humanity's New World is a city where the streets and parks, subways and schools are corridors of terror; a suburb where flight finds only what it flees; a day which is the hurried, steady gnashing of nerves, and a night which is tormented by the wail and revolving roof lights of police cars and ambulances. It is a language which uses violence to name even supposed measures of peace—the war against poverty; the battle for men's minds. It is the Midas myth of ubiquitous golden death.

CHAPTER 2

The Solitary Sex

Come alive with Pepsi.—*A soft-drinks advertisement*

The relationship of American men to American women increasingly astonishes not only foreigners but the Americans themselves. Further and further the masculine assertions of the frontier seem to have fled, under assault by fierce suburban Amazons, marching in club formation, with silver cutlery and embroidered guest towels, over the log cabins and ranches, lumber and mining camps, railroads and steel mills in the American dreams of their men. The ritual, like the folklore, remains virile, but the vigor has vanished, and in its place is a vast bewilderment, a sense—shared by men and women alike—of strayed sexual purpose.

For how long Americans have been obsessed with homosexuality may occasion wide disagreement; the obsession itself is now only too evident. In no country of the world do the armed forces display such care to exclude homosexuals, so that an assumed effeminacy has become a far from unknown way of escaping conscription. The GI, with his ubiquitous pinups and relentless lusting, is not altogether his own projection. In entertainment and propaganda his heterosexual appetite is diligently, often laboriously, stressed, and leagues of American women devoted to decency, whose sharp eyes rake through civilian films and books for sources of corruption, offer no complaint.

In no country of the world do men, in and out of uniform, take

51

such obvious pains to persuade others of their own manliness, shrinking from any suspicion of effeminacy with even more horror than advertising teaches them to have for any human smell. The fear of effeminacy runs deep and wide. American parents go in dread of rearing children whom their neighbors will regard as aberrations, and pay particular attention to securing a son from any accusation of being a "sissy." Clothes, games, and toys are chosen, from the earliest feasible moment, and frequently before, to distinguish the sexes and encourage them in their different similar roles. Baby girls loll in bikinis on the beach, and baby boys are introduced to the appointments of masculinity, from cowboy suits and guns to crew cuts and baseball, as soon as they can lodge them. Interior decorators offer sexually distinctive color schemes and furniture for children of any age: modern, with blue, red, or orange for boys; period, with yellow, pink, white, or green for girls.[1] The ritual of dating begins before the teens, with "coketail" and even dinner parties, to assist in devolping the "real" boy and the "real" girl. And since development seems, at the best of times, too slow, a "training bra" has made a successful appearance in the eight-to-ten-year-old female market.[2] Children are thus led to act out their sexual identities before they know what sex is about, and it is scarcely surprising that so many of them remain sexual actors all their lives. The anxiety of the parents cannot fail to transmit itself to the children, and not seldom promotes the very condition against which it is directed.

Public panic is reflected in the criminal code. Of all the states, only Illinois has legalized homosexual acts between consenting adult males; in several, such acts can be punished by terms of imprisonment twice as long as the maximum for armed robbery or second-degree murder. Other societies may have similarly harsh penalties but rarely if ever prosecute offenders. The provisions rust on the statute books, mere reminders of an ecclesiastical sway in the past. But in America, as in Britain until the recent legalization of homosexual acts between consenting adult males, the police have periodically padded their conviction records with arrests for homosexual offenses. And, much more even than previously in

Britain, such arrest, let alone conviction, carries a social stigma that scarcely any crime against life or property possesses. American homosexuals have reason enough to fear being found out, as American men have to fear being merely suspected.

The general anxiety is not without substantial nourishment. The legal and social censure of homosexuality makes it impossible to establish the number of practicing homosexuals, let alone the number of those who would be, if no such censure were involved. Kinsey in the 1940s estimated that only half of the male population remained exclusively heterosexual throughout adult life, while 4 per cent were exclusively homosexual, and 46 per cent had both heterosexual and homosexual experience.[3] More recently, in a study by Celia Deschin of venereal disease among 600 adolescents attending social hygiene clinics in New York City, 106 of the 265 infected boys, or 40 per cent, reported homosexual practices.[4] And R. H. Kampmeier, Professor of Medicine Emeritus at Vanderbilt University School of Medicine, citing an outbreak of infectious syphilis at Nashville, Tennessee, in which 47 per cent of the several hundred male contacts admitted to homosexual relations, suggests that homosexuality is more frequent today than it was.[5] In considering the large increase in cases of venereal disease over the past few years—an almost fourfold rise, from some 6400 to some 23,400, in infectious syphilis, and a rise of about 45 per cent, from some 225,000 to some 325,000 in gonorrhea, between 1956 and 1965—Kampmeier claims that "the promiscuity responsible for venereal disease . . . is often homosexual."

But whatever the estimate; whether the increase is more apparent than real; whether the incidence in America is indeed higher than in other comparable countries or just more closely examined and discussed, there is no society in which the homosexual appetite seems more in evidence. The abundance of photographs, magazines, and books more or less openly sold to cater to it makes the markets of Europe, or any other continent, appear puritanical in comparison. If accusations of a similar catering on the television screen [6] strike a note of hysteria, it is difficult to see programs like *Batman* as innocent in intention of their effective response—a national snigger. To a degree unmatched elsewhere, even in traditional Britain, certain parks, squares, streets, shops, hotels, and bars in America's major cities are known haunts of homosexuals, forced by the absurd social persecution into their furtive maneuvers. Homosexuality is extensive, and the awareness of it, in fear or explanation, all but inescapable.

Indeed, the homosexual is displacing the Negro and the Jew in American fiction as the symbolic social victim. Homosexuality has become a presence in the arts—when not as a theme, then as an essential ingredient in the personality and purpose of the artist—without parallel in other contemporary cultures, despite the influence of particular figures, past and present, in a few such as the British and the French. And by comparison with the arts in many cultures of the world, from the Senegalese and the Soviet to the Indian and Brazilian, its importance in America is prodigious.

Nowhere is the apparent extent of homosexuality more significant than within the black American community, in the face of the so long-propagated image of the Negro as so potently, intransigently heterosexual. And the evidence spreads far beyond the existence of prominent Negro homosexuals in letters and in the civil rights movement. Negro male prostitution flourishes in the cities, especially among the young of the ghetto streets. And poverty is only part of the explanation. "He was defeated long before he died," James Baldwin wrote of his father,[7] "because at the bottom of his heart, he really believed what white people said about him." The racial humiliation of the Negro father is inevitably a sexual humiliation as well, a debasement of his essential masculinity. The Negro mother triumphs over violation, as the symbol of suffering and survival. The Negro father succumbs, his ability to protect his family suspect, the symbol of impotence.

And racial degradation assails the natural family pattern directly. In the struggle for an ever-diminishing supply of unskilled jobs, Negro women are preferred, as clerks or servants, to Negro men. It is the men who make up the bulk of the sullen unemployed in the ghetto, who drift from drinks to drugs, from the home to the desperate family of the streets. There are 23 illegitimate for every

1000 live births to white women; to Negro women, there are 216. Only 1 in 10 white families is not "normal"—composed of a husband and wife; for Negro families, the figure is 1 in 4. Some 8 per cent of white households are headed by women; women head 21 per cent, or more than 1 in 5, of Negro households. Among whites, there are some 60 "disrupted marriages"—divorce or separation— per 1000 married women; among Negroes, there are 198.[8] In short, though American society is by tradition, law, and doctrine patriarchal, the Negro community is largely matriarchal in practice, and the consequent conflict cannot fail profoundly to disturb those who find themselves caught in it. The power, the protectiveness, the inviolability of the father is sought, by so many frustrated sons, in a sexual relationship with a male, and not seldom—not remarkably—with a white one, the representative of the racial conquest.

And if this helps to explain the apparently high incidence of homosexuality among Negroes, a similar conflict, between the proclaimed and the effective values of America in general, may well help to explain the apparently high incidence among whites. Outwardly America is patriarchal. In history and folklore, as in business and politics, women feature, in all but an insignificantly few instances, as mere accessories—the occasions or the rewards, not the agents, of crucial events. No woman signed the Declaration of Independence or blazed a name across the legends of the frontier; there have been no female Presidents, no female generals, no female pioneers of industry or finance. There is no American equivalent to Britain's Boadicea and Elizabeth I, France's Joan of Arc, or Russia's Catherine the Great, as a national symbol. Indeed, the penetration of the West in folklore, one of the cultural influences closest to American children, is aggressively male. Men are the sole agents of heroism, as the dominant themes, of violence and retribution, are essentially male.

And yet, in the supposedly patriarchal society of America today, women exercise a power that almost all foreigners find excessive and that amounts, in the view of many Americans as well, to an indifferently disguised dominance. They seem so much in command, so outwardly sure of themselves, shopping and traveling carelessly with their hair in curlers; dragging their business-drained husbands to concerts and lectures or going complacently alone; dressed somehow tightly but as splendidly as resources allow, with their men as a neutral background, at parties, in restaurants. Abroad and at home, it is they who seem volubly to express opinions, while their husbands so often nod or intermittently elaborate. It is they who fill the ranks of the major political parties and the multitude of respectable pressure groups outside of business, from local squalls of agitated mothers to the daughters of one or other historical event. They appear to have it both ways, the respect for their power and the courtesy for their weakness, like so many Boadiceas in crinolines. There seems something pale about the character of the American male, as there is something brightly colored about the character of the American female, like the plumage of birds inverted. Henry James was right to portray America in so many novels as an heiress, the proper home for the riches and morality—though not by any means any longer the innocence—of the New World.

Three of the most enduringly popular American comic strips—*Blondie, Li'l Abner,* and *Bringing Up Father*—reflect, indeed, a derisive despotism. In *Bringing Up Father,* Jiggs is a figure of pathos rather than fun, persistently pressed by his strident and muscular wife, Maggie, into the service of her social escalation; able to escape only by sneaking off in disguise; and subject, when discovered, to a storm of flying furniture. In *Li'l Abner* it is the women, such as Mammy Yokum, who outwit and control their lazy or boneheaded men. *Blondie,* of course, has long been remarked as a commentary on the subjugation of the husband in middle-class American suburbia. Dagwood is untidy, lazy, inefficient, greedy, and accident-prone, always having to be rescued from his blunders by the resourcefulness of his pretty wife, Blondie. (His boss is similarly bumbling, and terrified of his own wife.) His son, Alexander, and his daughter, Cookie, treat him with an indulgence close to contempt and effectively regard Blondie as the head of the family. And Blondie knows how to exercise the ultimate sanctions. In punishment for Dagwood's more serious misdemeanors, she banishes him from her bed. As one American anthropologist and psychiatrist has observed, "The boys of the Bumstead family stand a good chance of developing into homosexuals." [9]

Interestingly, a new comic strip, *Andy Capp,* has recently reached into the established popularity of the Sunday comic-strip supplement. The hero is a lazy, pugnacious, beer-swilling football fanatic who knocks his wife pleasantly about at the slightest provocation, and so commands her wry, but inwardly eager, subservience. The Capps are always broke; Andy is regularly out of work and filches the rent money for drink; and their home, like their clothes, should be the horror of middle-class America. The strip is, of course, not American at all, but British, a prized possession of the *Daily Mirror* group. The Capps as an American family would be incredible. Yet their popularity in America implies an appeal that is less horrible than wistful, a way for women as well as men to enjoy, at safe secondhand, a different relationship between the sexes.

What has happened to the American man since he planted the prairies with corn and covered the plains with cattle to sustain a dependent and respectful family? For one thing, he spends much less emotional time at home. When he is not at business in body, he is so in mind, tired by work and travel and worry, yet working and traveling and worrying still, to close the opening between his resources and the desires, expressed or supposed, of his wife and children. The sheer pressures of his search for success place the responsibility for governing the family in the hands of his wife, who runs not only the home but its relationship to the community. It is the woman who supervises local education, culture, and charity, through the Parent–Teacher Association and a multitude of committees and clubs. It is the woman who chooses the car, the house, and the neighborhood, the schools and summer camps for the children, the friends and leisure activities, to suit the social aspirations of the family. It is the woman who reads the latest fashionable psychological tracts and who disciplines, or refrains from disciplining, the children accordingly. It is the woman who dictates taste, not merely in furnishings, but in books, magazines, music, and the television programs that the children are permitted, or forbidden, to watch. It is the woman who, as the primary consumer in an economy dominated by consumption, dominates business itself.

"Never underestimate the power of a woman" has been the staple advertising slogan of the *Ladies' Home Journal,* with illustrations of how in a kaleidoscope of circumstances the husband's choice succumbs to the wife's. It is at the woman that most advertisements, in the press, on television and radio, on highway hoardings, and in neon explosions across the night, are directed— telling her not only how to dress and smell, what to cook and how to decorate her home and children, but what she would like her husband to wear or slap on his face after shaving, where she would like him to bank, or how she would like him to vote. For parties and candidates are, increasingly, commodities, to be sold by the exhortations and innuendoes, the exploitation of anxieties and frustrations, of normal consumer management. It is the wife for whom the car is in general displayed, with a young and beautiful woman lounging sensuously inside, offering just such youth and beauty to the possessor of just such chrome and plastic, or with a young and handsome man behind the wheel or at an open door, promising sexual adventure with the down payments. Similarly, it is the wife at whom the political campaign is mainly directed, emphasizing those themes, from stability to the good looks of the candidate, that seem most likely to attract her. It is no more surprising that men should more and more be elected to high political office for their good looks, professional or amateur, than that other commodities should more and more be sold for their packaging. The effective exclusion of women from all but a very few offices on the top floors of political power may not unreasonably be seen as evidence for, rather than against, the sway of women in contemporary American society.

And how should it be otherwise? The fundamental function of the American is to consume, for without rising consumption, as the exponents of the American system exhort the public, there can be no rising production, and without rising production, there can be no security of employment, let alone rising prosperity. Increased output is the requisite not only for further material advance but for virtual survival; the memory of the Great Depression is alive even among those who never experienced it, and the message of "climb or collapse" is assiduously disseminated. Nor will any sort of increased output do; it must be increased output for individual, and not collective, consumption. The public services are associated with the overweening power and exactions of government, with the welfare demanded by the idle poor and paid for by the taxes of the industrious and talented; any growth in their operations is declared, by the propagandists of private production, to erode the whole meaning and purpose of free enterprise.

The American system is a hymn to personal indulgence. "Pamper yourself, pamper him, pamper her," is the chant of the advertisements. They address not the community, far less the nation; they address the individual American, and in particular the individual American woman. "Buy," they cry. "Buy as a wife. Buy as a mother. Buy as a woman. But buy." Yet the Americans are in general already more lavishly fed, clothed, sheltered, and served by machines than any other people. What are they to buy? In the business recession of the late 1950s, President Eisenhower was asked just that question. His reply was, "Anything." But not even a public constantly advised of the duty, indeed necessity, to buy more and more will buy anything. It must be allured or alarmed into wishes, into wants, that it never felt before.

And that is the function of advertising. Of course such advertising is not directed at provoking or encouraging the desire for cleaner streets, cleaner water, cleaner air; more public playgrounds and swimming pools; more efficient, because better qualified and paid, teachers and trash collectors. It must not feed but starve any inclination for collective endeavor and purpose, any compassion and capacity for self-denial. It must foster acquisitiveness, envy, extravagance, ostentation, and, above all, vanity. It sets out primarily not to include but to exclude, to excite the pursuit of superiority through the ownership of what others have not got, and to make the measure of achievement and even identity the number and nature of possessions.

The society of competitive consumption is concerned less with the contents than with the wrappers, less with the functioning than with the appearance of things. Cars, refrigerators, and washing machines are sold as if they were dresses, so that a new cut of metal, strip of chrome, or color combination makes an existing appliance look worn out because unfashionable long before it ceases to give proper service. "Planned obsolescence" has become a phrase not of abuse or complaint, but of deliberate and even publicly proclaimed policy. Where styling cannot make the consumer change his appliances rapidly enough, built-in defects and the high cost of repairing or replacing essential parts insure that he will. To manufacture a bed or a vacuum cleaner to last a lifetime is to assault the whole structure of ever-rising consumption. It is tantamount to industrial sabotage.

The ideal object of consumption, therefore, if it is to last longer than a tissue, is shoddy but stylish, conveying a pride and excitement of ownership only until a new model makes its replacement immediately imperative. And the ideal subject of consumption must exist in an ecstasy of anxiety and acquisitiveness, always needing the latest offering of the market as an assurance, indeed a prerequisite, of identity. The man I met in Salt Lake City had the easy good looks promised by the advertisers of deodorants. Sitting in a café, sucking at a Coca-Cola, he seemed serenely self-absorbed. But when he began to talk about himself it was with bewilderment. He had failed twice in business. He did not blame anyone. He did not complain. He did not upbraid himself for his mistakes. It was at his car, five or six years old, that he struck. Repeatedly he apologized to me for it. Repeatedly he told me how ashamed he was to drive his wife and children around in it. Yes, they resented it. And why shouldn't they? Wouldn't he expect them to be proud of the best car that money could buy? Maybe they cared too much, or showed too much that they cared. But

Americans were like that. And that's why they got things done—most of them. Maybe it was different in Europe. Maybe they were brought up to expect less there. But here it mattered, the car you had. He knew many people who drove, sweating, on the hottest day with their car windows up, so that anyone who passed would think that they had air-conditioning. As he went on, explaining and asking and apologizing yet again, that car became in itself his failure to make money, and then not merely the source but the fact of his plainly failing relationship with his family. He hated that car.

And it was proper that he should. For what the America of private consumption ultimately requires is that the relationship between people should depend upon, and so give primary place to, the relationship between people and things. And inevitably this requirement fortifies, as it is fortified by, the increasing sense of strayed sexual purpose and identity. Commodities make the man. For how is a man to know what he is if he does not give out the masculine tang of a new cologne, or smoke the cigarettes that cowboys favor, or wear the underpants of athletes? It is not to him, but to his suit, that a woman responds, as it is not to a woman, but to her hair spray or nail polish, that a man makes love. A cosmetic firm offers "a whole wardrobe of faces." [10] The bra does not merely make a woman look beautiful; in itself "it's a rare American beauty." [11] Why have the man or the woman, when the clothes are the real thing? Across a stretch of naked hoarding around a building site on Madison Avenue, someone has scrawled: "Kiss the Beautiful Satin Lining of Her Coat."

But why make love to someone else's possessions when it is so easy to preserve your independence by making love to your own? Increasingly evident in American advertising is a sensual self-absorption amounting to a national narcissism. "If you're all woman and love it," proclaims a producer of brassières, "Lady Marlene 'Lady-Like' is designed for you . . . gently molds feminine curves—assures blissful uplift with never, never a letdown." [12] More and more, women are depicted caressing their own breasts, removing their brassières, or cavorting across meadows in their underwear with smiles of independent satisfaction. Whatever the state of their dress, they are seldom if ever sensually involved with a man; whatever the physical postures, they seem always to be looking inwards, at themselves, or at some neuter middle distance. When they show any hunger that is not for themselves, it is for an object, from tissues and lipsticks to cameras and cars, that seems, or seems to be becoming, sensually a part of them, and they stroke it or hold their faces close to it lovingly, as they treat their own bodies. They are seen and see themselves as complete in their private consumption.

More and more they withdraw and are withdrawn from the fantasy lives of men. Tarzan now does without Jane, and in one popular television series, *My Three Sons,* a grandfather, father, and three boys run a modern American home with the most desirable appliances and no women at all. In the celluloid romance of the West, the woman is increasingly dismissed as an interlude, if introduced seriously at all. Few cowboys seem to have wives or the prospect of any. The sunset toward which the hero usually rides in the final feet of film holds no small house with highchairs for the children. The quest is not only male but celibate. Indeed, it is chaste. The typical hero does not even make evanescent love; it is, far more, the villain to whom women seem to matter in that way. One long-lived Western television series, *Bonanza,* takes this monastic maleness to extremes. Among the quartet of heroes, a father and his three ripe sons, not one seems encumbered by a girl friend, let alone a wife.

That there is a strong homosexual element in all this is scarcely to be doubted. It is even more evident in advertising. From clothes to cigarettes, commodities clearly aimed at a male purchasing public are attached to images of the masculine often bordering on the pornographic. The possession of the commodity offers in fantasy not just the identity of the particular image but an act of intimacy almost, with the cowboy on his horse or the student in his jeans. Yet this is not the living relationship of a man with a man, but the dead relationship of a man with a commodity. And in its encouragement of this relationship, the consumer society is making masturbation the new meaning of free enterprise.

Manufacturers and distributors of cosmetics for men have increased their sales recently by between 100 and 200 per cent a year, to an almost half-billion-dollar annual business. The number and variety of products would have overwhelmed the courtiers of Versailles. And they are not the preserve of costly boutiques in the city; they stretch along shelf after shelf of suburban drugstores and even supermarkets. There are invisible face creams to moisturize the skin, hair sprays, hand creams, eye pads, and pick-up masks that make the face firm and alert, as well as some two hundred different sorts of men's cologne. With the Aramis Pick-Up Mask, "only you know what's going on, because it doesn't show on the skin." [13] Like the woman with a wardrobe of faces, the man can select his character from an array of bottles. The Fabergé company produces three different scents: Brut, which is "bold and brash"; Aphrodisia, which is "dry and sophisticated"; Woodhue, which is "crisp and sports-loving."

In this climate of consumer masturbation, it is only too likely that people will draw further away from one another as they draw closer to things, till sensation altogether submerges sympathy. Millions of Americans experience their strongest emotions not by living but by watching, so that they grow incapable of distinguishing between the person and the spectacle. In San Francisco, while I was there, a local club staged a strong-arm robbery in the middle of the day at the corner of two busy streets. Almost all passers-by stood and watched as the robbed woman screamed and the thief ran safely away.[14] Was this merely discretion, a refusal, even in a crowd, to tackle a single assailant?

Some six weeks before, in New York, an eleven-year-old boy fell from an overpass onto a disused track of the Long Island Railroad freight yards, hitting on the way a high-tension line that set his clothes on fire. For nearly five minutes he lay, trying feebly to beat out the flames and crying for help, while more than fifty people gathered at a nearby fence to watch him, without one of them making any move to help. And then a young mechanic, drawn by the crowd and the cries, ran across the street, pushed his way through to the fence, clambered over, covered the short distance to the boy, and saved him from being burned alive.

Those fifty people lining the fence were not being discreet rather than valorous; there was apparently little risk in going to the rescue. They were transfixed by the spectacle. This was not for them a boy burning; it was the burning of a boy. I spoke to not a few Americans about the incident. No one seemed surprised, let alone shocked, and most had similar stories with which to compete. Some tried to explain: such things just happened; it was the pace of America; there was no time; a certain selfishness was survival. But no one even tried to explain why those fifty people should not have gone on with their business, but hurried instead to watch. And I was left with the suspicion that those who did not, or perhaps could not, try to explain this would themselves have dropped what they were doing and jostled one another to the fence, had they seen the boy catch fire. There would have been time enough, from the way they talked, to enjoy the spectacle—not from cruelty, but because it was offered to them, a new sensation to consume. "They have no compassion," an emigrant from England teaching in Dallas complained. "They give a great deal, of course; but for themselves, not for anyone else. The act of giving is an experience of pleasure, or pride, or advantage, or duty, I don't know—but it's not compassion."

It is this capacity to subtract sensation from the people suffering it, without according the people themselves any more substance than belongs to the two-dimensional figures on the television tube, that promotes the wide syndication of a brutal comic strip on the Vietnam war [15] for entertainment over Sunday breakfast. It is this that allows a popular columnist to publish and expect his readers to find funny: "Buddhists keep setting themselves on fire to protest against the Ky regime. Not all Buddhists, of course—just the real diehards." [16]

The wisecrack is peculiarly American. It is for the most part a sort of stratagem, a self-depreciation to forestall depreciation by others.* And the purpose is to insulate the wisecracker from hurt, to cauterize his own emotions. Indeed, the essence of the wisecrack is its isolation, its separation of the moment and the person. It is not part of a developing perception or argument; it exists in itself. I remember uncomfortably a swimming party at the home of a show-business agent in Beverly Hills. All afternoon the wisecracks came, to dry rustles of laughter; but they seemed to mean nothing at all, to belong nowhere, to be lonely explosions of sensation. I asked the acquaintance, himself in films, who had brought me, why they went on, these obviously tired people, like this. He shrugged his shoulders. "It helps," he said. "It keeps things manageable. I remember when Marilyn Monroe killed herself. We were sitting round a swimming pool, and a guy came and shouted at us, 'Marilyn Monroe's pulled out the plug.' And after a few moments of babble we went on to other things." And then he added wryly, "Hardly anyone who knew her well was at the funeral. They didn't want to be connected in the columns."

The city of Los Angeles, let alone its lacquered enclaves for the rich, such as Beverly Hills, is not typical of America—yet; but if the consumer society has a natural capital, it is here, and more and more of America must become, in mood and manner, like it. For Los Angeles is the ultimate—so far, at least—in organized disintegration. Sprawling with its suburbs across hundreds of square miles—the wags who plant markers saying "Los Angeles City Limits" in the middle of the Nevada desert are playing with the truth—the city is built not for people but for cars. There is no park, no river, no square, no cathedral, no sudden fuss of shops even, to give the city a focus, for the sense of belonging to a place and its people, an enjoyment of social identity in the mere loitering of the eyes. If the city has a symbol, it is the fretwork of freeways speeding the cars from garage to business and supermarket and then back again to garage.

Public transport is rare and remote; there is small opportunity

---

* The stage and films have supplied American humor with the wisecracking woman, who usually fails to get a man and neutralizes her humiliation and sorrow with her tongue. Eve Arden and Celeste Holm are type-cast examples.

even for the ersatz civic coherence of the commuter. Scarcely anyone walks. For where is there to walk? The commercial center is
shabby and, despite the costly sport and culture monuments recently built nearby over buried slums, holds the attention of few
people beyond business hours.

"I get away from work as quick as I can," said a young woman
vastly successful at designing dresses for the young at heart, "and
then I rush down to the sea and stare, with my back to Los
Angeles." Others turn their backs in the distant seclusion of their
homes. The rich immure themselves behind long lawns and swimming pools, often in independent districts with their own public
services, from schooling to garbage collection. Private police stand
guard at apartment-block entrances, insuring the safety and separation of the inhabitants and their visitors. And so down the scale,
to the poorest, the consumer citizens have their separate suburbs,
districts, or streets, nicely commensurate, in the quality of services,
stretch of lawn or floor-space, view of mountains or sea or other
buildings, with income or debt bracket. Nor is the organized disintegration only economic. There are apartment blocks, streets, districts, that have become preserves of the young or of the old, on
the popularized assumption that the young and the old have
different tastes, interests, purposes, meanings, and only embarrass
each other's resources and appropriate pursuits by being together.

And yet, living exclusively among their equals in age and income, few show much desire to explore their neighborhood
and exercise the possibilities of social commitment. But then,
why should they? What is there to discover and enjoy? They
know what their neighbors must be like by looking at themselves.
And since their objective is usually to clamber up the consumer
scale as soon as they can, into a richer neighborhood and more
impressive possessions, why bother with the society of temporary
exile, a mere preparation? Only when their very estrangement from
other people is threatened—by radical turbulence at the universities, a new alarm at the condition of national security and the
efforts of subversion, laws against racial discrimination in the sale
of houses, or higher taxes for higher public spending—do they

abruptly search one another out, for the limited company of petition, protest, or suffrage. Their proper business is themselves, and the existence of other people in any role but the obviously serviceable is considered, if at all, with disquiet. Local preachers caught the mood when, during the Cuban missile crisis of 1962, they informed anxious congregations that a man might rightfully shoot intruders into his private fallout shelter.

Nowhere is this self-absorption more apparent than in crowds, when the separate citizens of Los Angeles are having fun alongside one another. On the beaches, lying or standing in private clumps, passing in awe before the commercial idolatry of Disneyland, seeing a show on Sunset Boulevard, they seem preoccupied, suspended, solitary, like the blind. However crowded and noisy, an American bar has a loneliness and silence seldom found in English pubs or bars in Western Europe. While I was staying in Los Angeles I was taken by a young real-estate agent on a boat for a day's fishing. There were some thirty of us in all, and we spent together several hours of a sunshine so smooth and lazy that I remember the day as all late afternoon. But no one fell gradually asleep, or hummed to himself, or just sat staring round the bay. Scarcely anyone spoke to anyone else, except to mutter an excuse as he bobbed under rods to follow his fish or change his share of the sea. They were there to catch. And their resolve was reinforced by the prospect of the jackpot, to which each had given a dollar at the captain's suggestion, and which would go to the one who landed the biggest fish. This was competition, and there was neither time nor wish for talk or idle quiet. They fished with fervor, throwing back the unpromising with impatience, while the captain and his two assistants gave sporadic cries of encouragement or predicted better luck at the next halt of the boat. I was not surprised when my companion, as we left the boat with his substantial but unsuccessful catch, told me morosely, "I can't stand fish—I mean, eating them." And he gave the whole lot away to the parking attendant.

Frank Lloyd Wright is reported to have said that "if you tilt the whole country sideways, Los Angeles is the place where everything loose will fall." He may have been referring only to the body of the city; but as a comment on its mind, this could not easily be bettered. For Los Angeles is the home of instant—and momentary—salvation, of sudden consumer ecstasies, from surfing and parachute-jumping to religious cults that scoop up converts in crowds and then dump them all at once in scandal or boredom. This is the city of sensation, of the search for something—anything —new. If it is the ultimate so far in the disintegration of place, it is the ultimate, too, in the disintegration of time.

The culture of consumption must stimulate but never satisfy, and nowhere in America does a city perform this function so well as does Los Angeles. It seems to promise everything, and so in the end seems to deliver nothing. From all over the country they come to the last frontier, for steady sun and soft beaches and clean air, a sense of space along the ocean and among the mountains, the promise of money in the largest, fastest city in the fastest-moving state, the offer of a pre-emptive share in tomorrow. But even the sun is subject to the law of diminishing returns. "You get tired of saying, 'It's a beautiful day,' every day," the taxi driver who had emigrated from Chicago complained to me. And then he added in astonishment, "You get tired of eating steak." The beaches are far more crowded than the streets and have at least as much litter. Largeness, fastness mean the factory and the motor car, and the clean air succumbs to the smog. Besides, the more money that can be earned, the more has to be spent, if the new life is to be explored and enjoyed, and the anxieties of debt are to advance rather than retreat. The spaces disappear as the city climbs up the mountains and conceals the sea. And tomorrow soon assumes the shape more of a threat than of a promise. Those new space-age industries, what do they mean? Psychiatrists on the West Coast report that the nightmares of their patients are mainly concerned with machines. In the end, the vast ocean asks rather than answers, sighs not comfort but despair.

The search turns frantically to sensation, a new experience that will absorb, if only for a little while, the asking and the despair. But the essence of the new experience is that it is so soon old. Los Angeles is in a constant fever of change. Restaurants open, fill quickly, then empty and close. Another fashion, another cult, denounces the irrelevance of the one now being followed. In a speeding car the eyes can focus only on the approaching front. God, too—why not?—becomes a gimmick.

"STOP THE WORLD—I WANT TO GET OFF—AND ONTO THE MOON!" MISS VELMA WILL TAKE A TERRIFIC RIDE ON A ROCKET TO THE MOON —HIGH ABOVE THE CONGREGATION—AND LAND ON THE MOON—AND PREACH HER ENTIRE SERMON STANDING ON THE MOON!! THE FIRST WOMAN TO PREACH A SERMON ON THE MOON!! OVERFLOW CROWDS! THE WORLD CHURCH 123 N. LAKE—NEAR BEVERLY & ALVARADO [17]

It is to be noted that "overflow crowds" represent an obvious attraction—if second to the sermon on the moon; but then, after all, Christ took his sermon no higher than the mount. The newness of a sensation is not enough. The sensation must be approved by the eagerness of others to experience it. For otherwise how is one to know that it is worth having? The consumer mind has no shape of its own; it must be pummeled into an always different shape by advertisers, salesmen, and, above all, public opinion. For where no sense of identity exists outside of separate sensations, identity itself becomes the reflection in other people's eyes. As Americans communicate with one another personally less and less, they do so publicly more and more. They may suppose that they do not need one another as people, but they know that they need one another as guides. They think, as they travel, in organized groups.

They check up on one another ceaselessly in public-opinion polls, on every issue of conceivable importance and not a few of manifest triviality. The results are widely noted in the press, and there is constant evidence of the allurement that a majority exercises. Indeed, the bandwagon is a factor that no one in conventional politics neglects. Most people everywhere want to be on the winning side; but with many Americans it is a chronic hunger, an assurance of their suitable identity. That is why so many products are advertised not by their quality or price, but by their leadership in sales. And if leadership in sales is to be neutralized by a rival, this must be done not again by quality or price, but by the recom-

mendation of celebrities. For in this culture of reflected identity
one can be certain that someone is worth imitating not by what the
person is or does, but only by the sufficient establishment of his
success.

where the *action* is
You will find this PREACHER   Rev. Bob Harrington
                                   "Chaplain of Bourbon Street"
                                   NEW ORLEANS
now in HOLLYWOOD!
NOTE   • You have read much about this most unusual preacher
         • Has appeared on the Joe Pyne Show
         • Guest on "It's Keene at Noon"

MONDAY NIGHT
(June 27th Only)   8:00 p.m.   Free Admission
THE GRAND   BEVERLY HILTON HOTEL
BALLROOM   BEVERLY HILLS [18]

The preacher's appeal, it is to be noted, lies substantially with
his appearances on television and in print, rather than with what
he may edifyingly have done or with what sort of person—short of
being found where the *action* is—he may edifyingly be. It is
assumed that since he has been a guest on a popular show he is
worth going to hear. What he has to say must be important, for he
is a celebrity. (And where else ought a celebrity to appear, preach-
ing or not, but in the Grand Ballroom of a Beverly Hills grand
hotel?)

The celebrity, of course, need not do anything edifying at all. He
or she may model clothes,* or have inherited a great deal of
money, or have been frequently divorced, or have acquired a
provocative reputation for trying—though failing, of course—to
escape publicity. The sole criterion is that the person should be
known to the public: whether by talent or quirk or the efforts of a
public-relations agency is irrelevant. There are celebrities who

_____

* A peculiarly glamorous profession in the consumer society, perhaps
because the dummy in a shop window does so as well, and successful human competition reassures people both of their surviving superiority to
artifacts and the ease of achieving fame.

become so simply by being seen often enough with other celebrities in places where celebrities are usually seen. Being celebrated becomes a career, sustaining itself profitably on advertising, television panel games, and gossip columns. Such professional celebrities are the heroes and heroines of the consumer culture; for they are not only supreme consumers—their very existence depends on their being always in the forefront of fashion—but also themselves commodities and consumed.

Los Angeles is their appropriate habitat. For here is Hollywood, the mass-production center of fantasies, where synthetic reputations are manufactured, packaged, and dispatched to millions of anxious and eager minds across the country. More and more films are made abroad now, where labor is cheaper and tax evasion even easier; but most large film companies still have their headquarters in Los Angeles and are mining a new rich vein in television shows. Here are produced the celluloid identifications of the Western, the spy adventure, and, above all, the domestic comedy, that animated equivalent of the *Blondie* or *Bringing Up Father* comic strip. Here is the industry of the "star" and the gossip column. And close by is Disneyland, that slum of the American imagination, with the metallic patter of its guides, its shoddy plastic wild animals and savages, its ubiquitous commercialization of history and folklore, and in its central exhibit, on the Art of Animation, the terrible record of Walt Disney's own decline, from an individual inventiveness and vision to the stock sentimentality of a corporate skill.

Of course Los Angeles is far more than an entertainment capital; it is a major manufacturing center, in the national lead with many of the newest industries. Indeed, by the side of real estate, show business in the widest sense is a financial midget. But the very nature of Los Angeles makes entertainment the city's symbol and seemingly its purpose. New York, too, is an entertainment center, the capital of book and magazine publishing, the theater, dress fashions, and those border industries, news coverage and advertising. But New York seems also still the economic capital of the nation. Wall Street towers over Broadway and even over Madison Avenue as a city symbol. Furthermore, New York, with its long history as a world financial center, its consciously cosmopolitan population, and its situation on the Eastern Seaboard as the nation's premier port, looks at Europe and the Old World. Los Angeles looks at America and the New. Despite its situation, on the ocean at the farthest frontier of the West, it is in outlook an inland city. And so, while New York represents still the culture of production, it is Los Angeles that stands the archetype of the consumer culture and, more and more, the meaning of modern America.

Here is the acme of display, the obsession with appearances. Buses take trippers through Beverly Hills to view the outside of houses where celebrities live, while individual enterprise may get from gas-station attendants free copies of maps with the homes of movie stars marked. Here the dominant architecture strives to combine the maximum of decoration with the minimum of function; here house after house looks like an Indian temple or a Spanish-American palace or a shotgun wedding of both. Here, where the exclamation mark passes for imagination, bars are built like bottles and restaurants like hotdogs, while wood fires burn in hotel lobbies at the height of summer. Here, in short, is the home of the "silicone lift."

"I went to talk to this producer, see," a film director explained to me, "and he asked me to wait 'cause there was this woman with an appointment, and she came in with her boobs bouncing, and smiling, like inwards. And when I got to see him afterwards, he had a dazed look. 'She had an operation,' he said. 'She used to be flat on top, like a boy. Couldn't use her. Now, did you see? They put silicone or something in them, and it swells them out and lifts them up. I've looked at plenty, but nothing like this. This is the end.' " And the director added sourly, "It doesn't last. They sag. Everything does here. There's supposed to be a woman"—he brightened suddenly—"she was among the first to have it done, and now she has to keep her hands above her head all the time."

The relationship of this consumer ethos to the confusion of sexual identity, the doubt and despair, was only too evident at the crowded and clearly fashionable strip-tease club to which a friend took me. On Sunset Boulevard one such club advertises an amateur night, when audience participation may lead to a new career and presumably in any event provide intermediate satisfaction. But the club I visited was carefully professional. Indeed, it called itself a college and offered applicants suitable training and diplomas. For tuition fees of $100, women over twenty-one, of "high moral character" and "voluptuous body," "seriously interested in the art of strip tease," might receive instruction in:

1. History and Theory of the Strip Tease
2. Psychology of Inhibitions
3. Controlling the Structural Components of the Anatomy
4. Applied Sensual Communication
5. Elementary Bumps and Grinds
6. Methodology of Teasing, Tantalizing and Titillating
7. Fundamentals of Taking-It-Off
8. Dynamic Mammary, Navel, and Pelvic Rotation and Oscillation
9. Experimental Workshop
10. Advanced Studies and Seminar in New Trends and Techniques of the Strip Tease

For men "of rare social acumen," apparently in need of teasing, tantalizing, and titillating at home, the club offered an

original gift idea. . . . Give her the authentic Teasing Togs direct from the famous Pink Pussycat of Hollywood. Consists of: pink G-string; 2 pink felt bosom bonnets; and sparkling navel jewel. One size fits all . . . also Curriculum of the Pink Pussycat College of Strip Tease (eye opening) and a basic lesson in Bumps and Grinds (give the final exam yourself!) The sooner you order, the sooner you'll know if she's a sport! Only $4.95 postpaid.[19]

The audience was overwhelmingly made up of middle-class couples in the thirty-to-forty-five age group, and though—for all I knew—they might have come from the wheat towns of Kansas or the studios of Twentieth-Century Fox, they had the look about them of local suburbanites. Waitresses with long pink tails hanging from their bottoms handed out two pink feathers to each man as he sat at his table, and there were few men in the large dark room who didn't wear these, like horns, in their hair. All but one of the strip-tease acts themselves were received with a kind of strenuous glee, as though the watchers were going through an act no less practiced, or exhausting, than the performance on the stage, or were being commanded, as in certain "live" television shows, by flashing lights to "Snigger!" "Laugh!" and "Clap!" But then the acts, despite the club's "eye-opening" curriculum, allowed little scope for variety or the unexpected, while anything more sexually deadening than breasts revolving luminous tassels at high speed—the climax of several performances—could scarcely be imagined. The whole mood of the show, it soon became painfully plain to me, was the excitement not of desire but of distaste for normal sexual relations, the fostering of a solitary sex for both men and women. Appropriately, the one act which seemed to produce a spontaneous response, through the astonishing completeness of its statement, was a strip tease performed, as the climax suddenly revealed, by a man. And the reception of this, a hilarity that seemed to me more than halfway to hysteria, was accorded as well to the male *compère,* with his peculiar patter of dirty jokes. I don't remember ever having heard anywhere before so many jokes on impotence and the voraciousness or frigidity of women. And nowhere would I previously have supposed that such jokes might be publicly received with such acclaim, such jubilation, by an audience of both women and men.

"I suppose you all know the difference between fear and panic. No? Well, it's fear when you find out the first time that you can't do it a second time. It's panic when you find out a second time that you can't do it the first time. Yes, funny, isn't it? But what is the difference between a prostitute, a nymphomaniac, and a housewife? Can anyone tell me? You, sir? No? The prostitute says, 'You're through!' The nymphomaniac says, 'You're through?' And the housewife says, 'I think I'll paint the dining-room ceiling yellow.' "

A few nights later I went to a huge pre-election Republican rally in downtown Los Angeles. One hundred young girls in red skirts, red berets, and white blouses with the word REAGAN stretched tightly across them entered marching with large American flags, placed them on the platform, and then lined up in a clapping corridor of honor for Senator Murphy, prospective Governor Reagan, and former Vice-President Nixon, each with his wife. Women of various ages in the audience blew kisses, squealed, and jumped up and down at Reagan's entrance and at any reference— frequent in the speeches that followed—to his film-star looks. There was, indeed, a persistent emphasis on looks—not only Reagan's own, but his wife Nancy's, Mrs. Nixon's, and those of almost every candidate being endorsed. (Anyone whose appearance had tactfully to be ignored was praised for enterprise and dedication.) One would have supposed that the coming elections were for bathing beauties of both sexes, not for the highest public offices in the state. Only America provided a rival attraction to Republican comeliness, and sustained applause greeted the many tributes to her as the greatest country on earth.

This, it rapidly emerged, was not a meeting to promote, let alone consider, ideas; this was a display of sensations. Apart from paying their repetitive respect to party stalwarts—"wonderful guys" and "lovely ladies"—and boosting the candidates and the country, the secondary speakers limited themselves to a protracted "Hiya, folks!" The main speech was given by Richard Nixon, and he managed in some forty minutes to say nothing that meant anything at all. With several years in politics myself, and some experience of the professional's acquired ability to sustain his cause with reverberatingly meaningless phrases, I had never before heard a speaker—let alone one of such political prominence—exhibit such a dearth of thought to such a glut of applause. "We believe that people must rely on themselves. People, not government, have made America great." How? And so? But no one heckled. No one asked questions. No one, it seemed to me, really listened. The audience was responding to the name and the sounds of the words, as it was expected to do. Why should the speech mean anything? Its purpose was to produce, like background music in shops, a mood. The Republican rally aimed to promote a private sensation, a sort of political orgasm by the manipulations of advertising. At the start of the meeting, with the mechanically drilled Reagan girls, the domineering flags, and the mindless enthusiasm, it was easy to remember films of prewar Nuremberg rallies. By the end, I was thinking far more of the relationship with burlesque.

Coherent thought is alien to the very nature of consumer politics. For the consumers themselves do not, must not, think coherently. They must merely respond in predictable ways to separate, almost invariably incongruous stimulations. Thus advertisements for pain-killers on television bear no relationship to the programs they interrupt or to any other advertisements that may accompany them. They must in a few moments produce the anticipated or actual sensations of headache, tension, irritability, and a wish for the sensation of relief through swallowing a particular powder or pill. Into a film of murder and mystery, or lulling romance, will suddenly break a discordant image barking out bargains for used cars and urging an immediate telephone call; the watcher is required to switch instantaneously from one mood to another, and then instantaneously back again. How should minds disintegrated by an endless series of isolated excitements expect a coherent political program and leadership? It seems only natural that a political proposal or measure should be considered distinct from, should even contradict, other proposals or measures within a single program; that political leaders should talk and act as though they were advertising ice cream as mother made it at one moment and a carbohydrate-free diet at another.

Not strangely, as the capital of consumer culture, Los Angeles has some of the most fractured local politics in America. Here there is neither the supreme party machine of a city such as Boston, nor control by a tight business oligarchy as in Dallas. City councilmen claim a vigorous democracy in consequence; but it is the vigor, distracted and distracting, of vested interests, not of people. The mayor himself is a partisan political figure, and one of immense authority, since he is head of the city executive and also effectively leader of his party in the populous south of the state. But his very external importance inhibits his local initiatives. And in any event the ultimate power resides with the fifteen councilmen, who comprise the city legislature and are by loyal practice independents. Theirs is the responsibility of picking a nonpartisan, generally beneficial way among the lobbies which combine, fall apart, and contend against one another for the promotion of particular measures. To be sure, the real-estate interest, with the bulk of its power in the suffrage of the middle-income groups and its leadership usually exercised by the major brokers, developers, and builders, is seldom, if ever, challenged. And few councilmen are imprudent enough to risk antagonizing the *Los Angeles Times* and its Chandler ownership. The oil and automobile lobbies are, as all over America, intimidating forces, and their influence in Los Angeles is only too evident in the derricks that crowd so many of the beaches and in the obsession with more and yet more freeways. But in the common run of civic affairs, it is the competition of less awesome pressure groups, of one special interest, one district, against another, that constitutes the substance of representative choice and the semblance of popular sovereignty.

Whether the democratic will can ever properly be determined by calculating and succumbing to the noisiest or richest or most efficiently organized of rival, indeed frequently exclusive, interests must very much be doubted. Far less doubtful is the socially disintegrating effect of such a system. The constituent districts, or even areas within a single district, see themselves increasingly not as complementary to each other, but as natural competitors for the city's limited resources. It is hardly startling, therefore, that when the Watts rioting broke out in the summer of 1965, most citizens of Los Angeles apparently did not know where Watts was. And this was not because Watts was a Negro area, subject to racial near-sightedness; almost all New Yorkers at least know where Harlem is, and there can be few whites in Chicago unable to point out the main Negro ghettos on a map. It was because those who live in one part of Los Angeles pay no attention to any other, until their interests seem somehow suddenly to be affected by it. No more appropriate comment could be provided than that, in a city all but completely out of control, the council should postpone its business while one member rises, in an apparently not uncommon procedure, to introduce his visiting relatives. "I want you all to meet my sister and niece from Missouri." His colleagues display a dutiful concern. And how should they not? He, after all, is a lobby in himself.

Santa Monica, one of the city's close suburban fragments, is the home of the Rand Corporation, a research institute "dedicated to the task of contributing to the public welfare, and specifically to the nation's security." [20] Founded with funds from the United States Army Air Force in 1946 to "study and research on the broad subject of intercontinental warfare other than surface," Rand has since expanded its territory to take in "Aero-Astronautics, Computer Sciences, Cost Analysis, Economics, Electronics, Logistics, Mathematics, Physics, Planetary Sciences, Social Science, and System Operations," for the over-all objectives of "decreasing the probability of thermonuclear or other war and of stemming or reversing the advance of Communism—the task of seeking peace but preserving freedom." Orwell might well have considered such an institute worthy of inclusion in the apparatus of 1984, for this is the nursery of the war games, the alma mater of Herman Kahn and his thoughts *On Thermonuclear War,* the center for such expert speculation as the probable response of the Soviet Union to the outbreak of war between the United States and China.

With some 1100 employees, Rand has an annual expenditure of around twenty-two million dollars now, two-thirds of it supplied by the Air Force and most of the balance by various other government agencies such as the office of the Secretary of Defense, the National Aeronautics and Space Administration (NASA), and the Atomic Energy Commission. Its own senior officials are scarcely more modest about its accomplishments and influence than are those restless libertarians who see in it the corporate *éminence grise* of the Pentagon. Rand Vice-President J. R. Goldstein declares that it has issued some seventy-five formal recommendations in the past fifteen years. "These have almost all been adopted or taken seriously, for example our recommendation that the Air Force move immediately into the ICBM [intercontinental ballistic missile] program." [21]

The institute proclaims its engagement in much research of a patently peaceable nature and intent, from "the technology and economics of water supply," begun in 1953, to urban transportation, begun in 1957, while published Rand books stretch from *The First Six Million Prime Numbers* [22] to *Teacher Shortages and Salary Schedules.*[23] But the bulk of its work, even in publishable form—and its major labors are top secret—is uncompromisingly concerned with America's military, political, and economic struggle against the enemy. The first major project, commissioned by the Air Force in 1946, was research into "the feasibility and military usefulness of an artificial earth satellite," and since then, whether it is examining *Prices and Production of Machinery in the Soviet Union, 1928–1958* [24] or *Air War and Emotional Stress: Psychological Studies of Bombing and Civilian Defense,*[25] its ultimate interpretation of the uses to which science should be put has remained the same.

I spent a little time with some leading members of the institute while I was in Los Angeles. I found them precisely hospitable, eager—if tense—talkers, and among the most openly lonely people I have ever met. Subject to constant security surveillance; with an armed guard checking their identities each time they enter the buildings where they work; without the companionship of challenge, either from colleagues holding different general opinions or from a rebellious and skeptical body of students; they are not so much employed as immured in their inquiries. Indeed, a university campus was considered and discarded as a site for the institute because "the difficulties of security classification and of doing interdisciplinary work, and the near absence of a well-developed body of thought and community of scholars dedicated to the study of national security as an analytic field, all argued against it." [26]

These arch-specialists are isolated not only from a cohesive urban culture, by the nature of Los Angeles, but from any real local relationships and even from one another by the nature of their profession. Since they come from different parts of the country and different backgrounds, to work alongside one another for a passage—sometimes lasting no more than a year or two—in their

lives, they establish little intimacy; and where they do form friendships, these seem—not unreasonably—to be with those in their
particular compartments of research. But their loneliness is not
peculiar to their situation alone; it is intrinsic to the whole cultural
disintegration of modern America. Socially adrift and morally
mindless, they are engaged in their intellectual masturbation, with
their fantasies the material of government policy probes to the
ultimate of human desolation.

We were sitting, several members of the Rand Corporation and
I, at a nearby restaurant on the edge of the ocean, eating shrimp,
with the pleasant sun on our faces. We talked about Los Angeles,
and I was finding them so clear about their disquiet: the dominion
of "nonpolitical politics," as one of them described it; the suburban fragmentation; the crime rate; the lack of any central city
culture. "Why are there so many golden tans?" a senior researcher
declaimed. "There's nothing else to do but lie on the beaches."
Only, in all this apparent social commitment, it suddenly seemed
to me, there was a real estrangement; not, after all, a disquiet, but
rather a disapproval. The city was a failure in terms not of people
but of functions; its efficiency, not its morality, was at fault. And
we got into an argument over the propriety of war games. But we
moved around, never closer to, each other. And I thought how
absurd it was that they should stretch out to Moscow and Peking
so confidently with their lonely minds, when they could not reach
me, nor I them, across so short a space of checkered tablecloth in
so easy, so sane a light.

Between Santa Monica and Beverly Hills, on the other side of
Sunset Boulevard from the Bel Air Country Club, stretches the
campus of UCLA, the University of California at Los Angeles.
Covering over 400 acres, and with a student body of some 27,500,
this is one of the most richly endowed universities in America, not
only in the extent of its equipment and the variety of courses it
offers, but in the caliber of its staff and students. Yet classes are
frequently so huge that students have no relationship at all beyond
that of receptacles with anyone who is supposed to teach them;
they might as well attend lectures on television, and indeed there is

closed-circuit provision for overflow classes. Not that any sort of attendance at lectures is necessary; there is a flourishing business in the reproduction and sale of lecture notes. Nor is it surprising that the lecturers are unable or unwilling to give sufficient of themselves to their students; to retain, let alone advance, their posts, they are required to produce articles or books that will not only reflect credit on their university—an essential exercise in the capitalism of higher education—but demonstrate their qualifications for the jobs they hold or hope to reach. For how else, in a culture of identity by appearance, is a teacher to be known, if not by his published works? A newly appointed young member of staff somewhere in the maze of the humanities recounted to me her interview with the vice-chancellor. He had welcomed her despite— the rebuke, the warning, and the bribe were inseparably implied —her thin record of publications. "Now if you were in the biological sciences"—he had smiled—"we would require fifty articles before you became an associate professor."

The ability to strike fire from the mind of a student, to communicate a regard for doubt and constant inquiry, is not a quality which a university so vast * and busy can check as evidence of excellence. Examination results, based on readily assimilable, readily classifiable information, and the publishable products of research—these are facts. And facts are what the public demands; facts are what must be provided, if industry and private wealth are to continue their subventions, and parents are to send their gifted children here rather than there. The successful modern American university is an essential aspect of the consumer society, and inevitably the student is treated not as a person with an intellectual—let alone a moral—need critically to understand his society and develop a dynamic relationship with it, but as so much raw material for specialization, to be sorted out as efficiently as possible, rejected as unsuitable, or processed, labeled, and delivered for an adequate return on the investment in capital, labor, and time.

* UCLA is only one of nine campuses—in a University of California that has almost 100,000 students enrolled and confers some 8600 bachelor or equivalent, and some 4500 advanced, degrees each year—all under central administration.

A young girl determined to register for the university summer
session invited me to go along. And as we strolled across the
campus, I paged through the *UCLA General Catalog,* with its jug-
gling of numbers, letters, and opaque instructions.

> The minimum number of courses (and units) for the bachelor's
> degree shall be 45 courses (180 units), of which at least 13 courses
> (52 units) shall be upper-division courses (courses numbered
> 100–199). After a student has taken 24 courses (96 units) toward
> the degree, no further unit credit will be allowed for courses com-
> pleted at a junior college. Not more than one course (4 units) in
> Physical Education 1 and 2, and not more than two courses (8
> units) in 300 or 400 courses may be counted toward the bachelor's
> degree. The candidate shall have attained at least a C (2.00) grade-
> point average in all courses undertaken in this University.

Passing over such recondite sections as Aerospace Studies—

> 21 A. World Military Systems (½ course). Lecture, two hours;
> leadership laboratory, one hour. Prerequisites: courses 1A, 1B, and
> 1C. This course continues the study of US Military Systems begun
> in Aerospace Studies 1B. The current weapons systems of US Army
> and US Navy are examined with emphasis on concepts for their
> employment.

—I reached English with relief. Here was such a multitude of
courses as made any English university I knew seem starved of
personnel, equipment, or ingenuity. Here one might proceed from
"100. Major British Authors Before 1800," all the way through
"242. Experimental Phonetics. (Formerly numbered 250 C. Same
as Speech 280 A and Linguistics 267 A.) Prerequisite: Speech 208
or Linguistics 207," to "300. The Teaching of English (Formerly
numbered 370). Required of candidates for the general secondary
credential with the field major in English and speech." It was a
portent.

When my companion and I finally found the correct section of
the correct administrative building, it was no more than the start.
From window to window we went, collecting one form here and
depositing it there, to collect another for deposit somewhere else;
asking and explaining and arguing; losing each other and ourselves
along the corridors; till my companion triumphantly enrolled and

received her "IBM Packet," five different cards, each with its tiny mysterious windows. "Look," she said wryly, peering through them at the ceiling, "my own, my very own personality." I turned to the woman presiding importantly over the packets. "Five cards? For one student? What does she do with them all?" She was clearly taken aback. "Oh, library, fees, courses . . ." And then she smiled with pride. "You get eleven cards for general enrollment."

It is, this immense campus with its own intractable traffic problem, its churches and cinemas, cleaners and police, another piece of Los Angeles, loose in a sheltered spread of rich real estate. It shares the anxious introversion of its consumer environment. Its inhabitants behave as though it belongs to them; in truth, it belongs to everybody and to no one at all. "The climate of Los Angeles is well suited to university work," proclaims *UCLA Summer Sessions 1966*. "Proximity to the ocean insures an even temperature without extremes." Such is one pride of the university. Another is the new Social Sciences Building. It is largely made of tinted glass, so that those working inside it live in a world of packaged light.

Los Angeles is special in the degree, not in the kind, of social— indeed, human—disintegration that it displays. For what is so massively evident in Los Angeles is evident as well, and ever increasingly, all over America. As Jane Jacobs has pointed out in *The Death and Life of Great American Cities*,[27] it is the old type of city street of mixed character, with residents from different income groups, with apartments and houses, shops and a restaurant or bar, which provides and preserves a sense of neighborhood, of social commitment and ease, so that the local delicatessen or newsstand is a place to leave messages or keys, and the pavements are kept safe by the eyes of curiosity and concern. Such streets are vivid; they beckon visitors and hold the interest of those who live in them. They are not tunnels between home and work, for the hurry of indifference or fear, and the haunt of violence.

A multitude of such streets supports the specialty shops and restaurants, busy libraries and theaters and concert halls and art galleries, the explorations in dress and food, in taste and in ideas, that constitute the peculiar creative quality of cities. But the territory of apartment towers, public or private in ownership, for families of similar income and status—sometimes a street, sometimes a cluster of blocks—is isolated from the city around by strips of grass, by police patrols, or merely by the invisible barbed wire of attitude toward those on the other side. Rich or poor, in pride or mortification, but always anxious, always exclusive, it looks inward, away from the city, whose attractions represent so many demands and whose life is a coherent society. Billions of dollars have been spent to resuscitate the cities. But the spending has been so directed as only to sustain and promote centrifugal consumption, the dispersion of self-absorbed people by price, as if they were goods in a department-store sale. Like the suburbs, with their drive-in shopping, eating, drinking, playing, their monotonous seclusion, too large and too small for the variety and vigor of street neighborhoods, these urban enclosures are places of desolate privacy, where fear hustles people off the pavements and indifference secures only a separate despair.

It is in the suburbs that the effects of this social disintegration struck me as most ruinous. Along the lake, north of Chicago, lies a preserve for families in the income region of $7500 to $10,000 a year. The wives don't work, though to do so might reduce the load of debt and disquiet which they and their husbands seem generically to bear; it is far more important to them that they should display their economic ability to stay home, as a flag of their status. Their kitchens and cupboards glitter with gadgets to cut the time taken up by housework. But what is there to do outside their doors, beyond supermarket shopping and the bored visits to other wives no less helpless to cope with the time that they have on their hands? The John Birch Society runs the nearest approximation to a bookshop, and an occasional itinerant lecturer, usually predicting disaster from Communist subversion and public expenditure, provides the personal communication of culture. Most husbands commute to their work in the city and return late and worn out, while the weekends, supposedly set aside for family "togetherness," are more frequently devoted to country-club obligations and the ritual of entertaining.

I was taken to visit a local school, dependent on the taxes of the community and regular fund-raising functions because the parents reject any federal government aid as degrading, an attempt to group them with the needy and failed. In the class where I spent most of the day, the children were nine or ten years old, but already as keenly ostentatious, in nail polish, jewelry for both sexes, and the obvious effort of their clothes, as Madison Avenue could reasonably require. The teacher, a friend from Chicago, asked me to talk about my old house just outside London, as an occasion for some agreeable history. So I talked about the design in beams and plaster, about the Tudor period when it was built, and then, because there is a thin tradition that Bradshaw, President of the Regicides, once lived in it, about the Civil War and Cromwell. Confident of my capacity to hold an audience even of children, and full of my long enthusiasm for Cromwell, I expected the rush of questions at the end—but never their nature. "What's the house worth?" "Have you a swimming pool?" "How much does a Rolls-Royce cost?" "What kind of car have you got?" One boy suddenly broke in with "My father is a Ph.D.," and a girl immediately followed with "My father is a vice-president." To cover my confusion I asked, "Of what?" "They make pipes," she said and went on to elaborate, while Cromwell and the surrounding centuries irretrievably receded.

As the class passed through the various subjects of study, my consternation increased. This was not permissive education; it was a disorder of petulant rivalry. Slouching over their desks, wandering up and down the aisles, defiant or indifferent when checked, jostlingly alert only when asked a question that gave them an opportunity to perform, they might have been playing baseball; and, indeed it was to baseball, with the appropriate running commentary of acclaim for the successful and jeers for the failed, that most of the gym period was devoted. On the classroom notice board were exhibited the encouragements to individual expression:

periodic elections for class president, secretary, treasurer, and librarian; selected compositions pinned under the injunction "To Be Admired!"

The interest in science of a sort was certainly high, assisted by equipment—from glossy colored charts to a small incubator for chickens—that would be regarded as lavish by most British children several years older. Browsing in encyclopedias appeared generally popular, and facts, from the business world to America's space program, were offered up proudly, if often irrelevantly, for approval. But there was little coherence in these little consumers, and during the English lesson, when they read or spoke at any length, they groped, as though lost in a foreign language. Over lunch, I questioned the other teachers in the staff room. I was fond of the one who had brought me to the school and knew her to be generous and intelligent, but I could not believe that her class was typical of the school, let alone other schools in the suburb. Yet the chorus of complaint from her colleagues was stupefying. A senior teacher seemed to sum up the collective dismay from the nods that accompanied her diatribe.

"Do you know how many of these kids come to us in a mental mess? In my own class there are two who visit psychologists and five others who should. And if you knew the parents, you'd understand. They live in a world of magazine ads, of wanting and worry and boredom. These kids never see their fathers. And what can their mothers teach them but how to want and worry and be just as bored, at six or seven years old? They're sick, these kids. They don't belong to anything or anyone, not even to themselves. They dream about swimming pools when they don't want to learn how to swim. You should see their brothers and sisters. They kill time by driving around and around the suburb in cars, just to keep moving.

"Discipline? You must be mad. They're down here, usually the mothers, in a flash, threatening everything from the courts to our jobs. I remember when a teacher meant something—not the old maid with the heart of gold whose pupil becomes President, like in the movies—but still, something worth while. Now they look at you as though you only teach because you couldn't make a go of it in business. And they're sure that you don't understand them. They're damn right. I don't. But why should the kids think any differently? It's enough that they can tell you how much you get paid, to the last cent almost. They should bring me apples? I'm just glad that they don't bring me the latest deodorant."

It's a long way from the North Shore suburbs of Chicago to Sun City, Arizona, but only on the map. Twelve miles from Phoenix there appears, suddenly from out of the flat surrounding haze, what looks like an enormous mirage of lawn and palm trees, pools, and buildings sleek in the sun, some with colonial porticos, some with Moorish tiles and wrought-iron tracery, some with brick and concrete contemporary fronts, and all improbably the same. And here live some ten thousand people, also all improbably the same. With the price of houses starting from over $12,500, and of apartments from over $10,500, where scarcely any opportunities for paid employment exist, the community is solidly middle class. It is also effectively closed to Negroes and Indians, though a few Spanish Americans have managed to slip in. But it is age that constitutes the essential criterion for residence in this city of "active retirement," with its promise of "lively adult living." Only those who are fifty years old or more—in fact, the median age is sixty-four—and who have no children of school age may "move into its attractive homes and begin to relax in its country-club-like atmosphere." Del E. Webb, president of the private corporation that developed Sun City, Arizona ("now duplicated in Sun City, California, and Sun City, Florida"), has a "philosophy" behind his ventures.

> The "way of life" we promise senior citizens emphasizes independence for men and women who have reached an entirely new social strata after their places in normal community life have been taken over by others on their retirement.
> In the average community there certainly is no way of controlling the age bracket of our neighbors or the number of their children. This we can control, thus avoiding the problem of mixing conflicting living patterns and, in many cases, forcing social contacts that actually constitute for our senior citizens an invasion of privacy.[28]

Here are three eighteen-hole golf courses, a cinema-size swimming pool, bowling greens and "hobby shops" (for talents from ceramics to sewing), with a library, little theater (the Sun City Players), "many card clubs," and opportunities for charitable work in nearby Peoria, a preserve of the poor. There are two shopping centers with supermarkets and a variety of basic stores; two banks and two weekly newspapers; a "modern medical center staffed by eleven physicians and dentists"; and a throng of different churches for the soul. The Del Webb corporation investigates needs, and acts. "Because a survey indicated retirement community residents often like to 'eat out,' a 250-seat restaurant–coffee shop–cocktail lounge is provided at the motor hotel." The citizens govern themselves, and "because residents serve without pay, and politics are frowned upon, the governing body has been able to recruit high-caliber talent." This says little for America at large, but perhaps no more is meant. Not that national politics are eschewed. Polling in important elections is high, and according to a Del Webb official, Sun City votes 70 per cent Republican and went 69 per cent for Goldwater in 1964.

Above all, here are ample opportunities for consumer division and display, for the purchase of identity within the limits set by multiple building for profit. Houses and apartments are priced by size, design, and variety of appliances all the way to over $25,000, and offer such choices as "The Shenandoah" (elusively Midwestern "for people who are socially inclined but still prefer a minimum of house responsibilities"); "The Navajo" (in no sense Indian, but "featuring a lanai surrounded by all the living areas of the house"); "The Aztec" or "The Contempo" (both in Plan 45—"an easy livin' house featuring a lanai and leisure room for relaxing and entertaining"); and even "The Crescendo" (which is nothing so much as something of everything else).

The latest offering, in the highest price range, supplies "the atmosphere of the Mediterranean . . . Spain, Italy, Morocco. This magnificent house, called the Mediterrania, contains those expansive features developed in the fine homes of the famous countries of Southern Europe . . . houses designed for entertaining and living in the grand sense of the word . . . and it also contains the best the industrial age has developed. In short, it represents the best of two worlds." Happily, even the cheapest homes have such morale-boosters as "cultured marble vanity top with large plate glass mirror" and "deluxe gold-plated Country Club shower head." Gardens, too, are available in several styles, by costly courtesy of a local concern, though climate sets rather stricter limits on these than on the buildings. And for those who want to make a show without an effort, there are pebbled fronts painted green to look like lawns.

It is so sad, so lost, so wrong, this city without children, without young men and women in the flush of new homes, new families. The still, hot streets, and cool shaded living rooms deny passion and struggle and change; deny time itself. It is as though the whole cycle of life had suddenly been broken, and this was the quiet, tired end. And one knows at once how sad, how lost, how wrong are all those other cities too, with their children and young parents, schools and jobs, which these older men and women have left, taking with them their integral place in time and humanity.

No less an authority than *Time,* in an admiring cover story on "builder Del Webb," [29] proclaimed:

> In a society that tends to judge who a man is by what he does, the vigorous oldster suffers a special stress. . . . A retired man finds himself not only without a job but without an "identification tag": someone accustomed to thinking of himself as a railroad man or an insurance executive is often seriously disoriented when he finds that he is no longer anything at all.

And so he acquires a new identity; he is old. If he is one of the "less well-off," to quote *Time* again, he may go to a drab boarding house in "such geriatric capitals as St. Petersburg, Fla., where 28.1 per cent of the population is 65 or over." Here he can sit on a pastel-colored bench in the sun, have his blood pressure taken for only 35 cents at a street-corner booth, listen to free band concerts, or "Eat Like a King for $1.60." The richer can go to such settlements as the Casa de Mañana in La Jolla, California, operated by the Methodist Church, where for something like $27,500 and a monthly maintenance charge of $200, the resident receives life tenancy of an ocean-view cottage, free meals in the community center, free linen, and cleaning service every two weeks. Or for those who cling to freehold and rather more independence, there are the Sun Cities and their various imitations.

Del Webb has ample cause for self-satisfaction. Sun City has paid off handsomely. The "turnover rate"—as a corporation official described the population shifts, in a phrase that I had always associated with merchandise—is, including deaths and moves from one home to another within the city, only 5 per cent a year, in contrast with the national average of 12½ per cent. And the citizens themselves eagerly protest their contentment to visitors. Earnestly they press your hand, show you their hobby shops, and explain, without being prodded, how safe and useful and easy they feel now, away from a world which treated them as obsolete. Some of them speak as though they fled here in panic. And a Del Webb public-relations officer confirmed the impression. "I suppose, after all," he said reluctantly, as if this detracted from Sun City's absolute virtue, "that they come, many of them, simply to get away— from the pace of today and the pressures represented in their children. Notice how often they use the word 'relax' here." But then "relax" is a favorite word in Del Webb publicity.

Perhaps the inhabitants of Sun City protest too much. Perhaps they do not feel nearly as safe and useful and easy as they pretend. Perhaps they are merely eager to conceal from others, even from themselves, their sense of rejection, the ruthless psychological enforcement of their retreat. But then, perhaps they really are contented. Perhaps they think it only decent that they should remove the irrelevance of their age from the rest of society. And that, surely, would be more sad and lost and wrong than anything else. For they would have accepted that life should properly be without integrity, without loyalty, without love.

The disintegration of time pervades the consumer society. Stories too good to be untrue, such as the one about the skating film star who could not stay in a house or hotel without twisting to a stop the hands of every clock in sight, magnify, but do not distort, the reality. The casinos of Las Vegas have no clocks or windows at all and provide breakfast, lunch, or supper at any hour, on request. In the constant artificial light, there is no day or night, only a perpetual moment. Las Vegas, of course, is another magnifying glass. But the news programs on television reach into almost every American home, twisting the hands of the clocks there to a stop. There is no progression in the treatment of events; there is an item of local news, then an item of international news, then an interview with a visiting celebrity, then sport, then suddenly local news again, and another item of international news, with abrupt changes of announcer and interruptions by advertisers.

The American press is no different. Stories begin on one page and end on another, often half or three-quarters of the newspaper away, in a disintegration of time and place alike. To move progressively from page to page is to read several beginnings together, then some endings and other beginnings, and then a rush of endings all at once. To read each news story from beginning to end is to jump backward and forward from page to page, till any semblance of progression in the paper disappears. Many papers, indeed, intersperse their current stories with items of trivial information, dressed up as news, to produce the sort of constant artificial light that envelops the Las Vegas gaming rooms.

It is scarcely wonderful that this disintegration of time and place should increasingly inform the conduct of government. The rhetoric and the reality draw ever further apart. Ever-mounting debt and disquiet are promoted in the cause of sound prosperity; ever more power is exercised by unelected officials, commanding ever wider areas of secret activity, in the cause of individual freedom and the open society; ever more terrible weapons of war are used in the cause of compassion, and ever more oppressive oligarchies abroad are supported in the cause of democracy. Things are less and less what they are, and more and more what they are made to appear. New laws to protect civil rights are introduced as a substitute for the enforcement of old ones. Big corporations swallow smaller ones and become bigger still, to safeguard the competitive society. Casualties on the battlefield are described as "light" or "moderate," to distinguish between the many and the more men killed and wounded.

Deception has ceased to be a mere propaganda device; it has become second nature, enabling the administrators to conceal from themselves, as well as from the public, the increasing incoherence of their policies and acts. Indeed, the administration no longer knows when it is telling the truth or not. It speaks in so many voices— military and civilian, advisory and representative, surreptitious and exposed—that official pronouncements may, and frequently do, contradict each other with equal authority. Besides, the policies themselves are more and more isolated from one another. Like an American newspaper, the administration jerks from one beginning to another, leaving the sequel for some column of some other page. Suddenly education is the domestic concern of government, then the beautifying of America, then air pollution, then civil rights, then education again, then the decay of the cities, and again civil rights. And each time a new concern is displayed, the old ones, previously so urgent, are shut away, as though the public can respond to the excitement of only one overriding need at a time. Nowhere is the separation more abrupt than between foreign and domestic concerns, and profound astonishment greets such efforts to connect them as the relationship between the civil rights struggle and the movement of resistance to the Vietnam war. Yet what could be clearer than the connection between the war and the condition of the American Negro, if only through the diversion of resources—political, economic, emotional—from public welfare to military effort?

It is a disintegration of the American personality that all these other disintegrations promote and express. The passion that Americans display for taking photographs wherever they go has been ascribed to their national delight in machines and the sense of technical mastery which a camera so readily lends. But Americans busy themselves, it seems to me, less in merely taking photographs than in taking photographs of each other or getting bystanders to take photographs of them. In this, are they not seeking a proof of personal identity, a witness to one instant of disintegrated time and place when and where they demonstrably exist? Such, surely, is the search of Lyndon B. Johnson. He has his initials. They mark his wife and daughters, his ranch, his radio and television business, every available possession that can promote acknowledgment of his peculiar integrity.

Yet integrity is just what has escaped him. His body reflects the conflicts in his nature and career. While his mouth acclaims dissent in a free society, his eyes assail it as assisting the enemies of the nation; while his eyes declare his deep concern for the poor, his mouth betrays his long association with a corrupt political leadership in Texas, his intimacy with oil barons, and the prodigious success of his radio and television operations; while his shoulders sag with his exertions for peace, his hands flaunt the impulse of American power. It is, paradoxically, his simplicity that gives him away. He cannot conceal the disintegration of his own personality. It is no wonder that so many Americans who find no cause for repugnance in his politics find it in his person. He reminds them too disturbingly of themselves. They cannot attempt to escape their own sense of disintegration by adopting his identity. His vanity is theirs.

The further apart reality and rhetoric diverge, the more elaborate and insistent the rhetoric becomes. A whole new language is being developed to support the claims of fantasy against fact. To be old is to be disagreeable, unwanted, and so the old are translated into "senior citizens." To be poor contradicts the American undertaking, and so the poor are translated into the "underprivileged" or "culturally disadvantaged." Everything is in a name. Appearance supplies, appearance *is* integrity. *The Wall Street Journal* [30] cites a Dartnell Corporation survey revealing that nearly four in every ten companies employ "ego-puffing titles for salesmen. . . . Among those in vogue: key account supervisor, executive representative, resident engineer, communications consultant." Employees, *Time* reports in its Modern Living department,[31] have taken delightedly to uniforms. Board Chairman Robert C. Townsend of Avis car rentals arrived at his office in Garden City, New York, one day wearing the company blazer. His subordinates hastened to follow his example. "There is no rule that says they have to dress alike, but it does give them a sense of community, a kind of feeling that even though they are No. 2, they don't look No. 2. Such corporate happiness could be catching. It has already caught on with the people at the Fidelity Bankers Life Insurance Co. of Richmond, Va. Fidelity has laid out $23,000 to outfit 117 employees with identical wardrobes because, as Fidelity's President Harold J. Richards explains, 'it furthers our *esprit de corps*.' . . . The only worry is over the day the boss might bark: 'You're fired! Turn in your clothes!' Fidelity has thought of that. An employee who stays on for a year can keep his uniform on leaving." The ripeness of appearance is all.

It is easy to slide into a conspiratorial interpretation of American society. So many Americans are so assiduously manipulated that the existence of a concerted effort by the various manipulators to direct the society for their common power and profit seems only too feasible. Yet are the manipulators not themselves manipulated, ultimately by their very victims? Among the denizens of Madison Avenue, many succumb to their own techniques and soon see advertising as a social service. But even those who recognize their devotion to deceit, who are only too ready to admit that their business is to take the public for a perpetual ride, must deceive successfully, and to do so must identify themselves with the consumer culture so closely that in the end for them also the appearance becomes the reality, and it is they who are taken for the ride. The proprietors of news dissemination and entertainment manipulate the public taste and are inevitably manipulated by it, in a constant vicious circle of commercialization. Labor is manipulated by union and management executives, who are in turn manipulated by the newspapers that they read and the television shows that they watch. The star in the White House, let alone a whole chorus line of lesser politicians, is more manipulated—by a multitude of lobbies seeking to shape public opinion to their particular purposes —than manipulating. The lobbies themselves—a major publishing force, under single-minded direction, as the Luce group of magazines has been; business interests of enormous resources and political energy, from the major oil companies to the American Medical Association; the traders of votes and patronage, in the offices of organized labor and electoral minorities by color, religion, or national origin; bureaucrats in powerful areas of government safe from the scrutiny of public discussion and the polls, like those in command of the intelligence services and the armed forces—seem the supreme manipulators. But then they are themselves manipulated by advertising, by entertainment, by the propaganda of other "pushers" in the consumer society. The claims of the latest deodorant, the wisecracks of the latest television comic, the hacking of yet another freeway through the city, the promise of yet another isolated refuge for the old—they pursue the general down the corridors of the Pentagon as they pursue the suburban housewife from breakfast to *The Late Late Show,* disintegrating his personality as they disintegrate hers. The consumer culture knows no master; to accept its purposes, to employ its techniques, is necessarily to serve it.

The essentially manipulated society is essentially passive. Its proper symbol is not the eagle but the pill.*

> Five to 10 million Americans with varying complaints each year take amphetamine tablets or capsules, and 20 million take barbiturates—all on their doctors' orders. More than 80 million prescriptions are filled for these two types of drugs that directly affect the mind as well as the body. Altogether, more than 13 billion doses were manufactured by 1000 drug companies, or enough to provide 24 doses (100 mg.) of sleeping capsules and 35 doses (5 mg.) of wake-up tablets for every American man, woman and child. At least half of the 13 billion doses of amphetamines and barbiturates found their way into illegal channels. Police departments everywhere reported increasing police activity and arrests involving illegitimate use of these non-narcotic drugs. . . .[33]

Yet this is very far from the full story. There are some 135 million Americans over the age of fourteen. Apart from the many

* Liquor comes a distant, but by no means unimpressive, second to the pill. According to U.S. government health officials, there are some 6,500,000 alcoholics in the country, and their number grows by 200,000 every year. A rising proportion consists of married middle-aged women of the middle and upper-income groups.[32]

millions who take amphetamine and barbiturates on doctors'
orders, and the many millions more who do so illegitimately, there
are unnumbered millions who take tranquilizers, in the belief that
though they do the same job as barbiturates, they do not bear the
same risks.

> Many of their trade names (Miltown, Equanil, Placidyl, Doriden,
> Noludar, Librium and Valmid, among others) have become house-
> hold words. These drugs depress the central nervous system to re-
> duce restlessness, relax the muscles, relieve emotional tension and
> induce sleep. The news about them is that they are . . . just as
> likely to create dependence as the older sleeping pills are.[34]

Such drugs may be bought only on prescription; but the readiness with which doctors prescribe them, and the profits they offer
to less respectable private enterprise, make the medical safeguards
a mere formality. The drug companies promote each new panacea
with the fervor of detergent manufacturers; on a single afternoon
that I spent with a Chicago doctor in his suburban surgery, he was
visited by four different salesmen from large drug companies, each
offering only a new tranquilizer with a lavish supply of free sam-
ples and a brochure of equally lavish pictures and prose. Other,
supposedly much milder, drugs, though of unpredictable sedative
or hypnotic effect when taken in large doses (antihistamines, anti-
emetics, and bromides) are freely promoted in the press and on
television, and freely sold over the counters of drugstores. Next to
drug-taking on such a mass scale, the numbers addicted to the
traditionally defined narcotics—some 56,000 according to the
relevant authorities, though the figure is certainly higher, since
many thousands must escape official records—receive a strangely
disproportionate share of public disquiet.

Such narcotics, of course, carry a social stigma which other
addictive drugs, however dangerous and squalid in their effects,
escape. Severe barbiturate addiction is no less degrading, physically and mentally, then severe addiction to heroin or cocaine. But
the suburban housewife can take barbiturates in the secure belief
that many of "the beautiful people," as well as many of her own
neighbors, do so as well. Indeed, she may find an identification

with the glamour of the gossip columns, as her husband may do with the glamour of the board room, in a dependence on sedatives. The source, however, is much deeper. The reasons usually given, by specialists in its problems and treatment, for narcotic addiction are no less applicable to the mass dependence on sleeping pills, pep pills, tranquilizers, and similar drugs.

Dr. Joel Fort, of the School of Criminology at the University of California, in a paper for the Congressional hearings on Drug Abuse Control, declared that addicts are "immature, suspicious, intolerant of stress or frustration, passive and overdependent." At the government hospital for the treatment of addiction, in Lexington, Kentucky, the main psychological provocations to drug dependence were found to be fears of sexual inadequacy and an inability to express aggression. Some 90 per cent of the patients at Lexington were described by doctors there as "impulsive, unstable, unable to plan ahead . . . childishly demanding and stubborn." A study of addicts by a team of scientists from the Research Center for Human Relations at New York University revealed that 97 per cent of the addicts interviewed came from homes where the parents were divorced, separated, or living together in open hostility. "The typical fathers were weak, unstable, pessimistic about their prospects in life—and failed to present a mature adult image on which the child could model himself. Many were either criminals or alcoholics. In contrast, the study showed that many of the mothers were overindulgent toward their sons." [35]

The attributes of drug addicts read like the attributes of the ideal consumer; and, indeed, psychological products of consumer society they in very large measure are. "Impulsive, unstable, unable to plan ahead . . ."—such is the right raw material for processing by business into a constant longing for something new to buy. And what is more likely a consequence of advertising than that such qualities should be encouraged, fortified, alongside an intolerance of stress and frustration? The consumer society offers beauty in a jar, romance in a motor car, self-assurance in silverware. And when the beauty, the romance, the self-assurance still elude their pursuers, it offers pills to relieve instantly the anxiety and the distress. It thrives by exciting easy expectancy and impatience with disappointment. It produces, as it exploits, the "childishly demanding and stubborn." Americans early grow accustomed to being indulged, because their parents are persuaded of their own ability to secure love only by buying it, and because indulgence is intrinsic to the competitive display that provides parents and children alike with their precise social identity. In this cultivation of the consumer mind the mother is the major agent, the banks between which love flows, in the form of toys and clothes, approval and consent, to the child. The father earns; but it is the mother who spends. And it is not the earning but the spending that is central to the developing consumers. Is it so strange, then, that the child should look increasingly to the mother for the source of meaning and satisfaction, and increasingly see in the father the servant, not the master? What is more to be expected than that the child should develop a sense of confused sexual identity and so "fears of sexual inadequacy"; should acquire, through the conflict of his own experience with the proclaimed male role of dominance, "an inability to express aggression"? The drug culture is the consumer society undressed.

The connection between drugs and the sexual act is far from remote. Whether in a needle or a pill, the drug enters the body, to bring temporary delight, indifference to the world beyond, a sense of meaning and identity. Is the widespread dependence on drugs not a search by women for a satisfaction that their men do not supply, that they will not allow their men to supply; and by men for the passive sexual role that their culture leads them to want while surrounding it with horror? Are drug addiction and the homosexuality with which the society seems so obsessed not related indications of the profoundly "passive and overdependent" nature of the American consumer? Is the very public horror surrounding homosexuality not a formal revulsion from, as it is a forceful recognition of, this passivity and overdependence, this mental inversion of sexual identity? In their flight from disintegrated place, time, and personality, Americans seek a refuge in yet deeper consumption, a spending that promises to transform, to restore, their natures. It is ironic and inevitable that in the process they should only advance their disintegration.

They are, so many men and women in America, a solitary sex, ultimately private, ultimately involved in a relationship not with others but with themselves, in a masturbation, moral and emotional when not physical, that hungers as it feeds. It is the perplexed, so often secret groping of adolescence, but without the gradual discovery and achievement that adolescence ought to bring. It is a relationship as dry and sterile as the things with which it is concerned. It never really takes, as it never really gives. It is sensation alone, without meaning beyond itself. And it defies every yearning of the human purpose. Its privacy is, must be, terror and guilt, hatred and destruction—an outraging of the self by the self —for it is a denial of life.

CHAPTER 3

The Open and Shut Society

Modern liberalism carefully emphasizes tact rather than
clarity of speech.—*John Kenneth Galbraith in* The New
Industrial State

America professes to be among the freest societies on
earth, and in many significant respects it is. No sympathy with the
struggle of poor peoples to revolutionize their condition, no understanding of the need for their organized sacrifice, and no belief in
the attainment of a finally far more profound freedom under socialism can conceal the fact that in America, under capitalism,
now, most citizens are possessed of a personal freedom not ex-
ceeded elsewhere and vastly exceeding that possible to the vast
bulk of mankind. The riches of America, the long security of her
frontiers, the reach of her power may help to explain this; they
cannot deny it.

It is not merely that in general * opposition to the policies and
even the nature of government may be outspoken; deep dissent
from prevailing values, social and economic no less than political,
may be expressed; and organizations to propagate such differences
may be promoted. These freedoms are, with varying limitations,
not uncommon to advanced industrial societies of more or less
capitalist commitment. What singles out America is the extent to
which they are formally guaranteed.

This singularity lies at the very source of the United States. The

* There are important exceptions—of time, place, race, employment, and
doctrine—which will subsequently emerge.

states of Europe begin with controls; America begins without them. Revolution, whether gradual or sudden, transformed the structure of power in Britain, France, Germany, Italy. The countries existed long before the changes that shaped their present order. But revolution became the United States. It informed the Constitution that governs still the relations between individual and society, and it was to the Constitution, rather than to a specific territory or nation, that communities subsequently acceded.

Influenced both by the dissenting character of much early colonization and by the recent experience of imperial control, this Constitution, in its Bill of Rights, established criteria of personal freedom some of which are denied even today in societies of the stanchest liberal allegiance. The prohibitions against establishing any religion (Amendment I), against imposing any excessive bail, excessive fines, or cruel and unusual punishments (Amendment VIII), and against infringing "the right of the people to keep and bear Arms" (Amendment II) reflect a restraint on government that few, if any, other modern states would regard as proper. Above all, the whole emphasis of the Constitution is not on the yielding of particular freedoms by authority to the person, but on defining the particular concessions by personal freedom to authority. As Amendment IX declares: "The enumeration in the Constitution, of certain rights, shall not be construed to deny or disparage others retained by the people." Such is the extent of America's formal dedication to a free society, and most Americans today are convinced that no freer society can reasonably be envisaged. Yet from the beginning there has existed, between the promise and the performance, a substantial discrepancy.

The protection and so the interpretation of personal liberties fell to the judiciary, and since judges generally came from the classes of property and established power, it was generally in the interests of property and established power that any conflict of rights was resolved. Under the direction of an early strong Chief Justice, John Marshall, the Supreme Court flexed its muscles, declaring in 1803 * the supremacy of the Constitution and of its interpretation

* *Marbury* v. *Madison.*

by the judiciary. "It is a proposition too plain to be contested, that the Constitution controls any legislative act repugnant to it. A legislative act contrary to the Constitution is not law. It is emphatically the province and duty of the judicial department to say what the law is." In 1810 the implications of such authority in such hands for the dominance of capital over the popular interests were made only too plain. The Supreme Court prohibited the State of Georgia from rescinding a flagrantly corrupt sale of Western lands * on the principle that this would impair the sacred obligations of a contract.

It is scarcely surprising that such exercise of the judicial power should have been extended to sanction slavery. And though, with the Civil War, the Constitution was augmented to proclaim full citizenship for all "persons born or naturalized in the United States," the crucial provisions of Amendment XIV—that "no State shall make or enforce any law which shall abridge the privileges or immunities of citizens of the United States; nor shall any State deprive any person of life, liberty, or property, without due process of law"—were subsequently employed by the courts less to secure the rights of Negroes than to protect the interests of capital from public regulation. Indeed, with the decease of Reconstruction and the return of the white South to political power, the Supreme Court connived at mob violence to intimidate Negroes from voting and, in a series of decisions that culminated in the *Plessy* v. *Ferguson* case of 1896, vindicated the spreading practice of racial segregation not only in the South but widely in the rest of the country. In his dissent from the judgment in the Civil Rights Cases of 1883, Justice Harlan of Kentucky assailed the record of the Supreme Court.

> Constitutional provisions, adopted in the interest of liberty, and for the purpose of securing, through national legislation, if need be, rights inhering in a state of freedom, and belonging to American citizenship, have been so construed as to defeat the ends the people desired to accomplish, which they attempted to accomplish, and which they supposed they had accomplished by changes in their fundamental law.

* *Fletcher* v. *Peck.*

Meanwhile, corporations prospered in virtual immunity from legislative interference. The ruthless rise of huge industrial and financial trusts—in manufactures such as steel and agricultural machinery; in the exploitation of natural resources such as coal and oil and timber; in communications, such as the telephone, the telegraph, and the railroads; in banking and insurance—fired public opinion to demand legislative action. The Standard Oil lawyer Samuel Dodd saw the trust as providentially inevitable.

> You might as well endeavor to stay the formation of the clouds, the falling of the rains, or the flowing of the streams, as to attempt by any means or in any manner to prevent organization of industry, association of persons, and the aggregation of capital to any extent that the ever-growing trade of the world may demand.

Congress tried none the less, and with the Sherman Antitrust Act of 1890 outlawed "every contract, combination in the form of trust or otherwise, or conspiracy in restraint of trade or commerce . . ." But the Supreme Court inclined to the view of Samuel Dodd and in an important test case of 1895 * held that mere control over 98 per cent of the nation's sugar-refining did not in itself constitute an act in restraint of trade. Only when the provisions of the Act were applied to labor unions did the government find the courts cooperative.

Indeed, in sustaining the sentence of six months' imprisonment against labor leader Eugene Debs for having disobeyed a federal injunction in the Pullman strike of 1894, the Supreme Court held that even in the absence of statutory law, the government possessed a dormant power to remove obstacles from interstate commerce. Time and again the courts acted to uphold injunctions against strikes, outlaw boycotts as conspiracy in restraint of trade, and so restrict picketing as to make it all but impossible within the law. In this collaboration of the judiciary with big business, the Constitution became a safeguard less against aggression by property and its political representatives, than against any resistance by the victims. Mass meetings of strikers were broken up by police, despite the constitutional guarantee of free assembly; strikers were arrested,

* *United States* v. *E. C. Knight and Company*

deported or imprisoned without trial, and newspapers shut down by state administrations, despite the constitutional rights to security of person, speedy and public trial for the accused, and freedom of the press. When public disquiet produced welfare legislation, the courts paraded to the defense of capital. Laws fixing a limit on hours of labor, providing for accident compensation, setting minimum wages, were struck down as depriving corporations of a fair return or workers of the right to work when and where they pleased, in defiance of the "due process" provision in the Fourteenth Amendment. Even two attempts by Congress to outlaw child labor, in 1916 and 1919, were defeated by the judiciary. No less a figure than Theodore Roosevelt attacked the courts as "agents of reaction" which had "left both the Nation and the States well-nigh impotent to deal with the great business combinations."

For the rich, this was liberty indeed. No income tax clogged the accumulation of enormous fortunes; no labor laws disturbed the pursuit of profits; no government regulations embarrassed enterprise. Public opinion was on the whole submissive, and government supine; capital insured the first by its control of all but a fringe of the press, and the second by buying parties and candidates, legislatures, and, where necessary, courts. A Vanderbilt or a Morgan could treat senators and judges as his servants because so many of them were. The Jeffersonian banner of agrarian democracy—that government is best which governs least—now fluttered over the forces of industrial oligarchy.

For the poor, liberty lay in a discreet acquiescence. The major corporations dealt promptly and powerfully with labor unrest: they could afford to hold out against strikes far longer than the strikers themselves could hold out against unemployment; they could recruit blacklegs from the immigrant ships; they could employ the most skillful lawyers to seek assistance from the courts; they could bribe or intimidate government into intervening on their behalf; and when public opinion seemed impervious to the usual propaganda of their press, they could raise the alarm of anarchy, revolution, and the despotism of the mob. They owned whole towns and counties, with the civil administrations in them; in the 1920s the Constitution itself was suspended in Harlan County, Kentucky, and in 1933 the United States Secretary of Labor was forcibly prevented from speaking in the streets of a Pennsylvania coal town. Henry Clews, the New York banker, spoke for capital when in 1886 he identified the strike with treason. "Strikes may have been justifiable in other nations, but they are not justifiable in our country. The Almighty has made this country for the oppressed of other nations, and therefore this is the land of refuge . . . and the hand of the laboring man should not be raised against it."

The ultimate power possessed by the mass of the whites—for the mass of the blacks had been dispossessed of all but their formal unfettering—lay in their votes, but this was a power that they did not know how, or care, or feel themselves able effectually to employ. Business backed, and commanded the policies of, both major parties, and if it watered the Republican fields more generously, this was because the Republicans for long seemed more successful at getting out the vote. On most important issues, especially those concerning the relations between capital and labor, the Democrats and the Republicans did not differ, and where they did, it was more for electoral excitement than for administrative change. On the state and city level, well-oiled machines packaged the voters for purchase by business, at a suitable commission in political office and financial opportunity. And where the prudent distribution of patronage did not keep the electorate loyal, intimidation or fraud could be pressed into service as well. But Americans in the overwhelming main accepted this system of unequal power and liberty. Persuaded of the country's infinite potential and their own chance of a prize one day in the great American treasure hunt, they saw the suzerainty of capital not as an oppression but as an inducement, as a promise rather than a threat. Reforms they might occasionally require, some limit set to the exploitation of people and resources, for the ease of their faith in the security of the present and the abundance of the future. But the Constitution was there as the assurance of their fundamental freedoms, and the courts were there to protect the Constitution against assault. If the laws they promoted were adjudged unconstitutional, then the laws were wrong. What was good for business, they were earnestly encouraged to believe and earnestly agreed, was good for America. And so, where they allowed the combination of capital to be native good sense, they joined in denouncing the combination of labor as alien conspiracy; where they accepted the right of businessmen to manipulate government, they swelled the cries of alarm when labor attempted to do so. Their real condition was revealed by one of the rich themselves, Frederick T. Martin.

> It matters not one iota what political party is in power or what President holds the reins of office. We are not politicians, or public thinkers; we are the rich; we own America; we got it, God knows how, but we intend to keep it if we can by throwing all the tremendous weight of our support, our influence, our money, our political connections, our purchased Senators, our hungry Congressmen, and our public-speaking demagogues, into the scale against any legislation, any political platform, any Presidential campaign, that threatens the integrity of our estate.[1]

There was, of course, revolt from a minority. Within the ranks of organized labor were two disparate forces—one reformist and opportunist, basically loyal to capitalism and pursuing the piecemeal spoils of collective bargaining; the other revolutionary and idealist, demanding the surrender of the existing system to socialism and not seldom meeting violence with violence. The first found its most effective form in the American Federation of Labor, which had recruited some two million workers by the outbreak of the First World War, but which concentrated on the craft unions, jealously pressing their advantages, and left the vast mass of semiskilled and unskilled alone. As one of its leaders, Adolph Strasser, propounded its purposes: "We have no ultimate ends. We are going on from day to day. We are fighting only for immediate objects—objects that can be realized in a few years." The second force emerged in sudden raging strikes, in militant organizations such as the American Railway Union of Eugene Debs and the Western Federation of Miners, in the Industrial Workers of the World, founded in 1905 with a formal dedication—the earliest such by an American labor organization—to class struggle. In the preamble to its constitution, the IWW firmly declared: "The working class and the employing class have nothing in common. . . . Between these two classes a struggle must go on until all the toilers come together on the political as well as on the industrial field, and take and hold that which they produce by their labor, through an economic organization of the working class, without affiliation with any political party." Before it was destroyed in 1918, for threatening to interfere with the war effort, it had won many important strikes and made significant headway in organizing such sectors of long neglect as lumbermen and dockers in the West and even migratory farm workers on the Great Plains; not until the formation in 1936 of the Committee for Industrial Organizations would anything like a similarly serious effort be made to mobilize unskilled and semi-skilled labor. Whether in the end the careful maneuvers of the AFL or the possibility of spreading support for the principles of the IWW did more to encourage a less intransigent attitude by capital, slow improvements in working conditions were made. But they followed only upon widespread industrial unrest. In the 25 years from 1881 to 1906 alone, there were some 38,000 strikes and lockouts, involving almost 200,000 establishments and over 9½ million workers.[2]

Political parties of labor, however, met with a derisory public response. Indeed the AFL itself never gave formal support to any of the socialist parties that entered the lists from time to time, and clearly preferred to try and play off the two major parties against each other. The Labor Reformers of 1872, with a platform no more radical than government regulation of railway and telegraph companies to insure fair rates, polled less than 30,000 votes nationally. In 1888 a Union Labor party arose to denounce Democrats and Republicans alike as "hopelessly and shamelessly corrupt" and demand government ownership and control of railways and telegraph lines; it polled less than 150,000 votes. A Socialist Labor party collected just over 36,000 votes in 1896. Then in 1900 the Social Democratic party joined the Presidential fray with a detailed program for nationalizing the principal means of production, and nominated Eugene Debs as its candidate. But, despite his appeal to militant labor, Debs polled under 95,000 votes, and though in subsequent elections he did far better, reaching a peak of almost 900,000 votes, or just under 6 per cent of the total, in 1912, socialism seemed unable to make any real impact on the electorate.

It was from among the struggling farmers of the Midwest and the South that a substantial political movement against the two-party subservience to capital emerged. The price of agricultural products had been falling steadily since the end of the Civil War, and farmers had been forced to borrow at predatory interest rates from Eastern finance. By 1890 the farms of Kansas, Nebraska, and the Dakotas had been mortgaged to a quarter of their value, and panic pursued the plunging cotton price across the South. Farmers' Alliances arose to demand currency inflation, lower interest rates, taxation of the rich, and public ownership of the railways; they attracted extensive support in the Congressional elections of 1890 to win three seats in the United States Senate and fifty in the House of Representatives. Elated, the leaders of agrarian revolt sought a coalition with industrial labor to confront both major parties, and at Omaha in July 1892 the People's party—popularly known as the Populists—was launched.

"Corruption dominates the ballot box, the legislature, the Congress, and touches even the ermine of the bench," the platform proclaimed.

The newspapers are largely subsidized or muzzled; public opinion silenced; business prostrated; our homes covered with mortgages; labor impoverished; and the land concentrating in the hands of capitalists. The urban workmen are denied the right of organization for self-protection; imported pauperized labor beats down their wages; a hireling standing army, unrecognized by our laws, is established to shoot them down, and they are rapidly degenerating into European conditions. . . . We have witnessed for more than a quarter of a century the struggle of the two great political parties for power and plunder, while grievous wrongs have been inflicted upon the suffering people.

Was this the Justice, the general Welfare, were these the Blessings of Liberty, to which the Constitution was dedicated?

The Populists demanded radical changes in the currency, the economic structure, the government, and the law of the country. With a Civil War veteran, General Weaver, as their candidate, they entered the presidential elections and polled just over a million votes, or 8.51 per cent of the total. For despite their appeal—"The interests of rural and civic labor are the same; their enemies are identical"—the industrial workers virtually ignored them. Out of almost 1,000,000 votes cast in Pennsylvania, only 8700 went to the Populists; out of some 400,000 in Massachusetts, only 3200.[3] The Populists recorded real strength only in the impoverished farming areas, especially on the Great Plains. Yet this regional concentration was not without benefit; it enabled them to collect twenty-two electoral votes—the first third party since 1860 to win any electoral votes at all. Attacking from their rural strongholds, they laid waste the Democratic vote across much of the South and West and seemed poised to sack the Democratic party itself. But the agrarian discontent within the Democratic ranks, excited to mutiny, seized the 1896 convention from the Eastern leadership, to nominate William Jennings Bryan as Presidential candidate. It was a revolt that put revolution to flight.

Bryan and the new Democratic command wanted to reform society but not reconstruct it. For all their demands—the due taxation of wealth, an end to the use of federal injunctions in industrial disputes, laws to protect labor, inflation of the currency to reduce indebtedness—and the rhetoric with which these were trumpeted, their program was not a summoning to upheaval such as had issued from Omaha. But those Populist leaders who shrank from the implications of their own insurgency, or who were dazzled by the glitter of imminent battle for at least some of their immediate objectives by the massed ranks of a major party, took control of the Populist convention and named Bryan as their candidate too. It was the fall of Populism as a force for fundamental change. The Populist attempts at collaboration between poor white and Negro disappeared down the gullet of the Democratic commitment to white supremacy. The search for a new system of power turned into a ranging through the old system for new accommodations. The sudden flow of freedom to dissent went to water the party meadows, and old professionals grazed on the new grass of democracy.

That capital was resisting merely some adjustment of its dominance was scarcely to be supposed, however, from the fury with which it fought the 1896 elections. It raised an enormous fund for the Republican campaign, sent its press ferociously into battle, and intimidated industrial workers with the threat of summary dismissal if they voted for Bryan, and of valueless dollars, wage cuts, and unemployment if Bryan won. The Republicans had nominated a creature of the Hanna political machine in Ohio, William McKinley, who had pledged himself relentlessly to oppose this "sudden, dangerous, and revolutionary assault upon law and order. . . ." He polled just over 7 million votes (50.88 per cent), to just under 6½ million for Bryan (46.77 per cent), and his electoral vote majority—271 to 176—was emphatic. The populous industrial states of the East and Midwest went solidly Republican, and it was clear that the mass of urban labor had not been captured by the cry for a primarily agrarian reformism. The election has been judged by historians the inevitable victory of industry over agriculture, of the factory over the farm. It was unquestionably a triumph for the manipulative power of money. Whether a bold Populism could ever have advanced from the farmlands to the city slums, for a frontal assault on the system, and whether such an assault, even if unsuccessful at the polls, would have produced profound structural changes in power, may be endlessly disputed. What is certain is that a Democratic party of agrarian outlook, enfolding anti-Catholic fundamentalism, hostility to emigrants from anywhere but "Nordic" Europe, and a seemingly insatiable appetite for degrading the Negro; trailing Cavalier legends of the ante-bellum South; and ultimately supervised by an alliance of rich

Southern planters and merchants with professional political bosses for the promotion of their joint interests, could not mobilize a national disaffection of the deprived.

In the rise and fall of Populism may be seen one aspect of that equivocal freedom which has made America at the same time so open and so shut a society. The size, gradual settlement, and uneven industrialization of the country produced regional patterns of prevalent immigrant origin, religion, and economic occupation— patterns held, by historical alignments (such as those of the Civil War) and by the federal nature of the polity,* in a political frame. This regional diversity and division have made both easy and difficult the promotion of new ideas and of any effective challenge to established power. Within a homogeneous regional environment, a popular movement has been able to spread all the more speedily for feeding on a local cohesion, but then has been brought up short at the frontier of a new regional cohesion, not seldom to turn back and furiously consume itself. The achievement of national power has thus traditionally required sufficient accommodations to excite, behind a common program and candidate, sufficient support in sufficient regions for a majority of the electoral votes. (A study of John F. Kennedy's reach for the Presidency reveals how crucial such strategy is still considered.) This has long given the immediate advantage to the existing major parties and, within them both, to such interests, whether of capital or of capital–loyal organized labor, as can command the resources, in ready adherents, money, and other means of propaganda, for a pervasive campaign. And it has long given the final advantage to the fundamental status quo, for massive coalitions of interest can far more easily be preserved than produced. By the nature of its polity, therefore, America encourages conservatism, and only a breakdown in normal functioning, such as occurred with the struggle over slavery and the secession of the Confederate States, or the deep economic depression of the 1930s, can provoke a powerful enough popular outcry

* Not only the existence of state administrations as objects of local allegiance, but the composition of the U.S. Senate by states and, above all, the state basis of the party nominations and electoral-college vote for President.

for basic change. Yet even then, the force of change emerges through the various processes of adoption and execution as rather less than the form, and is followed by a new conservatism, if not a period of retreat. Individual freedom is in practice far less the freedom to dissent than the freedom to acquiesce, and the society is nowhere in shadow more open than when it is in substance shut.

The huge vote for Bryan's reformism in 1896 shocked the business leadership and provided it with an additional incentive for promoting the thrust of America abroad. It was, of course, an age of imperial expansion—the principal powers of Europe were seizing colonies and commercial concessions with anxious indignation at one another's greed—but since Washington and Jefferson, American interest had been concentrated on the immediate environment, on securing and extending the frontier and on exploiting the country's abundant resources. When, with Monroe, it had looked beyond, it had done so defensively, to preserve its hemisphere from any further European political encroachments. Imperialism there had undoubtedly been from the beginning—against Indians, against Spain in America, against Mexico. The United States was an empire whose colonies had been absorbed because they were contiguous and whose colonized peoples had been swamped by massive immigration. But such imperialism had been excused by the necessity of its natural limits, and guilt had been an important if reticent party to repudiation of any further appetite. Now, however, the whole world seemed to beckon, and a cry arose from platform, press, and pulpit, led by Theodore Roosevelt and Henry Cabot Lodge in the Republican party, for America to fulfill her "manifest destiny." The mass appeal was easy to project: farmers would have augmented markets and so higher prices for their products; industrial workers would be assured of full employment and higher wages. And meanwhile capital might promise itself not only new areas of profitable and protected investment, but popular distraction from domestic discontents.

The first move, in 1897, against Spain, was largely excited by the anguished protests of capital, whose sugar plantations and mills were being outraged by the civil war in Cuba, and by the accounts of Spanish atrocities carried in American newspapers, such as those of William Randolph Hearst, not usually stirred by the different cruelties of power at home. "It is time," declared Senator Cullom of Illinois, the home state of Lincoln, "that someone woke up and realized the necessity of annexing some property." Yet the American public was not ready to accept so naked a version of that very imperialism which the American Declaration of Independence had with such eloquence defied; which the Constitution and traditions of America implicitly denounced; and which many immigrants associated with the regimes they had fled. The intervention against Spain had to be modestly dressed as the liberation of the Cuban people.

Within a few weeks American power had shattered Spanish command of Cuba. But that was no more than a beginning. Puerto Rico fell to America, and the Philippines. The Hawaiian Islands, where missionaries and sugar interests had already produced American control, were formally annexed soon after the war with Spain began. Yet the Senate showed an obstinate reluctance to ratify the peace treaty forced on Spain, with its surrender not only of Cuba to independence, but of Puerto Rico, Guam, and—for a payment of $20 million—the Philippines to the United States. It was Bryan himself who came to the rescue by urging his followers to vote for ratification as a matter of national honor; and, chaperoned by a declaration that the future of the Philippines was to be left undetermined, the treaty passed safely through the Senate. A rebellion by Filipinos, who wonderfully supposed that they should receive the same independence as had been promised to Cuba, was met with inflexible force, and in 1901 Cuba itself was compelled to accept an American protectorate. So vast a vulnerability as China could scarcely be ignored. In 1900 the Boxer Rebellion broke out, and American troops joined those from Britain, France, Germany, Russia, and Japan in avenging the massacre of missionaries and preserving commercial privileges. America herself sought no territorial presence, such as her allies had previously seized, but confirmed her adherence to the Open Door policy, by which she proposed to enjoy equally with the other foreign powers such access to Chinese markets as they had wrung from Chinese weakness.

For the elections of 1900, the Republicans renominated McKinley, with Roosevelt as running mate, and the Democrats, Bryan. While the Republicans campaigned on their record of achievement, with "ten millions of the human race . . . given a new birth of freedom," and on their resolve to crush Filipino rebellion, so as "to confer the blessings of liberty and civilization upon all the rescued peoples," the Democrats condemned "the greedy commercialism" of this policy and assailed the war against the Filipinos as "criminal aggression." What Spain had done in Cuba, the United States was now doing in the Philippines, and the Democratic platform considered it necessary to remind Americans that "all governments instituted among men derive their just powers from the consent of the governed; that any government not based upon the consent of the governed is a tyranny; to impose upon any people a government of force is to substitute the methods of imperialism for those of a republic." On domestic issues the two parties contented themselves in the main with restating their programs of 1896. And the Republican victory was vivid, with McKinley registering an increase of nearly 200,000 votes, and Bryan a decrease of over 100,000. Whatever the respective influences on the electorate of foreign and domestic policy differences, the Republican imperialists proclaimed the results as clear public support for America's world mission, and were emboldened accordingly.

In 1901 McKinley was assassinated, Theodore Roosevelt moved into the White House, and all residual timidity disappeared from the conduct of foreign affairs. The war against Filipino disaffection was relentlessly pursued, and the opening of China to American capital vigorously encouraged. Roosevelt wanted a canal across the Isthmus of Panama, for the swift movement of naval forces from ocean to ocean as well as for the promotion of American trade. But the Colombian authorities appeared inadequately amenable. A little Panamanian revolt against Colombian rule suddenly broke out, American warships were conveniently close to dissuade the Colombians from any effective response, and a treaty with the new independent Republic of Panama granted the United States, for $10 million down and $250,000 annually, perpetual possession of the area needed for the construction and proper functioning of a canal. For the elections of 1904, the Democrats nominated a conservative judge and turned their backs on the greater part of Bryan's reform program, while Roosevelt busily denounced the power of the trusts and the grossly inequitable distribution of wealth. This combination of assailing riches at home and bullying poverty abroad was crushing; Roosevelt polled over 7,600,000 votes (56.41 per cent), while the Democrats mustered just over 5,000,000 (37.6 per cent). The rich had little cause for agitation: they were secure in their command of the Republican party, confident of Roosevelt's allegiance to capitalism, and content with the course of "manifest destiny"; the Democrats were no longer pressing for reform, and the 400,000 or so who had voted Socialist in the election could be contemptuously ignored.

Roosevelt enjoyed himself. When Russia and Japan went to war and seemed near deadlock in 1905, he offered to mediate and opened their peace conference at Portsmouth, New Hampshire. In 1907 he sent a fleet around the world to advertise the power of the United States. And when the indebtedness of the Dominican Republic threatened to draw European intervention, he moved to take control of that country's finances and sent warships to warn off any resistance. This provided him with an occasion for pronouncing a new hemispheric doctrine. Monroe had aimed at excluding European imperialism; Roosevelt now aimed at establishing a right to American imperialism instead.

> If a nation shows that it knows how to act with decency in industrial and political matters, if it keeps order and pays its obligations, then it need fear no interference from the United States. Brutal wrongdoing, or an impotence which results in a general

loosening of the ties of civilizing society may finally require intervention by some civilized nation; and in the Western Hemisphere the United States cannot ignore this duty.

The new imperialism was given a new twist by Roosevelt's Republican successor, William Howard Taft, who proclaimed it the duty and the right of the American government to insure that American capital could operate freely in foreign countries. "This policy has been characterized as substituting dollars for bullets," he explained in 1912. ". . . It is an effort frankly directed to the increase of American trade upon the axiomatic principle that the government of the United States shall extend all proper support to every legitimate and beneficial American enterprise abroad." But that this "dollar diplomacy," as the Republicans called it, produced rather than precluded bullets, Taft himself made clear. Disturbances in Nicaragua resulted in the dispatch of American marines and the establishment of yet another protectorate.

With the elections of 1912, Woodrow Wilson won the White House for the Democrats, but his renunciation of imperialism provided no rupture in policy. In 1914 he sent marines to the Dominican Republic, and two years later ordered full military occupation, the suppression of the government, and the imposition of a new constitution drafted in Washington. In 1915 he sent marines to Haiti, where revolution had broken out, and placed the republic under American military control after an engagement that cost more than 2000 Haitian lives. Bryan, now Secretary of State, blandly explained: "The United States Government has no purpose of aggression and is entirely disinterested in promoting this protectorate." But its protection was to last till 1930. The marines stayed in Nicaragua, the State Department sanctioned an exacting bankers' loan to the republic, and Bryan negotiated a treaty which leased the Gulf of Fonseca and the Corn Islands to the United States. Then, in 1917, further to establish American power in the Caribbean, Wilson achieved the transfer by treaty of the Danish West Indies to American possession.

Meanwhile, the course of revolution in Mexico was increasingly engaging American interest. Wilson refused to recognize the government of a new military dictator, Victoriana Huerta, and so introduced a new instrument of American foreign policy—that governments might be legally ignored, with the threat implicit in this, for failing to meet the political, economic, or moral requirements of the United States. (To what absurd and dangerous lengths this precedent has been pursued is only too evident today, in America's long recognition of the Kuomintang rump on Formosa as the legal government of China.) But the mere failure to recognize the Huerta regime proved insufficient. In 1914 Wilson sent marines to seize the city of Veracruz, and only after Huerta's surrender of office were they withdrawn.

This new imperialism had profound effects on American society and the substance of personal freedom. First, it enormously invigorated and sped the movement from idealism to nationalism, from the view of America as a universal meaning and cause to the view of America as a particular place and power. If America had begun as a refuge and a revolution, she became more and more merely another state, with an anthem and a flag of the body rather than the mind. The celebrated toast of Stephen Decatur, the early-nineteenth-century American naval commander—"Our country! In her intercourse with foreign nations may she always be in the right; but our country, right or wrong"—would have brought to their feet few if any of those who first colonized America as an escape from the persecutions of Europe or who signed the treasonable Declaration of Independence. It was not at all the same as Patrick Henry's even more celebrated cry, "I know not what course others may take, but as for me, give me liberty or give me death!" And the spreading belief that it was, served only to produce such distortions of the original American purpose as the House Un-American Activities Committee and the whole frantic persecution of dissent to secure a society with freedom of expression.

Secondly, the new imperialism helped capital to propagate the equation of capitalism with patriotism. The American civilization that McKinley, Roosevelt, Taft, and Wilson were advancing by their interventions abroad was the capitalist organization of society in the main, and foreign regimes came increasingly to be regarded as conflicting with or conforming to American interests by the way that they treated not only private American capital but private capital as such. This, of course, fortified the influence of business lobbies in Washington seeking to identify their own interests abroad with the interests and even survival of the nation. Indeed, such lobbies have been only too evident in provoking such latter-day interventions as that which overthrew the radical democratic government of Guatemala in 1954, and in nourishing the growth of intransigent hostility toward the revolutions in China and Cuba. It is no trivial limitation on the liberties of individual Americans that the nation as a whole should risk conflict and even, in an age of nuclear weapons, annihilation, not—as most suppose, or rather, are led to suppose—always for the sake of its decent security, but certainly sometimes for the protection or recovery of investments by private American capital abroad. There are other consequences for the reality of individual freedom in America. The equating of capitalism with patriotism inevitably intimidates free consideration and dissemination of anti-capitalist views: to question the value of a particular economic system is one thing; to do so when this is generally regarded as disloyal, and by many as dangerously subversive, is another. In fact, the long emphasis in foreign policy on the economic rather than on the political nature of a regime has made capitalism seem more important than democracy. If a foreign dictatorship that cherishes private capital is obviously considered, as it so often has been, by the American political leadership and the bulk of the American press, as more serviceable, more admirable than a foreign democracy that fosters socialism, then Americans themselves must grow less and less resistant to demands for an abridgment of their own democracy in the cause of promoting or protecting capitalism.

Thirdly, the accelerated development of nationalism and of popular acquiescence in the equation of capital with country together increased the pressures for a bipartisan foreign policy. Despite the sporadic passion with which Democrats denounced the new imperialism of the Republicans, their leader, Bryan, sought Senate approval for the conquests from Spain in the name of national honor, and Wilson, the first Democrat to occupy the White House for sixteen years, repudiated expansionism only to pursue it. If the major parties did display some differences over international involvement after the First World War—differences largely confined to political entanglement in European problems—the Second World War brought them closer together in foreign policy than they had ever been. And when, some twenty-five years after Pearl Harbor, foreign affairs became a public issue of high heat, the leadership views of the two major parties were virtually interchangeable, and dissent depended upon a minority inside each. Over-all, there can be small if any doubt that the freedom of the individual American to propagate opposition in the area of foreign affairs through conventional processes has steadily diminished.

Fourthly, the new imperialism revealed, and materially furthered, the dependence of government on the calculated deception of the public. To be sure, government has always involved some deception, conscious or otherwise; but the careful costuming of conquest as philanthropy, of nationalism as idealism, involved a degree of deliberate and protracted deceit without previous parallel in American history. And the results were to be seen not only in the increasing manipulation of news and opinion by government, but in the increasing cynicism with which the public would come to regard its governors. In the confrontation of fact and authority which is so prominent a feature of American politics today, it is the confidence of individual Americans in their capacity to control events and effectively exercise by traditional means the freedoms they formally possess that has suffered most serious injury.

Finally, the new imperialism confirmed that schizophrenia in American attitudes to freedom long proclaimed by the treatment of Indians and Negroes. It encouraged American paternalism, a sense of superiority to those foreigners beyond the bounds of European power and cultural prestige, as poor, disorderly, and backward, ready and rightful prey for the benevolence of rich, orderly, and advanced America. That American interventions across the world were conducted in the name of freedom could not alter the fact that they infringed the freedoms of others. Is freedom inevitably indivisible? Certainly the whites of the South were imprisoned by their fears and hatreds no less oppressively than they imprisoned Negroes in social, economic, and political degradation. The lawlessness of the frontier that savaged Indians turned to rend the rights of whites as well. In denying freedom and equality with themselves to those peoples whom they captured to protect, did the mass of Americans not sacrifice their own freedom and equality? In promoting their nationalism and the power of their private capital, did they not make themselves the captives of both?

It was in time of war or threat of war that personal freedom came under fiercest attack from power in the name of patriotism. As far back as 1798, less than a decade after the Bill of Rights had been added to the Constitution, deteriorating relations with France and alarm at the radical disposition of Jefferson's Republicans excited the Federalist administration of John Adams to sweeping measures for the defense of the social order. An Alien Act directed at Jacobin agents and agitators gave the President the authority for two years to expel by executive decree any alien deemed by him "dangerous to the peace and safety of the United States," and although Adams never in fact deported anyone under this law, its mere existence was widely condemned by the Republicans as an invasion of liberty. More menacingly, the Sedition Act provided substantial penalties for anyone who spoke, wrote, or published criticism of the President, Congress, or government "with the intent to defame" or to bring them "into contempt or disrepute." Several Republican writers and editors were jailed or heavily fined, while the Republicans themselves raised an outcry against what they held to be a clear infringement of the First Amendment to the Constitution, with its ban on any law abridging freedom of speech or of the press. Indeed, the state legislatures of Virginia and Kentucky replied with resolves declaring the two Acts unconstitutional and developing the doctrine—which was to play a crucial role in the struggle over slavery, and which survives still as a claim of the recalcitrant South—that whenever Congress patently exceeds its proper powers, the individual state may interpose its authority between the federal government and the persecuted citizen. But the prospect of war with France receded, Jefferson won the presidential election of 1800–1801, and not only were the two controversial laws allowed to lapse, but those imprisoned under the Sedition Act were released, and all fines collected under it were repaid. In comparison with what was to come, the confinement of dissent was scarcely prolonged or severe.

At the start of the Civil War, Lincoln called for enlistments without the sanction of Congress and suspended *habeas corpus* in parts of Maryland, despite the protests of the Chief Justice. By order of the State or War Departments, military officers were empowered to arrest those suspected of espionage or disloyalty and detain them indefinitely, without trial, in military prisons. Lincoln himself required moderation but could not insure it, and the authority that he seized for subordinates was frequently abused by them. Then, at the same time as he issued the Emancipation Proclamation, he declared that all those who resisted the draft, discouraged enlistment, or were "guilty of any disloyal practice affording aid and comfort to rebels" would be subject to martial law, denied *habeas corpus,* and tried by court martial. Under this executive order over 13,000 people were arrested and detained by the military in the North, for offenses ranging from theft of government property to treason. In the South the exercise of central executive power was restricted by resistance from states jealous of their supposed sovereign rights; several, especially Georgia and South Carolina, even refused to cooperate in the strict enforcement of the conscription laws. But Jefferson Davis, President of the Confederacy, did obtain authority from his Congress to suspend *habeas corpus,* and where such suspension was ordered—as in Richmond, the Confederate capital itself—arbitrary acts were only too common.

Opposition to the war remained open and organized, however, especially in the North—for the most part among those, on both sides, who maintained that only the character of their war leaders stood in the way of necessary negotiations, and who discouraged recruiting or otherwise countered the war efforts of their govern-

ments. That such was so testifies to the large numbers, in North
and South alike, who withstood the pressures for conformity during war; and, relatedly, to the absence of any systematic campaign
by authority to eradicate disaffection. There was no general censor-
ship of the press in the North, and little interference with public
discussion of war aims and peace terms; in the South no newspapers were suspended or even censored, though there was frequent
and sometimes ferocious criticism of the Davis administration in
the press. Sentences by courts martial were mild in the main, and
pardons were not usually difficult to obtain with the coming of
peace. Pacifists and conscientious objectors suffered far less persecution than they were to do in an America at war under Wilson or
Franklin D. Roosevelt. Where personal freedom fared worse was
in the extent of arbitrary rule, with the substitution of military for
civil control, and in the economically selective enforcement of
military service.

Freedom and equality are intrinsically connected. If there were
no masters, there would be no slaves. If everyone on earth were
illiterate, the freedom to read would not exist at all. And this is no
less true for the effective enjoyment, than for the formal possession, of freedom. All men in a particular society may be formally
free to read whatever they please; but many, even most, may be
prevented, by inadequate education or by poverty and the high
cost of available literature, from enjoying any significant measure.
The difference in actual freedom between the rich and the poor has
always been central to a proper appreciation of America's open
society. And nowhere was this made more apparent than in the
way that conscription operated during the Civil War.

In March 1863, impelled by the failure of successive recruiting
drives to produce enough volunteers, Congress passed the first
United States Conscription Act. This allowed exemption from any
particular draft upon payment of $300, and from military service
during the entire war by provision of a substitute who would enlist
for three years. An immediate trade in men for the battlefield
developed. Since recruits were credited to the district of enlistment,
not of residence, rich communities satisfied their quotas by buying

recruits wholesale from the poor, so that while the poorer districts, forced to satisfy their own quotas from among those left, were virtually denuded of their able-bodied men, the richer often escaped the effects of the draft altogether. And when the poorer districts had no more acceptable recruits to send or sell, agents scoured the poorhouses of Belgium and Germany. The inequity of the law did not pass without comment. The first drawing of names provoked the Irish poor of New York City to four days of rioting, which was brought to an end only by the intervention of troops and the loss of several hundred lives.

The South, fighting for an independent existence and, it believed, the very survival of white supremacy, responded with less blatant discrimination to the call for sacrifice. But the complaint that this was "a rich man's war and a poor man's fight" had substance. When conscription was introduced, in 1862, it not only provided for substitution, as in the North, but exempted certain categories altogether, among them plantation overseers at the rate of one to every twenty slaves. So much evasion ensued, and so strenuous an outcry against the privileges of money, that most exemptions were, along with the right of substitution, soon dropped. But even then the rich who wished to escape military service found it far easier to do so—by bribery, influence, or claims that their presence at home was essential to the security of agriculture or trade or the professions—than could the poor.

One century later, in another war, the economically selective enforcement of military service again became a serious issue. Until recently, draft deferment was allowed to students attaining a set higher educational standard, though the correlation between affluent background and academic success was amply demonstrable. The inequalities of freedom to learn, planted in the economic inequalities of "free enterprise," were the inequalities of freedom to escape being killed on the battlefield. But the expansion of the Vietnam war and rising public protest against the injustices of the Selective Service System, not least from among the very children of the rich who benefited from them, have now reduced the academic safety routes to such needed skills as medicine and to sufficiently advanced graduate study. The possibilities of further discrimination remain. Exemption is provided for those whose jobs, essential to the economic welfare of the community, cannot otherwise be filled, and local draft boards, especially in communities of manageable size, are not indifferent to the influence of local wealth. Moreover, the local quota system diminishes vulnerability to the draft in proportion to the number of volunteers, and in districts with ready recruits from poverty, the rich have commensurate opportunities for escape. It would be surprising indeed if the obligations of military service should fall equally on all in a society where power is so unequally distributed.

If the Civil War displayed the despotism of which government was capable in times of emergency, the First World War displayed, too, the massive employment of propaganda to promote public intolerance and the resultant despotism of an inflamed majority. The Espionage Act of June 1917 and the Sedition Act of May 1918, concerned as they were only marginally with espionage and sedition, constituted the most damaging assault on personal freedom by government since the formation of the United States. The first provided penalties of up to twenty years' imprisonment and a fine of $10,000 for anyone attempting to obstruct the draft or to "cause insubordination, disloyalty . . . or refusal of duty" within the armed forces. The second extended such penalties to anyone who interfered with the sale of United States bonds, incited insubordination, discouraged recruiting, or should

> wilfully utter, print, write or publish any disloyal, profane, scurrilous or abusive language about the form of government of the United States, or the Constitution, or the flag, or the uniform of the Army or Navy, or bring the form of government . . . or the constitution . . . into contempt . . . or advocate any curtailment of production of anything necessary to the prosecution of the war.

Many states individually enacted similar or even more drastic laws of their own.

Apart from the pacifists, only the Socialist party provided any significant source of opposition to the war. Indeed, the Socialist convention at St. Louis in April 1917 castigated America's entry as a crime of the capitalist class against the people and pledged a "continuous, active and public opposition to the war through demonstrations . . . and all other means within our power." To deal with this challenge, the government used its new powers, under the Espionage and related Acts, systematically and ruthlessly, censoring and suppressing Socialist newspapers, prosecuting Socialist leaders, raiding and banning Socialist meetings. Eugene Debs, who had polled nearly 900,000 votes as presidential candidate in 1912, was sentenced to twenty years' imprisonment for a speech that was held, without apparent proof, to have had a tendency to produce resistance to the draft. Victor Berger, editor of the Milwaukee *Leader* and Congressman, was sentenced to twenty years in prison for editorials in his newspaper which attacked the war as a capitalist conspiracy, and, though twice re-elected by his constituents, was twice refused his seat by his fellow Representatives. The conviction of C. T. Schenck, General Secretary of the Socialist party, on a similar charge was upheld by the Supreme Court with an opinion from Justice Holmes celebrated for its introduction of the "clear and present danger" criterion.

> The question in every case is whether the words are used in such circumstances and are of such a nature as to create a clear and present danger that they will bring about the substantive evils that Congress has a right to prevent. It is a question of proximity and degree.

This was meant to establish a safeguard for freedom of speech, but it could easily enough be swung round, by judges of different outlook in situations of real or imagined emergency, and fired at that freedom instead. In its war ardor, authority struck at pacifists and conscientious objectors as well; several pacifists were prosecuted—a minister in Vermont was sentenced to fifteen years' imprisonment for citing Christ as an expert on pacificism—while a drive against conscientious objectors, supposedly exempt from the draft, placed many in military prisons.

The disregard of civil liberties was flaunted in the draft raids of

September 1918. Agents of the Justice Department's Bureau of Investigation,* assisted by members of the armed forces, special police, and volunteers from the American Protective League, an association of super-patriotic vigilantes founded by a Chicago advertising executive, fell upon the major American cities to hunt down "slackers." Men of possible service age who could not instantly produce their draft cards or evidence that their dates of birth exempted them were snatched from barbers' chairs, streetcars, restaurants, shops, even hospitals, and detained without warrant in prisons or hastily requisitioned public buildings for hours or days, until proof of their innocence was established. The total of those seized across the country was never disclosed, but over 60,000 men were taken into custody from the New York metropolitan area alone, and some 27,000 from Chicago. The Justice Department subsequently revealed that, on assessments made by its own Bureau of Investigation, 199 out of every 200 men arrested and detained overnight had been innocent.

Senator Hiram Johnson, the California progressive, denounced the raids as a manifestation of the American drift to militarism. And he later informed the Senate: "I got sixty letters in today's mail from men who had been subjected to humiliation and indignity, commending my speech of protest in the Senate. More than two-thirds of these were unsigned. Many of the writers frankly confessed that they were afraid to sign their names." But Senator Kirby of Arkansas spoke for the clear majority when he declared: "If in the necessary enforcement of this law in a summary way some individuals are inconvenienced or individual rights are infringed or invaded more or less, they must put up with that rather than that the law shall not be enforced." [4]

Only a public mood of patriotic delirium could permit such assaults on personal liberty, in defiance of the strictest constitutional guarantees, the strongest traditions, the most solemn declarations, and most sacred events in American history. And just such a public mood was what the government set out assiduously to promote. A Committee on Public Information covered the country

* From which the present FBI emerged.

with furious propaganda; under its direction newspapers, magazines, pamphlets, films, posters took the message of beleaguered civilization and German depravity into homes, clubs, cinemas, trains, shops, lecture halls, classrooms. In the hysteria of hatred and fear with which they responded, millions of Americans hunted out guilt by origin. German-American musicians were banned from many concert platforms; German books were withdrawn from circulation by many public libraries; the German language was dropped from study in many schools and even some universities; and a multitude of Americans experienced individual harassment for speaking German, or a foreign language that might have been German, or English in an accent of suspect derivation. The Governor of Iowa did not go so far as to require a specific accent, but did proclaim that "conversation in public places, on trains, or over the telephone" should be in English only.

To a public so aroused, any independence of mind appeared as disloyalty. Indeed, a mere failure to share in the general fervor, let alone any open expression of doubt over the purposes of the war or the conduct of the government, inflamed many Americans, not only as being unpatriotic, but as calling the propriety of their own commitment into question. It was not enough for them to feel themselves a majority; they needed the assurance of unanimity— and not just in passionate support for the war but in prevalent appearances. Their ideal was a 100-per-cent America 100-per-cent American. The eccentric who spent too much time in reading unusual books or listening to unusual music, who went walking too often mysteriously on his own, soon found his motives suspect and the indulgence of his community dependent on an exceptional display of his association with public opinion. Americans spied on one another, listened to private conversations in public places, and flooded the Department of Justice with reports of local espionage and subversion. But the most powerful pressures to conformity came, of course, not so much from what people did—the threats and accusations they made—as from what they did not do—the trust, the respect, the acceptance that they withheld and that is nowhere more wanted, more ceaselessly sought, than in America.

Alexis de Tocqueville in 1835 had declared the dangers of despotism by a majority in the democratic American republic.

> The authority of a king is purely physical, and it controls the actions of the subject without subduing his private will; but the majority possesses a power which is physical and moral at the same time; it acts upon the will as well as upon the actions of men, and it represses not only all contests, but all controversy. . . .
>
> Under the absolute sway of an individual despot, the body was attacked in order to subdue the soul; and the soul escaped the blows which were directed against it, and rose superior to the attempt; but such is not the course adopted by tyranny in democratic republics; there the body is left free, and the soul is enslaved. The sovereign can no longer say, "You shall think as I do on pain of death"; but he says, "You are free to think differently from me, and to retain your life, your property, and all that you possess; but if such be your determination, you are henceforth an alien among your people. You may retain your civil rights, but they will be useless to you, for you will never be chosen by your fellow citizens if you solicit their suffrages; and they will affect to scorn you, if you solicit their esteem. You will remain among men, but you will be deprived of the rights of mankind. Your fellow creatures will shun you [as] an impure being; and those who are most persuaded of your innocence will abandon you too, lest they should be shunned in their turn. Go in peace! I have given you your life, but it is an existence incomparably worse than death!" [5]

Was de Tocqueville's majority despotism the American exception, a response to occasional crisis, such as war? Or was it becoming the rule, in response to a developing sense of permanent crisis? The First World War produced not only political but economic upheaval in Europe. The fall of several royal dynasties and the rearrangement of frontiers were of little consequence to the commanders of property and power in America; the envelopment of Russia, and nearly of Germany, by Communism, and the proclaimed intention of the international Communist movement to confront the forces of capital across the world, alarmed them as they had never been alarmed before. Whatever appearances they might put on, especially at election time, they had always been sure of their capacity to dictate the shape of the American future.

But now history, which had so long seemed their sleeping partner, was discovered as having collaborated with the competition. It was a betrayal from which they never recovered, and alongside their fear of the enemy without flourished a fear of the enemy within, the secret processes of conspiracy and subversion.

Certainly there was evidence enough of disaffection at home. The revolution in Russia encouraged the few Communists and yet fewer anarchists in America, the force of whose numbers was scarcely increased by their passion for quarreling among themselves. But the massed ranks of labor were provoked less by the prospects of revolution than by the pressures of inflation. The purchasing power of the 1913 dollar dropped to 45 cents by late 1919, and wages fell further and further behind the leaping cost of living. Not since the Civil War had labor been in such distress, and the first year of peace was marked by 3600 strikes, involving more than 4 million workers. Business, however, with its hold on the general American faith confirmed by its unprecedented achievements of production during the war, had no intention of employing its enhanced resources and prestige to accommodate labor. Its cry was "normalcy," and by "normalcy" it meant not merely an end to wartime government meddling, but a subjection of labor such as had prevailed a quarter of a century before. In its struggle against the unions, it recognized that now more than ever could capitalism be profitably equated with country, and it set out to use such organizations of patriotic vigilantes as the American Protective League, which the war had spawned.

In this new siege psychology of the peace, with Russia now substituted for Germany as the barbarian at the gates, and Communist conspirators taking the place of the Kaiser's spies, anything radical, indeed foreign, even different, bore the imprint of the menacingly un-American. The first major engagement, in January 1919, was a general strike, led by the militant IWW, in the city of Seattle. The nation's press covered the strike as a first move by the Communists to conquer America, and the threat of intervention by troops, with the rising fright of the American Federation of Labor, brought the capitulation of the local unions in four days. This revealed more than the ease with which public opinion could apparently be mobilized against any challenge to the existing economic order; more, too, than the degree to which organized labor itself could be intimidated, by public hysteria, to fight only on those terms conceded as proper by capital: it revealed how in peace, no less than in war, the American democracy was increasingly becoming the despotism of a managed majority, and American freedom, the right not to dissent, but to comply.

A series of bomb explosions a few months later, clearly the work of a few crackpots, roused the government to a campaign of repression unparalleled in peacetime. The Bureau of Investigation, in which a certain J. Edgar Hoover was already playing a crucial role, vastly expanded its payroll of informers, its secret files of gossip and accusation, its claims to infallibility in recognizing and identifying the subversive. Almost half a million radicals were soon listed in its records, though the bureau provided no definition of radicalism, and Hoover himself was subsequently to cite a membership of 12,400 for the growing Communist party by 1922. A series of Red Raids, ostensibly aimed at subversive aliens and conducted under the authority of A. Mitchell Palmer, the Attorney General, culminated in a sudden swoop on 33 cities across the country in early January 1920. Some 10,000 suspects were seized, most of them without warrants, many of them with a gratuitous display of violence—some 400 in Boston were forced to march in chains—and held, frequently incommunicado, for questioning. Many, it afterwards emerged, were American citizens, and most had been arrested by mistake. The mere fact of foreign birth had apparently been sufficient to excite the suspicion of bureau agents, who had fallen upon innocent meetings where foreign languages were being spoken or on clubs whose membership was mainly foreign in origin. Even in the appetite of the time, this was too much for the stomach of several influential lawyers, clergymen, and politicians; a vigorous Senate inquiry exposed the more flagrant injustices of the raids, and those principally responsible for them busied themselves in shifting the blame onto one another.

The disquiet of a minority, however, had little effect on the general delirium. History textbooks were revised to promote the right attitudes in children; schoolteachers were required to take loyalty oaths; citizenship was denied to professing pacifists; and books, pictures, and films were scrutinized and censored by watch committees for signs of corruption and conspiracy. Religious "modernists" were expelled from colleges and seminaries, while several Southern states banned the teaching of evolution in schools supported by their funds. Symbolically, that onetime crusader for sweeping reform, William Jennings Bryan, now took the field for fundamentalism, with science supplanting the trusts as the object of his fury. Half the states passed laws to suppress radical labor agitation. West Virginia went so far as to outlaw any propagation of "ideals hostile to those now or henceforth existing under the constitution and laws of this State," while in 1920 New York expelled five Socialist members from the state legislature on the grounds that Socialism was "absolutely inimical to the best interests of the State of New York and of the United States."

From a single seed in 1915, the new Ku Klux Klan spread rankly through the early twenties, to cover the South, much of the Midwest, and even parts of the North. Anti-Negro, anti-Catholic, anti-Semitic, anti-foreign, it soon boasted more than five million members, an enormous income, and the subservience of important figures in both major parties.[6] In Indiana alone, outside the South, it owned the governor, the legislature, most of the representatives and both United States senators. Whole cities, with their churches and schools, fell openly under its dominion—year after year more evident in the crosses blazing at its meetings; the killings, mutilations, floggings, and kidnapings of those whose race, religion, or opinions it opposed; the lengthening intimidation that was its shadow. And then suddenly, in 1925, a sexual scandal struck the leadership, and the decline was as steep as the rise had been. But it said little for the state of liberty in America that collapse should have come less from outside resistance than from inside rot.

The fear of the foreign, in this nation of foreigners, led to a series of laws restricting immigration. Organized labor, forgetting or remembering too well its own origins, feared the competition of fresh arrivals; apostles of Nordic supremacy regarded with horror the mounting proportion of immigrants from southern and eastern Europe; business had more than enough manageable labor already and did not yearn for more foreigners with subversive doctrines in their baggage. There were even social reformers who saw no end to the slums for as long as ships supplied them with the European poor. A quota system, introduced in 1921 and made more severe in 1924, discriminated effectively against immigration from southern and eastern Europe; the National Origins Act of 1929 limited the total of immigrants in any one year to 150,000, with the number to be apportioned among the various European states according to the national origins of the American people in 1920. The open society was all but shut to outsiders. The flow of milk and honey was not for everyone. Few Americans, of course, now thought it necessary to erase, or at least amend, the inscription on the base of the Statue of Liberty;

> *Give me your tired, your poor,*
> *Your huddled masses yearning to breathe free,*
> *The wretched refuse of your teeming shore,*
> *Send these, the homeless, tempest-tost to me. . . .*

The attrition of reality made all the more requisite the nourishment of illusion.

Alexis de Tocqueville saw despotism by the majority as an inherent danger of the democratic system, and since the American republic was the major working democracy of the time, it is not marvelous that he should have done so; but the evidence of other democracies since then suggests a generally stronger propensity, especially in peacetime, to suppress minority dissent in the United States than in many, if not most, of these. One explanation lies in the siege psychology of dominant American business since the upheavals of the First World War; but there are other explanations, originating further in the past—in the Puritan, the colonial, and the racial experiences.

The first popular fit of intolerance within white America took place as early as 1692, with the New England witch-hunt. In an atmosphere of crisis following protracted warfare with the Indians and the repressive interventions of James II, accusations of witchcraft by some young girls in Salem stirred a public paroxysm of fear and hatred in which sensible people believed, or pretended to believe, the most lurid nonsense about each other, and anyone failing to join in the general cry ran the risk of denunciation as a witch. By the time that the special court to try suspects was hastily dissolved, after denunciation had begun to pluck at exalted citizens, 19 people, including a Congregational minister, had been hanged, and 150 were in prison awaiting trial.

The Salem witch-hunt has long provided material for the American artist, especially at times when dissent has come under more than customary pressure. For it not only possesses historical and dramatic priority, but reaches to the roots of the American identity. Puritanism was, in its very refuge from intolerance, intolerant; Roger Williams was banished from Massachusetts for propagating the principle of religious liberty, and Quakers were hanged in Boston. This early tendency to monopolize freedom embedded itself in the American character, to emerge in a variety of subsequent religious, political, economic, and social Puritanisms, of which Prohibition has been perhaps the most massively absurd. For the Puritan inheritance, it is never enough that the majority should behave as they believe to be right; everyone else must behave as they do, by the sanction of law or social disgrace if necessary, whether different behavior is innocent of injury to anyone or not. And it is never enough for everyone to act in the same way; everyone must think in the same way, too.

This factor is fortified by what may be termed the colonial mentality. The admiration, almost awe, of many, if not most Americans for "old" Europe—whether frank or furtive in an anxious boasting of American superiority—has been remarked by Europeans and Americans alike since the achievement of independence. The current hunt for European ancestors and coats of arms or for pre-Revolutionary American relatives is not new. Over 130 years ago de Tocqueville remarked: "There is hardly an American

to be met with who does not claim some remote kindred with the
first founders of the colonies; and as for the scions of the noble
families of England, America seemed to me to be covered with
them." [7] In part this is a response to the economic and social
dominance of "old" families, usually claiming a respectable if not
illustrious English origin and a lien on Anglo-Saxon virtue. But in
part, too, this reveals a sense of national uncertainty, illegitimacy
even, as though the rebellion of the thirteen colonies had ruptured
the natural relationship of father and child, to leave the child guilt-
ridden and searching still for an acceptable source of authority.
This search invests the majority in America with a peculiar power.
For it is the will of the majority that alone seems to provide an
indigenous source of authority, and to deny that will is not merely
to reject the views and wishes of most Americans, but to take from
America herself her justification.

Finally, at least as potent as either the Puritan or the colonial
experience has been the racial one. For as far back as white settlement goes in America, there has been white subjugation of colored
minorities. And this subjugation has bred a habit of majority despotism. A white majority that denies to colored minorities full and
real equality of individual rights is not likely to treat individual
whites in a minority of conduct or opinion with much tolerance.
The white American who refuses to accept a Negro or Puerto
Rican neighbor is the American who objects to eccentric opinions
in his white neighborhood.

Yet if America is therefore in some respects a special case, it
also shares with similar industrial democracies the effects of consumer culture. And if it seems to display such effects in pre-
eminent strength, this is because its consumer culture is by far the
most advanced. In his ever more urgent search for an identity,
which ever more tormentingly eludes him in the society of manipulated needs and satisfactions, of disintegrating time and place,
the American invests ever more faith in the majority, because it
provides, in the shifting reflection of itself, an easy and acceptable
identity for him to assume. And to him the very existence of a
minority represents a threat, since it challenges the general identity

that he has assumed and reminds him of the individual identity that he lacks.

Political restraints in the America that emerged from the First World War were less severe than economic ones, however; there is little room for the exercise of personal freedom in a slum tenement or on a farm whose harvests are consumed by mortgage payments. It is common to think now of the 1920s as a period of general if scarcely sober prosperity—short-skirted, glistening with beads, fast and eager. But the income from agricultural production was falling steadily, and most of the nation's farmers were sinking ever deeper in distress. Industrial production soared, but the rewards were far from equitably distributed. Indeed, the rich increased their share of the national income at the cost of the poor.

Percentage of National Personal Income, Before Taxes, Received by Each Income Tenth

	Highest Tenth	2nd	3rd	4th	5th	6th	7th	8th	9th	Lowest Tenth
1910	33.9	12.3	10.2	8.8	8.0	7.0	6.0	5.5	4.9	3.4
1918	34.5	12.9	9.6	8.7	7.7	7.2	6.9	5.7	4.4	2.4
1921	38.2	12.8	10.5	8.9	7.4	6.5	5.9	4.6	3.2	2.0
1929	39.0	12.3	9.8	9.0	7.9	6.5	5.5	4.6	3.6	1.8

Source: Gabriel Kolko, *Wealth and Power in America* (New York: Praeger, 1962), p. 14.

By 1929, therefore, 10 per cent of the population had almost 40 per cent of the national income, while half had rather less than a quarter. And as the share of the top tenth had risen from 33.9 per cent in 1910 to 39 per cent in 1929, so the share of the bottom half had dropped from 26.8 per cent to 22 per cent. Nor did taxation significantly affect this pattern. By 1913 the power of Congress to tax incomes had at last reached the Constitution, and the rich, enjoying unprecedented prosperity, had subsequently acquiesced in a whole host of taxes and tax increases to pay for the war; but from 1921 to 1929 a series of revenue acts slashed surtax, eliminated the excess-profits tax, and refunded enormous sums to corporations, so moving the burden of taxation down the economic scale.

With encouragement from the Republican administrations that presided over the 1920s, the big corporations got yet bigger, swallowing more and more of American finance and industry. From 1920 to 1930 the twenty leading banks almost doubled their share of all loans and investments, from 14 to 27 per cent. In the exploitation of natural resources, in industry, in trade, in public utilities, a few concerns expanded their dominance by merger, purchase, or the ruin of smaller competitors. By 1933 fewer than 600 such concerns owned 53 per cent of all corporate wealth in the country, leaving 47 per cent for nearly 400,000 other companies. And with the mounting power of big business went the mounting vulnerability of labor. More and more strikes were broken—often with the use of company militia or the help of state troops and federal injunctions—and union membership steeply declined, from 5.1 million in 1920 to 3.6 million in 1929. Unemployment was persistently substantial—though dwarfed in retrospect by the number of workless during the depression—and living standards for the bulk of the laboring population remained low. While the index of speculative profits rose over 400 per cent from 1923 to 1928, the index of wages rose only 12 per cent in the same period, an increase made meaningless by inflation.

Yet the twenties have gone down in American tradition as a kind of golden age, with spreading—if hectic—contentment. That it seems to have thrived on the very food that would suddenly kill it only sharpens this vision. All golden ages, by their nature, come to an end. But how did this one ever acquire its glitter? In part, no doubt, by contrast with the gloom that followed it. But in part, too, it was an age with the appearance of promise and general prosperity. Mass production promoted an illusion of diminishing inequalities. Not all cars and radio sets cost the same; but now it was not only the rich who could possess them. The expansion in ownership of such standardized products was prodigious. Within a decade from the close of the First World War, the number of cars in use grew from 9 to 26 million; within a decade from the opening of the first broadcasting station, at Pittsburgh in 1920, the number of radios in American homes reached close to 13 million. Advertising offered entrance to the boardrooms of wealth and the playgrounds of beauty at the price of a cigarette, a shirt, or a lipstick. And the development of the film industry allowed not only easy and equal entertainment for rich and poor, but an instant trip to high luxury, huge events, eternal romance.

Alongside this illusively comprehensive vertical mobility, and seeming to make it real, was an enormously accelerated horizontal mobility. The car sped migration from state to state, from country-side to city, from city to suburb. In the obsession with sheer move-ment, millions made heroes of—and identified themselves with—those who could drive or fly faster than anyone else. Living itself seemed to have changed into top gear, with the titillatingly risky, comfortingly respectable national sport of evading Prohibition, and the slick tabloids, rushing the latest crimes, the latest gossip, the latest installments in the serial of American achievement, with more or less appropriate pictures, into the American home.

Women, of course, did achieve vertical mobility. The war had opened a multitude of jobs in office and factory to them, and peace provided a series of appliances, from washing machines to cheap contraceptives, that reduced the captivity of the home. Women at last got their suffrage constitutionally enshrined, and took increas-ingly to public affairs. All in all, their emancipation promoted their role as the primary customers of the consumer society, and Amer-ica became in the process far more theirs than their husbands'. But this was a vertical mobility within, rather than across, the existing national pattern of inequality.

Need is both absolute and relative. In a climate of periodic cold, every human being needs clothing; in a conformist society, every human being needs a particular kind of clothing. Indeed, the needs of conformity may outweigh the needs of climate; women may shiver in short skirts rather than be comfortable but eccentric in long ones. A society may produce new needs essential to survival: before the First World War, motor cars were the toys of the rich;

in the United States today there are cities where public transport is
so poor that proper employment is dependent upon the possession
of a car, and rather than go without one, a family may, in an
emergency, reduce dangerously its expenditure on food. And necessities are none the less necessities for being essential only to a
sense of common citizenship: less than twenty years ago television
was a luxury in the United States; today it is a necessity, and slum
tenements without running water possess television sets.

The consumer culture is directed at proliferating such needs, so
that men, women, and children must buy and buy to escape feeling
deprived, humiliated, outcasts. Yet how may the mass of Americans satisfy their endlessly new needs without years of saving
alongside large and rapid increases in income? The traditional
Yankee morality of thrift, prudence, simplicity would have killed
the consumer culture in the womb. What the 1920s did was to turn
Yankee morality on its head and make virtues of extravagance,
recklessness, display. And the gap between needs and resources
was in part—necessarily just in part—closed by debt. Business
provided easy credit, and the public bought frantically on the installment plan, as though tomorrow could be reached only by making it today. By 1930 the total of private and public debt was
estimated at between $100 billion and $150 billion, or something
like a third of the nation's total wealth.

It was a measure of the American mood that the stock exchange
assumed such pervasive importance. By tradition, the twenties
were a time when typists and taxi-drivers joined bankers and industrialists in share speculation. Yet a subsequent Senate investigation revealed that at the height of speculative fever in 1929, only
1½ million people out of some 120 million in the country had had
any association with the stock market, and that of these far from
all had been speculators. In fact, some two-thirds of accounts had
been for cash, and only a third for margin transactions.

No less strange than the substantial inclusion of typists and taxi-
drivers in the folklore of the stock-market boom was the substantial inclusion of bankers and industrialists in the folklore of the
ruin that followed. The truth is that the depression sucked under

few of the rich; it was almost all the poor and many in the middle-income reaches who were submerged. The national income fell from some \$85 billion in 1929 to some \$37 billion in 1932; but interest and dividend payments, the staple of the rich, attained a new peak of \$8 billion in 1931, and throughout the depression never fell below the 1928 level. It was those without such security who paid; in 1932 there were 10 million unemployed, and a year later between 12 and 15 million. Many had participated in the prosperity of the twenties on credit, or by spending all they earned; many more survived the depression by sinking further or for the first time into debt.

Percentage of Total National Net Savings Owned by Each Income Tenth [8]		
	1929	*1935–6*
Highest	86	105
2nd	12	13
3rd	7	6
4th	5	2
5th	3	−1
6th	1	−2
7th	(Less than 0.5)	−3
8th	0	−5
9th	−1	−5
Lowest	−13	−9

Just as the realities of medieval Europe were distorted by the vision of court chroniclers and poets, so the realities of inter-war America were distorted by the vision of contemporary recorders. Those modern equivalents of the medieval court poets and chroniclers—the press, the radio, the cinema—saw and recorded boom and slump as power desired. For them, everyone made money in the twenties and everyone lost it in the thirties; in the version that they authorized, American society showed itself nowhere more free and equal than in the collective character of progress and setback, prosperity and loss.

How is it that their version survived the disaster of the depression? The disaster itself was accompanied by a plummeting in the prestige of the business community. Even worse than the scandals which buffeted the business leadership, with revelations of corruption and fraud involving some of the most eminent names in finance and industry, was the obvious bewilderment of business itself, its inability to understand, let alone solve, the crisis which had come upon the country and for which its own speculative delirium now seemed to have been largely responsible. Banks, the very fortresses of capitalism, fell before the onslaught of the slump. Farmers in Iowa and workers in mines and factories across the nation stirred in revolt. Thousands of ex-servicemen marched on Washington and camped within sight of the capitol to demand the immediate payment of their promised bonuses. Revolutionary concepts coursed through the intelligentsia as well as the ranks of rural and industrial unrest.

Yet some twenty years later, the prestige of business once more dominated American culture, and the opposition to capitalism was, if anything, less popular and more vulnerable to the despotism of the majority than it had been in the dog days of the twenties. For this the New Deal administrations of Franklin D. Roosevelt were initially responsible. Capitalism was made to function more efficiently by supervision and sustenance from the much expanded powers of the state, while its popular appeal was secured and enhanced by urgent measures of social welfare.

The grip of gold on the economy was loosened by ordering its deposit with the government and abolishing the right of citizens to demand it in exchange for paper money. A new currency issued and managed by the federal authorities thus ended the power of the private banks to dominate credit by the issue of currency commensurate with their own stores of gold. But despite demands from prominent progressives that the whole banking system should be nationalized, the New Deal left it in private hands, introducing such measures—among them, federal insurance of all bank deposits up to a fixed sum, and the separation of commercial and investment banking—as would protect it there. Bank failures, which had averaged a thousand a year during the heady twenties, all but ceased. Billions of dollars were lent to industry, railways, and insurance companies to assist their recovery, in a direct assumption by the federal government of responsibility for securing the interests of corporate investments. And, more important for the long term, various measures adopted by the state to control the stock market, the credit available for speculation, and the conduct of corporation officials strengthened the whole structure of corporate finance, promoted public confidence in the principal organs of capitalism, and inevitably advanced the dominance of the few large concerns over the many small ones. By the early 1960s, some thirty years after the coming of the new capitalism, Senator Estes Kefauver, former chairman of a Senate Subcommittee on Antitrust and Monopoly, could report:

> The core of the economic problem facing us today is the concentration of power in a few hands. . . . In 1962 the 20 largest manufacturing corporations alone had $73.8 billion in assets, or about one-quarter of the total assets of United States manufacturing companies. In turn, the 50 largest companies held 36 per cent; the 100 largest, 46 per cent; the 200 largest, 56 per cent; and the 1,000 largest, nearly 75 per cent. This left for all others—approximately 419,000 manufacturing concerns—the remaining one-quarter of the total assets.[9]

The federal government took powers over the agricultural sector as well. It paid farmers not to produce, so as to eliminate the glut in their commodities and force up prices. From 1927 to 1933 some 10 per cent of the nation's farm property had been foreclosed at auction, and farmers were organizing to intimidate purchasers and even the courts; to afford mortgage relief, the government provided funds for the refinancing of farm loans at far lower interest rates. Such measures of manipulation not only permitted the successful management of the immediate crisis, but enabled a much smoother development of industrialization and rural depopulation than had previously been possible.

Yet there could be no security for a capitalism that encompassed mass unemployment, persistent labor unrest, and so much visible poverty. The New Deal appropriated billions of dollars for urgent relief to the hungry and homeless, and found jobs for millions of the unemployed on public works. But more lasting methods of public subsidy were plainly required, and gradually over the years a system of substantial, if far from sufficient, social welfare, concerned in the main with old-age pensions and unemployment insurance, was established. Gradually, too, labor laws were passed to raise wages, reduce hours, assail the grosser forms of exploitation, promote the right of collective bargaining, and protect union members from victimization. Capital, however, did not in general take kindly to the changes. It ignored the new federal powers or, when required to notice them, fought them in the courts, with frequent temporary success. Strikes and lockouts swept the country. In 1935 and 1936, the Committee (subsequently Congress) of Industrial Organizations emerged as a militant rival to the AFL for labor leadership and set out to mobilize unskilled as well as skilled workers, especially in such sectors of the economy as the steel, car, and textile industries, which had so far resisted the unions. Using new techniques like the "sit-down," by which strikers seized the property of their employers and refused to leave or release it until their demands were met, it initially achieved remarkable success. But its militancy alienated a public opinion concerned now more to secure than to change, and the return to dominance of organized labor by the AFL marked what would be a long and—if selectively —profitable collaboration of the trade-union movement with the new capitalism.

The most impressive single symbol of the retreat from rugged individualism was the Tennessee Valley Authority, a government agency which rescued some 40,000 square miles, stretching across seven states, from neglect and waste, mainly by the construction and operation of dams, the manufacture of fertilizer, and the generation and sale of electric power. Business leaders attacked the scheme as a direct threat to the $12 billion invested in privately owned utilities and as likely to undermine private enterprise. But privately owned utilities were affected only by an impulse to greater efficiency, and the TVA promoted private enterprise for as far as its operations stretched. Within a few years, millions of desolate acres had been restored to cultivation; industry flourished in the valley; tourists crowded its restaurants, hotels, and artificial lakes; and river traffic stimulated trade for a vast area around. In the new capitalism, public projects fostered private enterprise by supplying at public cost the unprofitable amenities on which profitable private industry and agriculture depended.

Yet if the New Deal provided much of the infrastructure for the new capitalism—or the liberal society, as some of its exponents preferred to call it—it clearly failed to finish the job. Between 7 and 8 million were still unemployed at the inauguration of Roosevelt's second term in January 1937, and production was still far below its 1928 peak. Then in September a new economic shock wave swept the country; stock prices fell even more steeply than they had done in the crash of 1929, and the slump in industrial production was even sharper. Again the government eased credit and increased public spending; but the impact promised no real recovery. The vigor of the twenties seemed irretrievable. And then war came. From Europe and Asia orders poured into American factories, and domestic rearmament swelled these into a flood. Unemployment plunged, and production soared. Soon America herself was thrust into war by Japanese attack, and the economy entered upon an unprecedented expansion.

The annual production of wealth had fallen below $50 billion in the depression; in 1943 it reached $150 billion. But this considerable growth in industrial activity did not diffuse economic power; it contracted it yet further. The government declared its intention of favoring small concerns in distributing its orders, but it generally turned to the major corporations, whose existing plants could so easily be converted from peace to war production, whose already large facilities could so much more cheaply be enlarged, whose management was so efficient and so influential. By the close of 1943, 70 per cent of war business had gone to the 100 biggest industrial firms, and the construction of at least 100 plant extensions had been assigned to General Motors alone. The Department of Justice, under pressure from the military establishment, exhibited little enthusiasm for initiating antitrust prosecutions, and capital concentration proceeded apace.

Few of the business leaders themselves would have predicted many years of peace without a serious slump. But, in the event, the American economy scarcely paused for breath. The years of war had created a huge accumulated demand for consumer goods, and a program of relief and reconstruction abroad produced a ready market for the American surplus. As capitalism had learned to expand credit at home so as to encourage consumption, it now learned to expand credit abroad, so as to encourage there the consumption of American products. All this might soon enough have proved inadequate, however, if the war economy had had to turn into a peace one. Instead, the hot war merely became a cold one with hot intervals—as in Korea and later in Vietnam—and the expenditure on defense, with the development of ever more devastating weapons and ever more sophisticated methods of delivering them, continued to thrive. Twenty years after the end of the Second World War, military expenditure accounted for around half of the federal budget and some 10 per cent of the country's gross national product, while an estimated 9 per cent of the total labor force was engaged in work directly connected with defense. By the time of Eisenhower's election in 1952, to produce the first Republican administration since Hoover and the crash, business had regained its popular prestige because the mass of Americans felt satisfied with capitalism in its new form.

The accomplishments of the new capitalism have been widely advertised and generally acclaimed. Far less widely advertised and not at all acclaimed have been the oppressions of the American personality that this capitalism entails. The essential American has to consume more and more if American production is not to falter and fall; and since industrial progress may have satisfied all his old wants already, he has constantly to be provided with new—and more and more new—ones.

Now whatever form of society contributes most to the freedom of the individual, it is not a society that survives by the multiplication of wants. If the freedom to inquire, consider, propose, discuss, decide has small meaning for those without proper food or shelter, how much meaning can such freedom have for those who feel a deep and perpetual need for the newest products of American industry and salesmanship?

This insatiable consumption depends decisively on debt. For if a man and his wife and his children must wait to satisfy their needs until sufficient money has been saved, second thoughts may reduce the necessary sense of urgency, and production waste away on a regimen of prudence. During the 1950s consumer indebtedness rose three times as fast as did personal income, and by early 1960 the Federal Reserve Bank of New York could note that half of all American families were devoting one-fifth of their incomes to meeting regular payments for debt. One critic has estimated that, for the years from 1960 to 1963 some 88 per cent of consumer durables were bought on credit, and some 21 per cent of all consumer expenditure went on debt repayments.[10] In 1950 the average American family was spending some 11 per cent of its after-tax income on its consumer debt and mortgage payments; in 1960 the figure was 18 per cent. Nor was the market price of the products themselves altogether responsible. Instant heaven has its ushers, and they too have needs to satisfy. Stores, credit-card companies, car dealers, house-building and -selling concerns may provide entrance, but at an extra charge, not seldom largely concealed —the interest rate is quoted by the month, without due indication of this or of the annual effect—that may raise the final price by one-third, one-half, as much again, and even more. Recent Senate hearings have revealed interest rates of 289 per cent and higher for cars, and up to 285 per cent for television sets.[11]

The resultant anxieties, whether on the surface or submerged, gnaw not only at individual freedom, but at health and even sanity. American doctors seem to agree that money worries are responsible for much of the illness, mental or masked as physical, with which they have to deal. Certainly the incidence of mental illness in America is by general opinion very high. Television appeals for funds to treat sufferers proclaim a ratio of 1 in 10, and among the many doctors I have met in America there has not been one who did not think this estimate far too low. In recent testimony before a House of Representatives subcommittee, government health officials estimated that in a typical town of 150,000 people, 1 in 5 would require some form of mental-health treatment at some time in his or her life. New York is not, of course, a typical city; but its stresses are not all that more intense than those of other large cities across America. A report on mental health in mid-Manhattan a few years ago [12] concluded from extensive interviews that only 18 per cent of adults in the area were so well adjusted to their environment that they had no use for mental-health services; 23 per cent, or almost one-quarter, were seriously disturbed or incapacitated.

That there are, of course, numerous other sources of anxiety apart from—though not altogether unrelated to—money, is undeniable. There is the fear or fact of retirement, among those who have never known how to dispose of their leisure; there is widespread sexual stress, and the whole host of tensions and terrors produced by a disintegrating sense of identity; there are the strains of speed and noise, overcrowding and loneliness, violence and indifference in the increasingly incoherent cities; there is the never completely suppressed horror of nuclear war. But anxiety over debt, over the inability to meet commitments, with the consequences of dispossession and social contempt, must be high, if not highest, on the list.

Inequality is in itself an important purpose and product of the new capitalism. For inequality provokes new needs by reference to what the richer consume or the poorer cannot afford. Clearly, the figures for distribution of personal income before taxes show, despite the managed economy and welfare politics of the new capitalism, little movement to equality across half a century.

What movement there has been reveals an apparent drop in the share of the top 10 per cent, and then a flow of wealth not downward, but upward. Moreover, notably, with the sole exception of this top 10 per cent, the extent of rise diminishes with the order of wealth, and the extent of fall increases: the second tenth experienced a rise of 3.5 per cent in share of the total; the third, of 2.5

per cent; the fourth, of 1.9 per cent; the fifth, of 1.2 per cent; the sixth, of 0.8 per cent; and the seventh, of 0.3 per cent; while the eighth sustained a fall of 0.9 per cent; the ninth, of 2 per cent; and the tenth of 2.3 per cent.

Percentage of National Personal Income, Before Taxes, Received by Each Income Tenth [13]

	Highest Tenth	2nd	3rd	4th	5th	6th	7th	8th	9th	Lowest Tenth
1910	33.9	12.3	10.2	8.8	8.0	7.0	6.0	5.5	4.9	3.4
1921	38.2	12.8	10.5	8.9	7.4	6.5	5.9	4.6	3.2	2.0
1934	33.6	13.1	11.0	9.4	8.2	7.3	6.2	5.3	3.8	2.1
1941	34.0	16.0	12.0	10.0	9.0	7.0	5.0	4.0	2.0	1.0
1951	30.9	15.0	12.3	10.6	8.9	7.6	6.3	4.7	2.9	0.8
1959	28.9	15.8	12.7	10.7	9.2	7.8	6.3	4.6	2.9	1.1

The declining share of the top tenth is so eccentric, indeed, as to incite the closest scrutiny. And two explanations persuasively offer themselves. Throughout the capitalist world, and certainly not least in the United States, the upper reaches of business and the richer professions have long enjoyed substantial income-in-kind. Legally tax-free benefits, from cars, even planes, and private retreats in the mountains or by the sea, to medical care and club membership and entertainment, are bestowed by American companies upon their executives, representing important expenditures that would otherwise be possible only with a much augmented taxable income. And then, it is not unknown for the rich, with the connivance of their companies and the advice of skilled accountants, to reduce their tax liabilities by reporting rather less than their actual income. Between 1950 and 1953 the number of federal tax returns reporting high incomes declined, a phenomenon which the National Bureau of Economic Research found "puzzling" in view of "the almost certain increase in upper bracket salaries." [14]

Yet what matters even more in assessing the real effect of the new capitalism on inequality is the tax system itself. To hear rich

Americans discourse upon the cruelties of American taxation is to suppose an America moving headlong to the Communist millennium. The truth is very different. Since 1941, when seriously progressive income tax was introduced to pay for soaring military expenditure, the rich have increasingly shifted their tax burden from forms of income subject to high rates, such as salaries, to forms carrying far lower rates, such as capital gains, or no rates at all, such as tax-free interest. Thus, in 1932, when the highest possible tax rate on incomes of $1 million and over was 54 per cent, only 47 per cent reached collection; when, in 1938, the theoretical maximum was 72 per cent, only 44 per cent; and in 1957, when the theoretical maximum was 91 per cent, only 52 per cent. The enormous rise in federal revenue was achieved by extending the tax base. In 1939 only 4 million families and individuals were subject to federal income tax; by 1957 the figure was almost 47 million, and two-thirds of all reported incomes were taxed at the basic rate of 20 per cent. Despite persistent inflation throughout the period, the lowest taxable income for a married couple, which was $3500 in 1929, became $2500 in 1935, $1500 in 1941, $1000 in 1944, and $1200 in 1948.

In contrast, depletion allowances, by which a percentage of gross income may be deducted from tax supposedly as compensation for diminished assets, have permitted the accumulation of vast personal fortunes. This has been especially apparent in the oil industry, where the allowance is 27½ per cent; but almost all the extractive industries have enjoyed such benefits, if in varying degree. In 1942 Senator Robert M. La Follette, Jr., assailing the whole system, mockingly asked why, with allowances for so many different items, sand and gravel were not included. Sand and gravel soon were, at 5 per cent. As a result, companies, not a few of them mere façades for individual or family operations, have earned millions of dollars a year and paid little or no tax. Over a decade, Senator Paul Douglas noted in 1957, 27 cited oil and gas companies had yielded an average 17 per cent of their net income in federal income taxes, compared with the ruling relevant rate of 52 per cent.[15]

Furthermore, while those in the higher income groups employ lawyers and accountants to insure that they take advantage of every permitted deduction, those in the lower ones frequently assume more than their legitimate liabilities by sheer ignorance of the deductions they may claim. There is abundant evidence that the effective operations of federal income tax make little difference to the inequalities of personal income. And if federal taxation turns out to be far less progressive than supposed, local and state taxes are actually regressive.

Percentage of 1958 Total Income Paid in Federal, State, and Local Taxes, by Income Class [16]

Income Class (in dollars)	Share of Taxes (per cent)		Total (slight discrepancies due to rounding)
	Federal	State and Local	
0–2000	9.6	11.3	21.0
2000–4000	11.0	9.4	20.4
4000–6000	12.1	8.5	20.6
6000–8000	13.9	7.7	21.6
8000–10,000	13.4	7.2	20.6
10,000–15,000	15.1	6.5	21.6
15,000 and upwards	28.6	5.9	34.4
Average	16.1	7.5	23.7

The Tax Foundation's figures, moreover, exclude the severely regressive social-insurance taxes. These, while taking 7.3 per cent of the income earned by those in the $2000 or under category, for instance, take only 1.5 per cent of the income earned by those in the category of $15,000 and upwards.

The obvious consequence of such an economic system is to perpetuate poverty, and on a massive scale. Estimates of how many poor there are, and what proportion of the population they represent, vary widely. It depends, of course, on the definition of poverty employed. There are relatively few Americans who live on the level of the world's "underdeveloped" poor—though there are far more, in fact, than almost all Americans believe.* At the highest reasonable limit of definition, it may be held that all those who have less to spend than the upper half of the American population are poor, since in competitive America they have failed and are in want by the society's prevailing standards of consumption.

All lower limits are arbitrary and may stretch from starvation— for there is starvation still in America—through varying degrees of undernourishment, to a barely adequate diet with inadequate shelter or clothing or medical care. In 1959 the United States Department of Labor, in a survey of twenty American cities, estimated a "modest but adequate" budget for a family of four at around $6000 a year. Of this figure, $4000 represented the outlay on basic food, shelter, medical care, taxes, and essential work expenses, without provision for clothes, household equipment, education, or entertainment, let alone savings for an emergency. And the Health and Welfare Council of Philadelphia estimated that any family with less than $4600 a year could not afford ordinary medical and dental care.[17] Taking the much lower figure of $2500 a year as the borderline for an urban family of four, Robert Lampman calculated that 19 per cent of the American population, or some 32 million, were poor. At more or less the same time, the AFL–CIO, using a 1958 household income of $3000 and an income for individuals of $1500 as the frontier, found that 41,500,-000 Americans, or 24 per cent of the population, were poor. Michael Harrington[18] concluded that between 40 and 50 million Americans, "about 25 per cent of the total population," were poor, with "inadequate housing, medicine, food, and opportunity."

In 1963, with inflation having eroded the dollar yet further and with a median income of $6249 for American families, 19 per cent had incomes of less than $3000 a year, while another 18 per cent had incomes of between $3000 and $4999.[19] An estimate of 1 in

---

* After a nine-month study a private panel, reporting in April 1968, estimated that between 10 and 14½ million Americans were suffering from chronic malnutrition and hunger, and claimed that 256 counties in 20 states were "so distressed as to warrant a Presidential declaration, naming them as hunger areas" in which emergency feeding programs should begin at once.

4 Americans, or currently some 50 million, as poor, seems only too probable.

Poverty is thus very far from being the mere minor historical sediment of American society that most Americans believe. The suppositions that it survives generally in pockets of rural backwardness, or almost entirely among the colored, or mainly in the South, are simply mistaken. The Conference on Economic Progress,[20] which estimated the number of poor at 38 million, found that only 17 per cent lived on farms, only 22 per cent were colored, and only 43 per cent belonged to the South. If poverty has long been acknowledged among the Negroes of the cotton belt, the Indians of the Southwest, the Mexican farm workers of Texas and California, it exists as well among millions in areas of dying industry such as the West Virginia coalfields; among millions in the Northern cities who have been discarded by automation and other strides in efficiency; among millions of the aged whom social security provides with an economic twilight. Poverty is so far concealed because so much of it, as so much of America, exists in ghettos—Indian reservations; migrant labor camps; concentrations of the derelict, such as Skid Row in Chicago and the Bowery in New York; retreats for the old, such as the retirement towns of Florida; slums, white as well as black, sometimes at the center of cities, sometimes a mere huddle of shacks by the side of a silent road. The rest of America, living in its own economically stratified ghettos, and traveling from home to work and back again in cars along raised freeways or by rapid train, does not see these separate sectors of poverty, or sees each as distinct from the other, an isolated and temporary distress. That they might combine to make one-quarter of America is rarely suspected.

And this poverty is itself made all the more miserable by the neglect, the rot even, of the public sector. In the society of the new capitalism, private consumption is paramount, and public services are promoted only so far as they are of obvious encouragement to it. While main roads are expensively improved, to nourish the rising consumption of cars and gasoline, roads of urgent service to local communities, where there is not the density or wealth to promise a becoming economic return, remain unbuilt or fall into disrepair. Cities provide inadequate garbage collection, and home incinerators, which the poor cannot afford, yet further pollute an air already thick with the refuse of private industry. Commercial property encroaches upon drab and desolate public parks, and while the business districts bustle with rebuilding, public schools decay to the indifference of all but those whom they immediately serve.

The physical and psychological degradations of the poor ruthlessly reinforce one another. Squalor and worklessness foster the sense of failure, of personal inadequacy, in a culture that places such emphasis on personal success and on money as the measure; the sense of failure, of personal inadequacy, fosters the squalor and worklessness. The will wilts; a man who has been refused too many jobs stops looking at all. Helplessly the poor help to perpetuate their own poverty as they come to believe themselves incapable of anything else. And poverty, too, reproduces itself. There are many millions of children whose minds and bodies it must deform, preparing them only for their rejection by the competitive society.

To talk of personal freedom, of an open society, for the poor of America is to conceive of freedom as soul without body, and of poverty as body without soul. But it is not only to the technically poor that the reality of freedom is denied. For the vast numbers of Americans who live between the poverty line and a "modest but adequate level," or who have incomes at or just above that level, serious illness or economic recession threatens a sudden slide into the quicksands of the poor. For many of them, freedom means no more than a struggle, in debt and anxiety, to reach the higher levels of consumption without losing their foothold and falling to the bottom.

Yet how free are those other Americans, for whom the new capitalism seems to hold with some security the promise of ever-rising consumption, the millennium of endless needs endlessly satisfied? Money should be freedom; is that not its ageless offering? But it is possible, as the palace eunuchs of Byzantium or the concubines of the caliphs knew well enough, to be luxuriously enslaved. The new capitalism projects itself as a "people's capitalism," in which an ever-increasing share of the nation's productive wealth and so of control over the economy will be owned by the mass of Americans. Certainly more Americans—some 24 million by current estimate of the Securities and Exchange Commission —own stocks than ever before. But there are far more stocks available to own than ever before. What matters is how far stock ownership is concentrated. The Brookings Institute, in a celebrated survey, examined nearly 3000 corporations in 1951 and found that only 2.1 per cent of the stockholders owned 58 per cent of the common stock; 31 per cent owned 32 per cent; and two-thirds owned only 10 per cent.[21] That this high concentration of ownership should be reflected in control of such corporations—and of such economic and political power as the corporations wield—for the benefit of that ownership is scarcely incredible.

It is true that stock ownership has become rather less exclusive; but paradoxically this has invested even more power in the hands of the few large stockholders. The days of the dinosaurs, when an individual owned outright a big corporation, are over. It was, as everyone now knows, an inefficient era. In the new capitalism, with the big corporations far bigger and more important in the national economy, effective control does not require 51 per cent of the shares; ownership of a small percentage, where the next substantial holdings can be expressed only after the decimal point, may amount to control. And this reduction in the relative size of effective control has not only perpetuated the power of particular holdings in particular companies, while permitting enormous increases in capital, but promoted the expansion of this power into other economic interests.

As poverty perpetuates itself if left alone, so does wealth. It is not only that wealth feeds enterprise and self-assurance, as poverty starves them. Wealth in itself under American capitalism is enough. Anyone in 1913 who had simply invested $1 million across the board of the securities then listed would have been worth, forty years later, $10 million, after receipt of a further $10 million in dividends and rights meanwhile. C. Wright Mills has estimated [22] that 68 per cent of the very rich in 1950 originated in the upper classes, and that 62 per cent had relatives among the very rich of earlier generations. In 1925 only 56 per cent of the very rich had originated in the upper classes, and only 33 per cent had had relatives among the very rich of earlier generations. The mobile society is, in its upper no less than in its lower reaches, much less mobile than is extensively believed.

Adolph A. Berle, Jr., and Gardiner C. Means, in their influential book of the early thirties, *The Modern Corporation and Private Property*,[23] wrote of the increasing separation between ownership and control of the big corporations and their passing under the command of professional managers with no more than a tiny fraction of the total stock. The transfer of corporate power to the committee of experts is a major theme of Galbraith's book *The New Industrial State*.[24] Yet, in 1967, of the 500 largest industrial corporations in America, 150—or 30 per cent—were estimated to be under the control of an individual or members of a single family.[25] Moreover, "control" was cautiously defined as ownership of 10 per cent or more of the voting stock. Yet many of the corporations not included in the 150 were widely known to be powerfully affected by holdings of far less than 10 per cent. One member of the Mellon family, for instance, Richard K. Mellon, was the largest stockholder in the giant aluminum corporation Alcoa, with only 2.98 per cent; the largest stockholder in Gulf Oil, with 1.78 per cent; and the second largest stockholder on the General Motors Board of Directors, with .084 per cent (a fraction worth nearly $20 million). With all the devices for escaping inheritance taxes and disguising the full extent of ownership through the use of nominees, it would be surprising if many more of the big corporations than are commonly supposed were not effectively controlled by single, or small combinations of, large stockholdings.

That such control is not reflected in overt management is only to be expected. Men with commanding holdings in several big corporations can hardly manage such interests themselves with reasonable efficiency. The big corporations are, it is true, increasingly administered by professional bureaucrats who, if they have not in general risen from the ranks of the poor as some mythographers of the new capitalism suggest, are not in general, either, the heirs of family fortunes. In the estimate of C. Wright Mills [26] made in the early 1950s, 57 per cent of the top executives in the top 100 corporations were sons of businessmen, and 14 per cent, of men in the professions; only 15 per cent were the sons of farmers, and only 12 per cent the sons of wage or lower white-collar salaried workers. And the working-class element was rapidly diminishing. Of the top executives who were under fifty years of age in 1952, only 2½ per cent had come from wage-worker families. The typical executive has his roots firmly in the middle class.

Such men are not as independent as they are customarily portrayed, the trustees of numberless small stockholders and so, by an implied if scarcely justified leap, of the public interest. That they would retain their positions, or have reached them to begin with, by displaying indifference to the interests of the large stockholders is less than likely. The very managerial make-up of their minds disposes them to give concentration of ownership regard, if not reverence. But even if their allegiance to the interests of the very rich may be doubted, their allegiance to their own interests is surely obvious. And by virtue of their offices, they soon enough inhabit at least the lower reaches of the economic elite. The chairman of General Motors owns only .017 per cent of the corporation's stock, but his holding is worth some $3,900,000. The chairman of Chrysler owns .117 per cent of his corporation's stock, but his holding is worth some $2,380,000.[27] The contention of Galbraith in *The New Industrial State* that power has moved from capital to management is unconvincing. Managerial skill has merely become a commodity to be exchanged for capital, where corporate power continues fundamentally to reside.

That the interests of the economic elite are the same as the interests of small investors is far from self-evident. The executives are well paid for their services. But executives do not accumulate much capital, let alone live as lavishly as they usually do, on salaries subject to high tax. Their expense accounts and company benefits, representing after all resources that might otherwise reach the small investors as dividends, provide them with a substantial tax-free income. And increasingly they augment their income and capital through the provision of options. Introduced by the Revenue Act of 1950, the stock option has become an important instrument in the compensation of executives for the high taxes leviable on their salaries. An option on company stock may be offered to an executive at no less than 85 per cent of current market value, and be exercised freely after eighteen months. In an economy of endemic inflation, this almost invariably produces a considerable profit, subject to a capital-gains tax of only 25 per cent. By 1957, one-fifth of the total income in the category of those earning $100,000 a year and over was in capital gains, and 77 per cent of the biggest corporations had option plans. That such stock manipulation may promote the interests of executives at the expense of small stockholders is only too clear. Moreover, without provoking the law, executives may manage the level of corporation profit and investment from one year to the next for tax or personal investment purposes. There must be few large stockholders and executives who do not take some private advantage from the powers of management. The small investors are not as favorably placed.

More serious, however, is the interrelationship of concerns. Directorships and stockholdings connect competing companies in the same industry, companies in related industries, purchasing companies and suppliers, producers and distributors, industry and finance. That the director of a large purchasing corporation, with a seat and influence on the board of a supplier, will regard as paramount the interests of small stockholders in the supplying corporation is not probable. And if the interests of small stockholders are of such account, what may reasonably be supposed of the public good?

Despite the antitrust laws and the sporadic zeal of the federal government in investigating combinations, open and concealed, against the public interest, big business has grown inexorably bigger, and mergers have spread through every major sector of the economy. By the middle 1950s, less than 0.2 per cent of all manufacturing and mining companies employed half of all those working in these basic industries. By the 1960s, out of some 420,000 manufacturing concerns, the 20 largest had one-quarter, and the 100 largest nearly a half, of the assets possessed by all. If the new capitalism has proscribed national monopolies, it has permitted the development of a concentrated control difficult to see as different in its effects.

The impact of this industrial and financial concentration of power on the substance of personal freedom cannot easily be exaggerated. An obvious example is what has happened to the press. In 1910, almost 700 cities and towns in the United States had competing daily newspapers. By the beginning of the 1960s, out of 1461 American cities with daily newspapers, competition survived in only 61.[28] Moreover, in many cities today the same person or company owns the only radio and television station as well as the only newspaper, so virtually monopolizing the public communication of local and even state news and opinion. If there is a counteragent to this local concentration, it is national concentration. The dominant national radio and television networks absorb more and more independent local stations, and the dominant newspaper chains buy out local newspaper monopolies. Only the national news magazines with the largest or richest circulations acquire sufficient advertising to survive. And corporations commanding one communications medium expand into others; the radio and television networks have been moving not only into the cinema, to merge purchaser and supplier, but into book-publishing, by taking over established companies. Inevitably, the further that such concentration of ownership and management proceeds, the more closely will the communication of news and opinion tend to reflect the views of the national economic elite. The distinction between the shadow and the substance of freedom could scarcely be clearer. Anyone can publish a newspaper in America—provided that he has a million dollars or so for effective entry to a middle-sized town, and the ten, fifteen, or twenty million needed for a city.

It is not surprising that American newspapers are so predictably, drearily the same, so conservative in political outlook, so paranoiac about Communism at home and abroad, so hostile to the expression of any individual dissent—at least, when not emanating from the Right.

The similar concentration of ownership and control in industry as a whole is no less corrosive, if somewhat less patently so, of personal freedom. The power of the big corporations permeates every aspect of American life. Employees, mainly in the middle and upper ranks, accept sudden transfer from one end of the country to the other with a docility that would be regarded as slavish if the state made such demands. And corporations order the manners of employees, their social activities, their clothes and companions, with a prying paternalism that would be regarded as tyranny in the state. It is true that, in the end, an employee can far more safely clash with a corporation than with the state, far more easily abandon the one than the other. But before the end, it would be an unusually bold man who risked his economic present and future by refusing to comply with the standards of conduct laid down—so benevolently, after all—by his corporation. The intrusive state has, of course, the sanction of force. But the intrusive corporation has the sanction of dismissal and the inducement of promotion—not insignificant pressures for those loaded with mortgage and installment payments.

Much more important, since much more pervasive, is the influence that the corporations exercise on the whole character of American society. Through advertising and the commodities that they choose to make available, through the pressures that they apply for the promotion of private spending and the pressures that they apply against any public spending which seems to threaten their values and economic sway, the corporations together are crucial in shaping the culture of the consumer society. Their political pressures are formidable. Electioneering has become an ever more expensive process of manipulation, and candidates for important public office need, like the two major parties themselves, ever larger contributions from the business community. Corporation executives move to and from high office in Washington—whichever party holds the White House—with their demonstrated managerial abilities increasingly prized for the increasingly complex activities of government and the increasingly complex relations between government and business. But whether they are formally associated with government or not, the top executives of the top corporations possess a prestige and command resources that make their opinions, expressed or merely suspected, of enormous moment to authority at every level. At the local level, indeed, corporations so control the employment and prosperity of whole communities as to turn them effectively into the modern equivalents of rotten boroughs.

Are they at least, then, free—the top stockholders and executives of the top industrial companies and financial institutions? C. Wright Mills, that flail of the new capitalism, seemed to think so.

> . . . above a certain point in the scale of wealth, there is a qualitative break: the rich come to know that they have so much that they simply do not have to think about money at all: it is only they who have truly won the money game; they are above the struggle. It is not too much to say that in a pecuniary society, only then are men in a position to be free. Acquisition as a form of experience and all that it demands no longer need to be a chain. They can be above the money system, above the scramble on the treadmill: for them it is no longer true that the more they have, the harder it seems to make ends meet. That is the way we define the rich as personal consumers.
>
> For the very poor, the ends of necessity never meet. For the middle classes there are always new ends, if not of necessity, of status. For the very rich, the ends have never been separated, and within the limits of the common human species, they are today as free as any Americans.[29]

It is to be doubted. The appetite for money, as for power, seldom languishes with feeding; indeed, most of the evidence suggests that, if anything, it thrives. To be sure, the idle rich exist—usually with energetic agents to secure, if not increase, the riches which make such idleness possible. But they constitute a clear minority of the rich. C. Wright Mills himself estimated their proportion at 26 per cent. And it is to be wondered, by anyone who has remarked their way of life, whether they do not work rather hard at their idleness and whether they are not even more profoundly captive to personal consumption than are most Americans. The majority of the very rich, however, are far from idle. It is not unknown for them to boast that they work much harder than anyone they employ. Certainly they seem at least as dedicated to making money, however much they have, as anyone pressed to meet his monthly payments on a new television set. For in a society so dominated by money, how much money is enough? And in a society so relentlessly competitive, who can be satisfied with riches while there is anyone still richer, or threatening to become richer, in view? To suppose the very rich to be above the money system and accordingly free is like supposing a drug addict to be above the drug system and accordingly free because he has an assured access to all the drugs he can use.

But the bondage of the very rich is not just a psychological product of the system. It is also a social and political one. The success of the new capitalism is dependent upon more than the capacity of American factories and shops to excite in the individual American consumer an endless succession of new needs. American capital has long sought to secure client markets and sources of raw materials abroad, and since the end of the Second World War this quest has intensified. In 1950, the direct foreign assets of American corporations totaled $11.8 billion; by 1963, the total had become $40.6 billion, representing a rise of almost 350 per cent in 13 years.[30] One critic [31] has estimated the foreign market for the output of American and American-owned foreign firms at some two-fifths the size of the domestic. The often leading role that such interests have played in the development of American foreign policy is generally recognized. Yet since the era of Theodore Roosevelt's safaris it is no longer open season all over the world for private capital. Revolutions, some Communist, some seeming so to the tender sensibilities of American enterprise, have intervened. American economic power is far greater than it was at the turn of the century, but the forces of resistance to it are greater, too. It feels itself more and more seriously threatened. And even where the substance of American capital is insignificantly involved, its morale is significantly invested. A defeat anywhere for the cause of private enterprise saps the self-assurance of American capitalists. The very expansion of their power enslaves them further to fear. America maintains hundreds of bases, major and minor, around the world; trains and equips numerous foreign armies and police forces; and combats, directly or indirectly, with varying supplies of men and material, insurrection against regimes of private enterprise. And meanwhile she constantly augments her domestic arsenal with the latest developments in methods of destruction, to intimidate Communist power or overwhelm it in the event of an ultimate clash.

All this has produced a huge military establishment. And the expenditure on this establishment has been of huge—some would say crucial—consequence to the success of the new capitalism. Indeed, how far the protection of American investments and values abroad, and how far the support of the domestic economy, promotes such a military establishment is impossible to measure. But there must be few thinking Americans who are not aware that a substantial reduction in military expenditure would confront the economy with problems, of unemployment and unused industrial capacity, for which no acceptable solution seem at present available. For military expenditure is a form of massive state intervention in the economy that does not disturb the commanders of capital, who see it after all as furthering their interests. To substitute for most, let alone the whole, of current military expenditure an equivalent in other forms of public spending would be regarded by private capital as rank socialism, spelling the end of the American system.

Yet this suitable arrangement, by which something like one-tenth of the gross national product is conscripted by the government to defend the dominion of private enterprise, has unsuitable side effects even for the very rich. It has produced a military elite of unprecedented size, prestige, and power, increasingly remote in outlook and allegiance, not only from the mass of Americans, but from the economic elite to whose purposes it has long been seemingly subservient. To be sure, there is heavy traffic between the two elites. The military buys and the corporations sell, to the benefit of both, and where so many billions of dollars are annually involved, the relationship is scarcely casual. Moreover, the top executives of the military are valuable management material, and not a few have traded retirement for a place in the boardrooms of America's largest corporations. But the two elites are essentially different in origin and training, and by no means inevitably similar in purpose. The leading stockholders of the economic elite come in the main from families already very rich, where education and travel and international business connections have instilled some sense of the complexity in human affairs, even if only a belief in the superiority of manipulation to force. They know—who better? —that there are many ways of killing a cat. And the corporation executives who have risen to mingle with them have learned to know this, too. True, there are the Hunts and the Murchisons, with their simple Texan visions. But they are rogue elephants. The vast majority of the economic elite voted against Goldwater and his virtuous extremism in 1964. Whether a poll of the military elite would have produced the same result is to be doubted.

The military executives come in the main from middle-income country, and not seldom from its most unstable terrain. Few rise from the ranks, and it is at the select academies of West Point (for the Army) and Annapolis (for the Navy) that by far the bulk of those who reach the top are trained. There, and in the career that follows, social uncertainty is transformed, by a rigid exercise of obedience and command, into a sense of corporate identity, with its own precise stratifications, its peculiar dominions and obeisances. They are not the stratifications of the society outside. The military values are not civilian ones. And the stratifications, like the values, survive only in isolation. They must be protected from a culture in which money, not rank, is the measure of success, and the voting machine is, periodically at least, the voice of God. All this reflects a similarity and a difference of purpose between the economic and the military elite. Both elites want to perpetuate and as far as possible promote the power they enjoy. But for the economic elite, the military establishment is a means; for the military elite, it is an end.

It is a crucial difference, in the reaching of decisions on where American military power should intervene, the extent to which American forces should be directly committed, the limits to which a limited war should go, the occasions on which ultimate war should be risked. Indeed, the difference has already produced serious strains over the Vietnam war, seen by many, probably most, in the economic elite as having expanded beyond prudence, to the point where it is imperiling the American economy through excessive inflation; draining the nation's gold and eroding the dominance of the dollar as a reserve currency; provoking a domestic disquiet of unlikely profit to the new capitalism; and presenting America with a choice between the most damaging defeat and a confrontation of the most dangerous dimensions. Stocks on Wall Street now rise sharply with rumors of peace talks.

In nearly all issues of military intervention, the economic elite, let alone the mass of Americans, is effectively isolated from the relevant facts and the opportunity to evaluate them. And in an age of permanent conflict and nuclear missiles, the important military decisions have become far more rapid as well as far more risky. The only real protection for the members of the economic elite, not to speak of some two hundred million other Americans, with their constitutionally enshrined individual liberties, lies in the civilian supremacy of command, essentially exercised by the Secretary of Defense—an official, it is interesting to note, drawn with increasing frequency from the upper reaches of corporation management —and, of course, the President. But on men such as these the specialist advice of the military elite, and the information which that military elite chooses to convey as relevant, must assume immoderate influence.

The very isolation which contemporary conflict allows the military establishment, and which the military establishment itself only too fervently fosters as preserving its identity, promotes its power. Congress has long renounced any serious supervision; the chairmen of the appropriate committees are, by nature of their interests, generally deferential to military needs, and probes by maverick members can almost always be deflected in the cause of national security. Recently, indeed, despite objections from the Secretary of Defense and the President, the House Armed Services Committee amended the Defense Authorization Bill to establish a four-year term of office for the Joint Chiefs of Staff, instead of the indefinite term which facilitated Presidential control by the threat or fact of sudden dismissal. In the middle of the Vietnam war, the President chose not to veto the change.[32]

General MacArthur pronounced clearly the consequences of war for the relationship between military and civilian power. Before the Senate Armed Services and Foreign Relations Committees, he testified in 1951:

> The general definition which for many decades has been accepted was that war was the ultimate process of politics; that when all other political means failed, you then go to force; and when you do that, the balance of control, the balance of concept, the main interest involved, the minute you reach the killing stage, is the control of the military. A theater commander in any campaign is not merely limited to the handling of his troops; he commands that whole area politically, economically, and militarily.

MacArthur, of course, was dismissed from his command by President Truman because he appealed to Congressional and public opinion, for war with China, over the President's head and against his express orders. The comment of Max Lerner is typical today.

> In the struggle between President Truman and General MacArthur during the Korean War, the issue was not the merit of the strategic ideas of the two men but the question of where the final decision lay. In this sense the episode marked a constitutional crisis. MacArthur had strong popular support, which made President Truman's challenge to him an act of courage and seemed for a time to open the possibility of civil strife. But the tradition of civilian control proved too strong to be overthrown.[33]

Yet over the strategic conflict, MacArthur was firmly opposed by the Joint Chiefs of Staff; General Omar Bradley declared that it would be the wrong war, at the wrong time, in the wrong place, with the wrong enemy.[34] The military establishment deploys far more influence and power now than it did then, and all evidence suggests that it is far more cohesive. One can only wonder how much courage a President of the United States would now need to oppose the united view of his field commander and his Joint Chiefs of Staff. The Pentagon, that biggest single bureaucratic building in the world, with its computers and map rooms, its ubiquitous security guards, is five times the size of the capitol—an ominous enough symbol of military power in modern America and of the isolation on which so much of that power is based.

Speaking at Boston in 1951, General MacArthur proclaimed:

> I find in existence a new and heretofore unknown and dangerous concept that the members of our armed forces owe primary allegiance and loyalty to those who temporarily exercise the authority of the Executive Branch of government rather than to the country and its Constitution which they are sworn to defend. No proposition could be more dangerous.[35]

Nor is the expanding military establishment alone in eroding public control of government and the disposed processes of the open society. The proliferating demands of national security and the world-wide mission of the new capitalism have produced an underworld of power in the various intelligence agencies, of which the CIA is by far the most massive and important. With some 200,000 employees and a budget of several billion dollars a year, it is virtually an autonomous state, subject only to the suzerainty of the President. It has its own armed forces which, like its budget, are beyond any practical scrutiny by Congress. It places its own agents in American embassies, to deliver confidential reports and even sometimes pursue policies diametrically opposed to the official embassy ones. It has provoked or conducted numerous interventions abroad, from the organization of the 1953 *coup* against the Mossadegh regime in Iran and the armed assault in 1954 on the radical Arbenz government of Guatemala, to the Bay of Pigs invasion of Cuba in 1961 and, of currently most pressing significance, the promotion of a client anti-Communist South Vietnam, under the repressive control for nine years of its own protégé, Ngo Dinh Diem.[36] But its interests and activities have by no means been confined to such foreign interventions, or the infinite facets of professional espionage. As has recently been disclosed by enterprising journalists and disenchanted former accomplices, it has for years recruited amateurs to spy and influence policy in American student movements; has employed the personnel and facilities of American universities for various furtive purposes; and has subsidized, through unsuspected foundations, a multitude of American and foreign, supposedly independent cultural organizations, magazines, and publishing concerns. The ever-present hand of the CIA used in general to be seen as the fantasy of Communist propagandists and paranoiac radicals; few now can reasonably doubt its reality.

The dangers are only too clear. Of course the President possesses ultimate authority over the CIA. Yet how can he keep pace with its constantly multiplying activities? And how can the information that it gathers and imparts so secretly be sufficiently checked? The apparent facts and advice which it gave President Kennedy on the extent of disaffection and insurgent preparations in Cuba led to the Bay of Pigs fiasco; a less skeptical or more incautious President might have been led into a far more forcible adventure, with far more formidable effects. The very President who established the agency in 1947, Harry S. Truman, subsequently expressed himself disturbed at "the way CIA has been diverted from its original assignment," to become "an operational and at times a policy-making arm of the government." [37] Allen W. Dulles, for nine years Director of the CIA, himself had no doubts. "The National Security Act of 1947 . . . has given Intelligence a more influential position in our government than Intelligence enjoys in any other government of the world." [38]

The separate existence of a vast military and a vast intelligence establishment does not reduce but increases the incidence of decisions, involving risk to the very survival of America, on which the American people are never consulted and over which only one of their elected representatives has any real—if necessarily precarious

—control. The military and intelligence executives are not natural rivals, but natural collaborators. The boundary between the operations of the CIA and of the various military intelligence services is blurred. In fact, the budget of the CIA is folded into Pentagon expenditure, and members of the military establishment are often seconded to high office in the agency. As now in Vietnam, the CIA and military commands are generally the closest allies. But, above all, the purpose of the military and intelligence establishments are the same—to promote their identity and power by promoting not only their remoteness from representative government, but the international tension and conflict which are their excuse.

War, its approach and aftermath, have repeatedly assailed personal freedom in America, whether through the repressive measures of government or the repressive mood of public opinion. It was the relatively liberal administration of Franklin D. Roosevelt, indeed, that committed, soon after America's entry into the Second World War, the most outrageous single assault on the civil liberties of Americans in this century at least. By executive order, all Japanese Americans, some 110,000 men, women, and children, of whom two-thirds were American citizens, were evacuated from their homes and businesses in the three West Coast states to internment camps. No sabotage had taken place, and none was reasonably expected. Public opinion and the prejudice of the military leadership proved enough. Even before war broke out, its very approach provoked new attempts to smother dissent. In 1938 the House of Representatives established an Un-American Activities Committee, which at once began devoting itself to the persecution of the subversive in the shape of anything radical—all but invariably from the Left; and in 1940 the Smith Registration Act gave legal body to the doctrines of guilt by intent and association. But it was after the Second World War, with the onset of what seemed a permanent state of conflict, that the banishment of dissent looked like becoming a permanent condition of American society. In 1947 President Truman himself provided for the loyalty investigation of executive personnel, authorizing the Attorney General to prepare a list of subversive organizations and allowing even "sympathetic association" with any of these as evidence of disloyalty. It was preparation for a government service without independence of thought, let alone courage of criticism, and the prelude to what would soon be known as McCarthyism.

The loss of China to Communism, the Soviet intrusion into ownership of the atom bomb, spy trials, and the outbreak of the Korean war together worked on the old fears of conspiracy and betrayal to produce a clamor for ideological purge from much of Congress and the press, from influential business leaders, and from a swelling section of public opinion provoked to panic. Setting the pace was the Republican Senator from Wisconsin, Joseph McCarthy, whose technique of indiscriminate accusation and innuendo was supported by a facility for extempore lying and a practiced demagogic talent. But if McCarthy achieved a peculiar prominence in attacking the problem of free thought, his technique was employed by others, and his avowed purposes evoked a popular response, so that while many hastened to associate themselves with his campaign—among them, aspiring young politicians who would later transform themselves into liberal evangelists—few cared or dared openly to oppose it. As customary at such times, intimidation was greater than its cause.

The McCarran-Nixon Internal Security Bill of 1950 proposed making it illegal to conspire to perform any act that would "substantially contribute" to the establishment of a dictatorship in the United States, and though Truman resisted the measure, as "worse than the Sedition Acts of 1798," Congress passed it over his veto by acclamation. The Taft-Hartley Act required trade-union officials to take an oath disclaiming Communism, and many states and cities demanded loyalty oaths from teachers in schools and universities. Scholars and artists, pacifists and reformers, cultural deviants and dissidents of any kind might find themselves suddenly subject to investigation and purge. And however distant the suspect associations or opinions might be, they were evidence of current unreliability. Former Communists relieved their consciences or their fears by wholesale confessions, which plucked men and women from a past of sometimes short-lived and long-regretted radicalism into present inquiry, ruthless publicity, social reproach, and not seldom loss of employment.

For the Presidential election of 1952, the Republican platform assailed "the administration's appeasement of Communism at home and abroad," which had "permitted Communists and their fellow travelers to serve in many key agencies and to infiltrate our American life." General Eisenhower's inauguration was swiftly followed by the substitution for Truman's "loyalty" criterion of the even vaguer "security risk" as grounds for dismissal—so that personality, in particular as revealed by sexual inclinations, joined opinions and associations, past and present, as the suitable subject of official scrutiny—and nearly seven thousand government servants, without trial or indeed, for the vast majority, charge of any sort, lost their jobs because their employment was not "clearly consistent with the interests of national security." Yet McCarthy himself, emboldened by his contribution to the Republican victory and by the apparent lassitude of Eisenhower's leadership, now went too far. He extended his inquisition to the military, and the military turned on him. Eisenhower denounced him, the Senate censured him, and his personal influence disappeared outside fastnesses of fantasy such as the Texan oil rich and the suburbs of middle-class retirement in southern California.

The spirit of McCarthyism survived, however, not only in laws and administrative practices by which government at all levels sought to suppress disloyalty and un-Americanism, but in the fervor and social acceptability of unofficial super-patriotic groups, busily searching the press and television programs, libraries and art galleries, schools and universities, for signs of subversion. For a while, in the middle fifties, the judiciary invalidated the cruder attempts by government to cow dissent. But after 1958 it shifted its concern to national security, and in a series of judgments sustained the activities of legislature investigating committees, even when these were plainly directed at exposure rather than at eliciting information; endorsed the doctrine of guilt by association; allowed the right of a state to exclude from the bar candidates, otherwise qualified, who refused to answer questions on their affiliations; and upheld an act of Congress stripping native Americans of their citizenship if they voted in another country's election, on the far-reaching grounds that Congress might punish actions which embarrassed the conduct of foreign affairs.

Yet the real erosion of personal freedom in America lay less in the measures of government or the efforts of patriotic headhunters than in the overwhelming public response to the state of continuous crisis and conflict. For the vast majority of Americans, the very fact of the Cold War precluded any serious examination, let alone criticism, of their institutions and purposes, as virtually subversive. The existence of Communist societies and widespread upheaval abroad appeared not as a reason for reconsidering—if only to reaffirm—prevalent American values, but as an irrefutable argument for accepting such values altogether and whole. Nowhere was this more dismayingly in evidence than at the universities, supposedly the centers of skepticism and speculation, where compliance seemed all but ubiquitous.

The arrival of John F. Kennedy and his entourage of "new frontiersmen" at the White House appeared to promise a gradual repudiation of the long struggle against freedom of thought and association. But such repudiation as occurred was more rhetorical than real; the character and purposes of American society remained fundamentally unquestioned except by a few recalcitrant radicals; and the mounting militancy of the civil rights movement was still contained within the established frontiers of the settled American commitment. What the new civil rights leaders like Martin Luther King were challenging was not the new capitalism, but the failure of authority to insure its proper expansion to the South. And meanwhile organizations on the Far Right, most influentially the John Birch Society, promoted the conspiratorial thesis of American weakness by betrayal, and substantially assisted in Senator Goldwater's capture of the Republican party for the presidential election of 1964.

Johnson's landslide victory seemed to set a new high for the achievement of the new capitalism. The Democrats succeeded, more effectively than any party before, in uniting business, agriculture, the professions, organized labor, and the ethnic minorities behind a coalition of basic objectives. Indeed, the term "consensus" became the new catchword of politics, alongside Johnson's own slogan of the Great Society. While warfare kept the economy relatively taut, and the corporations accordingly no less contented with their growth than were the military and intelligence establishments with theirs, welfare augmented social security, even at last provided free medical care for the aged, and gave an influential place in the distribution of largess to the established leadership of organized labor and disgruntled minorities. The old cries of freedom and equality were lost in the clamor to induce and satisfy new wants, to summon new exertions for the climb up the charts of material accomplishment. To such criticism as detained attention, the response was, "But it works." The question "For what end?" was regarded as irrelevant.

How successful the system was proving itself to be! By its own standards, of technological progress, national wealth, and popular consumption, the new capitalism piled achievement on achievement. Yet all was astonishingly not well. Suddenly, it seemed, intellectuals were more numerously, and many of them more profoundly, alienated than they had been since the days of the depression at least. Labor and the minorities seemed less and less obedient to their recognized leaders. A rebellion against the whole character of American society was stirring among the young, and among the young of white middle-class success no less than the young of Negro deprivation. The relative rise in violence, against people and property, seemed far to outstrip—indeed, maliciously to mock—the relative rise in gross national product, so that the street was becoming a synonym for danger, and the city, for destruction. Most menacingly of all, a war being waged by America, involving the prestige and more—the government passionately proclaimed— the security of the nation, was not uniting but dividing Americans, not stilling but exciting dissent, to a degree unapproached for generations.

For this the government could scarcely blame itself. Despite persistent references to the importance of free thought and dispute in America, the President gave the lead in implying that any criticism of the war was an alignment with the Communist regime of Ho Chi Minh. Dissent was more than a betrayal of American principles; it was a betrayal of American men fighting and dying on the battlefield. And the administration could not ignore the possible parentage of protests. On the same day as opponents of the war marched through New York and San Francisco in April 1967, the White House announced receipt of a report on such activities from the FBI. The comment of columnist Clayton Fritchey was applicable not just to the latest administration, but to the basic development of American democracy itself. "President Johnson and his official family are all in favor of freedom of speech; they are only against the exercise of it." [39] Yet the protests against the war in Vietnam continued to mount, seeming both to emerge from and to swell a fundamental dissatisfaction. The first President of the United States, George Washington, had seen and warned against the tendency of American democracy to require a unanimity of opinion in times of crisis. "If men are to be precluded from offering their sentiments on a matter—which may involve the most serious and alarming consequences that can invite the consideration of mankind—(then) reason is of no use; the freedom of speech may be taken away and, dumb and silent, we may be led like sheep to the slaughter." Now, in one of the gravest crises to face America, more and more Americans were not only offering their sentiments, in defiance of their government's call to national unity, but examining the whole nature and purpose of a republic that had slid so smoothly, so prosperously, into such a crisis at all.

The American democracy has come a long way since the declarations of Washington and Jefferson. Yet in what direction? Has it not gradually, if informally, given way to a tyranny, unique in the popular election for a term of four years, and with a limit now on two terms, of the Tyrant? The system of checks and balances, the muscle of American democracy, has wasted till little is left under the skin. The judiciary presides over the sanctity of a Constitution more and more remote from the realities of power.

For how may it employ the Constitution to protect personal freedom from the expansion of the military establishment, the furtive activities of the intelligence agencies, the demands of policing American suzerainty abroad? How may it resist the increasing dominance, cultural and social no less than economic and political, of the major corporations? How may it secure the private citizen from the persistent manipulation of his personality? It may prevent easily enough the arbitrary seizure of the body. But it is the arbitrary seizure of the mind that matters far more, and how may it interpret its functions to prevent that? It confines itself to law in a society where law less and less reflects control. Indeed, the symbol of its helplessness has been displayed in its most celebrated modern achievement, its constitutional assault on race discrimination. For all the token submissions to its authority, segregation is more pronounced in the country at large since its rulings than it was before, and the isolation of the Negro from white America is more intense. The judiciary is the new capitalism in the clothes of a ceremonial priesthood.

How real, then, is the power of the legislative branch? Formally, to be sure, it remains immense. Congressional committees continue to supervise such executive agencies as the armed forces and the intelligence services. The Senate retains its right to confirm important executive appointments and treaties with foreign states. Above all, Congress still exercises command over taxation and so executive expenditure; still makes the laws of America. Yet supervision of the military and intelligence establishments has long lost any real meaning. Indeed, Congressmen are themselves not infrequently intimidated by the activities of the FBI. The confirmation of major executive appointments has become all but automatic, while the most significant foreign commitments seldom assume treaty shape and are in general—for the sake, of course, of national security—kept secret from the political populace. The budget, prepared and presented by the executive, is subject, in all its intricate detail, to amendment; but its basic structure is scarcely ever seriously questioned. The laws are the laws of Congress; but the crucial decisions, like the crucial powers, are effectively less and less dependent on the passing of new laws. Symbolically, the Vietnam war, involving by the end of 1967 some half a million American troops, has been waged for several years without ever having been constitutionally declared by Congress. To be sure, collisions between President and Congress still take place. But they have long ceased to be concerned with the fundamental character of American society. For Congress, too, is a ritual of the new capitalism, a sort of legislative drama to provide a public catharsis.

The home of Congressional power was the heterogeneity of American culture. Between representatives of the industrial cities and the farming communities, the slums and the suburbs, capital and labor, there was conflict and sporadic compromise. A President representing one coalition of interests frequently collided with a majority in Congress representing another. But now both President and the vast majority in Congress represent a single constituency—the suburban sprawl, the accommodation of capital and labor, the culture of suzerainty abroad and consumption at home. And election from that constituency requires more and more money, in keeping with the models of a consumer society and the methods by which its citizens are manipulated. A candidate, like any other commodity, has to be sold, by attractive packaging and expert exposure to the public. It is the appearance, not the content, that counts. There are still candidates with small material means who win elections, but they are scarcely the rule. Tens of thousands of dollars are generally needed to win a seat in the House; hundreds of thousands, sometimes millions, for a seat in the Senate; and more and more millions for nomination by a major party, let alone election to the Presidency. Candidates who are not sufficiently rich themselves need sufficiently rich backing, and such backing must most of the time come, in money or free packaging, from the constituents, whether Democrat or Republican, of the consensus—the economic elite, the press and television, the political machines of labor and the minorities. A fundamental split between President and Congress, short of a sudden brainstorm sweeping either, would mean a fundamental split in the consensus itself, and so the failure of the new capitalism. Indeed, it seems not too much to say that the sole surviving real power of Congress is to neutralize a President who does have a brainstorm: though whether, in an age of pushbutton annihilation, Congress would necessarily have the time, or, granted support for the President from the military leadership, the opportunity, must be suspect.

A final confinement of the central executive was for long the federal nature of American government, but the operations of the new capitalism have reduced this deliberate diffusion of power to little more than a formality. What states have excluded the giant corporations, to retain or procure some significant measure of control over the course of their local economies? Or resisted the mounting importance of central government patronage to their provision of public services, their managed prosperity? That states and regions differ, sometimes substantially, still from each other in the character of local administration and the treatment of individual citizens, so preserving and promoting immediate allegiances, can scarcely be denied. But paradoxically, since these differences are continuously being drained of resources, they reinforce rather than restrain the dominance of the consensus and its central representative. They increase the ease of manipulating the whole by playing off the parts against one another, as they diminish the impact of any particular part on the whole. In the mass consumer culture, local differences reflect more and more the rhetoric, less and less the reality of power. For, indeed, the further that the reality fades, the braver the rhetoric becomes. Governors and mayors enjoy authority without the equipment required to give it adequate meaning. If they have a place in power, it is not outside the ascendancy of the central government, as a counter pressure, but inside, contributing to the mood of the consensus and the adjustments of individual ambition to represent it. The forms of local government may seem of growing moment. The functions are fast receding reverberations of the past.

It is the palace that rules America—the President, with his prolific household of special advisers and press agents; his Cabinet, whose members owe their offices solely to his will; the heads of executive agencies, not least the military and intelligence establishments, whose information and advice condition his decisions. The Presidency has become more and more invested, like some ancient imperial throne, with a mystery of majesty, of collective identity and continuity, that commands popular awe and the due obeisances of those who minister to it, however unbecoming the particular incumbent may be. And certainly the power of the President is awesome enough. His domestic decisions—whether to encourage or inhibit the momentum of public expenditure; whether to favor the demands of social welfare or private profit; how the massive patronage of his office should be distributed; a multitude of interventions or inactions—significantly affect the lives of many millions. His foreign policy can affect the very existence of man. Yet whether he is a weak or a strong President is a difference of degree; he is the servant, not the master, of the system. Like innumerable tyrants before him, he effectively yields more of his freedom with every extension of his sway; increasingly his functions control him.

The truth is that America is not the open society that it pretends to be. And to reply that it is not the shut society of authoritarian Communism does not deny this. Of course it is not shut as Communist societies are shut. It is shut in a different way. The society of the new Communism is a totalitarianism of party. The society of the new capitalism is a totalitarianism of money. And just as the totalitarianism of party makes in the end everyone its victim, so in the end does the totalitarianism of money. That within the walls of party or money, freedom of a sort exists, is not to be doubted. But the walls are there, setting the measure, none the less.

The cells may seem larger, the windows wider, in the society of money than in the society of party; or, at least, they may seem so at present to more people. The totalitarianism of party developed to deal with a different situation, out of different circumstances. But where the reality of freedom seems to advance in Communist societies as their poverty retreats, so the reality of freedom in America —and in the many societies of the new capitalism following America's example—seems to retreat as riches advance. The two totalitarianisms appear to be approaching each other, for a meeting in the common bland manipulation of the person and the efficient processing of his freedom.

Is this, then, the inevitable accompaniment to industrial civilization, the price to be paid for material progress? There is, surely, no greater challenge to the human mind. And it is perhaps the greatest achievement of the American democracy, of the American meaning, that the challenge is being openly explored more profoundly by more people in America than anywhere else.

CHAPTER 4

The Insurrectionists

The trouble with this society is, it's overdeveloped and undernourished. It can't afford itself.—A New York City taxidriver

From time to time in American history men have arisen to dispute the prevalent interpretation of the American dream, to examine the ointment of realism and find it no more than a disguise for the discordance of reality. This, they have cried, is not the meaning of America, and they have set out to oppose the principles, expedients, or mere indifference of their society with a new call of their own. They have pursued not reform, but revolution, a fundamental reconstruction of politics, economics, morals, that would bring not the better but the best, a Utopia in the New World. And in this, whether excited by the ideal of sanctity or equality or freedom, they have been the real Americans. For the peculiar meaning of America in human history is that it was a pursuit before it was a people or a country, and pursuit not of an accommodation but of an ideal. Inevitably, as the pursuit became a people and then a country, and the interests of power and property promoted the cause of accumulation rather than choice, consolidation rather than change, it seemed that America had become the most conformist of societies, with whole generations sunk in a coma of compliance. But the pursuit has persistently reasserted itself in sudden surges of rejection and faith, which may have swept up only a small minority of Americans and ebbed to leave society seemingly little changed, but which have refreshed the American—and so, much more, the human—allegiance to the ideal. Such Americans, who have repeatedly refused to confuse freedom with safety, equality with prosperity, and happiness with fun, have given, and give still, America her purpose and excuse.

Indeed, no sooner had the Puritans settled their Promised Land in New England than one among them began disturbing their ordered peace by questioning its order. Arriving from England at Boston in 1631, Roger Williams brought with him the leveling social ideals and the religious individualism of the Seekers, a combination that scarcely recommended him to the theocratic magistrates of Massachusetts, who were adding property to piety in their refuge. For him the New Testament was a message of ultimate democracy, the brotherhood of men, Jew and gentile, learned and illiterate, in a commonwealth of love. His heresies were commensurately disruptive: he asserted that the civil power could exercise no decent jurisdiction over individual conscience; that the church had the legal status of a trading company, with its membership and creed of no more concern to the civil magistrates than those of any other corporation; that the state existed to promote the most freedom and well-being for the individual citizen, and, though possessed of the power to coerce, might properly employ it only to secure justice; and that the King's patent conveyed no rightful title to land, which should be bought from its owners, the Indians.

The elect of God were outraged and foresaw their measured gardens reduced to common pasture, if not wilderness. Williams was tried by the general court, required to recant, and, refusing to do so, was banished from Massachusetts. With four companions, he founded the first white settlement in present-day Rhode Island, at Providence, and, immediately establishing friendly relations with the local Indians, duly bought from them the land for his experiment. For here he set out to develop a new commonwealth, so solicitous of "liberty and equality, both in land and government," that it would not be seriously rivaled as an exploration in democracy and personal freedom anywhere in the world of the West for another century and a half, and must rank among the outstanding in history. The supremacy of the people was its body and soul, and Williams attempted to secure both by the provision of frequent elections, a single-chamber legislature, the joint and individual initiation of laws, the compulsory referendum, the right to revoke all laws, and appeal to arbitration. Unlike the American democracy to which Rhode Island would eventually, if reluctantly, accede, this commonwealth had no sacred constitution or separation of powers to modify popular sovereignty. A rigid constitution, on which age and custom would inevitably bestow an intimidating authority, Williams feared and discarded for one which the people might change or revoke altogether as their judgment persuaded. A judiciary with the power to review, interpret, and so transform the fundamental law was accordingly avoided, as was an executive able to exploit its constitutional independence so as to manipulate rather than express representative government. Furthermore, as an additional safeguard of individual liberty, the towns—which Williams regarded as voluntary corporations, in the same way as he saw the church—were given home rule within the structure of the state, and such was their subsequent fear of a centralized dominion that the legislature itself would be made to migrate from county to county till 1854.

New England Presbyterianism reacted rather as America currently reacts to revolutionary regimes abroad; anything that went right in Rhode Island was ignored or misinterpreted, while anything that went wrong was fed to public scorn and alarm as a sign of reprobation and anarchy. In Parrington's tart recital:

. . . for upwards of two hundred years the little commonwealth was commonly spoken of in such terms as Rogues Island and the State of Confusion; not indeed, till it left off following agrarian and Populistic gods, till it had ceased to be democratic, did it become wholly respectable. It was not so much the repeated turbulence of Rhode Island that was disapproved by the Boston magistrates; but rather the disturbing example of a colony at their very doors, which, in denying the right of the godly to police society, gave encouragement to evil-disposed persons in their own sober commonwealth.[1]

Without the support of influential friends in the English Parliament, and the charter that Williams secured through their efforts, the Rhode Island colony would have found it far less easy, if possible at all, to survive. The Boston oligarchs worked diligently to undermine so dangerous a precedent, and in 1644, and again in 1648, the colony was refused admission to the New England Confederacy unless it surrendered to the jurisdiction of Massachusetts or Plymouth. Its tradition died none the less hard. In its fear of a strong federal government, Rhode Island refused to attend the Constitutional Convention at Philadelphia in 1787, and only after the new United States Senate had passed a bill to sever commercial relations with it, did it ratify, in 1790, the federal Constitution—by a majority of two votes. The subsequent political and economic expansion of America did the rest. Where Roger Williams once established his democratic dissent there stretches today an indistinguishable part of the vast Northeast industrial and suburban sprawl, its political capital in the White House and the Pentagon, its economic in Wall Street, and its cultural in Madison Avenue.

Yet the tracks of Roger Williams are embedded deep in the development of America. His belief in religious freedom, not as a concession by a tolerant state but as a basic individual right, did much to promote an America with no prerogative for any religion, let alone any particular church. And in his view of the state itself as a voluntary compact of men for their mutual benefit, he was the precursor of Paine, Rousseau, Jefferson, and the Declaration of Independence.

From this Grant I infer . . . that the *Soveraigne, originall,* and *foundation of civill power* lies in the *People.* . . . And if so, that a People may erect and establish what *forme* of *Government* seemes to them most meete for their *civill condition:* It is evident that such *Governments* as are by them erected and established, have no more *power,* nor for no longer time, then the *civill power* or people consenting and agreeing shall betrust them with. This is cleere not only in *Reason,* but in the experience of all *commonweales,* where the people are not deprived of their naturall freedom by the power of Tyrants.[2]

More even than this, however, Williams was the first American prophet of that ever elusive, ever recurring American vision, the earthly paradise of liberty and equality through love. In his attitude to the Indians, his belief in equality beyond race, he is the precursor of Abolitionism and the modern civil rights movement. In his pursuit of personal freedom against the pressures of property and power, timidity, cynicism, and compromise, he prefigures Emerson, Thoreau, and the Transcendentalists; the poets of a rebel democracy, from Walt Whitman to Allen Ginsberg; the contemporary young insurrectionists in the protest of the campus and the streets.

The commitment of Roger Williams to his fellow men was total —political, economic, social, religious, moral—and he did not establish his own commonwealth to retreat from the remaining world. He bombarded the magistrates of Massachusetts with his exhortations. "I know and am persuaded," he wrote in 1637 to Governor John Winthrop, "that your misguidings are great and lamentable, and the further you pass in your way, the further you wander, and the end of one vexation will be the beginning of another, till conscience be permitted (though erroneous) to be free amongst you." [3] But in his retirement, albeit enforced, to the wilderness, he was the precursor of a distinct strain of American visionaries, the exponents of personal withdrawal, whose particular views he would not always have found congenial, but whose spirit of independence, rejection of social pressures, and ultimate longing for liberty he would have approved, no less than the right of individual search that they represented. Certainly the Beats of the 1950s and the Hippies who followed, like their more respectable predecessors who escaped to a European exile between the two world wars, are closer to the Rhode Island pioneers in mood and purpose than to either the early New England of the elect or the present-day America of obsessive consumption. And halfway between the total commitment of Williams and the retreat of the Beat or the Hippie from social management stands the figure of

John Noyes (1811–1886), who sought a revolution primarily of personal relationships in a new collective setting.

Converted to the belief that Christ had come again in A.D. 70 or thereabouts, and that man could achieve perfection this side of heaven, Noyes, a graduate of Dartmouth College and a Congregationalist minister, was dismissed from Yale for his heresies, and set out to establish the perfect society himself. One of the first militant Abolitionists, he renounced all allegiance to a government that countenanced slavery. But he was not to be sidetracked into campaigns of particular reform. He sought ". . . reconciliation with God, . . . a restoration of the true relations between the sexes, . . . a reformation of the industrial system, and . . . victory over death." He returned to the home of his family, in Putney, Vermont, and there organized the Putney Corporation of Perfectionists, with *The Perfectionist* as its organ.

It was scarcely surprising that Noyes attracted disciples. He raised women to an equality with men, liberating them from the drudgery of the kitchen, and from "the universal trap, the tyranny of child bearing"; dinner and supper were scrapped for access to a communal pantry, and "male continence" prevented "random procreation." Moreover, the leading Perfectionists came from among the first families of Vermont; Noyes himself was the son of a merchant, former headmaster of Chesterfield Academy, and Congressman, while his wife, Harriet, was the granddaughter of Mark Richards, a wealthy man and onetime Lieutenant Governor of the state. But they did not deport themselves as their station suggested. The Perfectionists practiced "complex marriage," by which they were all meant to love one another equally well and might cohabit among themselves with whomever they pleased, so as to lift the curse of conventional marriage, with its stress on the exclusive and indissoluble. Gossip in Putney and across the state became outcry, and in October 1847 Noyes was arrested for committing adultery and so breaking not only the Seventh Commandment but the laws of Vermont. For the grand jury which indicted him, such doctrines as Noyes had preached in *The Perfectionist* only augmented his offense. "In a holy community, there is no more reason why sexual intercourse should be restrained by law, than why eating and drinking should be—and there is as little reason for shame in the one case as in the other." [4]

Released on bail and warned of possible mob retribution, Noyes fled from Vermont to Oneida in New York, where an established group of disciples welcomed their prophet and his Putney faithful. The settlement was made up in the main of those from families of education, substance, and a Yankee respect for industry; it prospered and after three years numbered more than two hundred adults. Cohabiting couples and single women had sleeping quarters on one floor of a large community building, single men and boys had a dormitory on another, while parlor, dining room, and other day living quarters were on a third. In a Children's House all young were after infancy reared, not by their parents but by members of the community selected and trained for the purpose, so as to "prevent the idolatrous love of mother and child," and toys, like all property in Oneida, were held in common, so that children might grow up indifferent to—indeed, unaware of—personal ownership. It was a system not unlike that which would be adopted later by the agricultural settlement or *kibbutz* of the Zionist pioneers in Palestine. Noyes also instituted "mutual criticism," regular meetings at which the Perfectionists openly examined one another's faults in a collective cleansing process that had much of modern psychoanalysis in it and prefigured the group therapy of Alcoholics Anonymous or the Synanon method of treatment for drug addiction.

Noyes pursued the liberation of women with unremitting zeal. He redesigned their dress, lifting the skirt to the knee, and persuaded those in his following to accept this "uniform of a vital society" and even to wear their hair short as well. Above all, he continued to promote "complex marriage," which he angrily distinguished from the "free love" that most outsiders considered it to be; as he and his publications repeatedly explained, under his system each was married to all. Exclusive bonds between any two members of the community were strictly forbidden, and cohabitation was by mere agreement of those concerned, with the necessary negotiations conducted through a third party, and the conceiving of children reserved for "legitimate occasions." His definition of "legitimate" came eventually to mean an experiment in "planned, scientific procreation," a doctrine he had first enunciated in a pamphlet of 1848 called *Bible Communism,* and a special committee on "stirpiculture" was established to select the parents of community children.

Yet it was less doctrinal innovation than economic success that led to the disruption of the tiny Utopia. Starting with the sale of preserves, the Perfectionists proceeded to the manufacture of game traps, with the secret and celebrated craft of one convert, Sewell Newhouse, reluctantly imparted, after much "communizing and the democratic power of inspiration," to other members of the community. Before long they had taken on outsiders to help with mass production and were selling more than a quarter of a million traps a year, with the brand name Oneida-Newhouse as renowned across America as that of Colt for the revolver. Silk manufacture followed and, at a branch of the community in Wallingford, Connecticut, the production of tableware.

Such prosperity allured Americans who would otherwise have found the experiment of Perfectionism repugnant, and as visitors arrived in daily hundreds to view the bustling community and to return with bulging pockets of propaganda, the indignation of the clergy grew. The expulsion from Oneida of two unsatisfactory converts, one for his indiscriminate interest in sex and another for unreliability and exhibitionist conceit, brought lawsuits and scandal, and under the leadership of Presbyterian and Methodist clergymen, protest meetings against the "debauchery" at Oneida were organized, with the press joining happily in the hunt. The prophet's son, Dr. Theodore Noyes, a graduate of Yale Medical School, broke with the radicalism of community doctrines, while James Towner, an ambitious convert from Ohio, gathered a rebellion around him to oust the prophet altogether. In June 1879, warned by loyalists of a move to have him prosecuted for sexual irregularities, John Noyes fled to Ontario, from where he advised the abandonment of the practice, though not the doctrinal propriety, of complex marriage by the community.

What followed was a triumph for the American way of life from Wyoming to Wall Street. Some three hundred adults untangled themselves to marry in suitably permanent pairs, most under the simple laws of New York State, a few with elaborate weddings; and by a Plan of Division in 1881, communal assets were assumed by a joint stock company, Oneida Community Ltd., whose shares were distributed among claimants to the estate of Perfectionism. After years of furious proxy engagements, Dr. Theodore Noyes achieved control, and, under the supervision of another son of the prophet, Pierrepont Noyes, the company concentrated on the production of silverware. Putney, Vermont, had cause at last for pride. With the help of hired talents in design, and an advertising campaign that associated its products with a pretty girl drawn especially for the purpose, Oneida sold its Community Plate to successive generations of American newlyweds. The *Encyclopaedia Britannica* carries an appropriate quotation, apparently from the Oneida management: "The present company has 'no connection with the old beyond the personnel and traditions which it inherited from its 40 years' experience as a community.' "

In his emphasis on sexual freedom, Noyes is an important figure not only in the movement for women's rights, but in the whole line of social revolt through the liberation of personal relationships. And the end of the Perfectionist experiment was no less significant than the experiment itself. America has not always dealt with dissent through intimidation or indifference; increasingly it has merchandised it into the manageable, turned it into a profitably marketable contradiction of itself. What happened to Oneida happens still, and more formidably now with the development of mass communications. Insurrectionists are voluminously written about, interviewed again and again on radio and television, packaged and sold as celebrities, with their ideas treated as entertainment and fed to the national appetite for novelty, until for many the reception becomes the reality and dissent detumesces to canned applause. As one writer has described the process:

> To be a radical in America today is like trying to punch your way out of a cage made of marshmallow. Every thrust at the jugular draws not blood, but sweet success; every hack at the roots draws not retaliation, but fame and affluence. . . . Yesterday's underground becomes today's vaudeville and tomorrow's cliché.[5]

It is an overstatement, of course; not every radical becomes a celebrity, just as not every thrust at the jugular draws success rather than punishment, and not every radical become celebrity succumbs to his own celebration; but what it overstates is an essential part of the truth.

There remain insurrections invulnerable to intimidation or indifference, that resist the most concerted pressures for stability and survive the most seductive of merchandising techniques. They burst from time to time out of the wilderness between the promise and the performance of America, and they stubbornly pursue their purposes, gathering force, till the society must surrender, if only on negotiated terms, or be torn apart. Twice within American history, from the early 1830s to the late 1870s, and today, since the middle 1950s, such massive insurrections have centered on color, to sweep across the nature of American society. For the high visibility of the colored American draws eyes to the wilderness in which he wanders, and the eyes explore the wilderness itself, to discover how much of America it is.

The colored American is not a minority problem, to be accommodated at marginal cost in a spare room of American society. He is America herself, her achievements, her falterings, and her failures, the extent of her loyalty and the extent of her betrayal. He is pre-eminently the measure of the American meaning. It was the recognition of this that more than a century ago roused insurrectionists not only against slavery, but against the sort of society that could countenance it, and that rouses insurrectionists today, not only for the cause of civil rights, but increasingly for the cause of a new, different America.

In 1776 slavery was lawful throughout America, but it proved neither profitable nor popular in the North, and one state after the other there either proscribed it or provided for gradual emancipation. Indeed, even in the South influential voices spoke out against the principle at least; Washington and Jefferson, slave-owners both, expressed the hope that one day slavery would go, as harmful to slave and master alike, and Washington himself ordered in his will the emancipation of his slaves after the death of his wife. There were few hard-line defenders of slavery among the leaders of the Revolutionary generation, and in 1807 Congress passed an act against the slave trade. But it was the last gasp of Revolutionary inspiration. The development of the cotton economy in the South made slave labor immensely lucrative, and the planter class proceeded to raise slavery into the region's established religion, while the North looked on indifferently, stirring only to insure that the number of free Negroes with which it had to deal was not increased by immigration.

Despite the plantation propaganda that issued from the South, of course, not all slaves sang as they picked cotton in the sun or slept their leisure and old age away in the care of affectionate owners. Hatred and despair overflowed fear in countless conspiracies, two of which—in 1822 under Denmark Vesey, a slave in South Carolina, and in 1831 under Nat Turner, a slave in Virginia—surfaced in substantial insurrections. Public opinion in the North remained apathetic, but now there were those committed to disturbing its peace, even though its first irritated reaction would be turned against them.

William Lloyd Garrison was an enthusiast for personal liberty and righteousness, and against war, alcohol, tobacco, capital punishment, imprisonment for debt, and Freemasonry. But, above all, he was an enthusiast for the emancipation of the slaves, and this enthusiasm came to dominate his life. At first, under the influence of Benjamin Lundy, the Quaker Abolitionist, he accepted the need for gradual enfranchisement, but by 1831, when he started, at the age of twenty-six, *The Liberator,* with no money and only a borrowed press, his view had changed. Though as a pacifist he maintained that only moral pressures could properly be employed, he was convinced that emancipation should be immediate and that all schemes for sending the emancipated abroad were a compromise with prejudice and an abdication of responsibility. For him, the slaves had to be freed as full citizens of America, the equal heirs to the American commitment.

Indeed, it was on the terrain of the American commitment that he chose to give battle from the beginning.

> Assenting [he proclaimed in the opening number of *The Liberator*] to the "self-evident truth" maintained in the American Declaration of Independence, "that all men are created equal, and endowed by their Creator with certain inalienable rights—among which are life, liberty, and the pursuit of happiness," I shall strenuously contend for the immediate enfranchisement of our slave population. . . . On this subject, I do not wish to think, or speak, or write, with moderation. . . . I am in earnest—I will not equivocate—I will not excuse—I will not retreat a single inch—AND I WILL BE HEARD.

The North did not take kindly to such reminders from him or from other early Abolitionists. Yankee merchants were indignant at a movement that antagonized their Southern customers, and their newspapers reviled Garrison and his fellow mischief-makers as atheists and anarchists. Speakers at Abolitionist meetings were greeted with rotten eggs, stones, or the clamor of horns and bells. Mobs burned down the hall built by Abolitionists in Philadelphia and murdered Elijah Lovejoy, publisher of an Abolitionist paper, in Alton, Illinois. Garrison himself was seized by a Boston mob and paraded round the city with a rope round his neck. He complained that there was "contempt more bitter, opposition more stubborn, and apathy more frozen" in New England than among the slave-owners of the South. But the very persecution of the Abolitionists spread their message and brought them throngs of converts. In 1840 there were some 2000 anti-slavery societies, with a membership of near 200,000. It was the year Abolitionist forces formally divided, over the policies that Garrison pursued.

Garrison was a Utopian in the tradition of Williams and Noyes; he saw it as no part of his faith or his function to make a deal with

the ways of the world. For him, God and humanity, not the per-
suasions of policy, were the measure of what to say and do. The
churches did not respond to his appeals for vigorous support in the
struggle against slavery; he denounced and damned them. Many of
his colleagues objected, if not to his belief in the political equality
of women, then to his inexpedient advancement of it in supporting
their equal right to leadership of the Abolitionist movement; like
his increasing condemnation of the churches, they claimed, it
injured the cause of Abolitionism: he derided them for ignorance
or cowardice. The state countenanced slavery and depended on
coercion; he abandoned it.

> As every human government is upheld by physical strength, and
> its laws are enforced virtually at the point of the bayonet, we cannot
> hold any office which imposes upon its incumbent the obligation to
> compel men to do right, on pain of imprisonment or death. We,
> therefore, voluntarily exclude ourselves from every legislation and
> judicial body and repudiate all human politics, worldly honors, and
> stations of authority.[6]

The Declaration of Independence was his political gospel, the
meaning of America for him, and he judged both the laws and
even the Constitution by their conformity with it. Since the Constitution allowed the practice of slavery, he attacked it as itself iniq-
uitous, "A Covenant with Death and an Agreement with Hell." He
soon added the slogan "No Union with Slaveholders" to his ar-
mory and outstripped Southern extremists in fervor for disunion.
In 1854, at a Fourth of July meeting, he burned copies of the
Fugitive Slave Law and the Constitution, crying "So perish all
compromises with tyranny!" to a shout of "Amen!" from all but a
few in the multitude present. Only in 1861, when the Confederate
States seceded to take up arms against the Union, and he felt that
slavery itself would fall inevitable victim in the ensuing struggle,
did he finally cease to advocate disunion, and reconcile himself for
the time being to government and war. In 1865, with the victory of
the North securing Lincoln's Emancipation Proclamation, he announced the end of his Abolitionist career and stopped publication
of *The Liberator;* but the original motto of the paper, "Our coun-

try is the world—our countrymen are mankind," remained his dedication, and 1869 saw him, widely venerated, become President of the Free Trade League, advocating the abolition of customs barriers throughout the world.

Emancipation came, it may reasonably be charged, not by disrupting, but by preserving of the Union; not by exorcising, but by employing physical force; not by purifying Abolitionism of its compromisers and disciples of other iniquities, but by gradually expanding it, under the pressure of events, to encompass them; not by escaping, but by exploiting the political system. It came, so to say, not by affirming Garrison, but by denying him. Yet Garrison himself gave the proper reply to such a charge, long before events could supposedly sustain it. Speaking at Philadelphia in 1838, he declared:

> There are your men of "caution," and "prudence," and "judiciousness." Sir, I have learned to hate those words. Whenever we attempt to imitate our great Exemplar, and press the truth of God, in all its plainness, upon the conscience, why, we are very imprudent; because, forsooth, a great excitement will ensue. Sir, slavery will not be overthrown without excitement, a most tremendous excitement.

Paradoxically, it was an escaped slave, Frederick Douglass, the outstanding Negro leader of the period, who represented, in his astute and patient opportunism, the mood and the method of triumphant political Abolitionism. Born in Maryland in 1817, of a white father and slave mother, he learned to read and write with the secret help of his owner's wife, and before long put his knowledge to work by making out "free passes" for runaway slaves. Then, in 1838, he escaped himself, traveling as a sailor by railway from Baltimore to New York City, and from there proceeding, for greater safety, to Massachusetts, where he changed his name from Bailey to Douglass.

The flight of slaves to freedom provided Abolitionists with a sense of immediate purpose and achievement, and by the 1830s an elaborate system of escape routes, known as the Underground Railroad, was firmly established. Fugitives were passed from one

Abolitionist household to another, hidden by day and conveyed in disguise by night, for refuge in Canada or increasingly, as public opinion there changed to promise protection, the New England states. In Ohio alone, it has been estimated,[7] more than 40,000 fugitives slaves were helped to freedom between 1830 and 1860. It was no traffic for the timid. The law was rigorously on the side of the pursuers, and pursuit was relentless; escape was seen by both sides as a challenge not just to the property rights of the slave-owner, but to the survival of slavery itself. Yet the rewards far outweighed the risks, outside of the numbers saved from slavery. The Abolitionist conspiracy threw up heroes and heroines—Harriet Tubman, an illiterate field hand from Maryland, escaped herself only to return Southward again and again, guiding more than 300 slaves to freedom—who inspired widespread admiration if not imitation. The sight of slave-catchers at their work aroused a public indifferent to mere complaint, and mobs in the North soon began paying them the attention previously reserved for Abolitionists. Furthermore, the fugitives themselves provided the most effective propaganda. One of them telling his own story at a public meeting was worth a throng of second-hand descriptions. Frederick Douglass himself made a deep impression with an unprepared speech to an anti-slavery meeting at Nantucket in August 1841, and was appointed an agent of the Massachusetts Anti-Slavery Society, to stir audiences with his eloquence across much of the North during the next few years.

The American Anti-Slavery Society had been founded, with Garrison as its dominant figure, in 1833. But opposition to his policies gradually grew within the movement, and though revolt found occasion in his support for the rights of women and his assault on the churches, its causes lay more significantly in his refusal to collaborate with those who stopped short of demanding immediate emancipation, and, above all, in his resistance to working within the existing political frame. The 1838 convention of the New England Anti-Slavery Society voted to seat several women delegates, and a group of preachers walked out in protest. The following year Garrison prevailed again, at the convention of the national society, but this only further inflamed disaffection. In April 1840 the dissidents gathered at Albany and founded the Liberty party, to contest the country's Presidential election, and in May, when the national anti-slavery convention met and Garrison emerged victorious once more, they broke away altogether, to form the American and Foreign Anti-Slavery Society.

The Liberty party received a negligible vote in the 1840 elections, and the new anti-slavery society never rivaled the old in size or resources. But the split between the politicians and the prophets of Abolitionism was crucial none the less, for it led to the alliance of the former with the interests of free labor. In 1848 the bulk of the Liberty party joined forces with the anti-slavery moderates of the North and with the Free Soilers—who feared the extension of the slave and plantation system to the new territories in the West —to establish the Free Soil party, with the aim of preventing any expansion of slavery. Under the standard of "Free Soil, Free Speech, Free Labor, Free Men," the new grouping went into Presidential battle, nominating as its candidate Martin Van Buren—who had been Democratic President of the United States from 1837 to 1841—and polling nearly 300,000 votes, or just over 10 per cent of the total cast. It was an augury, but not for the impatient. In the elections of 1852 the party's vote dropped to 156,000, and it seemed that the mere exclusion of slavery from the new territories was not a demand sufficient to sweep a candidate into the White House.

During his early years in the North, Douglass had followed Garrison, but he steadily moved away from Garrison's policies, from his demand for disunion, his attacks on the churches, his exclusive pacifism, and his refusal to use the available resources of the political system. A break became inevitable. Douglass himself was an accomplished politician, ready to snatch occasion and turn it to his purposes, all the while working for a combination of forces and methods strong enough together to destroy slavery. He joined the Liberty party's national committee. In December 1847, against the passionate opposition of Garrison, who denounced all separate Negro organizations and propaganda as nourishing racial isolation, he launched his Negro newspaper, *The North Star,* in Rochester, New York, with the slogan "No Union with Slavery" for Garrison's own "No Union with Slave-holders." For him there was no inconsistency in working for the widest possible front against slavery, while promoting a powerful Negro movement to participate in it and influence its course. Nor did he want to discard the Constitution; he wanted to exploit it, so as to re-establish what he considered to be the original American commitment in the Declaration of Independence. He was present at the founding convention of the Free Soil party, and despite its severely restricted opposition to slavery, gave the new movement his general support.

He believed and warned that the South, in its very fear, would assert itself by exciting the expansion of slavery beyond popular endurance. And so it was to be. The Compromise of 1820 had admitted Missouri as a slave state to the Union, but in turn had drawn a line across the vast Louisiana Purchase area, north of which slavery was to be forever outlawed. Now, in 1854, under pressure from the South and with the object of conciliating sentiment there, Congress organized the two new Territories of Kansas and Nebraska, and, though both were north of the 1820 Compromise line, left them to decide for themselves whether to be slave or free. Douglass addressed one mass meeting after the other to stress the threat for all America of the new measure.

> The struggle is one for ascendancy. Slavery aims at absolute sway, and to banish liberty from the republic. It would drive out the school-master, and install the slave-driver, burn the school-house and erect the whipping post, prohibit the Holy Bible and establish the bloody code, dishonor free labor with its hope of reward, and establish slave-labor with its dread of the lash.[8]

He voiced a popular alarm. For it seemed idle now to suppose that slavery could be confined to the states where it already existed, let alone gradually wither away if left to itself.

The broad coalition that Douglass sought was on the way. The cry for a new party, to prevent the slave system from spreading across the country, arose from the churches and the universities, industrialists and farmers and free labor, and in July 1854 such a party was founded, to take the name of Republican, adopted by Jefferson for the popular party that had overwhelmed Hamilton's Federalists at the start of the century. At their first convention the Republicans chose John C. Frémont, the explorer of California, as Presidential candidate for the 1856 elections, together with the campaign slogan "Free Labor, Free Speech, Free Men, Free Kansas, and Frémont." Douglass criticized the limitations of the ticket, with its commitment to contain slavery within its existing borders, but gave Frémont his backing. "We have turned Whigs and Democrats into Republicans," he declared, "and we can turn Republicans into Abolitionists." [9] The new party went down to defeat, but narrowly enough—Frémont polled 1,340,000 votes to 1,838,000 for the Democratic candidate, James Buchanan—to encourage its supporters with the prospect of success at the next attempt.

It was at this point that the South achieved a victory which was to contribute generously to its defeat. Dred Scott was a slave who had been taken by his owner to Illinois, then to unorganized territory north of the 1820 Compromise line, and finally back to Missouri, where he sued for his freedom on the grounds of having twice resided on free soil. In March 1857, two days after Buchanan's inauguration, the Supreme Court, with five of its nine judges from the South, published its majority decision. Scott was a Negro and so not a citizen of the United States, with the right to sue in the federal courts; Scott was a slave, and a slave was property, and his owner did not lose ownership of him wherever Scott resided; the Compromise of 1820 had no validity, since Congress could not, under the Constitution, deprive citizens of their property without "due process of law." It was a decision that reduced Negroes everywhere in America to the status of objects. More, it made slavery national in scope. Slaves could legally be bought and sold in the cities of the North and put to work on plantations across the West. This not only outraged the most moderate anti-slavery sentiment; it threatened the very survival of free labor and independent farming, and the dominance of industrial capitalism. The judges had hoped to settle the issue of slavery once and for all by making it legal throughout the country. They stirred it up as never before. Douglass, assailing their decision in a speech on May 11, 1857, interpreted it as yet another move by slavery against freedom that would injure slavery itself.

> The whole history of the anti-slavery movement is studded with proof that all measures devised and executed with a view to allay and diminish the anti-slavery agitation, have only served to increase, intensify, and embolden that agitation. . . . This very attempt to blot out forever the hopes of an enslaved people may be one necessary link in the chain of events preparatory to the downfall and complete overthrow of the whole slave system.[10]

Civil war already raged in Kansas between free and slave forces for control of the territory. There came the attack by the Abolitionist John Brown, with eighteen men, on the federal arsenal at Harpers Ferry in October 1859, his capture, his trial, and his execution in December, to a surge of militant Abolitionism across the North. In May 1860 the Republican convention at Chicago nominated Lincoln as its candidate for the Presidential elections, and though Douglass sharply criticized the ticket for failing to face the issue of slavery head-on or even pledge the repeal of the Fugitive Slave Law, he endorsed it. The Republicans committed themselves only to keeping slavery out of the Territories, and expanded their appeal by promising protection for American industry and free homesteads for settlers in the West. A coalition of anti-slavery forces, industry, and free labor was formidable enough; with the Democratic party split into a Northern section that supported slavery no further than the principle of "popular sovereignty," and a Southern one that demanded protection for slavery even where, as in Kansas, the majority opposed it, a Republican victory was certain. In the event, Lincoln would have won even had his opponents united against him. He carried every free State and 180 of the 303 electoral votes. The South surrendered to hysteria, and secession followed fast.

Douglass saw his strategy of coalitionism and piecemeal victory vindicated. He contradicted Lincoln's claim that the Civil War was being fought simply to restore the Union. It "is," he declared, "a war for and against slavery; and . . . it can never be effectually put down till one or other of these vital forces is destroyed." [11] He turned his attention to the demand that Negroes be enlisted in the Union forces, but Lincoln feared the effect on the border states, and it was only in August 1862 that Negroes were at last officially allowed to be fighters. Nor did Douglass concern himself only with formal emancipation. In 1864 he proclaimed:

> No war but an Abolition war; no peace but an Abolition peace; liberty for all, chains for none; the black man a soldier in war, a laborer in peace; a voter at the South as well as at the North; America his permanent home, and all Americans his fellow-countrymen. Such, fellow citizens, is my idea of the mission of the war.[12]

But if it was an Abolition war, with emancipation pronounced by Lincoln on the first day of 1863, the peace was not for long, if fundamentally at all, an Abolition peace. Reconstruction gave the free slaves of the South their citizenship rights without the land or restructuring of the economy needed to give these rights real meaning. The slave was freed to struggle virtually on his own against the devastations of the past and the intimidations of the future. Symbolically, though Douglass was considered for important official posts—including direction of the Freedmen's Bureau—by both Johnson and Grant, he was not appointed to them. Indeed, with keen irony, it was in 1877, when Rutherford Hayes brought Reconstruction to an end and abandoned the Southern Negro to the tightening grasp of white supremacy, that Douglass was rewarded with his first serious official appointment, as United States Marshal for the District of Columbia. But such was the popular outcry at the possession of such a post by a Negro that Hayes did not reappoint him when his term of office ended, and made him Recorder of Deeds for the District instead. At last, in 1889, he achieved the diplomatic posting, as Minister to Haiti, for which he had been considered and rejected by the Reconstruction Presidents. But when he died, in 1895, white supremacy dominated the South as effectively as slavery had done, and the liberation of the black American would require another civil war, in the streets of American cities and deep within the American mind.

When that second civil war broke out, it would, like the first, reflect in racial issues a concern with the whole nature of American society; would represent, in significant measure, the rising of the person against corporate power, of American idealism against the American reality, of mind against money. More profoundly, therefore, than either Garrison or Douglass, it was Ralph Waldo Emerson who personified the moral insurrection of mid-nineteenth-century America and who prefigured the moral insurrection of the present. The criticisms that he made of his environment, and the remedies he sought, are startlingly valid today, though America seems to have changed in the meantime so much. Emerson could scarcely have foreseen the current dependence of the economy on the artificial excitement of consumer demand and expanding military expenditure, the extent of psychological management by business, the perplexed passivity induced by the capitalism of warfare and welfare, the perversion of higher education by the demands of private profit and national defense, the erosions of democracy by the exercise of electorally irresponsible power, the existence and effects of the threat to man himself by nuclear weapons. But what he saw was a culture that would foster just such developments, the essential temper of a society by which such developments would be accounted progress.

He was in the Utopian tradition of Roger Williams and New England Separatism, with its emphasis on the open mind and free, courageous inquiry. And like both Roger Williams and John Noyes, he did not stop with religion and philosophy but ranged, if rather reluctantly, since his temperament was less attuned to them, over politics and economics. He represented one cultural disruption and set out to promote another. Alongside the change from a static agricultural society to a dynamic industrial one, the old Calvinism of the elect and the reprobate gave place, among the intellectual first families of New England, to the Unitarianism of God's single beneficence and man's individual excellence. But Emerson was not satisfied. He moved on to Transcendentalism, which denied the personality of God altogether and visioned him instead as a universal force, evident everywhere in nature and operating through the moral law in every man. It combined the social perfectionism of revolutionary France, the metaphysical idealism of revolutionary Germany, and the mysticism of the English literary Romantics. It was an insurrection from within, and against, the spreading empire of the middle class, an attempt to substitute the liberty and equality of the spirit for the ordered confinements of industrial capitalism. It was for Emerson necessarily an insurrection of the whole man, destroying that distinction between the religious and the secular which had for so long allowed the discrepancies between promise and performance in America. He abandoned the church to proclaim the godhead of the individual mind.

In the journal which he kept from 1820, when he was sixteen, and which gives so vivid a record of his explorations, he wrote, at the age of thirty-six:

> A question which well deserves examination now is the Dangers of Commerce. This invasion of Nature by Trade with its Money, its Credit, its Steam, its Railroad, threatens to upset the balance of man, and establish a new, universal Monarchy more tyrannical than Babylon or Rome. Very faint and few are the poets or men of God. Those who remain are so antagonistic to this tyranny that they appear mad or morbid, and are treated as such. Sensible of this extreme unfitness they suspect themselves. And all of us apologize when we ought not, and congratulate ourselves when we ought not.[13]

He intended to do neither. He looked to the divine sufficiency of the individual, confused, coerced, confounded by laws and governments, schools and churches, factories and shops, but capable of asserting himself, of subduing his hostile environment, by steady self-reliance.

Was this the anarchism of anarchy? He acknowledged the accusation and met it with his principle of good will, a social love as the substance of the just republic.

> A man has a right to be employed, to be trusted, to be loved, to be revered. The power of love, as the basis of a State, has never been tried. We must not imagine that all things are lapsing into confusion if every tender protestant be not compelled to bear his part in certain

social conventions; nor doubt that roads can be built, letters carried, and the fruit of labour secured, when the government of force is at an end. Are our methods now so excellent that all competition is hopeless? [14]

He saw America, with a pertinence that has gained dismayingly in force since he wrote, as a place of captivity and fear and paralysis, where things were more important than people, and living had become a series of set, submissive gestures. There are affinities with Blake and Lawrence in the flashes of violence across his rejection.

Society everywhere is in conspiracy against the manhood of every one of its members. . . . The virtue in most request is conformity . . . if I am the Devil's child, I will live then from the Devil. No law can be sacred to me but that of my nature. . . . The doctrine of hatred must be preached, as the counteraction of the doctrine of love, when that pules and whines. . . . Men do what is called a good action, as some piece of courage or charity, much as they would pay a fine in expiation of daily non-appearance on parade. Their works are done as an apology or extenuation of their living in the world,—as invalids and the insane pay a high board. Their virtues are penances. I do not wish to expiate, but to live. My life is for itself and not for a spectacle. . . . The sinew and heart of man seem to be drawn out, and we are become timorous, desponding whimperers. We are afraid of truth, afraid of fortune, afraid of death, and afraid of each other. . . . Society acquires new arts and loses old instincts. . . . Men have looked away from themselves and at things so long. . . . They measure their esteem of each other by what each has, and not by what each is.[15]

Anything further from "rugged individualism," as expounded by the traditional American Right, than Emerson's call to self-reliance can scarcely be imagined. For Emerson, the free enterprise that pursued profit was imprisoned in property. And he was no less hostile to the aggressive covetousness of the traveling than to the defensive covetousness of the arrived. He viewed American politics as a tug of war between greed and fear.

. . . the two parties into which modern society divides itself,—the democrat and the conservative,— . . . differ only as young and old. The democrat is a young conservative; the conservative is an old democrat. The aristocrat is the democrat ripe and gone to seed;

—because both parties stand on the one ground of the supreme value of property, which one endeavors to get, and the other to keep.[16]

Yet he was no intellectual Luddite, seeking a way back to the past over the wreckage of machines. He objected not to the tool, but to its ascendancy over the mind because of the motive with which it was used. Indeed, he conceded that new tools could admit new possibilities for the liberating of man. He looked far into the horror of industrial civilization, but he was, like all insurrectionists of the American promise, an essential optimist, subject to bouts of bleak depression but never to despair. Even trade, whose contemporary havoc he so bewailed, seemed to him sometimes to have served, and to be serving still, some beneficial purposes. Yet the time had come to move on, before its devastations overwhelmed mankind.

The philosopher and lover of man have much harm to say of trade; but the historian will see that trade was the principle of Liberty; that trade planted America and destroyed Feudalism; that it makes peace and keeps peace, and it will abolish slavery. . . . Every line of history inspires a confidence that we shall not go far wrong; that things mend. . . . Our part is plainly not to throw ourselves across the track, to block improvement and sit till we are stone, but to watch the uprise of successive mornings, and to conspire with the new works of new days. . . . Trade was one instrument, but Trade is also but for a time, and must give way to somewhat broader and better, whose signs are already dawning in the sky.[17]

Such signs he saw in "all this beneficent socialism," from "the Communism of France, Germany, and Switzerland" to the Perfectionist communities of Massachusetts. What he sought, to be sure, was the ultimate dream of socialism, as of all humanism, the so-long-elusive prize of America herself—liberty without want, equality without conformity, peace without coercion, progress without subservience to man or machine. What he sought was a commonwealth of wisdom and love, and though he saw that it had never been found, he saw, too, that this was no excuse for not still seeking. "What answer is it now to say, It has always been so? I acknowledge that, as far back as I can see the widening procession of humanity, the marchers are lame and blind and deaf; but to the soul that whole past is but one finite series in its infinite scope. Deteriorating ever and now desperate. Let me begin anew; let me teach the finite to know its master." [18]

What did he achieve? He played no major role in the organized insurrections of American idealism. He believed in equal rights for women, but he gave only tepid support to the movements for their promotion. He opposed the government's predatory treatment of the Indian and eloquently assailed the removal of the Cherokee from an area of Georgia where gold had been discovered, but he did not devote himself to fostering public agitation for a new Indian policy. He protested, like Thoreau, against the Mexican War of 1846 as a war of conquest directed at expanding the slave power of the South; but, unlike Thoreau, he did not take his protest as far as refusing to pay his taxes. He abominated slavery, but long refused to identify himself with the Abolitionists. It was the mounting Southern challenge that moved him to militancy. When the Fugitive Slave Law of 1850, requiring all citizens to help in hunting down escaped slaves, was passed, he rebelled: "This filthy enactment was made in the nineteenth century, by people who could read and write. I will not obey it, by God." [19] Yet he looked still for some compromise that would come in peace. Believing that the Southern slave-owner was caught helplessly in his own trap, he proposed, before the Anti-Slavery Society of New York in 1855, that slavery be ended by granting financial compensation, on the British model, to the owners. The federal and state governments could donate the proceeds of public lands; the churches would "melt their plate"; the rich would give their thousands, and schoolchildren their pennies. He estimated the cost at $200 million, "to dig away this accursed mountain of sorrow once and forever out of the world." [20] But nobody seconded his motion. The North was not willing to pay, and even if it had been, it is improbable that the South would so easily have surrendered the pleasures of privilege and power which ownership of slaves conferred. Emerson drew steadily closer to the ultimatum of Abolitionism, and in 1859 lent his now considerable prestige to the late ill-fated adventure of John Brown, by publicly proclaiming him "a man to make friends wherever on earth courage and integrity are esteemed, the rarest of heroes, a pure idealist, with no by-ends of his own." [21] But he was never central to the practical struggle against slavery.

When he died, at the age of seventy-eight, in 1882, revered as the "Sage of Concord," it might have seemed as though he had spent his life singing to silence the sea. Southern white mastery had recently been redeemed by a general cynicism, and the nation had entered an era pre-eminent in the corruption of government and the open dominance of money. Yet the movement of American idealism achieved much, not only in the abolition of slavery, but in the more compassionate and rational treatment of the imprisoned, the blind, the deaf, the dumb, the insane; in the slowly improving climate of regard for women's rights; in the slowly improving conditions of labor; and not least, indeed, in simply having been, and so having reinforced faith in the infinity of the American promise. And there is little in this movement, if anything at all, that did not owe something to the rejections and aspirations of Emerson himself. He explored a territory which many others settled with the aid of his maps. They are settling it still, or using it as a base for explorations of their own.

Emerson has fed the ceaseless, if often subterranean, flow of American insurrection not only with his ideas but with his personal authority. And this authority is of no small significance. In a society of such profound cultural intimidation, of such persistent and powerful pressures to compliance, he has given to revolutionary thought the encouragement of his example, and to the insurrection of the individual the support of a distinguished tradition. As Emerson himself inherited the precedent of such insurrectionists as Roger Williams, so many of those crying today for a commonwealth of compassion rather than of computers are fortified, in themselves and against their lowering environment, by the precedent of Emerson and of a movement that did, after all, succeed in liberating America from one form of slavery.

It is true that Emerson's directions to the just republic are indistinct. Good will, love, the moral law, self-reliance are concepts to promote a mood rather than produce a program for the fundamental change of society. But the mood is essential to the production of a program, and as those more than a century ago developed from the mood of Emerson their specific campaigns, so too, today, new insurrectionists grope, in similar mood, for their own immediate and ultimate objectives. It is also true that Emerson, like so many American insurrectionists before and after, is far clearer and more certain about what he does not want than about what he wants. Yet no society changes without its investment and conquest first by the forces of rejection. Perhaps there are no clear and certain aspirations any longer credible. Too many revolutions in too many places have gone rancid. Perhaps the positive will come only by an accumulation of negatives. If one knows what one does not want, and resists rather than succumbs to it, one may get, by a kind of dynamic denial, finally close enough to what one wants. Certainly, in such a process, Emerson spoke for the incessant insurrection of American thought and art, of the whole human promise, when he cited the self-defeat of America's materialist reality.

> As long as our civilization is essentially one of property, of fences, of exclusiveness, it will be mocked by delusions. Our riches will leave us sick; there will be bitterness in our laughter, and our wine will burn our mouth. Only that good profits which we can taste with all doors open, and which serves all men.[22]

Henry David Thoreau (1817–1862) adopted many of his friend and mentor Emerson's ideas, but he gave them a new emphasis and from them reached out to others of his own. He went much further than Emerson ever did into the possibilities of individual withdrawal from social management, to develop and demonstrate a thesis of economic transcendentalism; he assailed the modesty of traditional liberalism with a pertinence even more manifest today than it was at the time; and he expounded a doctrine of civil disobedience that would make him, if only long after his death, one of the most widely influential thinkers that America has ever produced.

It was the economic subjugation and submissiveness, with their spiritual desolation, of his contemporaries that stirred his peculiar rage and resistance.

> It is very evident what mean and sneaking lives many of you live . . . always on the limits, trying to get into business or trying to get out of debt . . . always promising to pay, promising to pay, tomorrow, and dying today, insolvent; . . . lying, flattering, voting, contracting yourselves into a nutshell of servility, or dilating into an atmosphere of thin and vaporous generosity, that you may persuade your neighbor to let you make his shoes, or his hat, or his coat . . . making yourselves sick, that you may lay up something against a sick day, something to be tucked away in an old chest, or in a stocking behind the plastering, or, more safely, in the brick bank. . . . The mass of men lead lives of quiet desperation.[23]

His pass-key to escape was "simplify"; to live deliberately and deep, "to front only the essential facts of life." And so he went to live on his own in the woods, on the shore of Walden Pond, for two years and two months, from 1845 to 1847, supporting himself on what he grew or caught or made or earned with his own hands. The village of Concord, the ordered busyness of America in miniature, was a mile and a half away, and he would stroll there every day or two to hear the gossip. It was a withdrawal not from people, but from their culture of acquisitiveness, their captivity to things. And when he left his woods, it was not because the experiment had failed, but because it had succeeded; because, liberated, he "had several more lives to live, and could not spare any more time for that one."

Thoreau was not, of course, offering humanity a refuge along the shores of Walden Pond; such a reading would have small relevance indeed to the America of the suburban sprawl or to the multitudes over so much of the world whose lives have been simplified by circumstances to the very edge of survival. Nor did he intend a flight into the self; his uncompromising individualism was an uncompromising commitment to man, and he flung himself, at risk to his own physical quiet and even liberty, into the dominant social issue of the time. What he set out to establish, for himself and for others, was a sense of proper priorities: the superiority of man to his clothing; of experience to possessions; of leisure to abundance; of labor for its essential purpose to labor for an unallayable ambition and anxiety. And what could be of greater relevance than this to an America where prosperity is a ceaseless excitement of synthetic need, and where progress is the source not of peace but of panic, because men are afraid of their own machines, and because the purpose of leisure, like the purpose of labor, has been lost? What could be of greater relevance to a world where so many millions go hungry, diseased, and unschooled, because the resources to satisfy their wants are squandered instead on the manipulated consumption of luxuries and the development of yet newer destructive techniques?

In his revulsion from the ravening of America's competitive economics, his withdrawal into material simplicity, his exploration of the self, his interest in Oriental literature, thought, and religion, Thoreau seems close to the moral fugitives of the present—the Beats, the Hippies, the disciples of psychedelic drugs. But though he would have approved their withdrawal from acquiescence in a system which he himself would probably have found even more alien and degrading than the one that he spurned, he would scarcely have approved their flight, explicit or effective, into the self or private community, from the total commitment to total man. Fundamentally, despite his repute as a recluse, Thoreau is far closer in mood and in meaning to the insurrectionists of struggle than to those of flight.

It was the failure of the liberal to assume any real commitment at all, indeed, to his own humanity or to anyone else's, that Thoreau flayed.

What is the price-current of an honest man and patriot today? They hesitate, and they regret, and sometimes they petition; but they do nothing in earnest and with effect. They will wait, well disposed, for others to remedy the evil, that they may no longer have it to regret. At most, they give only a cheap vote, and a feeble countenance and Godspeed, to the right, as it goes by them. . . . The American has dwindled into an Odd Fellow, . . . whose first and chief concern, on coming into the world, is to see that the alms-houses are in good repair. . . . The soldier is applauded who refuses to serve in an unjust war by those who do not refuse to sustain the unjust government which makes the war; is applauded by those whose own act and authority he disregards and sets at nought; as if the State were penitent to that degree that it hired one to scourge it while it sinned, but not to that degree that it left off sinning for a moment.[24]

Thoreau's scorn is the scorn that infuses the current insurrection, whether of struggle or of flight, among American youth. Speech and article, play and poem denounce the liberalism that used such resounding regret to cover its retreat from resistance to McCarthyism; that so smoothly accommodates itself to racial oppression till sufficient rebellion stirs it into formal adjustments for the sake of some temporary peace; that grinds away freedom and compassion in the machines of further efficiency, to the tape recording of its own remote and repetitive rhetoric; that views poverty and discrimination through the opera glasses of public relief; that chants the canticles of democracy, while its planes drop napalm on Vietnamese villages to keep the world safe for a sterile anti-Communism; that acclaims the courage and idealism of a few as camouflage for the timorous time-serving of the many.

The response of Thoreau himself to crucial issues was very different. He refused to pay his poll tax in protest at his government's collaboration with slavery and was once imprisoned in consequence (if only for a night, since his family intervened to pay it on his behalf); publicly repudiated his allegiance to the Commonwealth of Massachusetts and the United States; on at least two known occasions assisted fugitive slaves on their way to Canada, hiding them and smuggling them aboard trains, in defiance of the law; spoke of John Brown as "the bravest and humanest man in all the country," and, more provokingly still, denounced his own neighbors for their "stagnation of spirit." For organized Christianity in America, he had only contempt. "Away with your broad and flat churches, and your narrow and tall churches! Take a step forward, and invent a new style of outhouses." [25] For authority, he had only defiance. He did not demand perfect government or no government at all. But he did demand *"at once* a better government" and, in order to achieve it, advocated civil disobedience.

How does it become a man to behave toward this American government today? I answer that he cannot without disgrace be associated with it. I cannot for an instant recognize that political organization as *my* government which is the *slave's* government also. . . . If the injustice is part of the necessary friction of the machine of government, let it go, let it go: perchance it will wear smooth,—certainly the machine will wear out. If the injustice . . . is of such a nature that it requires you to be the agent of injustice to another, then, I say, break the law. Let your life be a counter friction to stop the machine. . . . As for adopting the ways which the State has provided for remedying the evil, I know not of such ways. They take too much time, and a man's life will be gone. . . . Under a government which imprisons any unjustly, the true place for a just man is also a prison. . . . A minority is powerless while it conforms to the majority; it is not even a minority then; but it is irresistible when it clogs by its whole weight. . . . This is, in fact, the definition of a peaceable revolution, if any such is possible.[26]

The influence of Thoreau's essay on *Resistance to Civil Government,* or *Civil Disobedience* as it came commonly to be called, was hardly remarkable at the time it was published, or for several decades afterward. But it caught the attention of Gandhi in 1907, while he was in South Africa developing his doctrine of passive resistance as a reply to the policy of racial discrimination, and it impressed him so profoundly that he took a copy of it with him to prison, republished it in *Indian Opinion,* the paper that he was editing, and issued it as a special tract. It became the most celebrated work of American literature in areas of Africa and Asia struggling against foreign or indigenous race rule; and it remains a guide and an encouragement today wherever civil disobedience is being used as an instrument of insurrection. Not least, indeed, both in itself and through the medium of Gandhi, it has informed much of modern militant dissent in America, from the civil rights movement to the protest campaign against the Vietnam war.

"Let your life be a counter friction to stop the machine. . . ." In 1964 Mario Savio, a leading figure in the Free Speech Movement at the University of California in Berkeley, spoke at a meeting of fellow students before a mass sit-in that resulted in hundreds of arrests.

> There is a time when the operations of the machine become so odious, make you so sick at heart, that you can't take part, you can't even tacitly take part. And you've got to put your bodies on the gears and upon the wheels, upon the levers, upon all the apparatus, and you've got to make it stop. And you've got to indicate to the people who run it, to the people who own it, that unless you're free the machine will be prevented from working at all.

Williams and Noyes and Garrison, Emerson and Thoreau are usually associated with the idealist strain of insurrectionists, those pursuing an essentially moral change, through the struggle of the individual. And by this demarcation there is another, materialist strain, of those pursuing an essentially economic change, through the struggle of a class. Certainly, for Socialists such as Eugene Debs, the way to the perfect society lay through a revolution in the relations not primarily between man and man, let alone between man and God, but between capital and labor; not through discarding or depreciating material progress, but through subordinating it to collective instead of competitive profit and control. Yet this distinction invites, outside the precise definitions of metaphysical doctrine or influence, contradiction as soon as it is made. For just as the materialism of Debs was suffused with idealism, so too the idealism of Williams and Noyes, Garrison and Emerson and Thoreau was suffused with materialism. The latter searched for Utopia here, in this world, not in some indefinite heaven, and concerned itself consequently, in varying degrees, with expounding and encouraging the proper material relations between man and man; just as the former envisaged not only a society of material egalitarianism, but a moral Utopia, in which the total relations between man and man would be changed.

The correct distinction is, within the men and movements of American dissent, between those who have sought reform and those who have sought revolution, between those who have accepted existing American society as requiring mere adjustment to comply with the American promise and those who have rejected it as a denial of that promise altogether. Yet this covers and reveals a deeper distinction still—not, indeed, between the idealist and the materialist, but between the idealist and the realist, the prophet and the politician. For the truth is that revolution is the essence of idealism, as reform is the essence of realism. And just as professed reformers, impelled by a vision of what men can perfectly become rather than by a view of what men imperfectly are, have themselves become revolutionaries, so professed revolutionaries, impelled by a view of what men imperfectly are rather than by a vision of what men can perfectly become, have themselves become mere reformers.

To be sure, in the conflict between the two strains of American dissent, it is the realist, the reformist, that has consistently defeated the idealist, the revolutionary, as Douglass defeated Garrison in the conflict over the proper strategy of Abolitionism, and as Samuel Gompers defeated Debs in the conflict for the mind of the labor movement. Yet is it impertinent now to wonder, not in any sour distrust of success or mystique of martyrdom, but in a fresh exploration of reality, whether reform has outstripped the cause of revolution? Whether, if liberty, equality, happiness have always been the American goal of the idealists, their search is not as urgent today, however different in form, as it ever was?

Samuel Gompers was born in the East End of London in 1850 and thirteen years later immigrated to America, where he found work in a New York cigar-making shop. The cigar-makers talked or chose one of their number to read aloud while they worked, and Gompers soon became a favorite reader from among the books, pamphlets, and articles on economics, labor, and socialism produced in abundance by the presses of disaffection in Europe and America. He early became acquainted with Marx, who excited in him, as he subsequently described it, "some wild plans for human betterment." But such Utopianism early, too, alarmed him, as provoking endless passionate disputes over points of doctrine and inviting the indignation of public and police. Indeed, he came to regard the prophets of revolution as far more dangerous to his cause than the princes of capital. For his cause was not the disruption but the adjustment of the existing economic order, with a strategy of immediate campaigns to reduce working hours, increase wages, and improve conditions on the factory floor. As his movement grew in strength and attained its first objectives, it advanced to others, of a broader nature, such as the municipal ownership of public utilities and compulsory education with free schools and textbooks. But these advances were conditioned by the changing aspirations and circumstances of labor as such, and never challenged the assumptions of capitalism. Gompers himself was proudly a supreme opportunist. "At no time in my life," he was once to declare, "have I worked out definitely articulated economic theory."

Starting with the Cigarmakers' Union, which he made into a disciplined and businesslike body with high membership dues and insurance for sickness, accidents, and unemployment, he carried his message of craft unionism successfully along the higher slopes of labor. In 1886, after five years of preparatory organization, the American Federation of Labor took shape under his leadership, as an association of autonomous craft unions for more efficient industrial pressure; by the turn of the century it counted more than half a million members, and by the time that America entered the First World War, almost two and a half million, organized in 111 national unions and nearly 27,000 local ones. On the state level it bargained with political leaders for industrial legislation, and nationally swung its support to whichever of the major parties or candidates offered the best prospect of reform. The achievements of Gompers, who dominated the AFL for nearly four decades through his skill in negotiating with opponents and manipulating colleagues, his stocky pragmatism and self-assurance, were apparent enough in the increasing anxiety of employers and politicians to secure his collaboration or at least escape his open antagonism. But these were plainly within the limits that he set himself. When he died in 1924, the power and prestige of capitalism were all the greater for having been coaxed or threatened or pushed into soothing a substantial section of the country's working force with reforms, while the members of unions in the AFL constituted a sub-class of relative privilege within American labor. The mass of the unskilled remained unorganized, with the AFL encompassing less than a quarter of all workers in manufacturing plants, only a quarter of those in the building trades, a little over a third of those in transport, and a tiny proportion of women, recent immigrants, and Negroes. Indeed, though in its early years it called for the equal affiliation of all workers and even refused to admit the International Association of Machinists with a color-bar constitution, the AFL soon adjusted itself to the prevailing mood and in 1900 formally endorsed a plan for organizing Negroes in separate unions. When in 1910 he was accused of effectively keeping Negroes out of the movement, Gompers replied that they were, after all, only half a century from slavery. "It could not be expected that, as a rule, they would have the same conception of their rights and duties as other men of labor have in America." [27]

Eugene Debs, on the other hand, was one of America's prophets. Born in Indiana, of emigrant parents from Alsace, in 1855, he early started work in the railroad shops and in 1871 became a locomotive fireman. An active member of his railroad brotherhood, he helped to organize a local lodge and rose swiftly to election as national secretary and treasurer of the firemen in 1880. But he soon came to believe that craft unionism impeded the proper development of labor strength and that the future lay with the industrial union, combining the forces and aspirations of all employees—at least all employees of one color, for when he took the lead in forming the American Railway Union three years later, membership was open only to whites. The ARU attracted immediate support with its militancy and, after a successful strike in April 1894 against one of the country's major railroads, drew members in droves from the various brotherhoods.

Within its ranks were some four thousand employees of the Pullman Palace Car Company, which made and operated special chair, sleeping, and dining railroad cars. The company had built on the south shore of Lake Michigan the model township of Pullman, Illinois, and all employees were required to live there, in

Pullman houses at Pullman rents; to trade at Pullman stores, buy Pullman gas and water, and use other Pullman services available, at Pullman prices. Such coercive paternalism would have been provocative enough had it been coherent. But the company suddenly cut Pullman wages without cutting Pullman rents. It refused to negotiate with a grievance committee and dismissed the members. The employees replied with a strike, and Debs brought the ARU to their support, providing funds and, when the company rejected any arbitration, ordering all union members, in June 1894, to operate no trains with Pullman cars attached.

Representatives of the railroads formed a united front of intransigence in the General Managers' Association and discharged all workers who obeyed the boycott call. Railroad traffic was all but paralyzed across the Middle and Far West, and the General Managers appealed to President Cleveland for action to insure delivery of the mail. Two thousand troops were dispatched to Chicago, while some three and a half thousand deputies, paid by the railroads themselves, were raised and armed by the city's United States Marshal. Violence flared, with the burning of freight cars—by agents of the railroads, the union claimed—protest demonstrations and rioting by labor, parades of force and shootings by the militia. President Cleveland felt it needful to warn against the gathering of crowds in nine states of the Union. But the boycott held and even excited sympathy strikes. The United States Attorney General obtained a series of court injunctions against any form of picketing or boycott, and the indictment of Debs and three other officers of the ARU for having interrupted interstate commerce, obstructed the mails, and intimidated citizens in the free enjoyment of their rights. Debs saw that the sole prospect of success lay in expanding the conflict and called for a general strike, but Gompers proclaimed his firm opposition, and all but a very few unions in the AFL folded their arms. Debs was arrested for contempt of court, while some seven hundred other ARU members faced charges on counts ranging from murder to intimidation, and by early August the strike, along with the ARU itself, had collapsed.

While the AFL and the railroad brotherhoods congratulated

themselves on their judgment, Debs went to prison for six months. It was to be the wilderness of voices. He spent his sentence reading deeply in the literature of socialism and emerged no more a disciple of reform within the Egypt of capitalism but a prophet of Canaan through revolution. To the more than 100,000 people who massed to meet him on his release, he was the representative of an old, if still necessary, struggle; he set out to develop their discontent and yearning into a new one. At first he joined forces with several existing groups in a Social Democratic party, as whose candidate in the Presidential elections of 1900 he polled fewer than 100,000 votes. But in 1901 he seceded to establish the Socialist party of America, with the commitment, by "education and organization of the masses," to transform "the present system of private ownership of the means of production and distribution into collective ownership of the entire people." As its candidate in the elections of 1904, he collected over 400,000 votes.

Yet periodic campaigning for the polls was only one aspect of his total confrontation with capitalism. Through his weekly, *Appeal to Reason,* which was to climb to a circulation of over four million copies and enjoy a scriptural authority among most of its readers, he regularly denounced the crimes and corrosions of capital, as he recorded the struggles and sacrifices of labor. In response to his unceasing propaganda came large sums in tiny contributions, for the costs of defending labor leaders in the courts, the support of families bereaved by egregious martyrdoms, the promotion of industrial unionism. Through the Western Federation of Miners, he helped spread a militant labor movement across the West, along a trail of arrests, imprisonments, deportations, shootings, and sabotage. Then, together with William Haywood, secretary-treasurer of the federation, he moved toward "One Big Union of the Industrial Workers of the World," and in 1905 the Wobblies were born. The new organization, despite conflicts of personality and doctrine, achieved notable successes in recruitment and strike action among workers all over the country, and not least among the unskilled and recently immigrant, whom the AFL regarded as the rabble of labor. It broke through the color bar in unionism; even in western

Louisiana and eastern Texas it organized, during a series of lumber strikes in 1911 and 1912, thousands of blacks in the same union with whites. It pioneered a technique of struggle—to be adopted by largely middle-class students half a century later—in "free speech fights" against hostile municipalities; when these objected to its revolutionary propaganda and arrested its speakers, it replied with a continuous supply of propaganda and speakers till the local prison was no longer able to cope. And, above all, it asserted and disseminated its revolutionary faith in a wholly different, socialist America.

Debs ran as Presidential candidate of the Socialist party again in 1908, when his vote rose little above its previous total, and in 1912, when it more than doubled, to just short of 900,000. But the system he assailed was steadily changing shape, to preserve its nature, under pressure from broad movements of reform within individual states and the major political parties. The oligarchic character of the United States Senate had long been the target of attack, and in 1913 the Constitution was at last amended to transfer the election of senators from the state legislatures to direct popular vote. A parallel agitation produced the popular primary for party nomination to major offices, and a form of balloting more secret and so less vulnerable to bribery or intimidation than any that had previously prevailed. Beginning with Wyoming in 1889, one state after another in the Union surrendered the suffrage to women, until the Constitution itself was accordingly amended in time for the Presidential elections of 1920. When a massive coal-mining strike broke out in 1902, Theodore Roosevelt used federal power, in marked contrast to the way that Cleveland had used it during the railroad troubles of eight years before, to force arbitration on the employers and a settlement favorable to labor; and if he took little concerted action against the "malefactors of great wealth" he condemned, his rhetoric fostered the demand for reform. Taft started using the Sherman Antitrust Act against capital rather than labor, mildly endorsed the rights of trade unionism, and even brought the prestige of the Presidency to the support of the campaign for income tax. Wilson promoted firmer control over banking, stronger laws against trusts, and provisions to limit the use of injunctions in labor disputes. Alongside federal action, individual states took legislative steps to regulate working hours, control sanitation and safety in factories and mines, provide compensation for industrial accidents, improve public health, protect tenants against the grosser abuses by slum landlords, and restrict the profits of privately owned public utilities.

The socialist appeal of Debs was submerged by the general opinion that persistent reform and economic progress would, given time, deliver the American dream in the wrappings of capitalism. The mass of Americans simply did not believe the claims of the Socialist party convention at Indianapolis in 1912, that

> the capitalist system has outgrown its historical function, and has become utterly incapable of meeting the problems now confronting society. . . . It is this capitalist system that is responsible for the increasing burden of armaments, the poverty, slums, child labor, most of the insanity, crime and prostitution, and much of the disease that afflicts mankind. . . .

And then came the First World War. The armaments boom and the growing influence of the AFL—Gompers himself was appointed to the advisory commission of the United States Council of National Defense in 1917—drained labor support from the revolutionary left. Hysterical patriotism and fear of subversion encouraged the hunting down, arrest, and imprisonment of innumerable Americans known or suspected to have radical opinions. Debs himself, opposed to all war and to this one in particular as a capitalist conspiracy, was charged with violation of the Espionage Act and in September 1918 sentenced to ten years' imprisonment. Haywood and nearly one hundred other leading Wobblies were jailed for various offenses. While Debs was serving his sentence in the federal penitentiary at Atlanta, Gompers represented the AFL at the Peace Conference in Paris and was appointed chairman of the Conference Commission on Labor Legislation.

From prison Debs polled over 900,000 votes in the 1920 elections, and in December 1921 he was pardoned by President Harding. But the climate which he found on his release was hardly more congenial to his ideas than the one that had shut him away three years before. At the end of August 1919, a group of Socialists had seceded to establish the Communist party at a meeting in Chicago, and while revolutionaries excommunicated one another, America ignored them or persecuted them with ardent impartiality. What place was there for Debs in the era of the speed record and the speakeasy; the stock-market boom and the tabloid glamour of gang wars; the call of instant success, from messenger to millionaire, waitress to film star; the quest for the holy grail of the lucky break? There was place, as there was misery, enough. And if his body was all but burnt out, his faith was not. Until he died, in 1926, he believed insistently in the Second American Revolution, that would finish the work started by the First a century and a half before, and bring one day the commonwealth of freedom, equality, compassion, and peace.

Had he been able to see across the next three decades, he would doubtless have found much to dispirit him. The Socialists were to dwindle rapidly into a small band of faded reformists, their appeal pre-empted by New Deal liberalism and only their hatred of the Communists capable of waking a fierce but impotent passion. The Communist leaders themselves were to betray a cynicism and propensity for moral maneuvering, much more in the manner of Gompers than of Debs, that would range them, despite their zealous professions and the persecution which they increasingly attracted, with the reformers rather than with the revolutionaries. The Wobblies had already disappeared, in a distraction of factionalism, as a force of any significance. The Congress of Industrial Organizations was to display their militancy, if not their revolutionary commitment, during the depression, but would soon be assimilated to the new capitalism of manipulated needs, military nourishment, and social-security buffers. In 1956 the AFL and the CIO were to unite in a labor movement of 15 million members, with the resources, respectability, and objectives of big business, and under the management of George Meany, a proper disciple, in purpose and method, of Samuel Gompers. In a national enjoyment of political and economic dominance over much of the still largely poor and ill-fed world, the mass of Americans were to devote themselves to the culture of competitive consumption, superficial, vulgar, covetous, callous, and infinitely, intrinsically, unsatisfying. Debs would have been among the first, surely, to remark the depredations everywhere of this dominance, and the private loss and terror behind the whole burlesque of progress. And he would at last, surely, too, have recognized in the signs of black insurrection a powerful new groping for the American promise, that would lead a new generation, white as well as black, to question the very basis of American society.

In his own time, Debs saw no need for a separate Negro struggle. "We have simply to open the eyes of as many Negroes as we can and do battle for emancipation from wage slavery, and when the working class have triumphed in the class struggle and stand forth economic as well as political freemen, the race problem will disappear." [28] Racialism he identified as yet another of the system's ravages that would contribute to its downfall. "For capitalism the Negro question is a grave one and will grow more threatening as the contradictions and complications of capitalist society multiply." [29] It was a perception that events would confirm but, in doing so, set the strategy of Debs on its head. The struggle for socialism would not encompass and promote the Negro struggle; the Negro struggle would, by its separate existence, long outlast any serious struggle for socialism and eventually, indeed, revive it.

Populism, that mainly rural revolt against the subjugations of industrial capitalism, lost itself in the Democratic party among the demagogues of white supremacy. And by the early 1900s, the Negroes had been reduced throughout the South to a condition in some respects worse than that which had obtained under slavery. Slavery had denied them legal ownership of their bodies and minds, but had conferred on them the value and accompanying care of property. Emancipation gave them legal ownership without the effective means of upholding it, and made them the responsibility of neither master nor state. Indeed, they were if anything more vulnerable than before to violence, since their injury or death did

not diminish or destroy a negotiable asset, while their formal freedom incited assault from the fearful and frustrated white poor;
and they were far more rigidly segregated, outside acts of obvious
service, including sex. Moreover, slavery had provided, in the
crudeness of their captivity and the economic threat that it had
posed to free labor, a vigorous cause. Emancipation abandoned
them to the market operations of their ignorance, poverty, and
engrafted or enforced submissiveness; turned their former free-
labor support into indifference or antagonism; and deprived many
among them of even the sense that there was further struggle possible to conduct. Nor was their degradation restricted to the South.
In the North they no longer embodied the claim of free labor or
symbolized the mission of American idealism. Their mounting
numbers represented to most white workers a mounting menace
of competition, and their very need seemed to excite a guilty distaste in all sectors of white society. More and more were they
subjected to discrimination, in public places, in housing, in employment, in the labor movement itself, by emerging custom when
not by regulation. While successive municipal, state, and federal
administrations promoted reforms to modify the mastery of capital, they ignored or advanced discrimination against the Negro
under pressure from public opinion or particular lobbies, and with
the connivance of the courts.

The response of Booker T. Washington, born a slave on a Virginia plantation in 1859 and from 1881 head of a new Negro
college in Tuskegee, Alabama, was to turn from the political struggle altogether, as counter-productively provocative, and concentrate
on economic progress, in the hope that this would earn white tolerance and an eventual acquiescence in racial equality. To this end
he extolled the virtues of vocational training to blacks, and of a
docile, efficient labor force to whites, while recommending the
principle of segregation to both. "In all things that are purely
social," he was to write, defining this outlook in a celebrated sentence of his autobiography, "we can be as separate as the fingers,
yet one as the hand in all things essential to mutual progress." [30]
But his primary aim was the development of a Negro middle class

that would flow into the mainstream of capitalist America. And in 1900 he formed the National Negro Business League, "to give encouragement to people to stand together, to build up individuals in various connections and to show to the world the capabilities and possibilities of the race." [31] His blend of subservience and shrewdness was eminently successful. Donations poured into the Tuskegee Institute from Northern industrialists, and the Alabama legislature voted it an annual appropriation, while Washington himself was fêted at home, where he received an honorary degree from Harvard, and abroad, where he was received by Queen Victoria.

Yet Washington was not to have the field of Negro leadership long to himself. In William Edward Burghardt Du Bois, a distinguished sociologist who had been born three years after the Civil War and was now teaching at Atlanta University, the opponents of the Washington doctrines found their spokesman. With his *Souls of Black Folk,* published in 1903, Du Bois opened fire on the whole policy of accommodation as excusing and indeed encouraging the denial of civil rights to Negroes. In July 1905, with a group of Negro radicals from New England, he established, at a meeting in Fort Erie, Canada—once a well-known terminus of the Underground Railroad in the campaign against slavery—the Niagara Movement to promote a more militant approach. And in the following year, at a convention in Harpers Ferry—of John Brown fame—Du Bois outlined the movement's purposes in a message that would with time take on increasing meaning.

> We will not be satisfied to take one jot or tittle less than our full manhood rights. We claim for ourselves every single right that belongs to a freeborn American, political, civil, and social; and until we get these rights we will never cease to protest and assail the ears of America. The battle we wage is not for ourselves alone, but for all true Americans. [32]

The strategy that was adopted, however, and that would dominate Negro struggle for the next half-century, was less defiant than the choice of such meeting places implied. It was the conventional program for change—propaganda, petition, protest, pressure through the polls and through the courts. Nor would anything different have been fitting for the "thoughtful" and "dignified" membership that Du Bois sought to attract. The movement summoned the black masses to the struggle. But had the masses unaccountably responded, no one, it may fairly be supposed, would have been more taken by surprise than Du Bois himself. As it was, the Niagara Movement, with the power and patronage of the Washington school hacking at its slender trunk of intellectuals, was soon felled. Du Bois was undismayed. In 1909 he helped to form the National Negro Committee, which associated the Negro intellectuals with members of the commercial and professional class impatient at Washington's gradualism and with liberal whites of influence and means. In the following year the new movement changed its name to the National Association for the Advancement of Colored People (NAACP), and Du Bois became its Director of Publications and Research, the only elected officer who was not white.

In the complex character and career of Du Bois himself was expressed the multiple problem of Negro struggle. Were Negroes to unite with whites in a common movement for social change? Or were they to concentrate their forces in a movement of their own? What, indeed, was the objective to be: the development of a free and separate Negro community, organized along its own distinct lines for its own distinct purposes, or the total integration of Negroes in a racially indifferent society? How was either objective to be attained: by reform or by revolution? What allies among the whites could be won, without sacrificing an adequate momentum of reform or the reality of revolution? And in the absence of such allies, how was success to be achieved without powerful support from outside America? Did the proper allegiance of the Negro lie with America first, or with a country of color across the world? If constitutional forms of struggle repeatedly failed, were others to be tried? And of such others, which were likely to excite the desired change? Du Bois never resolved these issues for himself. They remain, for most Negroes, unresolved today. As in the record of Du Bois, so in the Negro struggle still, meet the integrationist and the separatist, the reformer and the revolutionary, the patriot and the internationalist, the politician of ordered pressures and the prophet of racial war.

During his long association with the NAACP, he was a crucial element in the alliance of the main Negro struggle with white liberalism. But he was, too, an avowed socialist, joined the Socialist party in 1911, and, though he left it one year later in despair at its indifference to the specific Negro cause, remained a stanch admirer of Debs himself. He was for more than a quarter of a century the outstanding Negro integrationist, yet throughout the period he sporadically and increasingly promoted the alternative of a separatist, self-sufficient, socialist Negro community. By 1934, indeed, his support for separatism and his demand that the NAACP should be clearly controlled by Negroes produced an open breach with other leaders of the organization, and he resigned. With the depression of the 1930s, he reaffirmed his belief in fundamental Marxism, but castigated the American Communists as dogmatic, purblind to the force of racial prejudice, and cynical in using Negroes only as "shock troops" in the battle for their private ends. Then, from the middle 1940s, he ceased his attacks on them, devoted himself more and more to opposing the hysteria of anti-Communism in American foreign and domestic policy, and as Chairman of the Peace Information Center was indicted, unsuccessfully, by the government in 1951 for having failed to register his organization as an "agent of a foreign principal." Ten years later, near the end of his life, he formally applied for membership in the integrationist American Communist party, now a mere political remnant with a minute Negro following, and left to settle in Ghana.

In *The Souls of Black Folk,* at the start of his career in Negro leadership, he had asserted the international character of the color conflict. "The problem of the twentieth century is the problem of the color-line,—the relation of the darker to the lighter races of men in Asia and Africa, in America and the islands of the sea." [33] And in the pages of *Crisis,* the mouthpiece of the NAACP which he edited from its establishment in 1910 to his resignation twenty-four years later, he set out to cultivate in the Negro a pride of race by celebrating the cultural achievements of the colored peoples and in particular the Africans across human history, and by giving consistent encouragement to a black American expression in art. Again and again in different ways he exhorted the Negro to recover "old ideals . . . old standards of beauty . . . not the blue-eyed, white-skinned types which are set before us in school and literature but rich, brown and black men and women with glowing dark eyes and crinkling hair . . . that harks back to the heritage of Africa and the tropics." [34]

Nor did he mean this to be a merely cultural involvement. Through the Universal Races Congress at London in 1911, which he attended, and the five Pan-African Congresses which he promoted—the first in 1919 at Paris, the last in 1945 at Manchester—he sought to establish a solidarity of African movements against imperial rule and an association between them and the Negro cause in America. He was thus not only the first important exponent of Pan-Africanism and a significant influence on many who were later to lead their peoples to independence, but the precursor of that radical alliance with color all over the world, though especially in Africa, in the Negro leadership of the late Malcolm X and of the Student Nonviolent Coordinating Committee (SNCC) today.

Indeed, though in practice he pursued the course of constitutional struggle and not seldom compromise, he was a prophet of apocalyptic racial revolution. Excited by the success of Japan against Russia in the war of 1905, he predicted a common awakening of the world's colored peoples, and warned that unless the whites changed their attitude and conduct a general race conflict would take place. And from then on, intermittently throughout his life, he spoke and wrote of the war that the "dark world" might one day wage against the white. The First World War itself he condemned as a quarrel among white plunderers over their colored victims, and though he patriotically swerved to view it, when America joined in, as a struggle for the very survival of democracy, he soon enough returned to his vision.

The World War was primarily the jealous and avaricious struggle for the largest share in exploiting darker races. As such it is and must be but the prelude to the armed and indignant protests of these despised and raped peoples. Today Japan is hammering on the door of justice, China is raising her half-manacled hands to knock next, India is writhing for the freedom to knock, Egypt is sullenly muttering, the Negroes of South and West Africa, of the West Indies, and of the United States are just awakening to their shameful slavery. Is, then, this war the end of wars? Can it be the end, so long as sits enthroned even in the souls of those who cry peace, the despising and robbing of darker peoples? If Europe hugs this delusion, then this is not the end of world war—it is but the beginning! [35]

There were predictions and interpretations of his subsequently seized upon by critics as contradicted by events. He saw Japan as the blade of the rebellious colored world; failed to remark its change into a power with an indiscriminately imperial appetite; explained its attacks on China, even its invasion of Manchuria in 1931, as an effort to save the country from white domination and as the prelude to a common front of colored resistance. Yet if he was mistaken in such details—not totally so, to be sure, for Japan was to prove the psychological blade of colored rebellion—his fundamental vision has acquired only force with time. Certainly there are not many today who would any longer rule out the prospect of extensive, even worldwide, race war as too improbable for serious unease. And the validity of his vision for America herself has scarcely been disproved by the rapidly rising violence of race in the cities.

The First World War produced an industrial boom in America at the same time as it cut off the supply of emigrants from Europe. Negroes thronged the routes to the cities of the North, drawn mainly by the sudden demand for their labor, but also by the promise of a less repressive environment. For many of these, the break with the South was a break with self-abasement, a plunge into the rapids of American expectancy. And not much less momentous a migration was that into the armed forces, with America's entry into the war. Nearly 370,000 Negroes enlisted, of whom some 200,000 were sent overseas. Treated as the equal of whites by the commerce of the streets and by the bullets on the battle-fields in Europe, they were subjected to common discrimination within the American Army, and, at home, to a more than custom-ary arrogance, as though to counter the pretensions of their uni-form. They did not always submit. In one outburst black troops at Houston, Texas, killed eighteen local whites; nineteen of them were hanged in consequence, and forty-one sentenced to life im-prisonment. No similar retribution attended whites who raged through American cities, mainly in the North, shooting and as-saulting blacks, burning and looting their property, during the summer of 1919.

Peace rebuked such expectancy as the war for democracy had raised. While a resurrected Ku Klux Klan spread across the coun-try, recruiting even more members outside the South than within it, agitation by white labor barred Negroes from all but a few trade unions and from whole regions of employment that war shortages had opened up to them. It was to the frustrations of these ghetto Negroes, their numbers and their needs constantly swollen by fugi-tives from the stagnant South, that Marcus Garvey, the spokesman of a new dispensation, appealed. Born in Jamaica in 1887, he went to London in 1912, where he met Africans from the British pos-sessions and was confirmed in his belief that the oppression of black men everywhere was related to the colonial prostration of Africa. Returning to Jamaica in 1914, he founded the Universal Negro Improvement Association, with the aim of "uniting all the Negro peoples of the world into one great body to establish a country and government absolutely their own." His ideas spread in the West Indies, but it was only after he settled in the United States in 1916 that they began to blaze. His movement acquired an immense following—in the millions, he asserted; in the hundreds of thousands, even its belittlers admitted—and the infrastructure for bringing the diaspora psychologically, if not physically, to an end. To a flag and an anthem were added such institutions as the African Orthodox Church, the Universal African Legion, the Uni-versal Black Cross Nurses, and, of course, a provisional govern-ment, with Garvey as president and a multitude of bizarrely deco-

rated dignitaries. The Black Star Steamship Line promised communication between the ends of the race and transport for exiles
home; *The Negro World* provided a mass-circulation running
gospel of Garveyism; a Negro Political Union, which issued a list
of approved candidates for the 1924 American elections, had a
marked effect on voting in the Negro districts of Chicago and New
York. But the Black Star Line sank under mismanagement and its
accumulation of debts, while Garvey himself was convicted of
using the mails to defraud, sentenced to five years' imprisonment
in 1925, and, after serving two years in the federal penitentiary at
Atlanta, where Debs had been before him, was pardoned and deported by President Coolidge, to drift into obscurity and die in
London in 1940.

The uniformed parades, the posturings in medals and plumes,
seem now the representative vanity of the whole "back to Africa"
project. There was no literal gathering-in of the exiles. Africa was
a destination, like the heaven of the Negro churches, that aroused
an ardor without any accompanying desire to depart. Yet the consequences of Garveyism remain all the same difficult to exaggerate.
In its turning away from the world of the whites, it provided a vital
alternative to the deadening sense of defeat, indignity, and despair
at continued economic failure, social rejection, and cultural contempt. "If you cannot live alongside the white man in peace, if you
cannot get the same chance and opportunity alongside the white
man, even though you are his fellow citizen . . . then find a
country of your own and rise to the highest position within that
country." [36] This call of Garveyism would inform the Black Muslim movement, much of the civil rights insurrection and unorganized individual Negro assertiveness to come. If the country was to
be essentially one of the mind, it would prove no less an object of
allegiance and a source of strength for being so. And if citizenship
of the country would increasingly involve violence against America, this was no more than the response, careless of self-destruction, to white intransigence that Garvey vengefully advised. He
warned of a whole world in racial disruption.

Black men, you were once great; you shall be great again. Lose not courage, lose not faith, go forward. The thing to do is to get organized; keep separated and you will be exploited, you will be robbed, you will be killed. Get organized, and you will compel the world to respect you. If the world fails to give you consideration, because you are black men, because you are Negroes, four hundred millions of you shall, through organization, shake the pillars of the universe and bring down creation, even as Samson brought down the temple upon his head and upon the heads of the Philistines.[37]

Relatedly and momentously too, Garvey raised the value of blackness to a Negro mass scarcely less disdained for it by the light-skinned in the Negro middle class than by the whites themselves. He denounced miscegenation and the evangelists of integration. Du Bois he called "more of a white man than a Negro" and "a mulatto whose white blood despised the black within him." Certainly if Du Bois pioneered the Negro intellectual's interest in Africa and appreciation of race, it is from Garvey that there dates the erosion of white sanctity, of the desire for white acceptance through mere mimicry, of the acquiescence in middle-class mulatto leadership, among the ghetto poor. He was crucial in the conquest of shame. As one of Garvey's counsel at his trial pronounced it: "If every Negro could have put every dime, every penny into the sea, and if he might get in exchange the knowledge that he was somebody, that he meant something in the world, he would gladly do it. . . . The Black Star Line was a loss in money, but it was a gain in soul." [38]

The America of the great depression promoted no potent new movement—the Nation of Islam, or Black Muslims, though founded at the beginning of the 1930s, achieved importance only after the end of the Second World War—in a Negro population distracted by general disappointment and distress. If Negroes looked, half hopelessly, to anyone secular for rescue, they looked to Roosevelt, for whom they broke their traditional allegiance to the Republican party. The small Negro middle class, when not pursuing the appearance of success in aping the manners of white respectability and consumption, continued attempting to produce reform through political lobbying and application to the courts. Some of the longing in the ghettos, swollen by Garveyism, flowed into the old channels of religion, to make the fortunes of new instant saviors such as Father Divine. But as the depression wore on, mounting frustration, especially among the young born in the expectancy of the Northern cities and barely brushed by the alleviations of the New Deal, detonated sporadically in picket lines, boycotts, and parades of protest. A riot raged through Harlem in 1935, a stone hurled in warning through the plate glass of American society.

The American Communist party, widely recruiting whites in revulsion at the dust bowl of the capitalist winds, lost much of its Negro influence by recommending, on the orders of the Comintern, an independent Negro republic in the black belt of the Deep South as a Stalinist solution to the problem of a "national minority." Stalin was not Garvey, and the Negro membership of the party was not in general drawn from the sharecroppers of Georgia or the cotton-pickers of Mississippi. Many intellectuals resigned or were expelled for their deviationist obstinacy, while the NAACP busily derided the strange new bedfellows of the Southern segregationists. At last, refusing to go down along with the black republic, the Communists rechartered the old policy of integration and manned it with a united Negro front. And in this new demand for energetic coalition, they were joined by leading Negro militants, among whom Asa Philip Randolph was pre-eminent.

Born in 1889, Randolph had been one of the young socialists who during the First World War and for a few years afterward had tried to build an alliance of white and black labor. But white labor, even at its radical edge, was unstirred by the call for solidarity across the color line, and Randolph turned to organizing blacks on the railroads into their own union, the Brotherhood of Sleeping Car Porters. Results were scarcely rapid. Founded in 1925, the Brotherhood was repeatedly rejected by the Pullman Company as a bargaining agent, and only in 1937, a year after its affiliation to the AFL, did it extract a contract, with improved working conditions, from the management. Meanwhile Randolph attached himself to the agitation for a nationwide movement that would unite

religious, social, political, and labor groups in a common cause
and mobilize those elusive black masses. In February 1936 the
National Negro Congress held its first meeting, at Chicago, with
over 800 delegates from nearly 600 organizations, to proclaim
deep Negro discontent and a series of objectives from the end of
segregation to the promotion of producer and consumer coopera-
tives. It encompassed radicals and moderates of varying complex-
ions, elected several prominent Communists to its National Council, and chose Randolph himself as its President. While the alliance
lasted, the movement thrived, and active local councils were
established in many cities. But with the conclusion of the Hitler–
Stalin pact, the Communist party's passion for the struggle against
fascism suddenly died, and its new strategy steered through the
third meeting of the National Negro Congress, at Washington,
D.C., in April 1940, a resolution condemning America's aggressive policy toward Germany. Randolph resigned and made a statement of racial as well as political rejoinder, subsequently published
as *The World Crisis and the Negro People Today.*

> The procedure, conduct and policies of the Negro Congress, as set
> up in this third national meeting, will make its influence in the
> affairs of the American Negroes, short lived. The American Negroes
> will not long follow any organization which accepts dictation and
> control from the Communist Party. The American Negro will not
> long follow any organization which accepts dictation and control
> from any white organization.[39]

Impatience with the traditional methods of pressure mounted.
Early in 1941 Randolph himself proposed a march of 100,000
Negroes on Washington to demand an end to racial discrimination
in defense-industry employment. The government judged the
gathering of such a number only too likely and grew more and
more alarmed at the domestic and international repercussions.
Roosevelt, by Executive Order, prohibited racial discrimination in
hiring labor for the defense industries and established a Fair Employment Practices Commission. The order did not provide for
effective enforcement, but it did constitute the first significant intervention by federal authority to promote Negro rights since the

collapse of Reconstruction and so demonstrated the advantages of militancy. The Congress of Racial Equality (CORE) was founded at Chicago in 1942 to conduct non-violent direct action and staged the first sit-in of the civil rights struggle.

The Second World War, far more than the First, hardened the mood of black America. European empire was expelled from many of its Eastern possessions, and American power mortified, by Japan. By the end of the war there were a million American Negroes in uniform, much less submissive to discrimination than they had been at the beginning; inside the armed forces themselves, several serious Negro riots, both at home and abroad, implied innumerable acts of individual defiance. Within wartime America, the Negro migration from South to North and West, and from countryside to city, gathered momentum with the industrial boom, labor shortages, and the mechanization of agriculture; and the peacetime massive military expenditure to safeguard the American way of life prolonged industrial prosperity and some demand for Negro labor. The urban Negro population rose from 6.2 million in 1940 to 9.4 million ten years later, while the rural dropped from 6.6 million to 5.6 million; by 1960 some 13.8 million Negroes would be living in urban areas, and only 5.1 million in rural ones. Indeed, at the start of the 1960s, a higher percentage of Negroes (72.4) than of whites (69.5) would be urbanized. And while more and more Negroes crowded into the spreading ghettos, more and more whites took flight to the spreading suburbs, so steadily increasing the Negro's relative as well as absolute numerical strength within the cities themselves. Aware of this, the Negroes no longer felt like visitors on sufferance; the cities were theirs and vulnerable to their discontent. It was a realization that would have a profound impact, and not least in the South. The intimidations of white supremacy were formidable on plantations or in small scattered rural slums. They lost much of their force against the solidarity of thousands in the streets, as events in Montgomery, Alabama, were soon to reveal.

One manifest result of the new demography seemed promising enough. The rising importance of the Negro vote in the densely populated industrial states began affecting the attitudes of the two major parties, and of their candidates for public office from City Hall to White House, on civil rights. And reinforcing this trend was the progress of the Cold War, which made overt racial discrimination an increasing impediment in the speech of democracy against Communism. Though there was some race rioting by whites in several cities during 1946, and even the proclaimed revival of the Ku Klux Klan, the political climate was not congenial to a return of such racial repressiveness as had followed the First World War. President Truman set up a Committee on Civil Rights in 1946, and when Congress refused to enact some of the recommendations for which he appealed, he made of civil rights a major issue for the elections of 1948. His generally unexpected return to the White House, on the sweeping support for him in the Northern cities and the failure of a separate Southern Democrat states'-rights ticket to carry more than four states, provided a lesson in the new significance of the Negro vote, even over much of the South, that was not lost on the professional politicians. The outbreak of the Korean war made moves to change America's racial image all the more urgent, while the achievement of formal independence by Asian and especially African peoples, with their own presidents and prime ministers, their own delegates to speak and vote at the United Nations, seemed to many American Negroes the final enforced retreat of immemorial white dominion.

The complex change in public opinion was registered by the judiciary, which had so loyally reflected the racist temper of the nation before. In case after case, usually brought on the instigation and with the resources of the NAACP, the Supreme Court struck at long inviolable forms of racial discrimination, outlawing the Southern white primary in 1944, segregated interstate travel in 1946, and various features of segregated education in the early 1950s. At last, in May 1954, it ruled against the very principle of segregation, in public schooling, to discard the "separate but equal" doctrine that it had laid down in 1896. "Separate educational facilities," it revealed, "are inherently unequal." But the famous victories for the most part merely glimmered at a distance or disappeared altogether as they were approached. The Southern Democrats and procedural maneuvers in Congress killed Roosevelt's Fair Employment Practices Commission and then, despite his vigorously fought electoral mandate for it, Truman's civil rights program. Southern local power evaded or ignored rulings of the Supreme Court in the belief that the federal executive could be bribed with concessions by Southern Congressmen on other issues, or, frightened by the implications of enforcement, would respond to defiance with no more than spasms of rhetoric. The white primary survived, as did segregation in interstate travel. The judgment against segregated education produced such a profusion of challenges and subterfuges in the South that it seemed as if compliance would have to wait for the lion to lie down with the lamb. In the face of effective federal inertia, the pass of change was held by local power. Yet how were Negroes to command local power in the South? There were counties with Negro numerical majorities where not a single Negro was registered to vote, counties where there were more adult whites registered to vote than could be found alive.

At the beginning of December 1955, black Mrs. Rosa Parks boarded a bus and sat down on a seat reserved for whites. She was ordered to move, refused, and was, of course, arrested. For this was Montgomery, Alabama, the very city where the Southern Confederacy, nearly a century before, had been born. But, for the first time, the local Negro community did not accept the customary course. Under the leadership of a young Baptist minister, Dr. Martin Luther King, Jr., it undertook a boycott of the buses till its demands—mainly the seating of passengers on the first-come first-served basis, with blacks starting from the back of the bus and whites from the front—were met. The bus company refused to consider Negro representations, authority arrested the boycott leaders on various charges, and other guardians of the Southern order set out to restore it by appropriate terrorism. But the boycott continued, to demand now an end to all segregated seating on the buses. It continued for more than a year. And it became much more than a boycott. King himself gave it the character of a crusade, an engagement by a community of fifty thousand people in passive resistance, with the Gandhian aim of conversion through the protest of love.

When, after a series of court orders, and with the lowering possibility that federal power would at last be forced to interfere, Montgomery desegregated its buses, this was the least of the local Negroes' accomplishments. The phenomenon of a whole Negro community, and of one moreover in the supposedly cowed and ignorant black belt of the Deep South, conducting so disciplined and protracted a campaign against discrimination, despite all the force of custom, hooliganism, and the law, stirred Negro pride and discontent across the country. The concept of struggle without hatred or violence, of resistance by personal sacrifice, had been lit first in the civil rights movement by the Congress of Racial Equality thirteen years before. Montgomery set it independently ablaze, above all among the young, who looked on it as in itself a protest against the morality of power and money. King and other clergymen were to establish in 1957 the Southern Christian Leadership Conference, to mobilize local black communities for further confrontations of conscience with white supremacy. But the mood of Montgomery was to appear less influentially in what King and his associates themselves undertook than in the related subsequent revolt by the student generation.

Montgomery also marked the start of a new impact by the Negro movement on the mind of America. It was the first important racial clash to be televised. The scenes of blacks singing and praying their determination in the churches and walking through the streets alongside empty buses, of jeering white by-standers and strutting authority, flashed to so many millions, white and black, in America, produced a sense of instant and vivid involvement that the press and the radio could not match. Nor were the scenes enclosed in America. On television screens across the world they challenged, as the Negroes knew they challenged, America's international pretensions. When, in September 1957, Governor Orval Faubus of Arkansas used first National Guardsmen and then white mobs to keep black children from entering, by court order, Little Rock's Central High School, President Eisenhower dispatched paratroops to the city, and made an address to the nation on the need to protect America's prestige and safety.

While black America stirred during the 1950s, white America lay in an apparent moral torpor of *Time-Life* values. The business of America was ubiquitously business, and not least at the universities, where students had to be dragged into criticism of their society by diligent professors or bewildered visitors. How far the mood was promoted by McCarthyism, and how far McCarthyism by the mood, may be endlessly debated. Promoting both was a liberalism blinded by fear of Communism and bankrupted by the success of the new capitalism that it had sponsored. Socialism had become little more than an optional history course at the less timid universities. The American Communist party, reduced by government persecution and ideological sterility to a coil of loyalists and FBI agents, lost any last appeal with the Soviet crushing of the Hungarian rebellion and the denunciation of Stalinism at the 20th Congress of the Soviet party. In 1957 the Labor Youth League, the American Communist youth group, disbanded altogether. Searching and original critics of American society there were, such as C. Wright Mills, whose *White Collar* was first published in 1951, and *The Power Élite* in 1956. But they were scarcely representative of the rising generation, and their influence surfaced only in the 1960s.

The rebels were the Beats, who turned their backs on the competitive frenzy of America to develop their own subterranean culture, with its idealization of the Negro, its sexual experiment, jazz and poetry, drugs and madness. It is not difficult to deride this café society of the barricades, with its distant thrusts at the commuter civilization, its individualism by cult, its flight from despair into the nerve endings. But it was essentially a moral movement. Its denials were declarations of value, and its withdrawal of acquiescence was the forerunner of a dynamic defiance.

Moloch! Solitude! Filth! Ugliness! Ashcans and unobtainable dollars! Children screaming under the stairways! Boys sobbing in armies! Old men weeping in the parks!

Moloch! Moloch! Nightmare of Moloch! Moloch the loveless!
Mental Moloch! Moloch the heavy judger of men! . . .
Moloch whose eyes are a thousand blind windows! Moloch whose
skyscrapers stand in the long streets like endless Jehovahs!
Moloch whose factories dream and croak in the fog!
Moloch whose smokestacks and antennae crown the cities! . . .
Moloch! Moloch! Robot apartments! invisible suburbs!
skeleton treasuries! blind capitals! demonic industries!
spectral nations! invincible madhouses! granite cocks!
monstrous bombs!

Howl by Allen Ginsberg, unreticent homosexual, propagandist
for pot, mystic, revolutionary, was first published in 1956 * and
represents a literary crest of Beat protest. Yet its denunciations
were essentially those that fired the Free Speech Movement on the
Berkeley campus eight years later, and fire the political radicalism
of the New Left today. The Beats were themselves generally indifferent or hostile to political agitation in the 1950s. They regarded organized protest as collaboration with the American system. But when organized protest against the system itself emerged
in the 1960s, not a few of the surviving Beats and their Hippie
relatives were drawn into the struggle. The Beats were more than a
portent; they were a prod. For what imbued both their own movement and the political insurrection that followed was a rapt concern for freedom in a society that seemed bent on burying it in a
mausoleum of smooth phrases. It was this concern, indeed, that
produced the clearest political contribution of the Beats, their at-
tachment of rebellion against a mercenary America to the symbol
of the Negro.

Meanwhile, in the late 1950s, other influences began to play on
the American campus. The Campaign for Nuclear Disarmament,
and new magazines such as the *Universities and Left Review* and
The New Reasoner † in Britain, nourished new thinking about
capitalism, about the Cold War, about the nature and purpose of
their own professed democratic society, among American students.

* By City Lights Books, San Francisco, in an edition called *Howl and Other Poems,* which was seized by the police, charged as obscene, and, after a long court trial, released.
† Merged as *The New Left Review* in 1959.

And the Cuban revolution, first welcomed by American liberalism
and then castigated as an aggressive betrayal when it began introducing structural economic changes and colliding with American
business interests, provoked a new skepticism toward the claims
of American foreign policy. From the Universities of Wisconsin,
Chicago, and California at Berkeley, groups and magazines of
radical complexion spread to Harvard, Columbia, and other campuses around the country.

It was a generation reared inside the terrible triumph of the
middle class, the abundant suburb under the abundant cloud of
nuclear warfare. The struggles, like the slump, of the 1930s belonged to another generation. The students of the 1960s had been
born to inherit a society of power and riches unparalled in place or
time, and the inheritance which so dazzled their parents seemed to
an increasing number of them no more than slick promotional
packaging around an obsolescent humanity. They saw no room for
themselves and their ideal of a free and peaceful, compassionate
and creative community in the America of artificially flavored
foods and television quiz shows, tax-deductible charities and the
latest missiles. The Old Left, which their parents now remembered
with an embarrassed nostalgia or a patronizing self-righteousness,
merely bored them, as the identification of their own deep disquiet
with a disloyalty bordering on treason angered and yet further
antagonized them. The yesterday of McCarthyism was a source
less of intimidation than of shame, that America had succumbed
so easily to the terrorism of a predatory demagogue. It was only
fitting, therefore, that their own first significant clash with authority should have been over the House Un-American Activities
Committee. In May 1960 the committee held hearings in San
Francisco, and hundreds of students from the Berkeley campus
and San Francisco State College, joined by stragglers from the
local Beat colony, demonstrated their opposition. That they should
have been accused so widely, in consequence, of being, or having
been misled by, Communists, further persuaded them, and others
of their thinking at universities across the country, that there was
something profoundly wrong with America. And what was pro-

foundly wrong seemed summed up in the treatment of the Negro. Already, indeed, some of them had attached themselves to the Greensboro revolt.

Montgomery killed one cherished myth of white complacency—that all Negroes in the South but for a few heady intellectuals were resigned to, if not entirely contented with, their condition. Another, robust since the mission of Booker T. Washington—that the educated middle-class Negro could be indefinitely conciliated by special, if still segregated, treatment—was killed at Greensboro, North Carolina. There, on the first day of February 1960, four students from a local all-black college sat down at an all-white Woolworth's lunch counter and ordered four cups of coffee. They were not served and they refused to leave until they were. On the next day they were joined by sixteen others from the college, and on the day following there were fifty sitting-in, with a few local white students among them. The new form of demonstration flashed to other towns in North Carolina, to South Carolina, Virginia, Tennessee. The demonstrators were set upon by outraged segregationists, arrested, imprisoned; and still their numbers grew. Students, mainly white, on campuses from San Francisco to New York, raised money for bail and fines, picketed nearby branches of the chain stores involved, and went South themselves to join in sit-ins and the risk of assault or jail.

The sit-ins were spontaneous, unled, uncoordinated. At last, with urging and a small subsidy from the Southern Christian Leadership Conference, some three hundred representative student militants, mainly from the South but with observers from nineteen Northern colleges, met at Raleigh, North Carolina, on the Easter week-end, April 15–17. Firmly they resisted pressures to attach themselves to SCLC, to CORE, or to the NAACP, each eager to assist and acquire this sudden young commitment; they wanted to keep the sit-in movement as their own, and they established the Temporary Student Nonviolent Coordinating Committee to direct and promote it. Throughout the summer the demonstrations continued. A young Negro teacher from New York, Robert Moses, joined the movement and was sent through the Deep South to

search out local militants. It was an early attempt to expand the
revolt beyond the student compass, and when in October a second
conference was held at Atlanta, among the 235 who attended were
the recruits that Bob Moses had made. This meeting slightly
tightened the movement's structure and adopted a founding declaration that would govern its purpose and methods for the next few
years. It was a revolt already groping toward revolution.

> We affirm the philosophical or religious ideal of non-violence as
> the foundation of our purpose, the presupposition of our belief, and
> the manner of our action.
> Non-violence, as it grows from the Judeo-Christian tradition,
> seeks a social order of justice permeated by love. Integration of
> human endeavor represents the crucial first step towards such a
> society.
> Through non-violence, courage displaces fear. Love transcends
> hate. Acceptance dissipates prejudice; hope ends despair. Faith
> reconciles doubt. Peace dominates war. Mutual regards cancel
> enmity. Justice for all overthrows injustice. The redemptive commu-
> nity supersedes immoral social systems.
> By appealing to conscience and standing on the moral nature of
> human existence, non-violence nurtures the atmosphere in which
> reconciliation and justice become actual possibilities.
> Although each local group in this movement must diligently work
> out the clear meaning of this statement of purpose, each act or
> phase of our corporate effort must reflect a genuine spirit of love
> and goodwill.

These students, most of them black, but with whites, from the
South as well, among them, represented an old insurrection
uniquely invigorated; for the first time in American history, it was
the youth who were raising the standard. The efficacy of their
creed, along with its appropriate methods, would come increasingly to be doubted by themselves. Fear, hate, prejudice, despair,
doubt, war, enmity, injustice would prove far more resistant than
they supposed. Yet that would not be for want of their own courage and faith, for some insufficiency in the love and the peace that
they offered. When they were clubbed down, they stood up again
to declare themselves; when they were jailed, they looked to re-

lease as an occasion to challenge jail again; and at their work they sang a whole new cycle of American songs, from the eye of their experience. They believed first in freedom, but next in America, her responsiveness to sacrifice. And so they sacrificed themselves unstintingly for a recognition, by the America that they knew, of the difference that they saw so plainly between right and wrong.

Was this not, after all, a time for trust? The sit-ins of 1960 had been widely successful. In states of the shallow South, where discrimination was less committed to ceremony, the surrender of one or two customs soon seemed preferable to a prolonged disruption of trade by demonstrations and, for chain stores, a costly attention to their far more important business in the North. America seemed ready to respond. Eisenhower, with his general, surely deliberate, lethargy, had left the White House, and in his place there was now one who had campaigned on the call for new frontiers, had addressed himself rousingly to the aspirations of American youth, and intervened, along with his campaign-manager brother, who was now Attorney General, to secure the release of Martin Luther King from imprisonment in Atlanta. Now, it was not altogether unreasonable to expect, federal power would exercise itself to protect those who upheld their constitutional rights against constant violation by a refractory racism.

In May 1961, at the instigation of CORE, seven blacks and six whites boarded two buses at Washington, D.C., to undertake a Freedom Ride through the Deep South and assert their right, proclaimed by the Supreme Court, to unsegregated travel and unsegregated use of terminal facilities. At the bus station in Rock Hill, South Carolina, police interfered, after a pointed interval, when riders were assaulted; at Anniston, Alabama, one of the buses was stopped by a mob and burned to its frame, while riders on the other were beaten, without a policeman in sight; and there were no police at the Birmingham terminal, where a mob with iron bars fell upon the riders as they walked through the white waiting room to the lunch counter. Since no bus would carry the riders farther, they took a plane to the planned rally in New Orleans, and the first Freedom Ride was over.

The Student Nonviolent Coordinating Committee (SNCC) immediately decided to continue the rides, and from Nashville, Tennessee, a busload of students descended on Birmingham. The White House, aroused by the reported beatings and bus-burning, now conferred with the Alabama state government over protection for the students. But when their bus reached Montgomery, there were no police at the terminal, and a mob attacked not only the riders but several newsmen and even President Kennedy's personal emissary. New riders arrived. The President pronounced the situation "a source of the deepest concern," but did little more than dispatch a few United States Marshals to Montgomery. Two buses of SNCC and CORE members went on to Jackson, Mississippi, where the riders were arrested as they tried to use white terminal facilities, and, refusing to pay the fines that the court imposed, went to jail. Attorney General Robert Kennedy called for a "cooling-off period" in an appeal clearly directed more at the Freedom Riders than at authority in the Deep South, and Martin Luther King's SCLC offered a "temporary lull." But the students, joined by clergymen, seemed not to have heard. Throughout the summer they traveled to Birmingham, to Montgomery, and on to Jackson, where more than three hundred of them were arrested. Like Stokely Carmichael, a young black student from Howard University who had been among the first Freedom Riders, many of them grew political muscle in a Mississippi jail.

Some of its members wanted SNCC to concern itself now with black voter registration in the Deep South. Since the federal government was demonstrably unwilling to confront local power, local power itself had to be wrested from its long white monopoly. Others argued that the movement should continue with its campaign of militant protest, its sit-ins at lunch counters, stand-ins at cinema box-offices, kneel-ins at churches, wade-ins at beaches. Meeting at Highlander, Tennessee, in August, the Coordinating Committee decided, typically, to do both. And typically, too, the students chose to challenge the order of the Deep South not somewhere in its pulp but in its hard and bitter core, in Mississippi, where selectively intricate tests and steady intimidation had kept

97 per cent of eligible blacks in the state off the voters' rolls, and where the average black income was, not unconnectedly, a mere third that of the average white one. In July, Bob Moses had gone alone to live and work in the counties on the Louisiana border, and here, into a moral wilderness rank even for Mississippi, followed a small party of SNCC fellow pioneers, most of them fresh from jail as Freedom Riders, to make a clearing, to help Negroes prepare for registration tests, accompany them to the courthouses, and demonstrate against segregation. Moses himself, whose courage and gentleness were to raise his name into an ideal for so many of the searching generation, withdrew to Jackson at last in January 1962. The civil rights workers and those local Negroes who had tried to register had been threatened, beaten up, jailed. And a Negro farmer who had attended registration classes had been murdered one morning openly, before three Negro witnesses. One of these had been prepared to testify if guaranteed federal protection; but the Justice Department in Washington had declared that such protection was impossible, and all three supported the murderer's plea of self-defense. The local Negroes were cowed now, while the White House appeared as indifferent as the nation. The news networks scarcely noticed the activities of a few young radicals, mainly Negro and with no celebrity appeal, operating in a dark corner of America.

The forlorn Mississippi engagement of 1961 and 1962, after the experience of the Freedom Rides, fired in the thinking of SNCC a train of disillusionment with the character of democracy in America. Kennedy's speech-writers rang increasingly hollow. A President who risked war to acquire Cuba for capitalism, but not even a skirmish to acquire the Deep South for democracy; who visited Berlin to proclaim "I am a Berliner," but not Mississippi to proclaim "I am a Negro"; who partly settled his new frontiers by appointing to the federal bench in the Deep South several champions of white supremacy, called into question the genuineness of his liberal commitment. At the same time, the prevalent agreement in the nation on his genuine commitment to liberalism, the prevalent allowance and expectation of a gap, even politic contradiction, between what should be said and what should be done, made the militants of SNCC question the whole liberal commitment, with the very meaning of American representative government.

They themselves increasingly practiced and preached a democracy of participation, by which decisions emerged from the dialectic of all those they affected. SNCC had always been a framework of coordination, not a pyramid of command; individual differences of aim and approach were not merely permitted, but encouraged, within the perimeter of collective engagement. Leadership of the traditional democratic type had been deliberately discarded, and Bob Moses himself was to resign in 1965 and even change his surname to Parris because of the following that had begun to gather around him. Indeed, the members of SNCC who had abandoned their campuses for the movement did not keep the word "Student" for the sake of nostalgia or some furtive prestige; they had changed, they had not abandoned, their studies. As in the Albany Movement of southwest Georgia, which they excited in October 1961 and which pulled down, through the persistence of the local black community, one racial barrier after the other across the next three years, they set out to learn as they taught, to help the Southern Negroes organize themselves and develop their own priorities and methods. As Moses described it in a talk on the fifth anniversary of SNCC's formation:

> What we have begun to learn and are trying to explore about people is how they can come together in groups, small groups and large groups, and talk to each other and make decisions about basic things, about their lives. I think that this has application everywhere in the country. Whatever we currently mean by democracy, we don't mean that people should come together, discuss their main problems that they all know about and be able to do something about themselves.[40]

It was a concept that often lost its way amidst white terrorism and black submissiveness, or just helplessly in the thicket of communication between those of different ages and backgrounds. But it did sometimes succeed, and then it was beautiful. Nor was Moses alone in remarking the relevance to all America. Increasingly it would come to inform the work of white radicals in the cities of the North.

The initiatives and methods of SNCC prodded the other civil rights organizations, and King's Southern Christian Leadership Conference began working within the Negro community of Birmingham, Alabama, for a massive assault on discrimination. On April 3, 1963, the first demonstrations took place, with sit-ins at lunch counters in downtown stores, and within a few days more than 150 protestors had been arrested. Then, on Good Friday, April 12, the Negroes began to march, and they marched day after day, chanting slogans, singing "We Shall Overcome," to meet the police dogs and firehoses of the Birmingham authorities. Hundreds, then thousands were arrested. Justice Department officials hurried from Washington to mediate between the city's two communities, helped by calls from big business in the North to local branches, and on May 10 a compromise program of phased desegregation and fair employment practices was adopted by the spokesmen of white commerce and black protest. Two days later buildings in the black area were bombed, and blacks rioted in response, burning stores and battling with state troopers and police. President Kennedy dispatched a demand for new civil rights legislation to Congress.

As impatience and resentment spread through black America, faith in the efficacy of non-violence faltered and fell back. Malcolm X spoke for a steadily swelling opinion in the ghettos when he denounced Martin Luther King and his strategy: "You need somebody who is going to fight. You don't need any kneeling in or crawling in." And King himself, while visiting Harlem in the summer, was pelted with eggs. More than two hundred thousand gathered at Washington in a Freedom March, under the leadership of A. Philip Randolph, in August, and though the mood was in the main carefully restrained, the speech by John Lewis, Chairman of SNCC, reflected the rising disillusionment. And then in the following month a bomb exploded at a Negro church in Birmingham during a Sunday-school class, and four children were killed. The news and the scenes that followed, of injured children and the funerals of the dead, fed a resentment that would flame across the ghettos in the years to come.

Meanwhile, throughout 1962 and into 1963 SNCC, with Bob Moses at its heart and with help from the other civil rights organizations, worked on voter registration in Mississippi. It was still a tiny movement of full-time devotion; it had only some 130 staff members scattered across the South, and of these only some 40 were in the state. Yet, in the company of mounting violence against their efforts—Moses himself escaped a bullet by inches—these few, often spread over many areas of activity, excited a wide striving and determination. The number of Negro voters grew. But the pace was so slow, and the price so high. In June 1963 Medgar Evers, Mississippi field secretary for the NAACP, was shot dead outside his home in Jackson. Thousands marched behind his body through the city in a demonstration of black anger without precedent in the history of the state. In the autumn the Mississippi movement was ready for a display of strength, and in response to the effective exclusion of Negroes from the regular election for governor, organized a Freedom Ballot, with Aaron Henry, NAACP state leader, as candidate. Civil rights workers and the local Negro militants who had emerged from the voter registration campaign, joined by a group of white students from the North, canvassed their way across the terrorism of the state, and when the ballot boxes, in churches and other meeting places, were cleared, some 80,000 were found to have voted, or some four times the number of Negroes on the Mississippi electoral roll.

Yet SNCC itself was not immune to the hardening of racial sentiment among Negroes across the country. There had been whites in the organization from the outset, who had left their colleges and families too, for equally demanding and dangerous work, equally small and uncertain salaries. They had earned places of trust and responsibility. But they were few. Now, for the summer of 1964, the Mississippi movement planned a massive voter-registration drive, and the campus mood in the North offered far more white volunteers than ever before. In November 1963 the

Mississippi field workers, all but a few from SNCC, met to consider the implications and in the end accepted them. The resistance displayed, however, the complaints that whites willy-nilly impeded the development of black initiative and self-assurance, and that they should work more among those of their own color, warned of the changing racial relationship even within the revolutionary commitment.

To the passion of Mississippi, then, they came, hundreds of white students from Northern campuses and often glibly liberal middle-class homes. And what they encountered was, inevitably, beyond their fiercest denunciations. The fear, the hatred, the collective white unreason belonged now not to tiny flat figures on a screen, but to people like themselves, distorted as though by some quality of the light. It was they who now experienced the violence, or watched as it was done not to symbols of a cause but to those whose hands they held in demonstrations, with whom they shared rooms and food, songs and sudden confidences. For the Northern white students who returned from the summer project in Mississippi, order, law and government, America herself would never be the same again. Not all of them returned. In June three civil rights workers, two of them white students from the North, disappeared in Philadelphia, Mississippi, and six weeks later their bodies were found shot and buried in a nearby earthen dam. White America responded with expressions of shock such as it had never extended to similar black victims, some of whom had indeed not even been noticed by the news services. Black America could scarcely fail to remark this. Nor could the Northern white students, in whose peculiar distress was an element of shame.

Yet no less influential than the cruelty of Mississippi was its kindness. The white students met among the Negroes they had come to help a simplicity, a courage, a humor, a compassion, a generosity that they did not have to sentimentalize favorably to contrast with the ostentation, the timidity, the grimness, the self-interest, the greed of competitive consumption. As one of them wrote in puzzlement:

There is some strong ambivalence which goes with this work. I sometimes fear that I am only helping to integrate some beautiful people into modern white society with all of its depersonalization (I suppose that has something to do with its industrial nature). It isn't 19th century pastoral romanticism which I feel, but a genuine respect and admiration for a culture which, for all the trouble, still isn't as commercialized and depersonalized as our Northern mass culture.[41]

They would return no less outraged by the subjugation of the Negroes, indeed far more so, because of the glad, giving qualities which survived in spite of it. Suffering in itself seldom ennobles, and they found abundant evidence of this in the degradations of want, in blacks cowed and apathetic or obsequiously brutal mimics of their white masters in the service of the jails. But the qualities which did survive, to snatch their admiration, seemed to indicate the wrong way which their own culture had taken, and they returned with a deeper insight into its loss, along with a clearer, more urgent sense of the need to challenge it. On their campuses, from Berkeley to Harvard and Columbia, they would be sources of a spreading insurrection, to liberate themselves and change the nature of their society.

Though the struggle in the South was for white America the substance of the Negro Problem, for black America the White Problem was in substance the same, if different in shadow, on both sides of the Mason-Dixon Line. Scarcely anyone disputed the Negro's right to vote, to use buses and trains, lunch counters at stations and stores, equally with whites in the North. But the Negro was segregated none the less, and the extent of his segregation, far from diminishing, was significantly increasing. The suburbs to which whites escaped from the tumultuous cities excluded Negroes by high housing costs and, where these proved insufficient, covenants more or less covertly arrived at.* And by such means, within the cities themselves, all but a few Negroes were kept in-

* While the percentage of whites living in central cities with a population of over fifty thousand dropped slightly, from 31.1 to 30 during the 1950s, the percentage of Negroes soared, from 29.2 to 50.5; and while the percentage of whites living in suburbs soared, from 14.7 to 22.8, during the same period, the percentage of Negroes rose from only 6.1 to only 8.4.

side, or absorbed by the steady growth of, the ghetto. Indeed, many major cities in the North displayed an even higher degree of segregation than the rising national average.* With the richer elements of the population taking their local taxes outside the cities altogether, or sealing themselves in their own neighborhoods, public amenities in the ghettos deteriorated, and schools lost more and more of such racial integration as they had achieved.

Segregation went much deeper than geography, however. With the technological climb of American capitalism, the demand for unskilled labor rapidly declined. The percentage of unemployed among Negroes had been only a little higher than that among whites in 1940 (16.8 to 14.2); but it fell less far, or rose much further, in the fluctuations that followed, till it became more than double (7.8 to 4.5, in 1950; 8.7 to 4.7, in 1960; 10.9 to 5.1, in 1963). And such figures disclosed merely a part of the picture. Estimates of unemployment which included part-time work or work so poorly paid that it scarcely permitted subsistence suggested a proportion among Negroes of over one-third, or several times that of any comparable incidence among whites.† Between 1960 and 1963, the average family income for Negroes dropped from 55 to 53 per cent of the average family income for whites.

In a society which assessed personal value by material consumption, this economic inferiority was psychologically as well as physically corrosive. The very structure of the black family diverged further and further from the nation's cultural model. The illegiti-

* See, for instance, the analysis of U.S. Census reports made by Karl E. Taeuber, of the Population Research and Training Center at the University of Chicago, cited in *The New York Times* of November 26, 1964. Taeuber postulated an index, on which zero stood for complete residential integration of the races, and 100 for complete segregation. Taking 109 cities, he found that the extent of segregation across the country had increased during the 1940s and 1950s from 85.2 on his index to 86.1. But cities in the North and Center had an index figure in 1960 of 88.4, and in eighteen cities of Illinois the figure was 90, with Chicago itself reaching 93 in 1963.

† In September 1967 the U.S. Department of Labor issued a report which, using this wider definition, revealed that 33.9 per cent of all urban Negroes were unemployed, with an estimate of 48 per cent for the Watts district of Los Angeles, 36 per cent for the Philadelphia ghetto, and 48 per cent for some areas of Chicago. (*The Progressive*, Madison, Wisconsin, Vol. 31, No. 10, October 1967, p. 4.)

macy rate was nearly ten times that of the whites; over three times as many black marriages as white ones were disrupted by divorce or separation; between two and three times as many black households as white ones were headed by women. And the discrepancies were widening.[42] In a culture which found more work for black women, in kitchen and office, as it found less for black men, and which had long mortified the black, especially the male, by racial contempt, the vaunted American claim of equal opportunity was a constant taunt, with past and present combining to clog the mind of the black child and soon excite, especially in the male, a hatred and a violence that were a refuge from humiliation and despair. It was hardly wonderful that a Black Muslim movement, with its counter contempt for whites as children of the devil, its strict hostility to any integration with them, its Garveyite glorification of the colored world, and its message of black self-sufficiency in all spheres, should have made such strides, in particular among the ghetto poor. By the end of the 1950s, it could count its "believers" in the tens of thousands and claim, not without evidence, to have influenced the outlook of millions.

In June 1964 the United States Senate at last passed the Civil Rights Act for which the late President Kennedy had asked. The provisions to outlaw discrimination by race in public amenities, even those privately owned, such as hotels, stores, and gas stations, had been strenuously opposed, and not only by representatives of the white South, as an intrusion by the law into the rights of the individual. It seemed to the sponsors of the act that they had promoted a momentous reform, and an unexpectedly easy one, as restaurants, beaches, cinemas across much of the South became indifferent to color without the predicted public upheaval. Surely this was an earnest of America's determination to encompass all citizens in her promise. Yet the Northern ghettos showed small appreciation. Black rioting swept New York City for five days in July, and no sooner had it begun to ebb there than it struck upstate Rochester, where the vast paternalism of the Eastman Kodak Company had cultivated a reputation for white enlightenment and relative black prosperity. By the end of September the storm of black frustration had broken over five more cities. There was no discoverable organization behind the rioting, though the authorities busily searched, and the established Negro leadership had no control over its course, though it intervened with anxious appeals.

Earlier, in May, President Johnson had confronted the perplexity of America with a new dispensation, in liberal succession to the New Deal, the Fair Deal, and the New Frontier—the Great Society.

> The Great Society rests on abundance and liberty for all. It demands an end to poverty and racial injustice—to which we are totally committed in our time, but that is just the beginning. The Great Society is a place where every child can find knowledge to enrich his mind and enlarge his talents. It is a place where leisure is a welcome chance to build and reflect, not a feared cause of boredom and restlessness. It is a place where the city of man serves not only the needs of the body and the demands of commerce, but the desire for beauty and the hunger for community. It is a place where man can renew contact with nature. It is a place which honors creation for its own sake, and for what it adds to the understanding of the race. It is a place where men are more concerned with the quality of their goals than the quality of their goods. . . .

Wrapped in the tinfoil eloquence of the speech-writer, this was so pervasive a denunciation of contemporary America, a call to change so profound, that, if it meant what it said, it meant no less than a revolution, in manners, procedures, values, aims. But did it mean what it said? Was American liberalism not promising more and more as it delivered less and less? The civil rights movement in Mississippi formed a Freedom Democratic party, and to the National Convention of the Democrats at Atlantic City in August came sixty-eight representatives, led by Bob Moses, to claim the Mississippi seats. Whatever the ceremony of selection in the state, theirs was the right, they declared, by their democratic basis, to speak and vote on behalf of Mississippi. Before the Convention Credentials Committee, Mrs. Fannie Lou Hamer, a black share-cropper in her late forties, testified to the beatings and the imprisonment that she and so many like her had suffered. "All of this is on account we want to register, to become first-class citizens, and if the Freedom Democratic Party is not seated now, I question America. . . ."

Waging the campaign for compromise, under the distant command of Johnson himself, were two eminences of American liberalism: Hubert Humphrey, who had led the Senate battle for the Civil Rights Act and whose Vice-Presidential ambitions seemed now to depend on the success of his maneuvers; and Walter Reuther, head of the United Automobile Workers. A compromise was reached. The convention overwhelmingly agreed that though the regular Mississippi delegates were to be seated, they would have first to pledge allegiance to the party ticket; that two of the Freedom Democratic party representatives might sit as delegates at large with the right to vote; and that henceforward at national conventions no delegations would be seated from states where citizens were deprived of the right to vote because of race or color. The liberals hailed this as less a compromise than a triumph. The Freedom Democratic party saw it as less a compromise than a defeat and, despite the urgings of Martin Luther King and other elders of the civil rights movement, unanimously rejected it. Nor was that all. To the anger, embarrassment, and sorrow of delegates, the representatives of the Freedom Democratic party staged a sit-in on the Mississippi seats and had to be removed. Their demonstration marked the divide between liberal coalitionism and radical defiance, between an Old Left of American reform and a New Left of American revolution. It marked the divide between realism and idealism. And it marked, in an unprecedented correspondence, the divide between the generations. In the Free Speech Movement that would soon envelop the Berkeley campus, one slogan declared, "You can't trust anyone over thirty."

The Berkeley insurrection did not come unprepared. The demonstration against the House Un-American Activities Committee had taken place in neighboring San Francisco some four years before, and across many months now a growing number of students had displayed their support for the civil rights struggle in the South and their hostility to local race discrimination. And each display of solidarity or protest in which the students took part encouraged them with the companionship they found. In March 1964 mass picketing of the Sheraton Palace Hotel in San Francisco culminated in a sit-in and several hundred arrests, with many Berkeley students involved. As one demonstrator described it:

> The lobby was filled, the lobby and the long corridors on either side, and we each realized, scanning the mass of a thousand faces, that *we were not alone.* One spent a lifetime, in America, hedging one's bets, keeping up one's guard, never letting anyone else look too deep for fear of being laughed at or looking foolish; but here we were a thousand strong, and, each in our own way, we knew that we believed, that we all believed, that we had some core of our lives to share with one another.[43]

And as the year wore on, through the Mississippi summer project and the clash at the Democratic Convention, students came to see or suspect the proper target of their collective protest less in Southern white supremacy or the more polite Northern forms of discrimination than in the whole quality of American life.

Of this quality, the University of California seemed to them a supreme example. It was so populous, especially at Berkeley, that few students ever even met those who presided over their studies. It was so preoccupied with results that the pressure on students to achieve satisfactory grades left little room for the desire to think. It was so up-to-date, so lavishly equipped with the latest in technical efficiency, that it seemed to be a regime of computers, by computers, for computers. It was so assimilated to the purposes of the new capitalism that it devoted enormous resources of talent and research to government-financed and -selected projects, generally related to defense, and served as one of the busiest recruitment centers in the country for the big corporations. And it was so contemptuous of the student's fundamental moral and intellectual interests that it effectively outlawed political and social issues from any serious individual inquiry or collective expression on the campus, by tight restrictions on the nature and activity of clubs, the content of posters, the organization and matter of meetings. In

short, students were increasingly persuaded that they were being
not liberated but manipulated, and for objectives that they feared
and despised, by their system of education.

Suitably, the university—and, within it, especially the Berkeley
campus—was regarded by those in the nation concerned with such
affairs as a settled frontier of liberalism in the Far West. Its
president, Clark Kerr, had refused to expel students arrested during the demonstration against the House Un-American Activities
Committee, since the protest had not been planned on university
premises, and the protestors had acted in their capacity as citizens.
He had even induced the regents to withdraw the ban against
Communist speakers on campus, though relieving disquiet by
simultaneously proclaiming new procedures to control the campus
presence of any "controversial" speakers at all. Indeed, he had
received the Meiklejohn Award, for his contributions to academic
freedom, from the American Association of University Professors.
And, as was only apt, he was the pre-eminent theorist of the
"multiversity" and its changing relationship to society. In his book
The Uses of the University,[44] he had placed the campus in its real
American context.

> The production, distribution, and consumption of "knowledge" in
> all its forms is said to account for 29 per cent of gross national
> product . . . and "knowledge production" is growing at about
> twice the rate of the rest of the economy. . . . The university and
> segments of industry are becoming more alike. As the university
> becomes tied into the world of work, the professor—at least in the
> natural and some of the social sciences—takes on the characteristics
> of an entrepreneur. . . . The two worlds are merging physically
> and psychologically.

In the new university, the key figures were not the students or
the professors but the administrators, the guardians of a "benevolent bureaucracy." Kerr himself did not necessarily defend such a
development. He merely regarded it as inevitable. And he was only
doing his own efficient best, it seemed, in helping it along at the
University of California.

In the middle of September, responding—it soon emerged—to

powerful complaints about student demonstrations in the Bay
Area, the university authorities, without consultation or warning,
banned club tables,* fund-raising, membership recruitment, posters, the "planning and implementing of off-campus political and
social action," from a strip of Berkeley sidewalk, a twilight zone of
city–university control to which such activities had been driven by
campus restrictions. "Off-campus" clubs, including even Youth for
Goldwater, formed a united front of opposition. Students picketed
the administration block and violated the ban, and at the end of
September five of them were summoned for disciplinary action. In
the inauguration of a policy which the students consistently pursued, to unite against any attempt at victimizing a few—Kerr later
commented on their "remarkable sense of solidarity"—more than
five hundred accompanied the five to their summons, declared that
they also had violated the rules, and demanded equal punishment.
The authorities added three more students to the list for disciplining—among them Mario Savio of SNCC, who had been in
Mississippi for the summer project and was fast now coming to the
front as the spokesman of the protest movement—and that night
announced the indefinite suspension of all eight. Several hundred
students who were sitting-in at the administration block now slept-
in till morning, when a Free Speech rally began with mass defiance
of the ban. Deans approached the CORE table and ordered one of
those manning it to leave. He refused, and they ordered the campus
police chief to arrest him. He refused to go peacefully, others
demanded to be arrested as well, and the police chief retreated for
help. A police car arrived, and hundreds of students, in a response
set off spontaneously by those with experience of the civil rights
struggle, sat down around it, while many more hundreds stood by.
They kept the car there for thirty-two hours, despite Kerr's threats
of large-scale police intervention, and moved only when Kerr himself signed a compromise agreement with nine student representatives, submitting the suspensions to the Academic Senate, declaring that the university would not press charges against the

* Literally tables from which students promoted club membership and
activities.

arrested man, and promising negotiations on the basic issues. Those thirty-two hours established the student insurrection. As one of its leaders subsequently wrote: "They furnished the emotional impetus for our fight, they were our signature on a promissory note of the heart. . . ."[45] The representatives of the "off-campus" clubs in the united front met and formed the Free Speech Movement, with an elected leadership for day-to-day decisions: students who were not members of the constituent clubs chose their own representatives at a special meeting, as did graduate students and even non-students (mainly drop-outs) in the campus community.

During the next five weeks it became clear that the authorities, despite the undertaking at the police-car sit-in, had no intention of negotiating on the basic issues and were waiting for student exhaustion to disintegrate the movement. Violations began again on November 9, with more than eight hundred students signing statements that they had manned tables. But by the Thanksgiving weekend, in the last days of the month, the movement was losing its way in the university's bureaucratic maze. And then, suddenly, the authorities cracked down with an announcement that Mario Savio and three other FSM leaders were being considered for expulsion. The students saw this as a calculated singling out of hostages and reacted with a noon rally on December 2, attended by some six thousand. Between one thousand and fifteen hundred then marched into the administration building and sat down, to sing their own Free Speech carols, to study and discuss, to pass around sandwiches and drinks, to hold an impromptu Chanukah * service and tell the story of the Maccabees with a Free Speech Movement gloss. As one of the Berkeley rebels has pointed out, joy was an intrinsic element in their rebellion, a sense of liberation hand in hand with a sense of the nonsense confronting them.

Certainly, we were seriousness personified; we've jail sentences to show for this. But faced with the absurd, in every sense, there is a dimension of response without which seriousness is meaning-

* A Jewish festival commemorating the successful revolt in the second century B.C., by Jews in Palestine under the leadership of the Hasmonean family, or Maccabees, against the rule and religious oppressions of the Seleucid king Antiochus Epiphanes.

less. We had it; it is hard to examine; but our ubiquitous "humor" is an essential testimony to our sanity. That "humor" was also an indelible stamp on our use of words like "democracy" and "moral commitment," which—for the first time in our American lives—had become alive and real. In a rhetoric fog of words without substance, we often treated ours lightly, as if leaning on them too seriously might again crush the life from them.[46]

It was Governor Pat Brown, embodiment of California's liberal regime, who now moved to crush this embarrassing demonstration on the state's foremost campus. In the early hours of December 3, police began dragging away the students. It took time, till the middle of the afternoon. Meanwhile the Academic Senate had roundly condemned the police intervention and come out overwhelmingly in support of the student cause. And a strike had begun which was to involve four-fifths of the student body and three-quarters of the teaching assistants. Five days later, the Academic Senate held the largest meeting in its history and by a ratio of almost eight to one upheld the right of students to the same freedom of political activity on the campus as they enjoyed alongside other citizens off it. With the students having cleared the way, the professors were now facing the "benevolent bureaucracy." Five months later the Byrne Committee, appointed by the regents, issued a report which rebuked the regents themselves, severely condemned the conduct of the university administration, and in general upheld the student case for free speech. It also accepted, after review by independent experts, a "reliable survey of student opinion," which had concluded that, before the December sit-in, some two-thirds of the students "supported the FSM's objectives and about a third supported its tactics." Subsequent surveys, the committee added, "showed that support increased after the December sit-in."

The Free Speech Movement groped toward revolution, and revolution, of course, it did not get. The poster that parodied the ubiquitous IBM card—"I am a UC student. Please don't bend, fold, spindle or mutilate me"—is no less valid today than it was during the demonstrations of 1964. Yet the FSM did achieve a great deal more than recognition by the university authorities of the students' right to collect funds for Freedom Schools in Mississippi or recruit members to political clubs on campus. It confronted, first, the national belief that insurrection could come only from the unfortunate, the failed, the misshapen—the colored, the poor, the backward, the victims of alien manipulation. The mass of the FSM was white, middle-class, academically successful, politically independent, and in the native strain of dissent. Attempts to suggest otherwise, by the press, the university authorities, and, not least, prominent social democrats of the Old Left, fell over the available evidence. Kerr himself began by declaring that "49 per cent of the hard-core group are followers of the Castro-Mao line," and that "up to 40 per cent of the hard-core participants" were from off-campus and were "very experienced and professional people . . . tied in with organizations having Communist influences." [47] But the nonsense of this was soon so obvious that he was careful not to repeat it. Professor Lewis Feuer, writing for the social-democrat *New Leader,* tried to smear the FSM even more rankly. Describing it as "a magnet for the morally corrupt," he lamented: "Intellectual lumpen proletarians, lumpen beatniks, and lumpen agitators wend their ways to the university campus to advocate a mélange of narcotics, sexual perversion, collegiate Castroism and campus Maoism."

The Byrne Report was clear in discounting both Communist and off-campus significance.

> We found no evidence that the Free Speech Movement was organized by the Communist Party, the Progressive Labor Movement, or any other outside group. . . . We concluded that "non-students" were not a crucial element in the disturbances or in the FSM. Of those arrested in Sproul Hall for example, 87 per cent were enrolled as students.

Among the "non-students," the report listed "recent alumni living near the University, and in some cases employed by it"; former students who "had retained their friendships on the campus and planned to return to formal studies"; and "wives of students, particularly graduate students." All such "were for all practical purposes part of the 'University Community.'" And the report summed up its findings on the accusations of alien influence: "Indeed, we found no evidence that any FSM leader was subject to *any* sort of 'adult' discipline. Even those who are close to the various revolutionary Marxist groups seem in most cases suspicious of the older generation of 'party line' Communists." Feuer's cry of "intellectual lumpen proletarians" was no less wild than his cry of "campus Maoism." As two separate and independent academic surveys of the FSM revealed, the majority of participants came from the most intelligent, scholastically most successful and advanced section of the student body, many of them the holders of important fellowships and other awards. In confronting the American view of disaffection through failure, the FSM confronted the whole meaning of American success.

It confronted, too, American liberalism, and in doing so revealed the character behind the camouflage. Kerr was on record as exhorting "each individual . . . to teach children, in the home and in the school, 'To be laws to themselves and to depend on themselves,' as Walt Whitman urged us . . . for that is the wellsource of the independent spirit." [48] Governor Pat Brown had exalted a similar independence, however embarrassing to authority, at the University of Santa Clara in June 1961.

I say: thank God for the spectacle of students picketing—even when they are picketing me at Sacramento and I think they are wrong—for students protesting and freedom-riding, for students listening to society's dissidents, for students going out into the fields with our migratory workers, and marching off to jail with our segregated Negroes. At last we're getting somewhere. The colleges have become boot camps for citizenship—and citizen-leaders are marching out of them. For a while, it will be hard on us as administrators. Some students are going to be wrong, and some people will want to deny them the right to make mistakes. . . . But let us stand up for our students and be proud of them. If America is still on the way up, it will welcome this new, impatient, critical crop of young gadflies. It will be fearful only of the complacent and passive.[49]

The humbug of American liberalism that was plumbed at Berkeley would soon be plumbed on campuses across the country in a confrontation with the politics of the Great Society.

Above all, however, the FSM confronted the inevitability of corporation America, its disintegrating cities and lives, its lonely suburban retreats and desperate ghettos; the clamor of its salesmanship; its obsession with display; its management even of learning as an element in the economics of organized waste; its civilization of things instead of people. And by confronting it, the movement did for white students what the Greensboro sit-in had done for black ones. The inevitable ceased to seem inevitable. Speaking on the steps of the university administration building, Mario Savio represented a generation of protest.

> The conception that bureaucrats have is that history has in fact come to an end. . . . Negroes will not accept an end to history here. . . . The most exciting things going on in America today are movements to change America. America is becoming ever more the utopia of sterilized, automated contentment. The "futures" and "careers" for which American students now prepare are for the most part intellectual and moral wastelands. This chrome-plated consumers' paradise would have us grow up to be well-behaved children. But an important minority of men and women coming to the front today have shown that they will die rather than be standardized, replaceable, and irrelevant.

At the time, the Free Speech Movement may well have seemed a solitary outburst of small and localized significance. When Barry Goldwater was not so much defeated as overwhelmed in the Presidential election of November, Johnson could reasonably claim to embody a liberal-led national consensus without parallel, a coalition of organized labor, the colored, and the white poor outside of the unregenerate South, with the bulk of the middle class and most even of the rich, in defense of the new capitalism. Not even Roosevelt in 1936 had reached Johnson's 61 per cent of the vote, and certainly few of the rich had succumbed to Roosevelt's allurements. But Goldwater had voted against the Civil Rights Act in the Senate and threatened to inflame the Negro by a moratorium on reform; antagonized business scarcely less than labor or the unorganized old and unemployed by his precipitate assaults on public expenditure; and alarmed moderates of every class by his calls for a more aggressive response to Communism abroad, especially in Vietnam, where Kennedy's commitment of 785 "advisers" in 1960 had already grown to 15,500 in 1963 and 23,000 in 1964. White Americans who had no intention of allowing Negroes to become their neighbors or the classmates of their children shrank from inciting riots across the country by an ostentatious racial rigidity; those on the upper slopes of consumption who interminably bewailed the tax demands of public welfare shrank from inviting economic upheaval by a return to the outlook of the 1920s; while those who did not doubt their democratic duty to resist Communism and its revolutionary relatives abroad shrank from bombing North Vietnam and stripping large stretches in South Vietnam of all vegetation, from sending massive reinforcements of American boys to defend the American way of life in the jungles of Asia, and from risking war with China and the Soviet Union. Johnson might not excite general confidence in his honesty—not least when taking flight into the distances of the Great Society—but slyness was by well-attested precedent no drawback in the White House and was certainly preferable to the zeal of an archaic evangelism. He promised at least to keep America much as it was: its racial and economic disaffection contained by periodic reforms; its new capitalism sustained by an alliance of business with liberal intellectuals and the established leaders of labor and the minorities; its clashes with Communism more or less carefully controlled.

Yet by November 1967, a mere three years later, the consensus had all the appearance of a national hangover; its embodiment was widely regarded, even by those who still helplessly followed his progress, as an irrevocable rake; and the Great Society, when mentioned at all, was a very sick joke. Black riots of mounting violence and devastation had swept through American cities in successive summers. The liberal intellectuals who had for thirty-five years constituted the conscience of the Democratic party were distracted but increasingly disaffected. Sections of organized labor, not least in the public services, were becoming troublesome. Selected areas of South Vietnam had been stripped of vegetation, North Vietnam had been bombed for more than two and a half years, and a million Americans were in the field, with no prospect of a stalemate peace, much less an American victory. Demonstrations against the war were substantial, and civil disobedience involved young Americans of unimpeachable family and campus. Not since the Mexican War of the late 1840s, in the intensifying struggle over slavery, had America been as openly and passionately divided over the engagement of American forces abroad. Where did the responsibility lie? The generations searched, saw, and replied differently. While their parents distrusted Johnson and his administration, large and growing numbers of the young distrusted liberalism and traditional democracy itself. The "credibility gap" that opened for the parents with Johnson's failure to quiet the cities and his expansion of the war through the adoption of policies he had decried, had begun to open for their children in the gilded Kennedy years. Alongside and influenced by the development of the mainly black SNCC, there had developed the mainly white and mainly middle-class radical movement of Students for a Democratic Society. The Berkeley Free Speech insurrection was not a solitary outburst of small and localized significance. It was a sudden dramatic exposure of the student unrest which had been stirring since the late 1950s and whose search for a new America its own course powerfully promoted.

The dissent which had first displayed itself at San Francisco, with the demonstration against political witch-hunting, was encouraged by the Greensboro sit-in and the subsequent militant struggle for civil rights in the Deep South. But the condition of the Negro was by no means the sole source of spreading disaffection. It interacted with the whole frozen posture of foreign policy. Students on Northern campuses, especially where socialist or other groups of ideological estrangement existed, grew increasingly critical of the motives behind America's anti-Communist crusade and increasingly sympathetic to the concept of a revolutionary Third World. They had watched the American government welcome the Cuban revolution as lending American economic dominance a democratic façade, and then turn to assail it as no more than an instrument of Soviet expansionism when it set out to place its economy on an independent socialist base. The island became for them a symbol of government deception and of the part played by private enterprise in America's commitment to the Cold War. They constituted still a tiny minority on the campuses, but an active and impassioned one which stirred widening circles of disquiet. A Fair Play for Cuba Committee was founded in the same month as SNCC, and campus chapters disseminated its message. C. Wright Mills, whose analysis of American society was so influential in the development of student radicalism, visited Cuba himself in 1960, and his subsequent book, *Castro's Cuba,* was an indictment of American policy not only toward the island but toward "the problems of the hungry world." Then, in April 1961, came the Bay of Pigs adventure, with rapid revelations of considered government dishonesty. And student distrust of the liberalism which President Kennedy so glamorously represented was scarcely dispelled by the experience of those from Northern campuses who went South to work with SNCC.

Ironically, it was the social democrats of the League for Industrial Democracy who gave this distrust an opportunity for organized expression, and so impetus to the disavowal by young radicalism of their own obsolescent ideology, when in 1960 they decided to establish Students for a Democratic Society as a student department. A group of thirty-five met at Ann Arbor, Michigan, in the last days of 1961 to set up an executive structure for SDS, and Tom Hayden, who edited the campus daily at the University of Michigan, was selected to prepare a manifesto for the founding convention. Hayden circulated copies of his draft, inviting suggestions and criticisms; and in the middle of June 1962, representatives of eleven functioning chapters and individual students associated with SNCC met at Port Huron, Michigan, and adopted what became known as the Port Huron Statement.

Its opening sentence set its mood. "We are people of this generation, bred in at least modest comfort, housed now in universities, looking uncomfortably to the world we inherit." For what they found was an America of intrinsic inconsistencies: the sentiments in the Declaration of Independence alongside the degradation of the Negroes; the proclamation of peaceful purposes alongside the heavy economic and military investments in the Cold War; the strides of science and technology alongside so much meaningless work and unemployment; the luxury of the American rich alongside undernourishment for two-thirds of mankind. The very complexity of life frightened Americans, as material advances diverted them, from any new thought or action. "For most Americans, all crusades are suspect, threatening. The fact that each individual sees apathy in his fellows perpetuates the common reluctance to organize for change. . . . Doubt has replaced hopefulness—and men act out a defeatism that is labeled realistic."

Students were generally indifferent to their function as citizens and preoccupied with social and academic status. But their apathy was, after all, only the proper product of universities that delimited the nature of controversy before controversy began. An "exaggerated compartmentalization of study and understanding" divided the student from life, while a "cumbersome academic bureaucracy" contributed to "the sense of outer complexity and inner powerlessness." Intellectual independence was smothered by "the value standards of business and the administrative mentality," and teachers took service with the corporate economy and the arms race. And the sense of helplessness on the campus mirrored the condition of American democracy, a "democracy without publics." The political system perplexed the citizen, paralyzed exploration of policy, and consolidated the irresponsible power of military and business interests. Each of the major parties harbored within itself greater differences than existed between them; the whole localized nature of party operations discouraged discussion of national and international issues; large constituencies, such as the Southern Negroes, migrant workers, and the poor, were effectively deprived of proper political expression; and a jostle of special lobbies spent hundreds of millions each year "in an attempt to conform facts about productivity, agriculture, defense, and social services, to the wants of private economic groupings." Politicians responded "not to dialogue, but to pressure"; their speeches and campaigns were based on a degrading conception of what their electorate wanted to hear; and the politics of personality and "image" had displaced the construction of issues able to afford each voter "a challenging and real option." Not surprisingly, Americans were "buffeted from all directions by pseudo-problems, by the structurally initiated sense that nothing political is subject to human mastery."

The Port Huron students rejected such individual and collective estrangement and helplessness.

> We would replace power rooted in possession, privilege, or circumstance by power and uniqueness rooted in love, reflectiveness, reason, and creativity. As a *social system* we seek the establishment of a democracy of individual participation, governed by two central aims: that the individual share in those social decisions determining the quality and direction of his life; that society be organized to encourage independence in men and provide the media for their common participation.

This was very different from the "rugged individualism" of the American Right, and the students underlined the distinction in their economic principles: ". . . the economy itself is of such social importance that its major resources and means of production should be open to democratic participation and subject to democratic social regulation." And they firmly ruled out violence, as a contradiction of the whole meaning that they attached to the individual. "In social change or interchange, we find violence to be abhorrent because it requires generally the transformation of the target, be it a human being or a community of people, into a depersonalized object of hate."

The Port Huron Statement showed, in its emphasis on a democracy of effective personal participation and on non-violence as an agency of change, the influence of SNCC; as, in its assault on the bureaucracy, with the subservience to government and private capital, of the universities, it prefigured the Free Speech Movement. It formulated the fundamentals of emerging insurgency on the campus, and inevitably, therefore, its iconoclasm did not spare the

altars of American social democracy. The students condemned the
Soviet Union for its "total suppression of organized opposition,"
its "intransigence and evasiveness," but they did suggest that it was
"increasingly disposed to real disarmament with real controls."
What stood in the way, they declared, was "our paranoia about the
Soviet Union . . . our own reluctance to face the uncertain world
beyond the Cold War, our own shocking assumption that the risks
of the present are fewer than the risks of a policy reorientation to
disarmament, our own unwillingness to face the implementation of
our rhetorical commitments to peace and freedom." The League
for Industrial Democracy was furious, summoned the student
leaders to a hearing, and meanwhile banned the distribution of any
material in the name of SDS. In the end, and with the intercession
of veteran Socialist Norman Thomas, the league climbed down and
allowed SDS its independence. But the experience convinced the
students that social democrats were not radicals and were not to be
trusted in a radical movement. And it confirmed them in the sense
of remoteness from the Old Left, its peculiar dissensions and preoccupations, that they felt. The doctrinaires of Communism and
the doctrinaires of social democracy seemed to them equally irrelevant.

They looked to Mills rather than to Marx, talked of elites rather
than classes, and saw the source of resistance on the campus rather
than in the proletariat. They accepted the need for profound economic change, of course, and it was they who first promoted a
concern with basic economic issues in the militant civil rights
movement. They attacked the involvement of American capitalism
with foreign as well as domestic racism, and it was they who were
to organize the picketing of the Chase Manhattan Bank in April
1965, to protest at American investment in South Africa. Yet their
economic ideology was as indefinite as their political one. Theirs
was a mood rather than a program, a revolutionary socialism of a
very old and a very new kind, a commitment to the liberation of
the individual through real community control of economic resources and political power. And if they saw what they did not

want rather more confidently than what they wanted, this did not dismay them—though there were those, especially from the Old Left, neither wanting nor not wanting anything very confidently any more, who supposed that it should. Certainly Roger Williams or Garrison or Thoreau would have felt more at home among them than among their orthodox critics. Indeed, recognizing the American failure of the old radical ideologies and their fertility in factionalism, these latest insurrectionists made no effort to develop a definite ideology of their own, depending instead on a few insights and ideals, and believing that experience and events would lead them to the social forms they needed. Action would produce ideology, not the other way around. And in this they were only being constant to the trust that they placed in people rather than institutions. Like SNCC in the South, they set out to be helped no less than to help. It was this allegiance to self-determination that so aroused their sympathies for the Cubans and for the Vietnamese, and so aroused their anger at the purposes to which American power was being put across so much of the world.

Gradually, and naturally, SDS moved toward doing in the North what SNCC had started doing in the South—organizing the poor for self-assertion. With a $5000 grant in August 1963 from the United Automobile Workers, it established the Economic Research and Action Project (ERAP) for community mobilization, and students went to live in the Northern and border slums: among poor whites in Chicago, Cleveland, and Appalachia; among Negroes in Baltimore, Boston, Newark, Oakland, and other cities. Encountering suspicion, fear, hatred, even violence, or dismissed with listless indifference, they did, none the less, sometimes succeed in developing, through rent strikes, resistance to predatory urban renewal, and other protest campaigns built on their dogged encouragement, a sense of community and of power in collaboration. And they sometimes succeeded, too, in producing an alliance —however small and localized—of white and black poor in a nation of fast hardening racial hostilities. It was from such successes that there emerged a concept of "counter-organization," "counter-government," "counter-society" even, to confront the America of machine politics, lobby government, and One-Dimensional Man.*

Yet the poor have by no means monopolized the hopes of the student insurrectionists. America's perplexed middle class—from which, after all, the insurrectionists themselves have mainly come —has more and more seemed a promising region of recruitment, under the stresses of competitive consumption and, above all, military expansionism. Indeed, only a comparatively few members of SDS have involved themselves in slum community projects. Most have joined and remained with the general, and growing, movement of opposition to the purposes of American society. And the impulse for this growth has been provided largely by the progress of the society itself. The Berkeley Free Speech Movement was provoked by a liberal administration whose velvet rhetoric could no longer cover its iron reality. The revolt against American foreign policy, which has spread the appeal and activities of SDS so far across the campus generation, has been similarly provoked by the divorce between liberal pretension and performance, for a youth so responsive to ideals and so scornful of traditional illusions. In February 1965 American planes began bombing North Vietnam in an extension of the war that the Johnson Presidential campaign had denounced as reckless and unnecessary when Goldwater had suggested it, and student protests intensified. Then, in April, Johnson dispatched some twenty thousand paratroops and marines to the Dominican Republic, where a rebellion was seeking to overthrow the military regime and restore the democratic constitution, on the pretext that fifty-five "foreign-trained Communists" were gaining control of the rebel forces. The intervention seemed defiantly to reveal the cynicism of American foreign policy, its resolve to protect dependable anti-Communist despotisms in the name of democracy rather than run the risks of permitting popular insurgency to take its course. And not unreasonably this reinforced

* The title which Herbert Marcuse gave to his influential study of advanced industrial society (Boston: Beacon Press, 1964), and which so well expresses the image of America held by the student rebellion.

student opposition to the Vietnam war as an attempt to sustain an American client tyranny against a popular revolution, whether Communist or not. SDS sponsored a protest march of thousands on Washington and was central to the organization of campus teach-ins on Vietnam across the country. At first the State Department sent representatives to defend its policy; but by the time of the huge Berkeley teach-in, of May 21 and 22, it had come to regard such participation as counter-productive.

The 12,000 who met at Berkeley were not exclusively young radicals. Norman Thomas and Dr. Benjamin Spock and Senator Ernest Gruening of Alaska were there to speak against the war. The movement of protest was stretching far beyond the campus and the New Left. But there could be little doubt of who were in the forefront of the movement, giving it its fervor and its meaning for the mass of those in the audience. Bob Moses—Bob Parris now—was a speaker, and Charles Cobb of SNCC; Mario Savio of the Free Speech Movement, and Paul Potter, a former president of SDS. "Why is it," Potter asked, "that Vietnam has brought us to a confrontation with America that other similar situations could not?" He cited the installation of dictators such as Ngo Dinh Diem by America in South Vietnam; the deceits in which the American government had been discovered; the mounting ascendancy of the American military establishment which the course of the war revealed; the "continued integrity and strength of the Vietnamese people." But, above all, he seized on the parallels that he saw between Vietnam and America.

> The murders in Vietnam are no different than the murders in the South. The refusal to deal with the needs and aspirations of people in Vietnam is no different than the refusal to deal with the need and aspirations of millions and millions of poor people in this country. And the refusal to allow the Vietnamese people to have the right to shape their own destinies is no different than the refusal in this country to allow ordinary people to shape their destinies in the places where they live and work. . . . What kind of a system is it that allows the United States or any country to seize the destinies of other people and use them callously for its own ends? What kind of a system is it that disenfranchises **people in the South**, that excludes

millions and millions of poor people all over the country from the
mainstream and promise of American society, that creates face-
less and shapeless bureaucracies . . . , that consistently places
material values before human values and still insists on calling itself
"free"; and still insists on calling itself fit to police the rest of the
world? . . . We must name that system. We must analyze it, we
must describe it, and we must change it and control it, or it will
destroy us.[50]

The Vietnam Day Committee, which developed at Berkeley out
of the teach-in, decided to employ civil disobedience in protest at
the war and in the summer started trying to stop troop trains in the
Bay Area. SDS itself launched a campaign against conscription for
the war, and students began burning their draft cards. The main
thrust of its attack, however, was directed at the system of selective service, which, by allowing a deferment of military obligations
to those who attained certain academic grades, effectively drafted a
far larger proportion of the poor than of the middle- and upper-
income groups. Indeed, in demonstrating against the nature and
processes of selection, often by refusing to take the required tests
themselves, SDS members not only demonstrated against their own
privileges, but made their own call-up much more likely.

No one who has spent time with the insurrectionists of SDS, in
their protest demonstrations or their ceaseless probing of their
purposes, in their search for liberation, of themselves and others,
on the campus and in the slums, can properly make light of them. I
have met those busily exploring experience in sex and drugs, music
and words, and those of a delicate quiet; those who were tormentedly
inarticulate, as though wrenching themselves from conventional
communication to reach some deep spontaneous level of understanding, and those whose easy eloquence welled up and spilt over
their coffee conversation; those who had read widely in the literature of politics and those who seemed to have read hardly at all.
Yet all of them cared—that is what set them so plainly apart—
about being free and truthful and kind and valid; about people
rather than things; and about all people everywhere, their liberty,
their equality, and their right to the pursuit of happiness.

For them, patriotism is now a betrayal, anti-Communism a device, liberalism a sham. The flag has come to mean bombers over North Vietnam and marines in the Dominican Republic, and they identify themselves with it only in shame and anger. To cries that they should condemn the persecution of dissident writers in the Soviet Union or the national imprisonment of Hungary, they reply that they do, but that they condemn too, and more insistently because it concerns them more closely, the persecution of dissidence and the racial imprisonment of Negroes inside America, with the containment by America of revolution outside so as to secure the investments of American corporations and advance the authority of American generals. And in response to the claims of liberalism, they point to its record. As Carl Oglesby, president of SDS, said to a protest march in Washington on November 27, 1965:

> This country, with its thirty-some years of liberalism, can send two hundred thousand young men to Vietnam to kill and die in the most dubious of wars, but it cannot get a hundred voter registrars to go into Mississippi. . . . [Some] will make of it that I sound mighty anti-American. To these, I say: Don't blame *me* for *that!* Blame those who mouthed my liberal values and broke my American heart. . . . We do not say these men are evil. We say, rather, that good men can be divided from their compassion by the institutional system that inherits us all. Generation in and out, we are put to use. People become instruments. Generals do not hear the screams of the bombed; sugar executives do not see the misery of the cane cutters: for to do so is to be that much *less* the general, that much *less* the executive. . . . This is the action of *corporate liberalism*. It performs for the corporate state a function quite like what the Church once performed for the feudal state. It seeks to justify its burdens and protect it from change. . . . Corporatism or humanism: which? For it has come to that. . . .[51]

Such are the true Americans, the faithful to the first promise, the insurrectionists created by their obstinate loyalty to the unique meaning of America. It is this loyalty, of SDS, of the early SNCC, of countless young Americans who have challenged and hoped, worked and readily given, under no particular initials, that informs what has come to be known simply as the Movement. The Movement is wherever there are those confronting corporate America, in Newark with a rent strike, in Chicago with demonstrations against effectively segregated schooling, in the grape-growing areas of California with a struggle by Mexican-American migrant laborers to attain elementary collective bargaining rights. And the Movement is, not irrelevantly, where Americans seem closest to each other: where there is a meeting of men and women in a common endeavor that reflects their exploration of one another and of their proper natures; where there is so much less a turning inward, on the self, and so much more a turning outward, to the infinite creativity of human relationships.

The Vietnam war has inevitably become its central preoccupation, but only its central one; it needs no reminding that the war is merely the pre-eminent among numberless symptoms of the national sickness. Its cause is liberation, and its very organizational forms express this concern. Like SNCC and the Free Speech Movement, SDS has deliberately discarded conventional processes of decision, for fear of the decay into bureaucracy that the separation of leader and led has everywhere produced. SDS has a National Council, and a national office at Chicago; it has a president and a national secretary. But its functioning has been coordinated, not ordered, in this way. It has set out to be a community of individual consciences and has astonishingly succeeded. The regard for every view represented that marks SDS meetings, the search by all who participate for a collective moral expression— what feasible application could such processes have, the realist asks, to the America that exists? Yet it is surely not unwarranted to ask in return whether the America that exists is the only America possible; and, if there are other Americas that can be made, whether the one that exists is all in all preferable to one in which such processes would be the natural application of democracy. Oglesby has said, "There is something very Emersonian about SDS." There is. It is the idealism of America, in an America being mutilated by realism.

An intrinsic part of the idealism that makes the Movement are the Hippies—or whatever they may from time to time choose to call themselves—the insurrectionists whose emphasis is mental rather than social but no less moral for that. Their particular instruments of personal liberation, whether LSD or predigested Oriental mysticism, astrology or psychedelic decor, are less likely to last than their loose pantheism, the sense of the mystery and relevance of all life that so much of America has lost. It is in this, their rejection of the compliant moral dying around them, the air-conditioned coffins of success, for the infinite value of the individual search, that they meet the strain of insurrection in the past and elsewhere in the present. In August 1967 a small group of them joined the tourists queueing to watch the New York Stock Exchange at work and, having reached the visitors' gallery, threw dollar bills onto the trading floor below. *The New York Times* reported: "Stockbrokers, clerks and runners turned and stared at the visitors' gallery. A few smiled and blew kisses, but most jeered, shouted, pointed fingers and shook their fists. Some clerks ran to pick up the bills. After a few minutes, security guards hustled the hippies out, to cheers and applause from the floor." [52] There is a partition now, of tinted glass, between the floor of the exchange and the gallery. How insurrectionists like Roger Williams and Thoreau would have enjoyed the original gesture, along with the exquisite propriety of the response!

On the edge of the Movement is the young Old Left, the Progressive Labor party (PL), and the W. E. B. Du Bois Clubs. The Du Bois Clubs are Marxist, of the Soviet revisionist variety. They are accordingly close to the American Communist party, but they belong to the protest generation of the 1960s and have not wholly escaped its iconoclasm. Their internal discipline is lax and has allowed substantial deviation from what the Communist party itself would regard as the correct attitude. Demonstrating against the Vietnam war, against political restrictions on the campus, against racial discrimination, the clubs have been part of the Movement's action. But its fundamental mood is not theirs. They are reformist, not revolutionary. They want to make America a more or less Soviet version of what she is, a civilization of things; theirs is not the Movement's intrinsic revulsion from the supremacy of consumption and the mechanization of personality—or, indeed, from the remote manipulations of bureaucracy and the corruptions of coalitionism. Their own policy is one of manipulation, of managed change through a coalition with liberalism in the Democratic party and the trade-union movement. Characteristically, throughout its participation in the Berkeley Free Speech Movement, the local Du Bois Club leaned toward moderation, not seldom seeming closer to the stand of the Young Democrats than to that of the New Left militants. Even the Byrne Committee reported: "We found that those FSM leaders who had been closest to the Communist party, while radical in their aims, tended to be more flexible than many other FSM leaders and to advocate comparatively cautious and 'responsible' tactics."

If the Du Bois Clubs are a collaboration with the America of performance rather than of promise, PL is a rejection of performance and promise together. Established in 1962—with the public split between China and the Soviet Union—in opposition to the Soviet alignment of the American Communist party, it pursues a Maoist policy of revolution, not only for America, of course, but for the whole world, and, accepting that violence is the only real agency of change, maintains that the American masses must arm and train themselves for the assault on capitalism, with its liberal and labor allies. For PL, the black riots in American cities prefigure and promote this end, and some of its members, prosecuted and imprisoned since, openly sought to give the Harlem rioting of 1964 a positive revolutionary impetus. Like SDS, it works in the slums to stir the apathetic and bewildered poor, but for Maoist education and violent resistance to authority rather than for demonstrations of collective integrity, protest and demand, the development of a new direct democracy. It has fostered crucial campaigns of the Movement. It defied the State Department ban on travel to Cuba by arranging student trips—the first in July 1963—and took the lead in forming the May 2 Movement during the spring of 1964, to organize student protest against American intervention in Vietnam. Indeed, its combination of ideological assurance and militancy has won over a few student radicals. Yet it has so far had no appeal for the vast majority of those in the

Movement, who are ready to concede the validity of the Chinese revolution for China, the Cuban revolution for Cuba, the Vietnamese revolution for Vietnam, but are concerned in economically advanced, ceremonially democratic America with the whole nature and functioning of industrial society, with an American revolution that must produce new creative forms of man's relationship to his work, of man's relationship to machines, of man's relationship to other men. Above all, neither within PL—itself increasingly bureaucratic—nor in the world it wants, is personal search and liberation the overriding aim. And such an aim, with the sense of the peculiar American promise to history, is the essence of the Movement.

The Movement cleaves still to the American meaning. Yet the very organization with which the Movement arose has turned its back on that meaning now. In January 1965, a few months after the refusal of the Democratic Convention to seat the Mississippi Freedom Democratic party, Stokely Carmichael and other members of SNCC moved into Lowndes County, Alabama, where white voter registration was well over 100 per cent and not one of the Negroes who comprised the vast majority of the population was registered to vote. There were the usual attempts at intimidation by whites, with uniforms and without; but the civil rights workers, particularly Carmichael, who advertised his contempt for local officialdom, slowly dispelled the submissiveness of the Negroes. It might have been a Mississippi student project of a year or two back; only there was a perceptible diminishing of faith now, a clenching of the heart. SNCC had also been working in Selma, not far away, since February 1963, and early in 1965 Martin Luther King and his associates moved there to help with voter registration. Within two weeks some 3000 people, including King, had been arrested, and on March 7 several hundred Negroes and whites set out on a protest march to the state capital of Montgomery. State and county officers attacked them, injuring some seventy, among them John Lewis, SNCC chairman. Repeated attempts to continue the march, day after day, were blocked, and for the first time in American history a sit-in was staged at the White

House, in protest, by civil rights demonstrators. On March 17, Johnson proposed yet one more civil rights law, which would enable federal officials to register voters where racial discrimination was manifestly being practiced by local registrars, and at last, on the 25th, more than 20,000 marchers, under federal court protection, reached Montgomery.

For Negroes the march on Montgomery revealed how little had changed since the bus boycott in Montgomery of nearly a decade before. The Negroes had then, by months of struggle, won the right to unsegregated seating on the buses. Yet Montgomery, like Alabama and almost all the Deep South, was still a fastness of white supremacy. The federal government remained unwilling to use the powers it constitutionally possessed to insure Negro rights; it acted only when events ran amuck, and then only by judicial maneuvers and formal legislative adjustments. Such progress as there was affected so few that for the vast mass of Negroes in the sharecropper shacks and servant slums of the Deep South, it was a passing parade, lighting their lives for a moment and then leaving them all the darker by contrast afterward. The only escape lay, as it had always done, in a train to the North. And for more and more Negroes in the rest of the country, the Deep South seemed a symbol of their own condition, except that there was now no North left for which to take a train. They, too, had marched down the highways of the American promise, and they had met barricades, made up not only of white evasion and indifference, but of their own past, their self-perpetuating degradation and poverty, their inability to compete successfully on the terms that America laid down for success. Civil rights legislation proclaimed new opportunities but did not give them jobs, or kill the rats in their tenements, or make suburbs of their ghettos. Humiliation and rage and despair grew all the stronger for having been fed so richly on hope. And the racial antagonism which was the result, America fostered with a foreign policy that appeared to cast the shadow of racial arrogance across the poverty of the world. The dispatch of American forces to the Dominican Republic and the expansion of the Vietnam war drew impassioned protests from black militancy.

The McComb, Mississippi, branch of the Freedom Democratic party spoke for a mounting Negro opinion, especially among students and civil rights workers, when it issued a statement in July 1965, calling on Negroes to defy the draft. "No one has a right to ask us to risk our lives and kill other Colored People in Santo Domingo and Vietnam, so that the White American can get richer. We will be looked upon as traitors by all the Colored People of the world if the Negro people continue to fight and die without a cause."

In August, the same month that Congress passed Johnson's Voting Rights Act, the worst black rioting in the country's history so far swept Los Angeles for a week. It spread far beyond the ghetto, to reach fifty square miles of the city; it consumed or seriously damaged some 600 buildings, among them supermarkets, department stores, office blocks; and it cost at least 34 lives, with more than 1000 injuries and some 4000 arrests. At the height of its fury some 10,000 Negroes were taking part, and some 13,500 National Guardsmen had to be summoned for armed patrol of the streets. There was evidence of rudimentary organization, if only by young Negro gangs, and attacks were clearly directed against whites and white property; Negroes wrote "Blood Brother" on windows and walls to protect their buildings, and if the fire was frequently indiscriminate, the assaults themselves were not. Nor, it emerged from subsequent investigation, were the rioters by any means exclusively the Negro poor and unemployed; significant numbers of middle-class Negroes participated, and many more approved. If it was a riot of the deprived, it was also a rising of race.

The SNCC voter-registration campaign continued meanwhile in Lowndes County. A clergyman was shot dead and another was seriously wounded that August, in front of three SNCC field workers, but two trials failed to convict the attacker, a part-time deputy sheriff. And crude fraud insured the election of only whites to the important local board controlling cotton acreages and subsidies, despite a massive Negro majority among the eligible farmers. Gradually, however, the Negroes began flexing their muscles. Under the encouragement and scorn of SNCC, and with the intervention at last of a federal registrar, their number on the voters' roll increased till it outstripped the white registration. In November SNCC decided to form a separate political party—the Black Panther—for Lowndes and six neighboring counties. Carmichael pressed for an all-black ticket, but local Negroes, still hopeful of white cooperation, insisted on an integrated one. No local white would associate himself. Early in May 1966 some nine hundred Negroes gathered at the courthouse in Hayneville, the county seat of Lowndes, to nominate their candidates, and most of them carried guns. SNCC had moved far from its 1960 founding commitment to non-violence and to the cause of racial reconciliation through love.

For a week, from May 8 to May 15, 1966, some one hundred and thirty members of SNCC, including twenty-five whites, met at a campsite near Nashville, Tennessee. Probing their experience and their purposes, they decided that integration was neither possible nor desirable in the America they knew, and that association with traditional white institutions was psychologically harmful to the Negro. John Lewis, their chairman, and a representative of their past commitments, expressed his intention of attending the White House Conference on Civil Rights, in the planning of which he had participated. The meeting elected Stokely Carmichael as SNCC chairman in his place and voted to boycott the conference. In its subsequent public announcement SNCC declared that "the foundation and consequences of racism" were "rooted in an attempt by Europeans and white Americans to exploit and dehumanize the descendants of Africa for monetary gain"; that white America had tried to shift the responsibility for black degradation "from the oppressors to the oppressed," and that the White House Conference was an example of this process; that "the executive department and the President are not serious about insuring constitutional rights to black Americans"; and that SNCC could not "in good conscience meet with the chief policy-maker of the Vietnam war to discuss human rights in this country when he flagrantly violates the human rights of colored people in Vietnam." And the statement concluded:

We reaffirm our belief that people who suffer must make the decisions about how to change and direct their lives. We therefore call upon all black Americans to begin building independent political, economic, and cultural institutions that they will control and use as instruments of social change in this country.

The whites in SNCC were henceforward to work among whites. And in future, Carmichael told the press, Black Panther candidates would be "protected by the toughest Negroes we can find in Watts, Harlem, Chicago, and Washington. . . ."

The American idealism that SNCC had raised so high at Raleigh six years before was abandoned for an idealism of blackness, whose agency was to be a revolutionary alliance of color across the world, with an immediate American application in Negro separatism. All that this creed now needed to blaze through black America was a slogan, and the slogan was inspired by Carmichael during the "March against Fear"—begun by integrationist James Meredith, the first Negro to register at the University of Mississippi—through Mississippi in June. He cried "Black Power," and the cry came back from the ghettos, from Negro students on Negro campuses and from Negro students on overwhelmingly white ones, from Negro politicians and Negro journalists and Negro preachers. It did not, of course, mean the same to them all—though for all of them it seemed to express the meaning of their need. For some it merely meant clearly measurable progress to integration through the attainment by Negroes of significant public office. For some it meant mobilizing racial resources to capture parts of America, such as the big cities where Negroes were or soon would be a numerical majority, as bases for the development of their own political, economic, and moral force. Integration was feasible only between equals, and equality would be an illusion until the long dependence of the Negro on the white was finally dispelled. But for more and more Negroes, especially among the young of the ghettos, and increasingly for SNCC too, integration was a deceit. "Black Power" was an end in itself, an assertion of value, and an assertion inevitably—for what other way did America offer them? —through violence. It was the fury of the rioter formalized. And it was all the more formidable because its despair was careless of self-destruction. "We built this country," said Rap Brown, Carmichael's successor as SNCC chairman, in July 1967, "and we'll burn it down, honkies and all."

Du Bois, Garvey, the Black Muslims had been implicit—sometimes explicit—warnings of such a response to the frozen white face of America. And then Malcolm X—whom assassination subsequently martyred—no longer warned. He openly preached the doctrine of hitting back at humiliation and hypocrisy and violence, and hitting hard. He said what many, perhaps most, Negroes felt and were afraid to say, or did not know how to say, and once he had said it, others felt able to say it, too.* And they did more, year after year, than merely say it. The Negro rioting of 1967 was far and away the most destructive in the country's history. And the shooting now no longer came only from the troops of authority. The summer riot was becoming guerrilla warfare. In July more than a thousand Negro militants from all over America attended a Black Power Conference in Newark, New Jersey. It was impressive testimony to the alternative that now faced America, of fundamental change or racial devastation. Indeed, there was evidence enough of rudimentary planning and training within the rage of the ghettos. And with a hundred thousand Negro soldiers serving in Vietnam, and scarcely fewer elsewhere in the armed forces, Black Power militants could not reasonably be ridiculed for anticipating skilled recruits to their cause.

In Chicago, at the end of August and the beginning of September, nearly two thousand insurrectionists, white and black, from a multitude of organizations across the country, including SDS and SNCC, attended the National Conference for New Politics, to consider the future course of their confrontation with the character of

---

* *Life,* in an article on militancy in the ghettos,[53] has a tart story to tell. "An aged Negro lady, nearing death, was trying for one last time to explain her lifelong religious devoutness to her alienated son, an extremist. 'Don't you *know* what I've been praying for all these years?' she implored. Her son sighed that he couldn't imagine. 'I've been praying,' the old lady snapped, 'that the good Lord would strike the white man dead.' Her son later said, 'It occurred to me right then I didn't really have *everything* figured out.' "

America. The call to conference had been a manifesto of the Movement.

We need doctors and decent houses and decent food in Harlem and in Harlems everywhere, because slums breed an infant mortality rate twice that in middle-class America. Yet we spend our money on napalm that burns Vietnamese children to death. In order to make children die abroad, we let children die at home. And the President says we have chosen the lesser evil, to avert a greater evil. What greater evil? That both the children of Vietnam and the children of Harlem should grow up and be free? . . .

We do not feel that we now can govern our government. We do not feel that we can even govern our own private institutions—the ones we work in—for our own good: our schools, our hospitals, our stores, our factories, our transportation systems. . . . Whoever runs America, it is not the American people.

We intend to end the destruction of Vietnam. We intend to end the destruction of scores of other countries by the economic and political pressures of the great powers to keep them poor and power-less. We intend to abolish the armies that consume the world's substance. We intend to begin the building of "Mankind"—which we know our children will have to continue. We intend to end poverty, fear and despair at home. We intend to end the bribery and subversion of our private associations, unions and churches by the secret agencies of "our" own government. We intend to make our government accountable to us. We intend to make our own work-places accountable to us. We intend to make the election process meaningful again. We intend to make it available to those who have always been excluded from it. We intend to use other kinds of tactics of creative disorder: sit-ins and marches, rent strikes and labor strikes and school boycotts. We plan to invent our own institutions, to found neighborhood governments based on neighborhood power. . . . We will not be trapped inside the old parties; and we will not be trapped outside of them. And if we should build a party, it will be not merely a party, but a movement. We intend to start now.

Yet American idealism and the idealism of blackness proved incompatible. The Negro delegates caucused separately and confronted the white ones with collective Black Power demands. Martin Luther King himself, symbol for a decade of the struggle for integration, with the millstone of the Nobel Peace Prize round his neck and scorned as wanting no more for Negroes than absorption into the American middle class by moral osmosis, had his keynote speech boycotted by many of the Black Power militants. And Floyd McKissick of CORE, widely regarded as the last representative Negro leader through whom the races might communicate, proclaimed to the conference: "No longer can black people be a plank in anyone else's platform. From now on *we* have to be that platform. . . . Therefore, you must let us withdraw from you, for our problems are different from white people's problems." Is this, then, where CORE, the first non-violent militant movement for integration in modern America, and SNCC, those brave dreamers of a few years before, had been taken by their idealism? For though Black Power spoke in the accents of realism, it was an idealism still—only of hatred now, not of love; of despair, not of faith. Theirs was the promise of America inverted by the American performance. Was not their violence, after all, in Rap Brown's phrase, as American as cherry pie? The conference accepted the Black Power demands by a massive majority, with the consequent decision not to establish a national party of white and black together for the building of Mankind.

As their protests broke against the moral indifference of power in America, white insurrectionists, too, began withdrawing from their non-violent commitment. At the large October demonstration in Washington against the Vietnam war, young members of the Movement clashed with troops at the Pentagon. And John Wilson of SNCC was quick to declare that Negroes had "gained a new respect for the white Left." Certainly, on campuses and in cities, more and more whites turned from peaceful protests as sterile. Acts of civil disobedience became deliberately more harassing, and representatives of the war policy and police encountered less and less a passive resistance. America was moving the white generation of protest, as she had moved the black one, from confidence in the creativity of mere moral confrontation. Would she go further and unite the divided protest generation only in giving up America for an idealism of hatred and despair?

CHAPTER 5

The Unhappy Americans

"What's the good of an American who isn't happy?"—A
character in the novel Giovanni's Room *by James Baldwin*

Every people has some prevalent creed, a set of assumptions about man and his purpose, about the functioning of the individual in society and nature, that may or may not be formalized in a religion, that may even be contradicted by the lip service of such organized religion as exists, but that informs the fundamental considerations of conduct and is an essential aspect of the common identity. Such a creed is the integration of experience by the collective mind, a communication of the present with the past in a language of values, interpreting environment in terms of a moral order—or disorder, indeed. For a creed need not reflect a manageable or even rational reality. What it must do is generally conform to experience, whether that experience is of an apparently manageable or unmanageable, rational or irrational environment. That is the basis of social sanity. For when creed and reality conflict, when sufficient members of a society find expectation generally contradicted by experience and their language of values unable to reconcile the present and the past, then the collective mind can no longer cope with events, life itself seems paralyzingly incoherent, and the society is likely to suffer a nervous breakdown, till reality is forced back into the mold of the creed, the creed is changed to accord with reality, or each is altered by the other to produce a new agreement.

There are creeds of terror, such as imbued the culture of the Aztecs and imbue still some outlying societies of the world's traffic, which correspond to the experience of a reality so cruel that only the existence of malignant and capricious gods, insatiable of propitiation, seems able to make sense of it. There are creeds, such as Hinduism, of acquiescence, corresponding to an experience of such consistent defeat, an environment of such steady distress, that the very condition of living is considered a punishment, and hope is confined to earning release from rebirth by a righteousness of submission. There are creeds of escape, such as have from time to time been associated with Christianity, corresponding to the experience of an environment so irrational, so morally unaccountable, that life is seen as a mere preparation for subsequent judgment and reward on the other side of the grave. Creeds such as these serve to stabilize the societies that possess them. They corroborate distinctions of status and power and wealth. They are creeds of agriculture rather than industry, of magic rather than science, of the landlord and the peasant rather than the entrepreneur and the stakhanovite. They are creeds of confirmation and continuity, not of challenge and change.

There are, too, creeds essentially of protest, the creeds usually associated with modern, highly mobile, industrial societies. They are concerned less with explaining than with transforming man's environment. They seek not propitiation, submission, preparation, but confrontation and triumph. They are the creeds of revolution, initially promoted to overthrow a particular system of privilege, and conscripting to the purpose, or developing from it, general doctrines of human liberation. For such creeds, man is capable of commanding his circumstances, he is at the center of meaning, and God, if retained as an authority at all, survives as scarcely more than a nod of approval. They are the creeds of humanism, stretching in a line through the fastidious freeman democracy of classic Athens and the explorations of the Renaissance, to the liberal capitalism and Communism of today. And in this line America holds a crucial place. The first modern nation formally to advance such a creed as the matrix of its institutions, the very measure of its identity, it has dominated, through its ideological no less than its expanding material power, much of human history ever since.

With an inheritance of British political and religious struggle, and in an opposition to British imperialism that promoted resistance to Britain's own compromise order, the Americans proclaimed a creed that reflected the radical excitement and confidence of insurgency, strong indigenous traditions of separatist dissent, the claims of capitalist competitiveness, and a Western era in which reason was ousting God in the government of a middle-class universe. Liberty, equality, progress, the mastery by man of his environment, the pursuit—the implied promise—of personal happiness informed the Revolution, to become, with its success, the orthodoxy of the new state. It was, whatever the private motives of some leading patriots—and it needs little digging in the records to uncover much unwholesome and undignified greed—a vast ideological investment in man, the dedication of a whole young vigorous society to the virtue of compassion and the limitless capacity of the individual human mind.

No revolutions have lived up to the statements of their creeds. For revolutionary America, liberty scarcely applied to the Negro slaves or the still fair game of the Indians; equality did not involve the eliminating of class discriminations or the reserving of natural resources to collective ownership and enjoyment; progress, man's mastery of his environment, and the pursuit of happiness concerned everyone, of course, but not without due regard to the rights of property and the differences of upbringing as well as effort. Yet the creed remained generally credible because it corresponded sufficiently to the experience of America. National expansion to the Pacific and beyond, to the open frontiers of a great power; the possession and exploitation of seemingly boundless natural abundance; the prosperity produced by massive industrialization, supported a degree of social mobility that bore a recognizable resemblance to the claims of the creed. Even the Negro seemed at last to have been included, with the abolition of slavery and constitutional amendments to secure his civil rights, while the Indian, driven out or defrauded of one retreat after the other, was at last, too, rescued, for a distinctive survival in tribal reservations. If immigrants from Europe often encountered fierce resentment from among those with whose labor they threatened to compete, they were soon displaced as targets by further arrivals, and the contrast of their new circumstances with their old made all but the most recalcitrant failure look like relative success. The city slums might flow with filth and disease rather than milk and honey, but their walls were not so high as to produce the despair of colonial Ireland or the ghettos in Poland and Russia. Full political rights accompanied naturalization, and while poverty still flourished side by side with citizenship, there were more than enough examples of rapid enrichment to excite the poor with the prospect of imitation, if not for themselves then at least for their children.

The Irish and the Jews, indeed, go far toward explaining the persistence of popular faith in the American creed. The shrewd mobilization of their votes, by their own political bosses, in the cities where they congregated, gave the Irish Americans a common sense of achievement and of increasing power in the government of so immense and muscular a society, while Ireland itself struggled on, with a common sense of deprivation, against alien rule, till partition provided the southern counties with a small and vulnerable independence. The career of the Kennedys, from Boston machine politics, through the amassing of an enormous fortune out of real estate and stock speculation, to Harvard, Congress, and the White House, has scarcely been the typical three-generation progress of Irish Americans; but it does catch in a gilded mirror an expressive profile of their experience. They have seen their Church, long subordinate and variously disabled, when not vigorously persecuted, in Britain, grow to the largest in America and the richest in the Catholic world, while their traditional British enemy has dwindled across the map into deepening dependence on American economic and military patronage. And in almost too pat a curl of history's lips, a people for centuries on the edge or outside of the law in their country of origin have become in their country of choice virtually synonymous with the police. The Jews, remaining largely where they arrived, in New York, came to exercise an influence over the culture of America out of all proportion to their numbers. New York City has long been the national center of art, entertainment, fashion, advertising, the communication of news and ideas, no less than the national center of finance; and its transmissions, from trade unions and liberal clubs as from publishing houses, television networks, and the film studios in its suburb on the West Coast, have not failed to reflect the gratitude of a people who felt that they had found a final refuge from the recurrent pogroms of their dispersion. If gentlemen's agreements of discrimination survived in such fastnesses of Anglo-Saxon virtue as old Wall Street law firms, covenanted residential areas, and country clubs, the magnitude of the Jewish population in New York City, with the manifest evidence of its cultural impact, made of these merely trivial irritants.

There have always been Americans aware of the unresolved contradictions between reality and the pronouncements of their creed. What was the substance of liberty enjoyed by the poor, the physically and intellectually undernourished? How was the liberty of others to be secured against the liberty of each to exploit labor and natural resources as far as his means allowed and the market made adequately lucrative? If the processes of democratic government could not control the economic relations of men so as to protect individual liberty from the power of capital and the appetite of profit, then they were little more than ceremonial. A man might starve without sufficient payment for his work or even the opportunity to work at all, while in possession of a vote the formal equal of that cast by the president of Standard Oil. Whatever liberty might mean, it surely implied—as the Declaration of Independence bore forcible witness—the right to life. And what, indeed, did the proclamation of equality imply? All babies were created equally without teeth, but only a profuse innocence would suppose that this symbolized the further reality of their condition. The heir to a strip of tenement floor, educated at the local slum school some part of the way and entering employment on the sole strength of his need, was scarcely the equal of the heir to a million dollars, educated at the best of schools and universities, and promoted in his father's firm from clerk to director on the strength of no more than the absence of serious deficiencies. Similarly, all Americans possessed an equal right to influence public opinion and the conduct of government; but in the exercise of that right, most of them were far from equal to those who also possessed newspapers or enough money to provide the major political parties with persuasive subventions. Of progress itself, there appeared to be ample evidence. The country clattered and boomed with the advances of inventiveness and investment—railroads, mechanical reapers, canned peaches, motor cars, movies. But the forests were heedlessly despoiled, to encourage the encroachments of the desert; factories and mines spawned bleak streets of cramped and crippled lives; mass production turned much of human work into a set series of mechanical movements. Whom, after all, did progress serve—the one who owned the coal mine, or the many who mined the coal? Was it even ultimately progress? If man was busily mastering his present environment, was he not in the process producing another, more formidable still, to master him? The reality of American humanism was competitive, not cooperative, a search for individual success too often exclusive of, generally indifferent to, the collective benefit. How likely was happiness in such a society? Fun, yes—an industry grew and grew to afford more and more of it; satisfaction of a sort, of course—business and advertising provoked increasing occasions for partial or temporary satisfaction: but happiness? The very pursuit seemed to excite estrangement and misery, while the content was mocked by the lavish provision of impatient substitutes.

Fundamental disaffection was seldom allowed to reach far, however; the appearance of hesitant questionings among the many was soon enough answered by reforms. Some restraints were placed on the exploitation of labor and natural resources, and on the more primitive attempts at operating monopolies; inheritance and progressive income taxes promised to reduce the opportunities for the accumulation of flagrant fortunes; Social Security proposed to alleviate the more extreme forms of poverty; the demands of efficiency drew light and color, background music and psychologists into the factories and office blocks; the responsibility of private business not to conflict with the public welfare became a platitude eagerly propagated by private business itself. As technology and industrial enrichment transformed America from a mainly producer to a mainly consumer society, the bulk of the population began to enjoy the benefits of motor cars and washing machines, packaged foods and paper tissues, on a rising flow of income and credit. The pressures of real estate and related industrial interests promoted the provision of easy mortgages for private homes, and new millions entered into the preoccupations of property. For most Americans by far, the national creed reflected, as it reinforced, the performance and above all, always, the promise of their lives. Only in the Great Depression did doubt develop on a sufficient scale to threaten upheaval; but the very greatness of the depression made it seem alien, a lurch of nature against the American system. And the adjustments of the system which it produced, with the unprecedented prosperity that attended the Second World War and the subsequent military preparations against Communism, seemed effectively to have answered such misgivings as had emerged.

Liberty and equality were a national heritage. There were exceptions, of course. But that millions of Negroes enjoyed neither was, for many Americans, at least as much a reassurance as a rebuke. If Negroes were openly deprived of the vote in the South, and segregated in more or less involuntary ghettos across the country, this confirmed by contrast the advantages which belonged to being white. Similarly, the differences between American standards of liberty and equality, and standards prevailing in so many other countries, made the differences among Americans themselves seem insignificant. First Communism in Russia, then Fascism in Europe, then Communism again in one place after another, encouraged Americans to congratulate themselves on the reality of their rights. Indeed, the Cold War virtually ostracized serious criticism of American society. The political instability in democratic European states of close historical and immigrant ties, such as France and Italy, with the economic difficulties of politically stable Britain,

invited no sideways straying from the American alternative to
Communism. And who could deny the progress of America, her
industrial dominance, by the middle of the twentieth century? On
her own she was consuming half of the world's raw-material output. And if no state matched her in riches and power, none
matched her in generosity either. From her abundance she gave, to
help the economic recovery of Western Europe and even Japan, to
help and guide the industrial endeavors of the poor world from
India to Brazil. That the motives of the government might be
politic did not decry, indeed needed and used, the support of
many Americans for such help as a proper manifestation of their
creed and meaning. From the very inauguration of their separate
identity, Americans had considered themselves, part as apologists,
part as pathfinders, morally involved in the rest of mankind; the
long, if now fractured, tradition of providing a refuge for the poor
and persecuted of the earth, or at least of Europe, had reinforced
this attitude; and the enjoyment of material pre-eminence would
have seemed hollow without the conviction of moral pre-eminence
as well. Moreover, for a people whose whole consumer culture
placed such emphasis on the reaction of others as a measure of
achievement, the expected appreciation of those who benefited by
America's bounty was no little sign of America's success. And in a
society where nothing succeeded like success, the sheer scale of
national success intimidated doubt. If happiness still eluded most
Americans, that was, surely, not America's fault, but somehow
their own.

Yet all the while a disquiet was developing, stretching, searching
under the crust. Exploiting the mood of bewilderment and frustration that followed the fall of China to Communism and accompanied the costly Korean war, McCarthyism threatened the very
forms of liberty with a paranoiac patriotism. But McCarthy over-
reached himself, to clash even with the military leadership, and the
threat receded alongside the decline in his personal career. A
threat remained—much more dangerous for drawing so much
deeper from the system of power—to the substance of liberty,
from the growth of lobby government. Eisenhower himself, General

before becoming President, and leader of the party more closely associated with big business, felt it necessary to warn, in a farewell message at the end of his second term, against the encroachments by the "military–industrial complex." And Kennedy eloquently expressed the groping unease of America in his election campaign. He subsequently did much to increase it. The disclosure of government's lying in the Bay of Pigs invasion; the increasing evidence of "managed" news, admitted and excused by the executive as in the national interest; glimpses of the irresponsible power exercised by the intelligence services, made more and more Americans wonder what real control they possessed over the conduct of their affairs. Then came the Cuban missile crisis of October 1962, and the possibility of nuclear annihilation lost the almost horror-movie remoteness that it had had for so many millions before. The mounting realization that America was no more immune to destruction now than the tiny islands she used for her nuclear tests, regardless of how many missiles she accumulated or military bases she established beyond her boundaries, did for the nation's sense of security what the Soviet Sputnik had done for its sense of technological dominance. And as these sources of confidence diminished, so increased the anxious and angry sense of manipulation by unseen and unaccountable government agencies, of captivity to managed news, of distance from significant discussion and decision, of divorce from power. What meaning did the vote, the speech, the Bill of Rights itself retain when survival, no less, depended on the response of a single man to secret advice in an age of instant retaliation? Then Kennedy was assassinated. The spreading suspicion of surreptitious agencies everywhere at work, and of deceit as second nature now with authority, encouraged a wide section of American opinion, in any event surprised by the news of Far Left fanaticism in Dallas, to discard the official version of what had occurred, even when it was presented over the signature of an otherwise highly respected Chief Justice. And, all other considerations of what had occurred aside, the fact of the assassination seemed to symbolize the rising violence of American life, the crumbling ledge of manifest destiny at home and abroad that made both the substance and long-supposed objectives of American liberty ever more suspect.

The disquiet that had been seeping seemed suddenly to burst through the crust with the Johnson administration. During the latter Eisenhower and the Kennedy years, the businessman's character and aspirations of the Soviet leadership had become increasingly apparent; the desire of the Soviet Union, especially after the Cuban missile crisis, to reach a more or less clear accommodation with America, so as to reduce the risks of nuclear war and allow a significant diversion of resources from armaments to consumer goods, had been too plainly expressed for easy dismissal; and the public Sino-Soviet split had made all customary talk of a monolithic Communism hell-bent on world revolution absurd. Under Kennedy, American policy had been moving—the neighborhood of China excepted—toward the sponsorship of social democracy rather than the use of dependable dictatorships, as the shrewder and more congenial answer to the challenge of Communism in the poor world. Johnson reversed this movement. His dispatch of American marines to the Dominican Republic, where popular rebellion had broken out against the military regime, on the grounds that a few dozen "foreign-trained Communists" were among the rebels, restored the American posture of assertive suzerainty and support for reliable despotisms in the hemisphere. More inflammatory yet, he not so much broke as shattered his 1964 Presidential campaign pledges, made in response to Goldwater's then seemingly extremist calls for a more formidable effort in Vietnam, not to enlarge the American commitment there. "We are not about to send," he had proclaimed at Akron, Ohio, on October 21, "American boys nine or ten thousand miles away from home to do what Asian boys ought to be doing for themselves." Within a year the number of American boys sent nine or ten thousand miles away from home to fight in the rice fields and jungle of South Vietnam had risen from little more than 20,000 to little less than 200,000. Was this what the democratic process was about, the election of a President to adopt and pursue opposition policies that he and his associates had so persuasively assailed as dangerous, unnecessary, and futile? Distrust among Americans in the word, deed, and intentions of their political leadership—become a cliché in the phrase "credibility gap"—widened and deepened as the American military involvement in Vietnam continued to mount, American casualties commensurately increased, and periodic assurances from the White House and the Pentagon that the war was going well and that no new initiatives needed to be taken were constantly contradicted by events.*

As criticism of the war ineffectually grew within Congress itself, the sense of powerlessness felt by many private citizens expanded to encompass many of those holding public office, and especially those belonging to the party of the administration. The executive seemed to have acquired a decisive dominion over all expressions

---

* At the very basis of America's vastly expanded involvement in Vietnam, it eventually emerged, had been executive deception. It was the supposed attack by North Vietnamese torpedo boats on two innocent American destroyers patrolling the Gulf of Tonkin in August 1964 that had excited Congress to give the Johnson administration a virtually free hand in conducting the Vietnam war, that had excused the bombing of North Vietnam by establishing for many Americans the aggressive character of the regime there. But hearings by the Senate Foreign Relations Committee in early 1968 disclosed a different scenario. The two American destroyers had been not, as Defense Secretary Robert S. McNamara had claimed, on "routine patrol" but on an intelligence mission. They had not been, despite Secretary McNamara's categorical assurances, unimplicated in, even unaware of, South Vietnamese raids against the north then taking place. Indeed, Captain John J. Herrick, commander of the American task force in the gulf and himself aboard one of the two destroyers, USS *Maddox,* had been so manifestly convinced otherwise that he had requested air cover. Above all, there had been no certainty of an attack on the two destroyers. Captain Herrick had informed the Pentagon by telegram, a few hours before the outraged American administration had ordered retaliatory strikes against North Vietnam, that "review of action makes many reported contacts and torpedoes fired appear doubtful. Freak weather effects and over-eager sonarmen may have accounted for many reports. No actual visual sightings by *Maddox.* Suggest complete evaluation before further action."

Senator Fulbright, some three and a half years later, declared that he regretted "more than anything I have ever done in my life" his major role in steering the Gulf of Tonkin Resolution through the Senate. "If I had known of that one telegram, if that had been put before me on the sixth of August, I certainly don't believe I would have rushed into action. . . . It never occurred to me that there was the slightest doubt . . . that this attack took place." Senator Albert Gore, Tennessee Democrat, spoke for many Americans: "I feel the Congress and the country were misled . . . I know I have been misled."

of government. Where had the checks and balances, with which
the system had been so carefully furnished, gone? What sanction
did liberty retain beyond the removal, after four years in office, of
a President who in the meantime might break every promise he
had made in order to be elected? Was any President any longer
able to control the enormous resources of power under his formal
command? How far was he the master and how far the servant of
the insatiable military establishment, with its huge and swelling
importance to the economy, the huge and swelling claims that it
communicated for national security? How could he check the advice and keep pace with the activities of the secret services? The
revelations of massive bribery and manipulation by the Central
Intelligence Agency, within America and involving the most respectable institutions of proud independence, confirmed and promoted fears that liberty was being steadily undermined. Whether
the President had authorized such planned corruption or whether
he had simply not been told seemed equally alarming.

America's actions abroad accorded less and less with America's
creed. Wars which killed and maimed American soldiers in large
numbers were hardly to be welcomed; but they had never been
seriously assailed for as long as Americans in general considered
them to be concerned with self-defense or with succoring the liberties of mankind. The Vietnam war, like the relatively minor Dominican intervention, impressed many Americans as concerned with
neither. Indeed, in their flourishing suspicion toward the assertions
of their government and the haggard commonplaces of the Cold
War, more and more of them saw the fighting in Vietnam as
excited by American arrogance rather than by American security,
as morally indefensible and politically calamitous. The changing
client regimes in Saigon—whether military or civilian, similarly
despotic and corrupt—made the excuse of America's commitment
to the defense of the free world unconvincing; the increasingly
apparent popular base of the insurgent forces in South Vietnam
gave more credit to the claims of a revolutionary nationalism,
Communist-led or not, than to those for territorial aggression by
the North; while the escalating provocation of China and, if for

separate reasons, of the Soviet Union, in America's escalating intervention, promised the prospect less of accommodation than of collision with either or both. Not least, with the intensifying of the fighting, the spectacle of a poor peasant society resisting the greatest military and industrial power on earth contrasted more and more disturbingly with the vision that Americans had been taught, by history, religion, romance, to have of themselves and of what was proper. It needed a notable patriotic squint to see the Vietnam war as a struggle by America against superior odds with the weapons of virtue. The reports of devastation wrought by American bombs, as of graft and cynicism in the Saigon regime nurtured by American money, projected the image of Goliath rather than David. And this was not a foreign war like others in the past, whose clashes and casualties reached America suitably processed. Television delivered them raw and immediate to the home. Mothers and wives watched sons and husbands struck down before their eyes—even in "living color"—and a struggle that increasingly involved cities and villages did not spare women and children or cover the humanity of the enemy with uniforms and set battle scenes.

As the Goliath image was reflected in rising foreign criticism of America's intervention in Vietnam, unease among Americans increased. The emphasis on appearances in their consumer culture, no less than their traditionally "decent respect to the opinions of mankind," sharpened their sense of estrangement from themselves. And they were dismayed rather than comforted by their government's new apologies for the war, such as the Secretary of State's specter of a billion Chinese brandishing nuclear weapons, in terms of expediency. The ready arguments of national status might ring less hollow than the coinage of a crusade, but they were not the arguments of the American creed. Was the ultimate meaning of America for mankind, the hope and the protection of the oppressed and the needy, to be abandoned for "face" and naked calculations of power? Dissent stirred questioning; questioning, dissent. And the present probed into the past and the future. Had the commitment of Americans always been crucially to liberty?

The liberty of others no less than of themselves? And if liberty was to be their crucial commitment again, as it had been presented in the Revolution that shaped America, what would this mean for the relations of Americans to one another and to humanity everywhere?

The issue of liberty, made so importunate by the war in Vietnam, merged into the issue of equality, made so importunate by the simultaneous war in America's own cities. For long, the equality of the Negro had meant no more to Americans, nearly all blacks as well as nearly all whites, than his effective inclusion in the formal rights of citizenship. Partly in response to changes in the world outside; partly, to a reviving idealism, especially among the young, within America; partly, to the growing importance of the Negro vote and to pressure from the growing militancy of Negro impatience, more and more white Americans had come to regard the Negro's political and social subjugation in the South as an intolerable taunt, to the integrity of American democracy and its international role. They had encouraged the courts to interpret the Constitution with less regard to the susceptibilities and power of Southern white supremacy; they had moved their elected representatives to introduce reforms; they had sympathized with, even sometimes substantially promoted, demonstrations of Negro protest. But with the Civil Rights Act of 1964 and the Voting Rights Act of 1965, many of them supposed the Negro Problem to have been solved. The Negro had the protection of the law in securing equal access to places of public resort and, above all, to the voters' rolls throughout the country. If he was not grateful, he was expected at least to be satisfied. He was, it became clearer as riot succeeded riot, not satisfied at all. Indeed, the imposing reforms seemed only to have further excited his discontent and to have made his impatience more militant still. He dismissed the form of equality as so much fraud and, pointing to the degradation of the spreading ghettos, expressed his demand for the force, by a rising rage of race against property and person. Far from having been solved, the Problem appeared more insistent than ever.

In late July 1967, after ghetto explosions in several cities—the most destructive in Newark and Detroit—President Johnson appointed the National Advisory Commission on Civil Disorders to examine what had happened, why it had happened, and what could be done to prevent it from happening again. It was no body of inflamed radicals. There was widespread criticism of its exclusively moderate character. No Martin Luther King, let alone Stokely Carmichael, was among its number. Its two black members were symbols of a much enfeebled reformist strain, while among the nine whites was Herbert Jenkins, Chief of Police in Atlanta, Georgia. It was a commission of the middle way.

It reported in March 1968, and its pronouncements were little short of apocalyptic. "Our nation is moving toward two societies, one black, one white—separate and unequal. . . . To pursue our present course will involve the continuing polarization of the American community and, ultimately, the destruction of basic democratic values. . . . What white Americans have never fully understood—but what the Negro can never forget—is that white society is deeply implicated in the ghetto. White institutions created it, white institutions maintain it, and white society condones it." [1]

The commission detailed the degradations of ghetto life and found not the least provocative of them to be racism among the police. Carefully it answered white complaints that blacks were not escaping from poverty, as white immigrants had done, by their own efforts. It examined the drop in the demand for unskilled labor; the more profound discrimination suffered by the Negro than had been suffered by the white immigrant; such crucial cultural differences as the cohesive immigrant family and the disintegrating Negro one; the decline in the power of the big city political machines. "The immigrants usually settled in rapidly growing cities with powerful and expanding political machines, which traded economic advantages for political support. . . . By the time the Negro arrived, these political machines were no longer so powerful or so well equipped to provide jobs or other favors, and in many cases were unwilling to share their influence with Negroes." [2]

The commission predicted the direst results from the failure by

America to take adequate emergency action. It expected the black population in the cities to increase by 72 per cent in the next 17 years, to almost 21 million, while the continued exodus of whites to the suburbs diminished urban resources and employment opportunities. "In prospect, therefore, is further deterioration of already inadequate municipal tax bases in the face of increasing demands for public services, and continuing unemployment and poverty among the urban Negro population. . . . Large-scale and continuing violence could result, followed by white retaliation, and, ultimately, the separation of the two communities in a garrison state. Even if violence does not occur, the consequences are unacceptable. Development of a racially integrated society, extraordinarily difficult today, will be virtually impossible when the present black ghetto population of 12.5 million has grown to almost 21 million. . . . No American—white or black—can escape the consequences of the continuing social and economic decay of our major cities. Only a commitment to national action on an unprecedented scale can shape a future compatible with the historic ideals of American society." [3]

The commission proposed a crash program of new schools and new types of school; new jobs and new homes; higher levels of welfare assistance, with uniform national standards and the financing met almost entirely from federal funds; various ways of changing public opinion and the character of such public services as the police. It was a program that experts costed at between $10 billion and $20 billion a year,[4] or around one-fifth of annual military expenditure. But in response to the cry of alarm from the commission, to such respectable evidence of the yawning gap between creed and reality in America, came a shrug of authoritative shoulders. The chairman of the House Appropriations Committee stated that the money for such a program was not available. The Secretary of Housing and Urban Development declared that the commission's proposals were not impossible—just highly improbable: "We've gone about as far as we can go." Vice-President Hubert H. Humphrey, onetime crusader for the deprived and now knight of the Johnsonian garter, allowed the commission's claim that the nation was moving toward separate and unequal societies "may be true, although it's open to some challenge." The burden lay not on the government, but on "our free society." Former Vice-President Richard Nixon deplored the report's "undue emphasis" on white racism and called for sufficient force to put down future rioting: "Until we have order we can have no progress." President Johnson himself did little more than comment that the commission had spent an "unprecedented amount of money—millions of dollars" to compile its report.

The commission had written its own epitaph. It concluded its report by citing a statement from the testimony of the "distinguished and perceptive scholar" Dr. Kenneth B. Clark.

> I read that report . . . of the 1919 riot in Chicago, and it is as if I were reading the report of the investigating committee on the Harlem riot of '35, the report of the investigating committee on the Harlem riot of '43, the report of the McCone Commission on the Watts riot.
>
> I must again in candor say to you members of this Commission—it is a kind of Alice in Wonderland—with the same moving picture reshown over and over again, the same analysis, the same recommendations, and the same inaction.[5]

Yet it was not altogether the same. As white Americans watched city after city fired by riot, more and more of them felt impelled to consider why the Negro was not, after all, satisfied. And in doing so, more and more of them began to consider the nature of American equality. If the Negro was impoverished by poverty; if slums made bad schools and bad schools made slums; if inadequate skills and high unemployment and segregation, like fear and hatred and despair, fed each other; if inequality bred inequality—was this not also true, if with differences of degree and even kind, for whites? Was American society as vertically mobile as Americans had always been led to believe? Leaving aside the plainly poor—and that there were far more of these than most Americans had suspected, a spate of studies also made plain—was it reasonable to claim equal opportunity for white children? Did a home insecure with accumulated debt, a school overcrowded and underequipped, an environment with little provision for the excitement and exercise of the mind, allow a preparation for the highly complex conflicts of free enterprise equal to that provided by a home secure with accumulated capital, a school with small classes and large facilities, an environment with resources for travel, attendance at the more serious universities, access to the challenge of ideas? And did not the differential influence of family and acquaintance reinforce the effects of upbringing for employment and the pace of promotion? To be sure, the process was not invariable. Yet if some even from a background of poverty could become rich or intellectually distinguished, what did this do but confirm the discrepancies in general, presenting exceptions to assert the rule? Were the operations and objectives of free enterprise not intrinsically exclusive? In short, was substantial equality of opportunity feasible without substantial equality of circumstances? And was inequality of opportunity not also denial of liberty?

The Negro embodied the new bold probing disquiet. His Problem had to be solved, to make not merely the cities of America safe from rising racial violence, but America herself safe in her traditional assumptions. Yet a solution to the Negro Problem seemed only to recede. A society that prided itself on its riches could not, or would not, supply sufficient finance for the purpose; a society that prided itself on its abundance of skills and techniques appeared without the very ones now needed; a society that prided itself on its flexibility was revealed as rigid where suddenly it mattered most; a society that prided itself on its power saw itself as weak and frighteningly vulnerable. Why? The easy answer was the Vietnam war, which absorbed so much urgent expenditure of public care, endeavor, and wealth that there was little left for the issue of racial inequality. Yet did America really lack adequate resources of will and material to resolve the racial issue while waging a war in Vietnam? Or was it that the very interests which led America to pay for the war in Vietnam were opposed to her paying for the equality of the Negro; that a nation which would send its soldiers into Vietnam was a nation which would send its soldiers into the ghetto? Were the war in Vietnam and the war in the cities of America not, after all, variations on the same theme—the failure of the American system? Was the betrayal of liberty in the Vietnam war not the natural companion to the betrayal of equality in America? And did not both betrayals involve a further betrayal, of progress itself, by the American experience? Progress had always been taken for granted. It was an American trait. Steadily the nation grew richer and stronger. Yet its difficulties, its anxieties seemed only to grow as well. Indeed, far from progressing toward total conquest of their environment, were the Americans not progressing toward total defeat?

The most popular modern measure of American prosperity, the sale of motor cars, no longer promised ease and speed of movement but approaching paralysis. The more cars that were used, the more space in city and suburb was surrendered for freeways, for the widening of streets, for parking lots, for a profusion of drive-in amenities, to avoid chaos; the more space in city and suburb that was surrendered for such expedients, the more cars were used, and the prospect of chaos advanced. The mounting dependence on the private car sapped public transport, and the more that public transport was sapped, the more dependence on the private car inevitably mounted. People fled from the congestion and confinement, the pollution and noise of the cities, to make cities of the suburbs, and the countryside retreated as fast as it was pursued. People fled from one another to make life more formidable for themselves. Traffic grew still less tractable as still more commuters rushed to use the roads. Travel took more and more time, more and more tolerance, more and more risks, not fewer. A tiny mechanical fault, a single momentarily inattentive driver, and cars screamed and crumpled into one another or shuddered to a helpless crawl for hours on end. Not solely but, to be sure, not negligibly, the car corroded the quality of civilization in America. While highway was added to highway, slashing the country with gleaming assurances of escape to nowhere, theaters and cultural clubs and specialty shops in the cities closed down for want of sufficient custom; parks decayed into desolations of old newspapers and loneliness, or lairs of crime; communities became towers of apartments, where neighbors spoke to each other, if at all, only in the elevator between floors. Yet even to this, a stream of refugees, usually the middle-aged with married children, was returning from the more dreary and demanding disintegration of drive-in restaurants, drive-in movies, drive-in shopping centers, drive-in neighborliness; the initiation rites of cruising and petting parties for the youth, and the ritual of cocktail and barbecue and country-club petting parties, Parent-Teacher Associations and Community Drives, for the married; the togetherness and separation of the suburban diaspora.

The progress of the motor car offered less the long-pledged liberation than a predatory despotism. With ever higher parking charges and tolls for new roads, bridges, tunnels, underpasses, overpasses, bypasses; with the ever higher costs of necessary new models and their minimum maintenance, more and more of the American's personal income was consumed by his car, as more and more of the community's income was consumed in efforts to accommodate it. At the start of the 1960s, the price of acquiring, maintaining, and operating motor cars topped $37 billion, with a further $10 billion spent on highway construction. The total outlay on education, public and private, at all levels was some $23 billion, or less than half. This peculiar order of priorities would not have mattered so much if education had still employed sufficient funds for the purposes that it was expected to serve. But instead, increasingly undernourished, the public-school system, the bones of the country's education, displayed the softening of rickets. This was not because Americans had small regard for the public school. A distrust of higher learning as the buttress of a religious, political, or economic elite and as a reproach to those whose circumstances had denied them such benefit was certainly part of the frontier and fundamentalist traditions; it survived, with an infusion of right-wing super-patriotism, in suspicion of the universities, their often foreign-sounding professors and now rebellious students. But the public-school system had long held a central place in the popular creed. For successive generations of immigrant children, it had been the passage to assimilation. And for almost all Americans, it had been the prerequisite of liberty and equality, the premise of progress. Through its impartial processes, the advantages of wealth would lose their force as the ravages of poverty were repaired; the intelligence of every child could be developed to its natural extent, for the adjudications of a truly free enterprise, and a just society, without privilege or deprivation by background, would be promoted. Not impertinently, therefore, teachers, and especially the female staple, had long enjoyed large public regard, with fiction and film celebrating their impact on future Presidents and other great men. Yet by the 1960s they had become a sort of intellectual peasantry, earning in the main substantially less than skilled manual workers, and with many of them, indeed, earning less than the prevalent definition of a living wage. And the economic drawbacks were matched by others—the frequent anxious meddling by parents in the regime of the classroom, encouraged by the declining status of the teacher no less than by the declining standards of the school; the frequent overcrowded classes, required to admit yet more pupils; the frequent inadequacy and shoddiness of equipment; the frequent confusion of bureaucratic paperwork seemingly increasing in inverse ratio to its educational relevance. That there were still so many teachers whose training and talents could command far higher incomes and prestige, at probably less effort, in business, yet who continued in teaching all the same, was a sign of some surviving peculiar satisfaction to be gained by service in the public schools. But inevitably many good teachers gave up the struggle, and the more of them who did so, the further the standards of public schooling fell, and the greater grew the pressure on the remaining teachers of more profitably marketable training and talents to give up as well.

Inevitably, too, education became ever more unequal. Public schools in rich suburbs, supported by generous local taxation and special fund-raising drives as part of the social round, could afford to escape the cruder corruptions of the system, spending some $1000 a year per pupil; possessing spacious buildings, with lavish modern equipment; employing a ratio of 7 or more qualified teachers to each 100 pupils enrolled; experiencing few failures by pupils to finish their studies; and sending a far higher proportion of high-school graduates to college than the national average of 50 per cent. A public school in a city slum, however, forced to rely all but entirely on the reluctant funds provided from outside the community, was likely to spend less—not seldom far less—than half the $1000 per pupil afforded by its rich suburban counterpart; possess dilapidated buildings and equipment; employ a ratio of 4 or fewer qualified teachers to each 100 pupils enrolled; experience many failures by pupils to finish their studies; and send a far lower proportion of high-school graduates to college than the national average. Resources, from good teachers to library books, flowed upward, from those schools and sections of society that needed them more to those that needed them less, in a momentum of imbalance. And instead, therefore, of reducing discriminations by background, the public-school system reinforced them, to make equality of opportunity even more of an illusion than the heritage of the home allowed. Further, outside the public system of education altogether was the private school, catering in the main to children of the very rich, at fees of around $2500 a year, and perpetuating the existence of a coherent elite.

The failure of American education to promote equality of opportunity has not, of course, distracted attention from its failure to fulfill other proclaimed purposes. As more and more Americans are coming to recognize, the rich endowment of a school is no guarantee of a good schooling, though poor endowment may well guarantee a bad one. In a culture of consumption, concerned so much less with the meaning than with the appearance of achievement, the schools are concerned much more with such measures of success as the acquisition of college places than with the quality of the education they offer. The consequence is a vicious circle of declining standards. The impetus at every level is not the development of aptitudes to their natural extent, for critical, dynamic service to the individual and the community alike, but the delivery of so many duly packaged minds as quickly as possible from one class to the next.

How are these minds to cope with an America so complex, so

demanding of sophisticated skills, vastly more in need of subtle and skeptical intelligence, of nurtured imagination, than it was only a few years ago? Progress of a sort has made obsolescent many conventional attainments of schooling; computers function efficiently today at the level of college entrants. The possibilities of far more leisure alarm Americans incapable of employing with any real pleasure or profit the leisure they already have. Choices profoundly affecting their lives confront Americans unprepared by the developed range of their thinking to assess at all significantly the implications.

The manifestations of failure by the society are striking. Even the military Selective Service test proves mentally insurmountable for something like one-quarter of those taking it, and the United States Department of Labor has estimated that the proportion of high-school drop-outs may reach almost one-third of all students during the 1960s.[6] It is not irrelevant that America has, of all advanced industrial states, much the highest rate of unemployment and public dependence on Social Security. Project Talent, a national testing program at the start of the 1960s that involved some 450,000 students, revealed that 99 per cent of those in high school could not write a five-minute theme without making mistakes in English. Certainly it is startling how commonly those who are in, or have completed, high school in this richest of democracies fumble and grope their way through their own language.

And higher education, molded by the material it receives and the pressures for results, diligently parodies itself. Credits are accumulated and degrees accordingly acquired at avowed universities, by passing tests—often through the memorizing of merely bought or borrowed lecture notes—on a clutter of courses, from a tiny slide of literature or the whole history of civilization to the proper preoccupations of ambitious brides. The bachelor's degree has lost all resemblance to a record of higher education. Yet the culture of consumption responds not by demanding that substance be given to the symbol, but by pursuing other symbols whose substance is not yet so suspect. If the bachelor's degree loses sufficient status, the master's degree becomes the threshold of achievement; if the master's degree then proceeds to lose its status, the doctorate has to be sought instead. The Free Speech Movement at Berkeley and similar recent campus insurrections reveal a deep and widespread discontent among the most intelligent and academically successful American students at the fundamental disrespect with which their minds are treated. It would not be unreasonable to assume, among students less articulate, and at lower educational levels as well, a growing sense of frustration, of bewilderment, of remoteness from an environment which their studies do so little to explain. For more and more Americans, in suburbs and slums alike, education seems less and less pertinent to the conditions and challenges of their society and, far from expressing and promoting collective progress, calls into question the whole nature and purpose of the progress they have supposed themselves to be enjoying. Their environment looms more hostile, more mysterious, more out of their control, with every apparent effort to understand and subdue it.

The air in the cities wears away the features from stone statues; it is only to be expected that living Americans should feel some unease at the silent activity of such air on themselves. Fertilizers are used with such abandon that the concentrated nitrates in the soil poison the water supplies of towns. Chemicals kill birds and animals alongside the particular pests at which they are directed. Manufacturers and salesmen press a profusion of competing synthetic remedies, in bags and bottles and sprays, on the public, without the slightest idea of how they may combine, or many of them themselves ultimately act, to affect plant, animal, and human life. "Some would-be architects of our future look toward a time when it will be possible to alter the human germ plasm by design. But we may easily be doing so now by inadvertence, for many chemicals, like radiation, bring about gene mutations. It is ironic to think that man might determine his own future by something so seemingly trivial as the choice of an insect spray." [7] America's attempts to command her environment appear increasingly incoherent and irrational. The constantly expanding use of chemical aids is advised, by the government as well as by interested private industry, for agricultural production. Yet enormous public subsidies are provided for the withdrawal of enormous acreages from farming. Until the consequences of such needless chemical saturation are far more clearly known to be on balance beneficial than they are now, the agricultural policy of the nation is a game of blind-man's buff, with immediate market profit as the blindfold. Similarly, suburbanization proceeds in bland disregard of what water and farmland requirements may be in a few years' time. The society squanders its resources as though permanent abundance were no less than the obligation of history. But there have been too many recent signs of history's inattentiveness or betrayal for the old confidence. Just as manifest destiny was shaken by the Soviet Union's initiative in space satellites and by the imminent possibilities of nuclear devastation during the Cuban missile crisis, so it is being shaken yet further by the spectacle at home of an America unable to cope with the appetite of the private car and the problems of public transport, to provide a proper education for her citizens, to prevent the decay and disintegration of her cities or the steady poisoning of her earth, water, and air. The democracy is anxious, and one would expect its anxiety to be producing a mighty endeavor at controlling the negligent expenditure of national resources. But the system whose characteristic operations excite the anxiety mightily resists any such endeavor as a threat to its very survival.

For more and more Americans, accordingly, the whole structure of their society appears antagonistic to concerted and coherent action for the collective benefit. During the Eisenhower years Congress agreed to appropriate $41 billion for a highway program—the largest public-works project in history, as Eisenhower himself described it—that paved further vast areas of America to advance the already unmanageable dominion of the private car. Yet proposals, involving expenditures of around $100 billion, for a program to secure clean water, or make the air in the cities safe, or subsidize the construction of low-income housing—let alone proposals demanding far greater expenditure to defeat the economic degradation of the Negro—meet insuperable opposition or inertia in Congress and Administration. But then a highway program serves the interests of rich and influential business lobbies, such as the car and oil industries, while the cause of clean water or safe air or low-income housing—let alone the cause of Negro equality—does not promise such profits to private enterprise as seem likely to compensate for the necessary expansion in public power. Indeed, outside of roads and, of course, defense—whose insatiable requirements are supposed essential for the protection of capitalism, provide private enterprise with exuberant profits, and constitute an acceptable way of taking up the slack in the economy—the business leadership vigorously discourages any rise in public expenditure above the level of pork-barrel politics. The traditional priorities of America are the priorities of private production, consumption, and profit. "Why can't history's most affluent, technologically advanced society act to make the black man a full participant in American life?" asked *Newsweek*.[8] And it replied:

> The inescapable truth is that so far America hasn't wanted to. On that point, there is, indeed, an American consensus—spelled out rather clearly in the way a democratic society allocates its resources. America spends $75 billion for defense but only $7 billion on welfare for the poor, $17.4 billion for tobacco and liquor but only $1.6 billion for the war on poverty, $3.2 billion for cosmetics and toiletries but only $400 million a year for the training of adult unemployed.

Some of these contrasts may have unhelpful implications. There is no reason to suppose that, in "history's most affluent, technologically advanced society," the eradication of poverty would require the surrender of the cocktail habit, or the training of the adult unemployed deprive the American armpit of deodorant. An American democracy less feverishly engaged in consumer emulation might well spend less on its drink and cosmetics, less on its packaging, its gadgets, its fun, and far less than the many billions of dollars dissipated annually on advertising.* An Amer-

---

* In 1962 more than $12 billion went on advertising media alone (*Statistical Abstract of the United States: 1963*, Washington, p. 846). Paul A. Baran and Paul M. Sweezy in *Monopoly Capital* (New York: Monthly Review Press, 1966) estimate that, together with "outlays on market research, public relations, commercial design, and similar services carried

ican democracy at all significantly engaged in raising the collective quality of its civilization would certainly spend far more than it does on education, public transport, town planning, the pro- tection of health, the elimination of slums and unemployment. An American democracy fundamentally engaged in promoting the liberty, equality, progress, happiness of its members, let alone of men everywhere, would regard as mad the squandering of one- tenth its national product and so much more of its highest human talent and training [9] on a military posture that substitutes fear for faith, cruelty for creativity, the sustenance of poverty and preju- dice for the explorations of generosity and reason.

But this, like the *Newsweek* reply, begs the basic question. Is America in force, as in form, a democracy, so that the allocation of national resources is a deliberate popular decision? Are Ameri- cans generally agreed that it is more important to spend so many minds and so much money on the military establishment and its activities than it is to arrest and begin reversing the decay of the nation's cities; or that the provision of clean and sufficient water should be neglected while the provision of still more highways should be heedlessly pursued? To maintain merely that Americans have a free and periodic choice at the polls is to disguise the narrow limits within which that choice really operates. Voters are presented with the opportunity to decide not between the claims on national resources of urban recovery or defense, secure water or new roads, but between two versions, more or less the same, of an over-all policy promoting the priorities of private enterprise and proclaiming itself the sole alternative to anarchy or labor-camp socialism. The existence of two, in practice exclusively competi- tive, political parties, each containing similar elements of reform and reaction, and both committed to winning power by wooing the uncertain center of the electorate, is a patent recipe for the regime of confirmation by debasement rather than of progress by explora- tion and change. As in American television, so in American poli-

out by advertising agencies and other specialized firms," advertising ex- penditure each year "now probably exceeds $20 billion. And this does not include the costs of market research, advertising work, designing, etc., carried on within the producing corporations themselves" (p. 119).

tics, the appeal is aimed at what is measured, by the controlling networks and within the confines they lay down, to be the lowest common denominator of taste, fear, and aspiration, and the measure becomes the medium in a downward-floating vote of effective popular choice and engagement. Indeed, like television, the political processes increasingly invite disdain, doubt, or apathy. The recent rise of street pressures aside, Presidential contests that register polls of less than two-thirds the number of voters do not reflect a democracy in its prime. The mass of Americans constitutes a sort of second chamber, with functions of review carefully circumscribed to approving one of the two, in general barely distinguishable, drafts set before it. It is proprietorship, with its corporate management, that commands the nation's resources between and beyond the ceremony of the polls. Those who profit most from the nature of the social system are in the strongest position to affect the course of its development, and their strength is not unpredictably directed toward reinforcing the basis of their profit. The fundamental movement of the society is toward becoming and, willy-nilly, seeming more of what it is, as age establishes personality and reveals it in the lines of the face. In so far as America is plutocratic rather than democratic, she grows more plutocratic rather than less, less democratic rather than more. And the further that her personality is realized, the further it appears removed from the ideas that have for so long been supposed to inform it.

The failure of American democracy, the essential failure of professing democracies so far, has been the failure properly to deal with the independent power of property. It has never been difficult for defenders of American democracy to identify the betrayal of Communism: the ideological concentration on general economic liberty, equality, and progress, to the neglect or cost of their political and intellectual counterparts; the substitution in practice of bureaucratic power, self-seeking and remote from popular control, for the discriminations of private capital. Surely, had Communism not existed, it would have been necessary for the developing social system of America to invent it. For how else could it so success-

fully for so long have concealed its own betrayal, the widening
separation between the creed it proclaims and the reality it promotes? Yet to conceal betrayal is not to cancel it. Indeed, like the
effort to deny the assertion of time in the lines of the face, conceal-
ment usually ends in revealing betrayal more clearly, more repel-
lently. So, through their very acceptance of the claims made by
democracy in contrast with the performance of Communism, more
and more Americans are all the more disturbed by the performance of their own system. Told how much liberty they enjoy,
they feel themselves less and less free; told how much equality,
they feel themselves more and more unequal; told how much
progress, they feel themselves slipping backward into an environment out of their control and even understanding. Above all, and
relatedly, told that they should be happy, they feel themselves
engulfed in a profound American unhappiness.

Everywhere reality contradicts their creed. The economy is supposed to serve them. Instead they seem in helpless service to the
economy. Far from their ordering its course, its use of resources,
its employment of labor, its processes of production and consumption, it seems to be ordering them, with the sanctity of profit and
the sanction, if they disobey, of decline and depression. The market, ceaselessly interpreted by ambiguous oracles, seems increasingly mysterious and demanding. The more they are informed that
they themselves are masters of it, the more subject they seem to its
moods and its exactions. They know or suspect that the major
corporations cooperate as they compete, producing merchandise
and manipulating consumption for motives that have little or nothing to do with the general welfare. Nor is such disillusionment or
distrust by any means the monopoly of sophistication. Folklore
abounds in the suppression of inventions, such as the permanent
electric-light bulb or razor blade, that threaten powerful and persuasive economic interests. And, folklore aside, Americans whose
faith has withstood the buffetings of personal experience have been
advised, by sufficient recent writings and scandals, of how shoddy,
deliberately obsolescent, dangerous even, are the products they
exert themselves to possess. If so many of them submit, it is be-

cause they see no way of doing otherwise within the nature of their society; the system presents itself as a package deal, with liberty, equality, progress, happiness inseparable from the operations of the market. But while they submit, they see that this is not what America set out, and ought, to be about. They submit to the ubiquitous intrusions of advertising, the littering of their environment, the fragmentation of their lives, by conflicting titillations, allurements, alarms, commands. From the tale of little George Washington and the cherry tree to the prescripts of science, they are taught that they owe to one another, as America owes to them all, reverence for truth and for facts. But they are surrounded by lies and by fantasies, and they learn that their prosperity, their distinctive American survival indeed, depends on their acceptance of lies as truth, of fantasy as fact. They submit, but with a deep sense of outrage at being deceived and a deep sense of guilt at their own deceit.

History, tradition, the themes of patriotic hagiography root reward, mental and material, in work; security in integrity; the creative relationship of individual and society, the very essence of the American creed, in compassion. Yet Americans meet on all sides the mental devaluation, even punishment, of work, with the irrationality, even irony, of success. The "lucky break" presides over their daydreams because it appears to provide the most consistent explanation for the escape of others from mediocrity. Their purveyors of fact and fantasy alike busily recount to them the accidents of attainment to fame and luxury—the stock-market scoop, the gush of oil from the dying farm, discovery by a talent scout or by riches in the guise of love. Nor does the cultural commitment to honesty, to candor, find much support in the American experience. Business and labor leaders, Congressmen and intimates of the President, widely respected representatives of intellectual independence and righteousness in universities and churches, turn out to have been long engaged in criminal or, if legal, obviously unsuitable activities. And, not unaccountably, Americans believe that what has been eventually revealed to them constitutes merely the tip of what remains, through bribery, influence, cunning, or again luck, concealed. Their romance is crowded with the corrupting and the corrupted. And if the bad men usually come to a bad end— they are sometimes allowed a last-minute escape into reform— this corresponds, by the nature of romance, to the wish rather than the thought.

Similarly, Americans find integrity on all sides assailed, assail it themselves, assiduously to undermine their security. Ever more emphatically the impetus of their prosperity is waste, accelerated production and consumption by accelerated decay in functioning or style. The cry of their impatience and their anxiety is for the new, for the latest in objects and in human beings. There can be few if any societies on earth where it is more of a mortification to be old. Frantic efforts are made by the no-longer-young to appear younger, to disguise their own obsolescence, as with the objects they pursue, by their packaging. To look young, rich, successful, by every device of display and credit, is to be desired, to be desirable, to be reassured of value by the appreciation, the envy of others. It is a conspiracy whose means and ends are inextricably self-defeating. For in this devotion to the semblance of security, security itself, of employment and purpose, of personal solvency and self-assurance, of living as a continuous discovery and development, is, has to be sacrificed. And how many are the Americans who declare this, in the fearful suspense of their faces, the aging agelessness of their overture to death.

The salesmanship of self, the self's predatory dependence for purpose on being purchased by others, is the obsession with self, the exclusion of all other selves except as purchasers. Compassion is incompatible, is impossible. For compassion belongs to people, not to goods. And compassion is the movement of integrity, in an environment of relentless disintegration. The craving not for achievement but for the appearance of achievement, the competitive display of status and possessions, promotes a centrifugal momentum, in society and personality alike. Just as the city disintegrates into streets, districts, suburbs of consumer separation, so the personality disintegrates into separate experiences of consumption. The model American consumer is a little Los Angeles—suddenly a

Beverly Hills with the acquisition of a new motor car, suddenly a Watts with the sight of a neighbor's new appliance, and the crowded emptiness of a freeway in between. Of what relevance to him are those other models, of history and romance, whose lives lay essentially in a creative communication with other men, in a sense of personal service and collective accomplishment? The model consumer, despite the moralizings in such scriptures of consumption as *Time* or *Reader's Digest,* never intervenes when he can to rescue someone from suffering, even if his intervention is plainly without risk. For he responds not to another person suffering, but to the suffering of another person, as a new experience to be enjoyed. The harassed housewife in need of a headache powder on the television screen and the woman knocked down by a car in the street are similarly mere sensations. What meaning has liberty for him, beyond the constant opportunity to escape from himself into appearance and sensation? What meaning has human equality, when his only real relationship is with things, in a rivalry of illusions? What meaning has progress, in a society of such exclusive instant excitements and ends? But there are few if any model consumers in America. For model consumption demands a total surrender. And Americans yearn for the ideals that they betray in the process of betraying them. They yearn for the liberty to be wholly themselves, while they strive to seem something more and to become something less. They yearn for the dignity, the decency of equal individual value, while they vie in discarding both. They yearn for a progress that will release them from need and subjection, while they feed a system that confines them in need and subjection ever more closely. They yearn for reason in their work, integrity in their environment, compassion in their relationships, the further that they drive these from their lives. They yearn to belong to each other, the more self-wrapped and separate they become. They yearn to be happy, as perhaps no people has ever yearned to be happy—for did they not covenant with history for happiness?—but they are not happy, and the more that they feel this, the more unhappily they yearn.

History seems bent on mocking them. They who tamed the wilderness and thrust the frontier across mountain and desert and unamenable Indians, whose lean heroes strode into the fantasies of half the world, have problems of fat now and are intimidated in the mere presence of life. The America of the pioneer column and the stockade has become the America of the Polaroid camera and the sedative. And the promise that was the steel mills of Pittsburgh and the wrestling with the earth of the West is the promise of the suburban golf course and the retirement cities in the Arizona sun. When was it that they were the most masculine, the most active of peoples? Americans seem now to themselves—and know that they seem so to others—the most feminine, the most passive in their souls. And it is a femininity somehow sexually estranged, its image no longer the bountiful mother, but rather the rich divorcee collecting her master points at bridge. Indeed, sex itself, like the primal energy of America, seems to have thinned as it spread, till it is everywhere and nowhere at once, in toothpaste and motor cars, at drugstore bookstalls and businessmen's lunches and children's birthday parties, in the city like a bitch in heat rubbing itself against the sky.

In not the least cruel of its taunts, history has taken the Americans, so decently respectful to the opinions of mankind, so longing, so needing to be loved, and surely so deserving, and delivered them up to hatred instead. They who fled from, to deny and defy, privilege and oppression, who made an America for the deprived, they are now widely decried as the custodians of privilege and oppression, and the deprived claim to be making an America against them. They see themselves as properly the first champions of democracy; yet men, in the name of democracy, storm their embassies and abuse their flag. They, who opened up a whole new world by wresting, from an empire of landlords and merchants and generals, the right to popular rule, find now their most ardent admirers and allies among landlords and merchants and generals, seeking to keep intact from popular unrest the old world of rule by riches and by force. It is as though time had stood reason on its head. For why should revolution regard the first of revolutionary nations as its foremost enemy? Why, if Communism is the extinguishing of all real liberty and equality, of all progress beyond the exaltation of the state, do so many of the poor and the oppressed respond so readily to its beckonings? Why should a new creed of protest be needed, when the old so successfully survives to serve? Yet the very act of asking reveals the answers. President Johnson is reported to have told American troops in South Korea in 1966: "Don't forget, there are only two hundred million of us in the world of three billion. They want what we've got and we aren't going to give it to them." [10] He was no more than voicing, with unwonted honesty, what most Americans brood over in an embarrassment of fear, anger, and guilt. America may remain a call, but it is no longer an offering. The Statue of Liberty stands guard now in New York over tightly restricted and stringently controlled immigration, admitting the fresh rather than the "tired"; the rich, in reputable resources, rather than the "poor"; the useful to American power and prosperity rather than the "huddled masses yearning to breathe free."

America, once the embodiment, for most of mankind, of liberation and the future, is now become, for most of mankind, the embodiment of captivity and the past. From a multitude of military bases and missions around the world, America supervises her peace, ostensibly to prevent or confront Soviet or Chinese expansionism, effectively to intimidate or resist any attack on the existing structure of power. On the pretext of protecting democracy, she clasps to her national interests the most repressive and corrupt of regimes. And when popular disaffection rises in revolt against her clients, she speeds to their support, with counter-insurgency specialists, military supplies, and, should such prove insufficient, substantial forces of her own. Collective self-determination, by armed struggle when peaceful means are clearly precluded,* was the crucial commitment of the emergent American identity; such self-determination is crucially what American policy toward much of

* That the harassment of loyalists was part of this struggle, the record of the American patriots leaves no room for doubt.

the world today is directed to denying.* Stability was the cry of the order against which America rebelled; stability is the cry of the order which America now represents. The cause of a nation masquerades as the cause of mankind, and the morality of privilege wraps itself round in the rhetoric of democracy. If there are shades, how those of George III and Lord North must be fluttering with laughter!

The irony is perfect. For Americans themselves, whose dominant response to history was hope, and who peered so impatiently at the future, respond now to history with fear and look back longingly over their shoulders at the past. Change itself seems to menace them, and safety seems to lie in digging trench after trench against time. A nation which has not suffered foreign assault on its soil for well over a century vaunts a vaster arsenal for war, and with it warnings of the consequence such war might have, than any other ever. Signs to nuclear fallout shelters in city streets, broadsheets in hotel bedrooms on how to behave in the event of nuclear attack, periodic air-raid exercises, like the incessant assertions of American military might, wither the heart. And the newscasts every day, with their coverage of the current war, keep the paint looking fresh on the shelter signs. Nor is peace, even, a prospect without foreboding. The overriding search by private business for more and still more profitable efficiency is producing machines without the means of assessing, let alone controlling, their social effects. It is no accident that so much American science fiction deals with the mastering of man by his own contrivances. Indeed, science itself, which seemed once a daydream of endless if indistinct delights, is now become a nightmare, where the mind runs in terror from the sound of its own feet.

The land of refuge is more and more the land of escape, so many different devious ways of escape. Here are women entertaining not as honest whores but as strippers, as statues of ostrich feathers and fruit, as lines of synchronized kicks and twitches, as

* There are reflections to be found, of course, in the conduct of Communist great power; but there is small comfort in catching sight of one's face in the mirror of one's denunciation.

rabbits or cats or stranger animals still with bare breasts and aprons; here are contests and prizes for every aptitude, from composing cake-mix jingles or answering the phone with the correct slogan, to eating meat pies or staying awake; here is sport of every conceivable and previously inconceivable kind, with a constant supply of predigested diversion, from syndicated gossip columns to the peculiar domestic comedy of television; here there is always music, in elevators and along corridors, through supermarkets and across car parks; here are comic-strip supplements and sorority raids, psychedelic dance-ins and debutante parades. Without doubt, there is fun in America, available as nowhere else and never before in history. But it is fun without joy, fun without quiet, a thirst seeking desperately to quench itself on salt water. For more and more Americans, fun offers no escape, only a dismaying repetition of reality, and today is turned quickly into tomorrow with dogged drinking or a bedside bottle of barbiturates.

Reality is, on its own, formidable enough. But its increasingly obvious betrayal of expectancy—this makes it unbearable. It denies every claim of the American identity; it seems to deride all possibility of happiness. It requires a creed of terror or acquiescence or escape. And it meets a creed of protest, seeking confrontation and triumph. How long can a people sustain so profound and pervasive a contradiction? Like the individual who finds himself less and less able to explain and face his experience, the society itself must, sooner or later, suffer a nervous breakdown.

And the approach of such a breakdown is, surely, being signaled, by the high and rising incidence of mental and closely related physical illness; by a widespread unrest, a hectic movement from place to place, job to job, mate to mate; by an increasing retreat into drugs that deflect, soothe, or silence the mind. It is being signaled by deepening divisions, of bewilderment, distrust, and antagonism, between races, generations, neighborhoods; between parent and child, man and woman, man and man. It is being signaled by an irritability, encountered more and more often, that spins suddenly out of control. It is being signaled by a violence, appalling in its extent and apparently irrepressible growth, imbued with a hatred of other people. It is being signaled by a mounting hysteria of strain that seeks release in some sharp, overwhelming solution.

History rules out nothing any longer, including its own end. The power now possessed by America would make a breakdown there, such as overtook the Weimar Republic, dangerous to the limits only of man's capacity to destroy. But if one takes civilized survival for granted, an American breakdown, mild or severe, would continue for as long as its cause, till the American creed was changed to accord with reality, the American reality was changed to accord with the creed, or both were changed to a new, as yet unsuspected, correspondence.

That there are Americans who feel themselves sufficiently at home in reality cannot reasonably be doubted. For them, the American creed is as obsolete as the horse, outside of the political racecourse and pageantry, and must change from challenge to acquiescence, with terror and escapism if necessary as attendants. The existing system of power and priorities must be preserved and promoted, if only because no alternative ought to be risked. For them, property takes precedence over people, and prosperity needs no purpose beyond itself. The vast private corporation, with its single-minded pursuit of profit, its efficiency of scale and integrated economic processes, its paternalist conciliation of labor, and its separation of the person from responsibility, is the proper product of American culture. Under its sway, America must provide steadily rising material standards for all but a few million unfortunates by race, place, personality, and the selective operations of the market. If big government itself, like big business, must grow bigger, with the executive and its agencies engorging more power yet, this must be a process ultimately responsible to property and subserving the morality of profit. Certainly the expansion of the military establishment is to be supported, not only to protect and where practical advance American interests and investments, but to waste the increasing surplus of the economy and encourage an urgent and submissive patriotism. That stresses must develop, through racial disaffection, residual poverty, strides in industrial efficiency, and military engagements abroad, is only to be expected. But economic manipulation and an adequate display of force have contained these in the past and can surely do so in the future with the help of new techniques. Management of the news is an already old-fashioned form of adjusting public opinion. The progress in cybernetics, the application of war-game method to the problems of social conditioning, the passivity of consumer culture, the sense of dependence fostered by specialization, the widespread use and acceptance of mood-inducing drugs, all promise unprecedented opportunities for programing popular responses. What the society wants is an appropriate creed, and the diffusion of this, in the projected darkness of a struggle for survival against Communism—especially a Communism allied to a different race—seems by no means impossible. The more anxious, the more uncertain, the more alone Americans become, the more receptive they must be to a creed of obedience, of confirmation and continuity.

There are other Americans, not least among the young, for whom the existing system of power and priorities is a perversion of the whole American meaning. For them, people should take precedence over property, and profit should be subject to the question "at whose expense?" just as prosperity should be subject to the question "for what purpose?" They, too, see the vast private corporation, with its singleminded pursuit of profit, its relentless efficiency, its separation of the person from responsibility, as the proper product of American culture—but of an American culture that has failed by betraying its own humanist morality. For them, America has become "the corporate society," and that is its indictment. They themselves pronounce the responsibility of the person for every act done, by his corporation or government, in his willing name, with his assistance or connivance. It is the Nuremberg ethic, extended beyond war to all the significant moral operations of society. Americans working for the United Fruit Company or for Dow Chemicals are no less guilty of exploiting virtual serf labor in the Latin American banana republics or of providing napalm with which Vietnamese peasants will be burned, because these are legally acts of impersonal entities. Indeed, every American who supports a system that allows—more, by its nature promotes—such acts is personally responsible, personally guilty.

These other Americans see in the progress of their economy a process that confines instead of liberating the mind; that satisfies some old needs only to excite new and more numerous ones; that increases, not diminishes, privilege and discrimination. And they see in the truculent expansion of the military establishment and other agencies not responsible to the electorate the essential denial of democracy at home and abroad, the divorce of people from power in the apotheosis of property. If, they maintain, the prosperity of America depends upon the mounting contribution of expenditure on armaments, then the economic structure of America must be changed. If America's foreign investments require the perpetuation of luxury alongside want, and the cherishing of repressive regimes, then such investments must be abandoned or transformed to human advantage. If America's national security requires persistent intervention in the affairs of other peoples, the policing of poverty to prevent the spread of popular resistance, then there is something wrong with the American nation, and what is wrong must be righted rather than secured. For such Americans, the reality of America is a hideous inversion of the American creed. In the name of the individual, America uses the individual, even the individual whose interests she seems so lavishly to serve, to serve the nation, instead of using the nation only to serve the individual, and moving toward the use, and ultimate elimination, of all nations for the service of individual man. The nation exists not to express and promote the profound collective strivings of the individuals in it, but to express and promote the principles of power on which it is based, to express and promote its increasingly alien nature. For the faithful of the American creed, accordingly, what is needed is not a flight from collective institutions and commitments, but a true endeavor to achieve them: to make power the prerogative of people, not of property; to make prosperity cooperative, not competitive; to make progress the instrument of liberty, equality, and compassion, not of captivity, privilege, and indifference; to put reason, to put dignity, in the place of greed and fear; to advance the value of the individual by involvement in the value of every individual everywhere. For them, the American creed must be the basis for the establishment of a new reality—not by a romantic retreat into the past, but by an exploration of the future, for new social forms to accord with the force of human purpose, to depose at last the despotism of the thing and liberate the democracy of the person.

The conflict between the two Americas, of creed and reality, is taking place not only between the partisans of each, but within the minds of most Americans, torn between the two. And this conflict has been enormously intensified by the Vietnam war and by the blazing of the ghettos. Without either, the conflict would still, of course, have existed and increased, for it is intrinsic to the whole developing derangement of American life. Indeed, had neither yet begun, American society would be in the process of bringing both about, firing the ghettos with frustration, and a war, if not in Vietnam then somewhere else, with its foreign engagement to stability. But the ghettos are already burning and there is already a war in Vietnam, and the two together, far more than the sum of each separately, concentrate the multifarious failures of the American system. Such concurrent poisoned streams, with all the others, such as the educational rot and the crime rate, newly regarded in relation to them, indicate a system polluted at its source.

More and more, therefore, is opposition taking to the streets, proclaiming the system incapable of responding in any significant measure at all to normal democratic pressures for fundamental change. Even labor, so long seemingly comfortable in the many mansions of the new capitalism, is stirring with violence, seldom noticed beyond its immediate neighborhood only because the corporate mind is directed to the greater violence of the war in Vietnam and the rioting in the ghettos. Negroes, mainly from among the poor, but also in important and mounting numbers from the middle class and especially the intelligentsia, commit, encourage, or condone civil disobedience and violence, convinced that the system is essentially unprepared to yield more than the rhetoric of racial equality. And whites, mainly from the triumphant middle class, and within it especially from the intellectual elite, are moving to civil disobedience and even, among the young, violence, because government is proving itself impervious to moral protest and secured from any effective popular participation and control by resourceful private lobbies, entrenched party officialdom, a creeping paralysis of Congressional conservatism, and an executive of proliferating powers virtually invulnerable for the Presidential term, if not ultimately invulnerable altogether. Moreover, the system, by its nature, cannot be satisfied with mere acquiescence; it needs and insists on collaboration. And so the draft forces members of the very generation most widely opposed to the Vietnam war to fight it themselves or face long imprisonment. And it is the children of privilege, of rich homes and costly education, the heirs to American success, who are in the forefront of the protest movement on the campus and in the streets.

For such insurrectionists of the American creed, and for more and more Americans being drawn by the challenge of their disaffection—as for their counterparts in allegiance to the American reality—the failure of the society is the failure of the liberal consensus, the regime of accommodation between creed and reality through "moderate" and "reasonable" men and measures.

> The reasonable man has become the enemy of this society at this time. His reason has been soured by compromise and his moral conscience traded for a conscience of conciliation. The capacity to ask fundamental questions appears to have been lost. The criticism of the war, in the mass media and in Congress, has been generally marginal and directed to practical, tactical critiques. The worst thing that reasonable men seem capable of saying about our attempt to control another people's destiny is that it is not working out very well; if we were winning, it would no doubt be considered a good war.
>
> . . . it is the reasonable men of the liberal center who have created the conditions that have brought this society to crisis. . . . They cannot revitalize the system by simply wishing the left or the right away. If there is a danger of America becoming a garrison state, it is a real potential because the reasonable men in power for the last 20 years allowed what former President Eisenhower called the military-industrial complex to develop all out of proportion to our

national needs. Since they had narrowed the channels of power and
contained the efficacy of dissent by consensus, there were no unreasonable men in power to challenge their myopic assumptions. This
lack of fundamental opposition to men—or ideas—in power has
been the greatest danger stemming from the liberal consensus.[11]

It is this liberal consensus that presides over the corruption of
America's natural environment: the decay of the public services,
from buses to schools; the disintegration of the cities and the
despair of the ghettos; the delights of the shops and the dismay of
the streets; the culture of display, estrangement, and manipulation,
of the imperious machine and the desolate personality. It is this
liberal consensus that has mouthed the American creed while
busily feeding the contradiction of the American reality; that has
served property in the name of people, the corporation in the name
of personal responsibility, bureaucracy in the name of individual
liberty, the dominion of business lobbies and generals and secret
agencies in the name of democracy, the nation in the name of
mankind. For the truth is that informing the new liberalism is an
old trinity—capitalism, nationalism, realism—the power and the
privilege and the pragmatism of money. And on those principles,
the pursuit of happiness is essentially exclusive; it divides men, not
unites them, and so succeeds only in denying them their American
desire.

If there is a single word which the insurrectionists of the American creed use for the principle of their own pursuit, it is "love."
This not unusually meets a polite disparagement as a principle for
the management of so complex a society. But it is not easy to
dismiss the failures which the use of the word "love" as an over-all
contrast implies. And, indeed, the failures of America may not
improperly be summarized as lovelessness. In this, materially the
richest and strongest civilization of history, there is a fear and a
hatred, rather than a love, of life itself. Here in the very use of
language there is a withdrawal from living, a lowering of circumlo-
cution over the light of experience. Here is the antithesis of humanism, a society of machines which does not know what to do with
people, which would be so much more efficient, so much more

profitable—if not happy, for how can machines be happy?—without people altogether and with equipment performing the essential processes of production and consumption.

Is humanity to witness yet again, and perhaps for the last time, the self-inflicted blood-poisoning of humanism? Is America now at the stage that Athens reached when, transformed from a selective democracy into an imperial interest, it destroyed the whole society of a small island which wished only to stay outside its suzerainty and purposes?* Is the Renaissance promise that has been the development of American democracy to end in the inverted idealism of the *condottieri,* the devotion of ambition and courage, intellect and imagination, to the achievements of death?

Are the loneliness and anger, the perplexity and terror being turned to a violence that is only the other side of a desire to die? So many Americans seem finally defeated as human beings, by so much tension that has grown intolerable, by too much hoping too often denied. They are beyond unhappiness as they are beyond life. Behind the waiting in their eyes, is there a different, dark American dream—of liberty, equality, the pursuit of happiness in an annihilation of the mind? As they watch the aggressions of the machine, the spreading rubble of riot and war, is this where the answer meets them, in the stare of the lidless electric eye, among the sirens and the fire? Must the meaning of America end in the computer rooms of General Motors and the Pentagon, or the last first quiet of the Plains?

Yet if there is hope for the survival of humanism anywhere among the present devices of industrial advancement, it is here, in America. So much of mankind is American now—Italians and Russians, Australians and Japanese—building busily, as America builds, a civilization of appliances, of material exaltation, of exclusive authority, careless of the cost. But in America, where that civilization has so far reached furthest, at least important numbers

---

* Melos, in the Aegean Sea, refused to join the Attic League and declared its neutrality in the Peloponnesian War. In 416 B.C. the Athenians attacked the island, slaughtered all men of military age, and enslaved the women and children. Thucydides saw this act as inviting the retribution of the Athenian fall.

have begun to care about the cost, to ask why such a cost is necessary, to cry from the midst of their success its violations and turn instead to the creed that answered their earliest need. If there is an escape from the vinyl world of moral manipulation, of the gleaming blank corporate and bureaucratic state, and in the end the whining of the wind along lost streets, it is in the unhappiness that so many Americans have found among the promises blinking perpetually across their sky.

REFERENCE NOTES

Chapter 1: Violence and the Divided Hope

1. Quoted in D. W. Brogan, *Politics in America* (New York: Harper, 1954).

2. Quoted in Henry Steele Commager, *America in Perspective: The United States through Foreign Eyes* (New York: Mentor, 1948), pp. 28–29.

3. Cotton Mather, *A Christian at His Calling: Two Brief Discourses, one Directing a Christian in his General Calling; Another Directing Him in his Personal,* 1701. Quoted in Moses Rischin (ed.), *The American Gospel of Success* (Chicago: Quadrangle, 1965), pp. 25–26.

4. For an extensive treatment of the ways in which revivalism and the culture of the frontier contributed to popular suspicion of learning and the learned, see Richard Hofstadter, *Anti-Intellectualism in American Life* (New York: Knopf, 1963).

5. For a study of the leading nineteenth-century capitalists, see Stewart H. Holbrook, *The Age of the Moguls* (New York: Doubleday, 1953).

6. Alexis de Tocqueville, *Democracy in America,* translated by Henry Reeve (London: Longman, Green, Longman, & Roberts, 1862), vol. I, p. 43.

7. Quoted in Arthur Mizener, *The Far Side of Paradise* (Boston: Houghton Mifflin, 1951), p. 57.

8. F. Scott Fitzgerald, "The Sensible Thing," in *All the Sad Young Men* (New York, 1926), p. 219.

9. F. Scott Fitzgerald, "Handle with Care," in *The Crack-Up,* Edmund Wilson (ed.) (New York: New Directions, 1945), p. 77.

10. Justin Kaplan, *Mr. Clemens and Mark Twain* (New York: Simon & Schuster, 1966).

11. 1960 Census figures. Ben J. Wattenberg and Richard M. Scammon, *This U.S.A.* (New York: Doubleday, 1965), pp. 462–63.

12. Sinclair Lewis, *Babbitt* (New York: New American Library, 1961), p. 212.

13. Warren Leslie, *Dallas Public and Private* (New York: Grossman, 1964).

14. Neiman-Marcus newspaper advertisement, quoted in John Bainbridge, *The Super-Americans* (New York: Doubleday, 1961), pp. 136–37.

15. Carol Estes Thometz, *The Decision-Makers: The Power Structure of Dallas* (Dallas: Southern Methodist University Press, 1963), p. 100.

16. Ibid., p. 101.

17. Alexis de Tocqueville, op. cit., vol. I, p. 310.

18. D. H. Lawrence, *Studies in Classic American Literature* (New York: Viking, 1964), p. 62.

Chapter 2: The Solitary Sex

1. Martha Weinman Lear, *The Child Worshipers* (New York: Pocket Books, 1965), p. 24.

2. Ibid., pp. 106–107

3. Kinsey, A. C., Pomeroy, W. B., and Martin, C. E., *Sexual Behavior in the Human Male* (Philadelphia, W. B. Saunders, 1948).

4. Deschin, C. S., "Teenagers and Venereal Disease, a Sociological Study of 600 Teenagers in New York City's Social Hygiene Clinics," *Public Health News,* 1962.

5. "If homosexuality was equally frequent in the past, it is difficult for me to believe that E. Gurney Clark and Ann Sweeney would not have stumbled into it more often in the studies in our clinic 25 years ago. . . ." "Venereal Disease in the Teenagers," *Medical Aspects of Human Sexuality,* New York, vol. 2, No. 3, March 1968.

6. Wendell Hall, "The Fag-Jag on the Boob-Tube," *FACT,* vol. IV, issue I, January–February 1967, pp. 17–23.

7. James Baldwin, *The Fire Next Time* (New York: Dial, 1963), p. 15.

8. Figures from the 1960 Census. Ben J. Wattenberg and Richard M. Scammon, op. cit., pp. 265–67.

9. Dr. Abram Kardiner, quoted in "The Fag-Jag on the Boob-Tube," *FACT,* vol. IV, issue I, January–February 1967, p. 22.

10. Coty, in *The New York Times Magazine,* March 19, 1957.

11. Gossard, in ibid.

12. Ibid.

13. Aramis Master Plan, offering "aids that suit your private and public life." Estée Lauder, Inc.

14. *San Francisco Chronicle,* July 13, 1966.

15. "Tales of the Green Beret," a property of *The Chicago Tribune.*

16. Jack Wilson, "Potomac Fever." Seen in the *Albuquerque Journal,* June 13, 1966.

17. Advertisement in *The Los Angeles Times,* June 25, 1966.

18. Advertisement in ibid.

19. The Pink Pussy Cat, 7969 Santa Monica Boulevard, Hollywood 46.

20. *The Rand Corporation—the First Fifteen Years,* November 1963.

21. Quoted in "Is Rand Corp. Really a 'Dark Presence' Behind the Defense Throne?" by Willard E. Wilks, Armed Forces Management Bureau Chief, West Coast, February 1966. A Rand handout.

22. C. L. Baker and F. J. Gruenberger, *The First Six Million Prime Numbers* (Madison, Wisconsin: Microcard Foundation, 1959).

23. Joseph A. Kershaw and Roland N. McKean, *Teacher Shortages and Salary Schedules* (New York: McGraw-Hill, 1962).

24. Richard Moorsteen, *Prices and Production of Machinery in the Soviet Union, 1928–1958* (Cambridge, Mass.: Harvard University Press, 1962).

25. Irving L. Janis, *Air War and Emotional Stress: Psychological Studies of Bombing and Civilian Defense* (New York: McGraw-Hill, 1951).

26. *The Rand Corporation—the First Fifteen Years.*

27. Jane Jacobs, *The Death and Life of Great American Cities* (New York: Random House, 1961).

28. This and similar quotations are from Sun City publicity material.

29. *Time,* August 3, 1962.

30. *The Wall Street Journal,* June 7, 1966.

31. *Time,* July 1, 1966.

32. Report from Washington in London *Evening Standard,* May 13, 1968.

33. *The Drug Takers,* a *Time-Life* Special Report (New York: Time-Life Books, 1965).

34. Ibid., p. 112.

35. Ibid., p. 114.

Chapter 3: The Open and Shut Society

1. Frederick T. Martin, *Passing of the Idle Rich* (New York: Doubleday, Page & Co.), p. 149.

2. S. E. Morison and H. S. Commager, *The Growth of the American Republic* (New York: Oxford University Press, 1962), vol. II, p. 246.

3. Charles A. and Mary R. Beard, *A Basic History of the United States* (New York: Doubleday, 1944), p. 333.

4. Quoted in Fred J. Cook, *The F.B.I. Nobody Knows* (New York: Macmillan, 1964), pp. 68–69.
5. Alexis de Tocqueville, op. cit., vol. I, pp. 309, 311.
6. William Peirce Randel, *The Ku Klux Klan* (Philadelphia: Chilton, 1965).
7. Alexis de Tocqueville, op. cit., vol. II, p. 207.
8. Gabriel Kolko, *Wealth and Power in America* (New York: Praeger, 1962), p. 48.
9. Estes Kefauver, *In a Few Hands* (New York: Pantheon, 1965), pp. 189–90.
10. H. Magdoff, "Problems of United States Capitalism," *Socialist Register 1965* (London, 1965), pp. 62–79.
11. *Sunday Times*, London, July 30, 1967.
12. "Mental Health in the Metropolis: The Midtown Manhattan Study," 1962.
13. Gabriel Kolko, op. cit., p. 14.
14. *The National Economic Accounts of the United States* (Washington, D.C.: Government Printing Office, 1958), p. 110.
15. John Bainbridge, op. cit., pp. 75–85.
16. *Allocation of the Tax Burden by Income Class* (New York: Tax Foundation, 1960), p. 17.
17. Ben H. Bagdikian, *In the Midst of Plenty* (New York: New American Library, 1964), p. 137.
18. Michael Harrington, *The Other America* (New York: Macmillan, 1962).
19. Ben J. Wattenberg and Richard M. Scammon, op. cit., p. 478.
20. *Poverty and Deprivation in the United States,* 1962.
21. Lewis H. Kimmel, *Share Ownership in the United States* (Washington, D.C.: Brookings Institute, 1951), pp. 43, 46.
22. C. Wright Mills, *The Power Elite* (New York: Oxford University Press, 1959), p. 107.
23. Adolph A. Berle, Jr., and Gardiner C. Means, *The Modern Corporation and Private Property* (New York: Macmillan, 1933).
24. J. K. Galbraith, *The New Industrial State* (Boston: Houghton Mifflin, 1967).
25. Robert Sheehan, "America's Money Kings: A Boardroom Guide," *The Times*, London, August 7, 1967.
26. C. Wright Mills, op. cit., p. 128.
27. *The Times*, London, August 7, 1967.
28. A. J. Liebling, *The Press* (New York: Ballantine, 1964), p. 3.
29. C. Wright Mills, op. cit., p. 163.
30. Figures from *Survey of Current Business,* October 1964.
31. H. Magdoff, "The Economic Aspect of Imperialism," *Monthly Review*, November 1966, vol. 18, No. 6.
32. Marcus Raskin, "America's Night of the Generals," *Ramparts*, vol. 6, No. 1, July 1967.

33. Max Lerner, *America as a Civilization* (New York: Simon & Schuster, 1957), p. 917.

34. S. E. Morison and H. S. Commager, op. cit., vol. II, p. 912.

35. *The Reporter*, December 16, 1954, p. 3.

36. For a detailed account, read David Wise and Thomas B. Ross, *The Invisible Government* (New York: Random House, 1964).

37. In an article syndicated by the North American Newspaper Alliance, *Washington Post*, December 22, 1963.

38. Allen W. Dulles' speech at Yale University, February 3, 1958.

39. Quoted in *The Progressive*, vol. 31, No. 6, June 1967.

Chapter 4: The Insurrectionists

1. Vernon L. Parrington, *Main Currents in American Thought*, 1927. This quotation is from the paperback edition (New York: Harcourt, Brace), vol. I, "The Colonial Mind," p. 73.

2. Roger Williams, "The Bloudy Tenent," in *Narragansett Club Publications*, vol. III, p. 248.

3. Roger Williams, *Narragansett Club Publications*, vol. VI, p. 51.

4. Quotations cited in Stewart H. Holbrook, *Dreamers of the American Dream* (New York: Doubleday, 1957), pp. 3–30.

5. Jack Newfield, *A Prophetic Minority: The American New Left* (New York: New American Library, 1966), p. 211.

6. *William Lloyd Garrison by His Children* (New York, 1885), vol. II, pp. 230–31.

7. Arthur Meier Schlesinger, *Political and Social History of the United States, 1829–1925* (New York: Macmillan, 1925), p. 93.

8. Philip S. Foner, *The Life and Writings of Frederick Douglass* (New York: International Publishers, 1950), vol. II, p. 279.

9. Ibid., vol. II, p. 65.

10. Ibid., vol. II, p. 412.

11. Ibid., vol. III, p. 15.

12. Ibid., vol. III, p. 403.

13. *Journals of Ralph Waldo Emerson* (Boston, 1909–14), vol. V, pp. 285–86.

14. Ralph Waldo Emerson, *Essay on Politics*, 1844.

15. Ralph Waldo Emerson, *Self-Reliance*, 1841.

16. Ralph Waldo Emerson, *Napoleon; or, the Man of the World*, 1850.

17. Ralph Waldo Emerson, *The Young American*, 1844.

18. *Journals of Ralph Waldo Emerson*, vol. IV, p. 242.

19. Ibid., vol. VIII, p. 236.

20. Quoted in S. E. Morison and H. S. Commager, op. cit., vol. I, pp. 649–50.

21. "John Brown," a speech delivered at Boston by Emerson on November 18, 1859.

22. Ralph Waldo Emerson, *Napoleon; or, the Man of the World.*
23. Henry David Thoreau, "Economy," Walden, 1854.
24. Henry David Thoreau, *Resistance to Civil Government,* 1849.
25. Henry David Thoreau, *A Plea for Captain John Brown,* speech delivered on October 30, 1859, and published in 1860.
26. Henry David Thoreau, *Resistance to Civil Government.*
27. *American Federation of Labor History, Encyclopedia Reference Book* (Washington, D.C., 1919), p. 300.
28. Eugene Debs, *International Socialist Review,* November 1903.
29. Ibid.
30. Booker T. Washington, *Up From Slavery,* 1901. New York, 1929 edition, pp. 221–22.
31. *Report of the Fifth Annual Convention of the National Negro Business League* (Chicago, 1905), p. 45.
32. W. E. Burghardt Du Bois, *Dusk of Dawn* (New York: Harcourt, Brace, 1940), p. 90.
33. W. E. Burghardt Du Bois, *The Souls of Black Folk* (New York: McClurg, 1903).
34. W. E. Burghardt Du Bois, *Crisis,* No. XII, 1916, pp. 216–17.
35. W. E. Burghardt Du Bois, *Darkwater: Voices from within the Veil* (New York: Harcourt, Brace, 1920), pp. 49–50.
36. Quoted in Harold R. Isaacs, *The New World of Negro Americans* (New York: John Day, 1963), p. 135.
37. Amy Jacques Garvey (ed.), *Philosophy and Opinions of Marcus Garvey* (New York: Universal Publishing House, 1923), vol. I, p. 77.
38. Quoted in Roi Ottley, *New World A-Coming* (Boston: Houghton Mifflin, 1943), p. 79.
39. Asa Philip Randolph, *The World Crisis and the Negro People Today,* quoted in Gunnar Myrdal, *An American Dilemma* (New York: McGraw Hill, paper, 1964), vol. II, p. 1249.
40. Transcript in *Movement,* the SNCC California paper, April 1965.
41. Quoted in Jack Newfield, op. cit., p. 95.
42. For exact figures see U.S. Census reports, or Ben J. Wattenberg and Richard M. Scammon, op. cit., pp. 265–66.
43. Gerald Rosenfield, "Generational Revolt and the Free Speech Movement," *Liberation,* December 1965—January 1966.
44. Clark Kerr, *The Uses of the University* (Cambridge, Mass.: Harvard University Press, 1963).
45. Michael Rossman, "Barefoot in a Marshmallow World," *Ramparts,* January 1966.
46. Ibid.
47. Quoted in Hal Draper, *Berkeley: The New Student Revolt* (New York: Grove Press, 1965), pp. 59–60.
48. Quoted in ibid., p. 45.
49. Quoted in ibid., p. 103.

50. Transcript in *We Accuse* (Berkeley and San Francisco: Diablo Press, 1965), pp. 143–44.

51. From the transcript in Paul Jacobs and Saul Landau, *The New Radicals* (New York: Random House, 1967), pp. 260–65.

52. August 25, 1967.

53. June 10, 1966.

Chapter 5: The Unhappy Americans

1. *Report of the National Advisory Commission on Civil Disorders* (New York: Bantam, 1968), pp. 1–2.

2. Ibid., p. 15.

3. Ibid., pp. 21–23.

4. *The Progressive,* Madison, Wisconsin, vol. 32, No. 4, April 1968.

5. *Report of the National Advisory Commission on Civil Disorders,* p. 483.

6. David Lyle in *Esquire,* September 1967, p. 182.

7. Rachel Carson, *Silent Spring* (Boston: Houghton Mifflin, 1962).

8. *Newsweek,* November 20, 1967.

9. "Between one-half and two-thirds of the present engineering-science research and development manpower of the nation is now devoted to military work." Seymour Melman, professor of industrial engineering at Columbia University, in "American Needs and Limits on Resources: The Priorities Problem," *New University Thought,* vol. 5, nos. 1 and 2, p. 5.

10. Quoted by David Lyle in *Esquire,* September 1967, p. 116.

11. "The Redress of Their Grievances," *Ramparts,* vol. 6, no. 5, December 1967, p. 33.

INDEX

Abolitionism, 189, 191, 192, 193, 202–203, 210
Adams, John, 120
Adams, John Quincy, 20
Advertising, 59, 61–63, 76, 137, 307
AFL, *see* American Federation of Labor
AFL-CIO, 217
Alamo, 15, 32
Albany Movement, 242
Alien and Sedition Act (1798), 120
American Anti-Slavery Society, 192, 193
American Association of University Professors, 252
American Communist Party, 217, 222, 228, 229, 234, 271, 272
American creed, 285, 292, 309, 310, 317, 319-22
American Federation of Labor, 106, 107, 129, 142, 211, 212, 214, 216, 217
American Protective League, 126, 129
American Railway Union, 107, 212, 213
Anniston, Ala., 239
Arizona, 14, 42
Athens, ix, 282, 323

Baldwin, James, 54
Bay of Pigs, 165, 166, 261, 289

Beats, 234–36
Berger, Victor, 125
Berle, Adolph A., Jr., 154
Bill of Rights, 6, 8, 9, 101
Birmingham, Ala., 42, 239, 240, 243
Black Muslims, 226, 227, 248, 278
Black Panthers, 276, 277
Black power, 277–80
Bloom, Sam, 36
Boston, Mass., 29, 40, 76, 130, 133, 179, 181, 189
Bradley, Omar, 164
Brotherhood of Sleeping Car Porters, 228
Brown, H. Rap, 278, 280
Brown, John, 196, 203
Brown, Pat, 255, 257
Bryan, William Jennings, 109, 110, 112, 113, 114, 116, 118, 131
Buchanan, James, 195
Byrne Report, 255–57, 272

California, 14, 42
California, University of, 80–83, 250, 251, 252, 253, 255, 260, 266, 267
Capitalism, 17, 117, 144, 218; new capitalism, 146, 151, 153, 160, 161, 171, 174, 175, 176, 234, 251, 320
Carmichael, Stokely, 240, 273, 276, 277, 295

Catholic Church, 284
Central Intelligence Agency (CIA), 165, 166, 167, 292
Chicago, 48, 84–87, 126, 226, 270
China, 113, 114, 118, 288, 292
CIA, see Central Intelligence Agency
Cigarmakers' Union, 211
CIO, see Congress of Industrial Organizations
Civil disobedience, 208, 320, 321
Civil rights, 36, 102, 231, 232, 245, 248, 276, 294
Civil Rights Act (1964), 248, 294
Civil War, 102, 121–23, 124, 196–97
Clark, Kenneth B., 297
Cleveland, Grover, 213
Clews, Henry, 105
Cobb, Charles, 267
Cold War, 170, 231, 287, 292
Colombia, 115
Communism, 128–29, 168–70, 176–177, 282, 308, 309, 314, 318; Russian, 287; see also American Communist Party
Compromise of 1820, 194, 195
Confederate States, 111, 121, 190
Congress, U.S., 120, 121, 122, 173, 174, 175, 231, 291
Congress (Committee) of Industrial Organizations (CIO), 107, 142, 217
Congress of Racial Equality (CORE), 230, 233, 237, 239, 240, 253, 280
Conscription, see Draft
"Consensus," 171, 174, 175, 258, 259, 322
Constitution, U.S., 6, 9, 10, 11, 101, 102, 181, 190
Consumption, 58–61, 68, 98, 138, 145, 151, 312
Coolidge, Calvin, 226
Cooper, James Fenimore, 19
CORE, see Congress of Racial Equality
"Corporate society," 318
Corporations, 103–106, 136, 154–55
Credibility gap, 260, 291
Creeds, 282, 283, 287, 310, 311, 314, 315, 316, 322; see also American creed
Crèvecoeur, Hector St. John de, 12

Crime, 24, 48; see also Violence
Crisis, 222
Crockett, Davy, 19
Cuba, 113, 118, 165, 166, 236, 260–261, 272, 289, 290
Cullom, Shelby Moore, 113

Dallas, Texas, 29–49, 289
Danish West Indies, 116
Davis, Jefferson, 121
Debs, Eugene V., 103, 107, 108, 125, 209, 210, 212–18
Declaration of Independence, 5, 7, 10, 11, 117, 190
Defense, expenditure on, 144, 160–161, 306
Defense Authorization Bill, 164
Democrats, the, 20–21, 105, 109–11, 115, 116, 170–71, 249–50
Depletion allowances, 148
Depression (1929), 59, 138–43, 227, 287
Detroit, Mich., 295
Dickens, Charles, 3
Diem, see Ngo Dinh Diem
Disney, Walt, 71
Disneyland, 71
Dissent, 38–39, 100, 161–71
Dodd, Samuel, 103
Dominican Republic, 115, 116, 266, 274, 290, 292
Douglas, Paul, 148
Douglass, Frederick, 191–97, 210
Draft, 51, 121–26, 268, 275, 321
Dred Scott decision, 195–96
Drugs, 95–99, 271, 316
Du Bois, William E. B., 220, 227, 278
Du Bois Clubs, 271, 272
Dulles, Allen W., 166

Eastman Kodak Company, 248
Economic Progress Conference, 151
Economic Research and Action Project, 265
Education: 300–304; cost of, 300; in Chicago, 77–79; in Dallas, 37; higher, 303; inequality of, 301, 302; segregation in, 231–32; in seventeenth century, 18–19
Eighth Amendment, 101

Eisenhower, Dwight D., 21, 169, 234, 239, 288, 290, 305
Emancipation, 191, 197, 218
Emancipation Proclamation, 190
Emerson, Ralph Waldo, 198–204, 209
Equality, 5–6, 122, 131, 285, 287, 294, 297–98
Espionage Act (1917), 124, 125, 216
Evers, Medgar, 244

Fair Employment Practices Commission, 229, 232
Fair Play for Cuba Committee, 261
Faubus, Orval, 233
Federal Bureau of Investigation (FBI), 29n., 126n., 130, 172, 173
Feuer, Lewis, 256, 257
Film industry, 71–72, 137
First Amendment, 101, 120
Fitzgerald, F. Scott, 26, 27–28
Florida, 14, 151
Foreign policy, 118, 160, 173, 314–15
Fort, Dr. Joel, 97
France, 120, 121, 287
Franklin, Benjamin, 9, 11, 22
Free Soil party, 193, 194
Free Speech Movement, 208, 235, 250, 254–58, 260, 263, 270, 272, 304
Free Trade League, 191
Freedom Ballot, 244
Freedom Democratic party, 249, 250, 275
Freedom March, 243
Freedom Rides, 239, 240
Frémont, John C., 195
Fritchey, Clayton, 172
Fugitive Slave Law (1850), 196, 202
Fulbright, William J., 291n.

Galbraith, John Kenneth, *cited,* 100; 154, 155
Gandhi, Mahatma, 208
Garrison, William Lloyd, 188, 189, 191–94, 209, 210, 265
Garvey, Marcus, 225–28, 278
General Managers' Association, 213
Georgia, 102, 121, 202, 242
Ghettos, 247, 248, 287, 294–95, 320

Ginsberg, Allen, 182, 235
Goldstein, J. R., 78
Goldwater, Barry, 42, 43, 170, 258, 266, 290
Gompers, Samuel, 210, 211, 217
Graham, Billy, 40
Grant, Ulysses S., 197
"Great Awakening," 18
Great Britain, 14, 52, 235, 283, 284, 287
Great Society, 171, 249, 259
Greensboro revolt, 237
Gruening, Ernest, 267
Guam, 113
Guatemala, 118, 165
Gulf of Tonkin, 291n.

Habeas corpus, 121
Haiti, 116, 197
Hamer, Fannie Lou, 249
Hamilton, Alexander, 9, 10
Harding, Warren G., 216–17
Harlan, John, 102
Harlan County, Kentucky, 105
Harper's Ferry, 196, 220
Harrington, Michael, 150
Harvard College, 18, 220
Hawaii, 113
Hayden, Tom, 261
Hayes, Rutherford B., 197
Hayneville, Ala., 276
Haywood, William, 214, 216
Hearst, William Randolph, 113
Henry, Aaron, 244
Henry, Patrick, 9, 10, 117
Hippies, 235, 270, 271
Holmes, Oliver Wendell, Jr., 125
Homosexuality, 51-55, 98
Hoover, J. Edgar, 130
House of Representatives, U.S., 174
House Un-American Activities Committee, 167, 236, 250, 252
Huerta, Victoriano, 117
Humphrey, Hubert H., 250, 296
Hungary rebellion, 234, 260
Hunt, H. L., 42, 45

Illegitimacy, 54–55, 248
Immigrants, 12–13, 110, 284
Immigration laws, 132
Imperialism, U.S., 112–20
Income, personal (tables), 135, 147

Indians, American, 15, 25, 119, 120, 151, 283
Industrial Workers of the World (IWW), 107, 129, 214–17
Industry, 3, 17, 135, 158
Integration, 228
Intelligence agencies, 165, 167, 173, 289, 292
International Association of Machinists, 212
Internment camps, 167
Interposition, 120–21
Irish, 12, 123, 284
Italy, 287
IWW, see Industrial Workers of the World

Jackson, Andrew, 15, 20, 21
Jackson, Miss., 42, 240–41, 244
Jacobs, Jane, 83
James, Henry, 26n., 56
Japan, 115, 143, 224, 230, 288
Japanese-Americans, internment of, 167
Jefferson, Thomas, 6, 15, 21, 25, 121, 188, 195
Jenkins, Herbert, 295
Jews, 284, 285
John Birch Society, 84, 170
Johnson, Andrew, 197
Johnson, Lyndon B., 42, 93, 170, 249, 250, 258, 259, 260, 266, 274, 290, 295, 297, 314
Joint Chiefs of Staff, 164

Kahn, Herman, 78
Kampmeier, R. H., 53
Kansas, 107, 194–96
Kefauver, Estes, 141
Kennedy, John F., 111, 170, 239, 240, 259, 260, 261, 290; assassination of, 289; and civil rights, 241, 243, 248
Kennedy, Robert F., 239, 240
Kennedy family, 284
Kentucky Resolves, 120
Kerr, Clark, 252, 253, 256, 257
King, Ginevra, 27
King, Martin Luther, 170, 232, 233, 239, 240, 243, 250, 273, 279, 295
Kinsey, Alfred, 53
Korean war, 231, 288

Ku Klux Klan, 131, 225, 231

Labor Reformers (1872), 107
Labor unions, 103, 106–107, 211–15
Labor Youth League, 234
Ladies' Home Journal, 58
La Follette, Robert M., Jr., 148
Lampman, Robert, 150
Langdon, Olivia, 27
Las Vegas, 91
Lawrence, D. H., 49
League for Industrial Democracy, 261, 264
Legislative branch, 173
Lerner, Max, 164
Lewis, John, 243, 273, 276
Lexington, Ky., hospital, 97
Liberal capitalism, 282
Liberator, The, 188, 190
Liberty party, 193
Lincoln, Abraham, 11, 21, 121, 190–191, 196, 197
Lobbies, 77, 94
Lodge, Henry Cabot, 112
Los Angeles, Calif., 65–77
Louisiana, 241; Purchase, 14, 25, 194
Lovejoy, Elijah, 189
Lowndes County, Ala., 273, 275–76
Loyalty investigations, 167–69
Loyalty oaths, 131, 168
LSD, 271
Lundy, Benjamin, 188

MacArthur, Douglas, 164, 165
McCarran-Nixon Bill, 168
McCarthy, Joseph, 168–69, 288
McCarthyism, 168–69, 234, 236, 288
McComb, Miss., 275
McCormick, Cyrus, 22
McKinley, William, 110, 114, 117
McKissick, Floyd, 280
McNamara, Robert S., 291n.
Madison, James, 9, 10
Malcolm X, 223, 243, 278
"Manifest destiny," 112, 115
Maoism, 272
Marcus, Stanley, 32, 35
Marcuse, Herbert, 266n.
Marshall, John, 101
Martin, Frederick T., 106

Massachusetts, 18, 109, 133, 179, 181
Massachusetts Anti-Slavery Society, 192
Mather, Cotton, 17
Means, Gardiner C., 154
Meany, George, 217
Meiklejohn Award, 252
Mellon, Richard K., 154
Mental illness, 86, 145–46
Meredith, James, 277
Mergers, 157
Mexican revolution, 116
Mexican War, 14, 202
Mexicans, 151
Military establishment, 162–67, 173, 267, 292, 317–19
Military expenditure, 161
Military-industrial complex, 289
Mills, C. Wright, 154, 155, 159, 234, 261, 264
Mississippi, 240, 244–45, 249–50
Mississippi Freedom Democratic party, 273
Mobility, 137
Money, 4, 21–28, 30, 34–35, 146, 176
Monroe, James, 112, 115
Montgomery, Alabama, 232, 233, 237, 240; protest march, 273, 274
More, Sir Thomas, 7
Moses, Robert (Negro militant), 237, 238, 241, 242, 244, 249, 267
Motor cars, 299, 300
"Movement," the, 269, 270, 272, 273, 279
Murphy, George, 75

NAACP, *see* National Association for the Advancement of Colored People
Narcotics, 96, 97
Nashville, Tenn., 240, 276
National Advisory Commission on Civil Disorders, 295–97
National Association for the Advancement of Colored People (NAACP), 221, 222, 228, 231, 237
National Conference for New Politics, 7, 278
National income, 135, 139

National Negro Business League, 220
National Negro Committee, 221
National Negro Congress, 229
National Origins Act, 132
Nebraska, 108, 194
Negro World, The, 226
Negroes, 15, 102, 151, 173, 212, 218, 224, 228, 283, 298–99, 320; in Dallas, 30; divorce rate, 248; draft defiance by, 275; and equality, 294; in ghettos, 247, 287, 294–95; and homosexuality, 54, 55; illegitimacy among, 248; insurrection by, 187; labor, 230; and male prostitution, 54; marriages among, 248; migration by, 230; riots by, 248, 275, 278, 295; segregation against, 287; unemployment among, 247; in Union forces, 197; and U.S. imperialism, 119; urban population, 230; vote by, 230, 231, 232, 294; voter-registration of, 273, 275–76; voting rights, 287
Neiman-Marcus (Dallas), 32, 33, 36
New Deal, 140, 142, 143, 217
New England Anti-Slavery Society, 192
New England Confederacy, 181
New Leader, 256
New Left, 235, 250, 267, 272
New Left Review, 235n.
New Mexico, 14, 42
New Orleans, La., 239
New Reasoner, The, 235
New York City, 71–72, 248
New York Stock Exchange, 271
New York Times, 22n., 247n., 271
Newark riots, 295
Newhouse, Sewell, 185
News, management of, 289, 318
Newspapers, *see* Press
Newsweek, 306, 307
Ngo Dinh Diem, 166, 267
Niagara Movement, 220, 221
Nicaragua, 116
Nixon, Richard, 75, 297
Nonviolence, 238
North Star, The, 194
Noyes, Alfred, 209
Noyes, John, 183–86

Noyes, Pierrepont, 186
Noyes, Theodore, 185–86

Oglesby, Carl, 269, 270
Old Left, 2?6, 250, 264, 265, 271
Oneida, N.Y., 184, 185, 186
Oneida Community Ltd., 186
Open Door policy, 114
Oregon, 14
Orwell, George, 78

Palmer, A. Mitchell, 130
Pan-African Congresses, 223
Panama Canal, 114
Panama, Republic of, 115
Parks, Rosa, 232
Parrington, Vernon, 180
Parris, Robert, see Moses, Robert
Paternalism, 119
Pentagon, 78, 165
"People's capitalism," 153
Perfectionists, 183–85
Personal freedom, 100, 101, 117,
    119, 120, 122, 124, 152, 157, 158,
    167, 173
Philadelphia, Miss., 245
Philippines, 113, 114
Plessy v. Ferguson, 102
Police, 37, 239, 240, 295
Politics, 19, 21, 135
Pollution, 304
Population increase, 40–41
Populism, 110, 111, 218
Populists (People's party), 108, 109,
    110
Port Huron Statement, 261, 263
Potter, Paul, 267
Poverty, the poor, 135, 150–52, 266
Presidency, 163–64, 166, 174–76,
    292
Press, 91, 157; in Dallas, 38
Prices and Production of Machinery
    in the Soviet Union, 1928–1958,
    79
Primaries, 215
Primitivism, 19
Progress, 286, 288, 299
Progressive Labor party, 271, 272,
    273
Prohibition, 133, 137
Project Talent, 303

Property, power of, 308
Providence, R.I., 179
Public opinion, 69, 119, 318
Puerto Rico, 113
Pullman, Ill., 212
Pullman Palace Car Company, 212;
    strike, 103, 213
Puritanism, 133
Puritans, 17, 18, 22, 179
Putney, Vermont, 183, 186
Putney Corporation of Perfection-
    ists, 183

Quakers, 133

Race rioting, 231, 248–49
Racial experience, 134
Racialism, 218
Racism and police, 295
Radios, 137, 157
Rand Corporation, 78–81
Randolph, A. Philip, 228, 229, 243
Reader's Digest, 312
Reagan, Ronald, 43, 75
Reconstruction, 102, 197
Red raids (1920), 130
Reform, 209–10
Religion, 8, 12, 101, 131, 133, 182
Renaissance, 282, 323
Republican party, 21, 105, 195, 196
Research Center for Human Rela-
    tions, 97
Reuther, Walter, 250
Revenue Act (1950), 156
Revivalism, 18
Revolution, American, 7, 101; creed
    of, 282; as idealism, 210; versus
    reform, 209
Rhode Island, 179, 180–81
Richards, Harold J., 94
Richards, Mark, 183
Rochester, N.Y., 248
Rock Hill, S.C., 239
Roosevelt, Franklin D., 140, 167,
    227, 229, 258
Roosevelt, Theodore, 104, 112, 114,
    115, 117, 215
Rusk, Dean, 293
Russia, 115; see also Soviet Union
Russian Revolution, 129
Russo-Japanese War, 115

Saigon, 292
Santa Monica, Calif., 78
Savings, percentage of (*table*), 139
Savio, Mario, 208, 253, 254, 258, 267
Sayre, Zelda, 27
Schenck, C. T., 125
SCLC, *see* Southern Christian Leadership Conference
Security, 311
Sedition Act (1918), 124, 125
Seekers, 179
Segregation, racial, 102, 173, 231–233, 247, 287
Selective Service System, 123, 268; test, 303
Selma, Ala., 273
Senate, U.S., 10, 113, 173, 174, 215
Shays's Rebellion, 8–9
Sherman Antitrust Act (1890), 103, 215
Sino-Soviet split, 290
"Silicone lift," 72
Sit-ins, 237, 239, 243, 273
Slave labor, 188
Slavery, 15, 102, 188, 190, 202, 218
Smith Registration Act (1940), 167
SNCC, *see* Student Nonviolent Coordinating Committee
Social Democratic Party, 108, 214
Social welfare, 23–24, 142, 172
Socialist party of America, 214, 215, 216
Socialism, 234
Socialists, 209, 217
South Carolina, 121
Southern Christian Leadership Conference (SCLC), 233, 237, 240, 243
Southern Methodist University, 35
Soviet Union, 264, 290, 293
Spanish-American War, 112–13
Spock, Benjamin, 267
Stalin, Josef, 228
Stevenson, Adlai, 21, 42
Stirpiculture, 185
Stock options, 156
Strasser, Adolph, 106
Strikes, 104–107, 142, 215
Strip-tease, 73, 74
Students: as civil rights workers, 245–46; insurrection of, 250–72

Students for a Democratic Society (SDS), 265–70, 272
Student Nonviolent Coordinating Committee (SNCC), 223, 240–45, 254, 260, 261, 263, 265, 269, 270, 273, 275, 276, 277, 280
Suburbanization, 305
Suburbs, 299
Sun City, Ariz., 87–90
Supreme Court, U.S., 101, 102, 103, 195, 231

Taft, William Howard, 116, 117, 215
Taft-Hartley Act, 168
Tatum, C. A., 36
Taxation, 147–49
Taxes (*table*), 149
Teacher Shortages and Salary Schedules, 79
Teachers, 301
Television, 62, 91, 138, 157, 233
Temporary Student Nonviolent Coordinating Committee, 237
Tennessee Valley Authority (TVA), 142
Texas, 14
Texas Centennial, 35
Texas Instruments Corp., 35
Thomas, Norman, 264, 267
Thoreau, Henry David, 202, 204–208, 209, 265, 271
Thornton, R. L., 32
Thucydides, ix, 323
Time, 312
Tocqueville, Alexis de, 3, 25, 128, 132, 133
Towner, James, 185
Townsend, Robert C., 93
Tranquilizers, 96
Transcendentalism, 198
Truman, Harry S., 164, 166, 167, 168, 231
Tubman, Harriet, 192
Turner, Nat, 188
Tuskegee Institute, 219, 220
Twain, Mark, 22, 26, 27–28
Tweed, William, 22

Underground Railroad, 191
Unemployment, 136, 139, 143, 303; in Dallas, 29; among Negroes, 247

Union Labor party, 107
Unitarianism, 198
United Automobile Workers (UAW), 265
United States Council of National Defense, 216
United States v. *E. C. Knight & Company*, 103n.
Universal African Legion, 225
Universal Black Cross Nurses, 225
Universal Negro Improvement Association (Jamaica), 225
Universal Races Congress (1911), 223
University of California at Los Angeles (UCLA), 80–83, 266
USS *Maddox*, 291n.

Van Buren, Martin, 193
Vanderbilt, Cornelius, 22
Vesey, Denmark, 188
Vietnam, 163, 167, 172, 174, 259, 260–70, 272, 274, 290–94, 298–99, 321
Vietnam Day Committee (Berkeley), 268
Violence, 48–49, 171, 320, 321; in American expansion, 15; in Dallas, 29; and disappointment, 7; and money, 24; in movies, 5
Virginia Resolves, 120
Voter registration, 240, 244
Voting rights, Negro, 287
Voting Rights Act (1965), 275, 294

Walden Pond, 205
Walker, Edwin, 42
War of 1812, 14, 20
Washington, Booker T., 219–20, 237
Washington, D.C., 14, 140, 229, 243, 267, 269, 280
Washington, George, 9, 10, 172, 188
Watts riots, 77, 275
"We Shall Overcome," 243
Weaver, James B., 109
Weaver, Robert, 296
Webb, Del E., 87, 89, 90
Weimar Republic, 317
Western Federation of Miners, 107, 214
Westerns, 4–5
Whitman, Walt, 182, 257
Williams, Roger, 133, 179–82, 203, 209, 265, 271
Wilson, John, 280
Wilson, Woodrow, 116, 117, 119, 215
Winthrop, John, 182
Wisecrack, 64
Witch-hunt (1692), 133
Women, 45; rights, 183, 184, 186; suffrage, 215
World War I, 124, 128, 216, 223
World War II, 143–44, 167, 230, 287
Wright, Frank Lloyd, 31, 67

Young Democrats, 272
Yale University, 183, 185